Networking Essentials

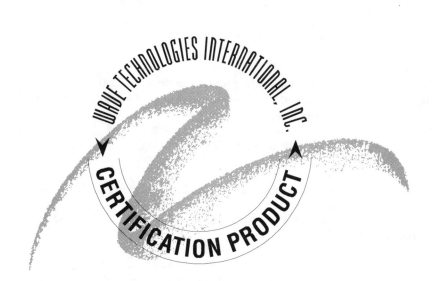

Wave Technologies International, Inc.
MNT4-COR1-7072A
Release 2

Networking Essentials
MNT4-COR1-7072A
Release 2
©1988-1998 Wave Technologies International, Inc.
All rights reserved.

Trademarks:

10 9 8 7 6 5 4 3 2 1

Contents

Introduction

COURSE PURPOSE

Local area networks (LANs), once the exception, are now the rule for business computing. As they have become more common, network operating systems and devices have become easier to use. However, they still have special management and support requirements.

During this study module, we will remove some of the mystery surrounding network devices. This includes a look at hardware components and a wide range of transport protocols. You'll see how the parts fit together to build both the local and wide area network environments.

The manual will discuss implementation factors. These include features and benefits, cost concerns, performance issues, and troubleshooting basics. The manual will also address ongoing management issues such as performance monitoring, trend monitoring, user administration, and security management.

This self-study manual is designed for anyone who wants or needs to know more about local and wide area networking. It is likely to be most helpful to those in a support or management position. The course also covers the requirements for Microsoft Certified Professional exam #70-058.

By design, these materials have only one optional exercise. However, you should take advantage of all chances you may have to practice setup and configuration procedures discussed in the manual.

The exercises in this self-study product are designed to be used on a system that is designated for training purposes *only*. Practicing the exercises on a LAN or workstation that is used for other purposes may cause configuration problems, which will require a reinstallation and/or restoration from a tape backup of the original configuration. Please keep this in mind when working through the exercises.

COURSE GOALS

During the self-study course, you will be provided with the information you need to complete the following:

- Identify the basic characteristics for local area networks (LANs) and wide area networks (WANs).
- List and describe the layers of the OSI networking model.
- List and identify the use of common network devices.
- Describe the procedure for installing and configuring network adapters.
- List common network protocols.
- Identify the best network protocol for a given networking situation.
- Describe the physical characteristics of a LAN.
- Identify internetwork connectivity hardware by sight.
- Define the roles of clients, servers, and peers on a network.
- List the most common network operating systems.
- Identify potential network bottlenecks.
- List fault-tolerance procedures.

Remember, there is always help available online. Please refer to the Support pages in Getting Started for further information regarding online support.

LAN Basics

MAJOR TOPICS

OBJECTIVES

At the completion of this chapter, you will be able to:

- Describe the primary difference between Local Area Network (LAN) and Wide Area Network (WAN) configurations.
- List the basic features and benefits provided by a LAN.
- Compare and contrast peer-to-peer and client/server configurations.
- List the hardware and software components that make up a LAN.
- Explain the significance of the OSI model.
- Describe the seven layers in the OSI model.

PRE-TEST QUESTIONS

The answers to these questions are in Appendix A at the end of this manual.

1. At what layer of the OSI model are the most consistent and complete levels of agreement found among network manufacturers?

   ....

   ....

2. Which LAN model, client/server or peer-to-peer, provides the greatest amount of centralized control and security?

   ....

   ....

3. What network software component is installed at the workstation to provide access to shared resources?

   ....

   ....

4. The Data Link layer of the OSI Model is commonly described as what two sublayers?

   ....

   ....

5. In most cases, WANs involve data transmission across _____ carriers.

   ....

   ....

INTRODUCTION

Only a few years ago, PC-based networks were the exception in the business community. Recently, such networks are nearing the status of being the standard for business communities.

Several factors have helped to fuel this growth. Ongoing support of legacy systems has become prohibitively expensive for many organizations. At the same time, PCs have become faster, more powerful, and less expensive. All the while, the quality of networking software has improved so that it provides more features, greater stability, and better security.

During this chapter, the basic building blocks of a network and the features commonly provided by network operating systems will be covered. Both the local area networks (LANs) and wide area networks (WANs) will be reviewed. Specifically, what makes each unique and situations where each is appropriate. Finally, time will be spent discussing the OSI model as a common point of network reference.

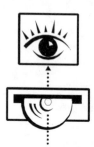

Stop now and view the following video presentation on the Interactive
Learning CD-ROM:

    Networking Essentials
        Overview
        The OSI Model

CHARACTERISTICS OF LANS

This section presents an introduction to Local Area Network (LAN) concepts. This includes a comparison of local and Wide Area Networks (WANs). The following topics are discussed within this section:

- LAN Legacy

- LANs and WANs

- LAN Features

- LAN Types

- LAN Components

- LAN Software

- LAN Hardware

- Networking Your LANs

- Network Scale - How Far is Local?

- LAN to WAN

Networks have become a standard part of business computer environments. Given the work environment, a network may be either a LAN or WAN.

LAN Legacy

PC-based networks can trace their heritage back to what are now often referred to as legacy systems, mainframe and minicomputer hosts accessed through dumb terminals. There are a number of similarities between these configurations, such as centralized storage and backup, access security, and central management of resources. There are, however, a number of differences:

Traditional Host	PC-based Network
Centralized Processing	Distributed Processing
Dumb Terminals	Intelligent Stations (PCs)
Custom Applications	Off-the-Shelf Applications
High Expansion Costs	Modular, Inexpensive Expansion
High Management Overhead	Moderate Management Overhead

Rather than choosing between a traditional host or PC environment, many companies have chosen to integrate their legacy systems into their PC network. This often leads to a more orderly transition, as well as providing benefits from each environment.

LANs and WANs

In the simplest of terms, a LAN is a number of computers running specialized communication software that are joined through an external data path. Basic LAN characteristics include:

- Relatively small geographic area, usually no larger than a single building.

- Direct high-speed connection between all workstations and servers.

- Shared hardware resources and data files.

- Centralized management of resources and network security.

Wide-area networking expands this basic LAN model by linking LANs and allowing them to communicate with each other. By traditional definition, a LAN becomes a WAN when it crosses a public right-of-way, requiring a public carrier for data transmission. More current usage of the term usually includes any situations where you expand beyond your own premises. A WAN is characterized by:

- Wide geographic area, ranging in size up to national or international.
- Low- to high-speed links.
- Remote links may be operational LANs or independent workstations.

With the exception of a WAN's wider area of operation, the benefits and features of LANs and WANs are the same.

LAN Features

The features built into most LAN operating systems provide a number of benefits to the organization and the end user. These include:

- Standard PC hardware

    Standard PCs are used as network servers and workstations. In some cases, Macintosh systems may be used as well. This allows a great deal of design flexibility, ensures relatively easy maintenance, and helps to keep costs to a minimum.

- Resource sharing

    Workstations share storage space and network peripherals such as printers and CD-ROMs. This helps to reduce hardware requirements and expense. Easy access to shared peripherals also helps to improve user productivity.

- Common applications

    Most LAN applications are LAN-aware versions of standard PC applications. This reduces the user's transition time when moving to a network environment. In addition, network licensing is usually less expensive than a similar number of stand-alone licenses.

- File sharing

  Users can easily transfer files to one another, improving productivity. Shared file access also allows for multiuser applications, such as database applications, traditionally supported through mainframe or minicomputer hosts.

- Data security

  Centralized data storage means that user data can be backed up in a timely and reliable manner. This reduces the chance of data loss and is a key tool in failure recovery. Data loss is expensive in both direct costs and lack of productivity.

- Fault tolerance

  Most network operating systems provide a number of fault-tolerance features such as Uninterruptible Power Supply (UPS) support, disk mirroring, disk duplexing, and disk striping with parity (RAID 5). This improves reliability and minimizes network downtime.

- Centralized security

  LANs provide centralized control over access to both the network and its resources. Access security can be customized to meet organizational requirements. This helps to protect sensitive data from loss, destruction, theft, or unauthorized disclosure.

- Communications

  Most LANs provide a messaging system that allows users to communicate. The LAN also forms a basis for easier implementation of more sophisticated systems, such as electronic mail and Internet access.

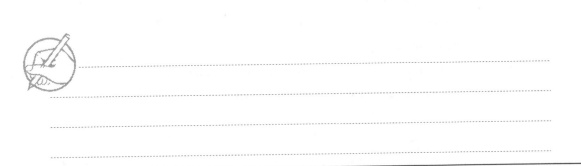

LAN Types

There are two LAN terms that we need to discuss before we go any further. LANs fall under one of two general types:

- Client/server

    In a client/server environment, you have separate systems providing resources (servers) and accessing resources (clients). Resource and security management are fully centralized. The software running at the server, called the network operating system, can either be like Novell's NetWare or can run on another operating system like LAN Manager.

- Peer-to-peer (Workgroup)

    In a peer-to-peer environment, often referred to as a workgroup solution, systems both provide and receive services. Each workgroup member acts somewhat like a server. Resource and security management is handled at the individual system level. The software providing these services may run as a separate application or may be integrated into the operating system.

LAN Components

LAN components can be divided into two basic categories: software and hardware. LAN software includes:

- Network operating system (NOS)
- Workstation shell
- Applications and data files

LAN hardware includes:

- Servers
- Workstations
- Shared peripherals
- Connection hardware (network adapters)
- Cable plant
- Support hardware: bridges, routers, brouters, and gateways

Let's take a closer look at each of these components.

LAN Software

The main difference between a stand-alone PC and one designed to function on a network is the software it is running.

The network operating system (NOS) runs on the server in a client/server network configuration. The NOS turns the PC into a network server. Examples of NOSs include Microsoft LAN Manager, Novell NetWare, Banyan Vines, and IBM LAN Server.

NOTE: LAN Manager is bundled as the network component of Windows NT Server.

Each workstation runs a workstation shell, often called a requester component or a redirector, which allows it to access the network and use shared resources. With most LAN products, the same requester supports both DOS and Windows.

The final software components are end-user applications and data files. Some applications allow users to share data files and access shared data. This functionality is often built into an operating system, such as Windows 95 or Windows NT Workstation. More advanced applications take advantage of the network by allowing users to access shared databases, communicate with each other through electronic mail, or even collaborate realtime with video conferencing and other advanced solutions.

LAN Hardware

The hardware components of a LAN are those that you can see and touch. These may vary slightly by NOS type, but most are standard for all LANs.

Servers on most LANs are standard PCs. Some configurations now also allow the use of RISC-based systems as network servers. The server (or servers) will contain the shared disk storage and shared peripherals. Shared peripherals may include printers, modems, CD-ROM drives, or other devices.

Most NOSs support PCs and Macintosh systems as workstations. Enough flexibility is built into the NOS to allow workstation operating system selections to match user requirements.

Each server and workstation will have at least one network adapter, sometimes called a network interface card (NIC). This provides the physical connection between the PC and the cable plant. The cable plant is the communications path between the server(s) and workstations. Depending on the network configuration, it may contain additional connection devices, such as bridges, routers, and gateways.

Networking your LANs

So far, most of this discussion has been limited to LANs. As LANs become more widespread and as users begin to desire access to remote information, pressures develop to connect two or more LANs together.

The majority of personal computers in the United States are not even connected to a network today. Most of those that are connected to a LAN use it for basic file sharing and printing operations. As the industry evolves, more users are attaching to networks and networks are offering new levels of services. These services increasingly depend on connectivity across a wide geographic region. In fact, in recent years, many corporations have had to look at wide-spread connectivity.

These pressures to link LANs may result from:

- Physical limitations of LANs
- Common user needs in different locations
- Needs to improve resource management and troubleshooting efforts

The decision criteria to consider when linking networks include:

- Organization structure.
- Network management style.
- Flexibility/scalability requirements.
- Consistent interface.

Network Scale - How Far is Local?

Basically, a LAN can be defined as a network contained within a building. It may consist of a collection of small, departmental LANs connected through some type of backbone facility.

Even within a building, distance limitations of LANs may become an issue, along with the questions of mixing different types of networks and computers, such as PCs, hosts, and terminals.

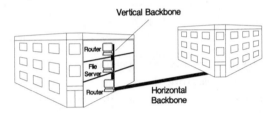

There are several terms that are used to describe a network that covers a region larger than a single building. These are Campus Area Networks (CAN), Metropolitan Area Networks (MAN), and Wide Area Networks (WAN). The term Wide Area Network is used generically to refer to any configuration that links LANs together.

A Campus Area Network is formed when networks in nearby buildings connect to each other. As within a single building, a backbone may connect multiple floors or departments. A backbone will also typically be used to connect multiple buildings. Since traffic may be relatively high, both speed and distance requirements may be of particular importance.

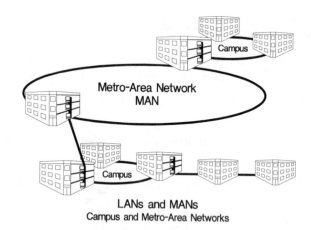

LANs and MANs
Campus and Metro-Area Networks

As it becomes necessary to establish connections across town, the network is called a Metropolitan Area Network. Depending on the distances and facilities available, these connections to more distant sites may involve telecommunication links provided by the local telephone company.

Metropolitan Area Networks provided by specialized carriers, such as Metropolitan Fiber Corporation, allow firms to purchase LAN-oriented bandwidth with wide-area linkages. However, in most environments, the cost for metropolitan- and wide-area bandwidth remains a serious concerns.

A global network may span multiple enterprises, in multiple states, in multiple nations.

LAN to WAN

Connections between cities almost always require some type of telecommunication links unless there is access to satellites or some other form of wireless transmission. In any case, the wide range of transmission speeds that may be involved in the complete wide area network may have considerable impact on the performance of applications running across the network.

In most cases, WANs involve data transmissions across public carriers. This can take several forms, such as dial-up lines, dedicated lines, packet switching, or other carrier options.

The issues surrounding LAN to WAN migration are not just the tremendous difference in cost, but also the presence of multiple vendors. By law, local exchange carriers (LECs) can only provide local access while an interexchange carrier (IXC) must connect services across local access transport areas (LATAs).

DEFINING THE OSI MODEL

This section will define the layers of the OSI model. This is the model for comparing network operating systems and communication. The following topics are discussed within this section:

- OSI Model
- OSI Physical Layer
- OSI Data Link Layer
- OSI Network Layer
- OSI Transport Layer
- OSI Session Layer
- OSI Presentation Layer
- OSI Application Layer

This model was designed as a guideline for building network components. Though compliance varies by manufacturer and by protocol, it provides a good baseline for comparison and consistent terminology.

OSI Model

This course will occasionally refer to the Open Systems Interconnect (OSI) model developed by the International Standards Organization (ISO). The OSI model provides a standard means of describing the data flow in a network and how it is managed.

While a number of companies have endorsed and agreed to apply this model within their own products, few follow its guidelines exactly. Some use their own networking model. However, most of these closely parallel the OSI standard, allowing a common point of reference for discussing network devices and concepts.

OSI Physical Layer

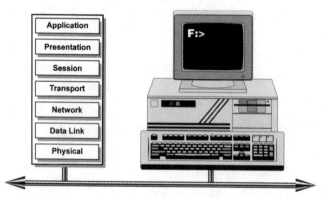

The Physical Layer defines the mechanical and electrical characteristics of the medium and network interface hardware. In other words, it describes the cable, and how it is attached to the network adapter.

Items defined at this layer include:

- Media

    This defines the cable characteristics. Examples include coax cable, fiber optic, and twisted pair.

- Transmission method

    Transmission types, including broadband and baseband, are defined at this level. Signal characteristics, such as signal strength, are specified.

- Topology

    The topology defines how connections are made between stations. These include bus, ring, and star.

The best level of adherence to standards is found at this layer.

OSI Data Link Layer

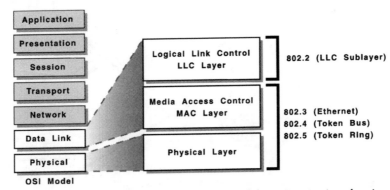

This layer specifies how to ensure error-free delivery of data. It organizes data into frames (structured data packets). This layer also adds control information in the form of a packet header. The header includes the source, destination address, frame length, and upper-layer protocol used for communications. It monitors for acknowledgment of transmitted frames. Should an error occur, it will retransmit the most recent frame.

The IEEE 802 specification divides this layer into two sublayers:

- Logical Link Control (LLC)

    The LLC, common to all 802 series specifications, defines error and flow control. It ensures the integrity of end-to-end transmissions.

- Media Access Control (MAC)

    The MAC defines access control. There are a number of specifications defined, including 802.3 (CSMA/CD or Ethernet), 802.4 (Token Bus), and 802.5 (Token Ring).

Hardware (or node) addressing is used to define source and destination addresses at this level.

OSI Network Layer

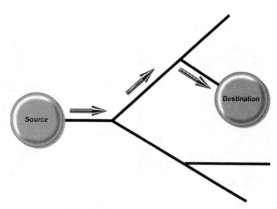

The Network Layer is responsible for data routing in a multiple segment network. This is referred to as Network Layer addressing. This layer:

- Translates addresses.

  Logical addresses, such as machine names, that have passed down from upper layers are translated into physical addresses that the data link layer can use.

- Determines best routing.

  It determines the best route for the data packet to take through the network to ensure timely delivery. Routing may be calculated or determined through a static table.

- Manages network traffic.

  Problem areas such as packet congestion are managed by this layer.

Network addressing on small LANs is not difficult because the nodes are all on the same logical network.

Some transport protocols do not support the Network Layer.

OSI Transport Layer

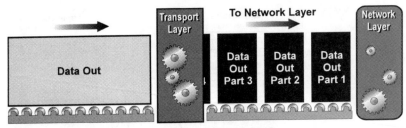

The primary responsibility of the Transport Layer is to make sure data gets from point A to point B in order and without errors. It often compensates for the lack of reliability in the lower layers. This layer provides:

- Repackaging of large data blocks into smaller packets.
- Flow control, packet sequencing, and sequence checking.
- Resynchronization with timeout and retransmission.
- Error detection and recovery.
- Transport connection multiplexing.

The Transport Layer monitors for receipt of each packet. If the destination system is not able to accept data as fast as it is being sent, the sending station can reduce the rate of packet transmission. There are two types of data transfers:

- Connection-oriented

   Data transfers are verified as correct and an acknowledgement is sent.

- Connectionless

   Data transfers are not verified as correct and no acknowledgement is sent.

OSI Session Layer

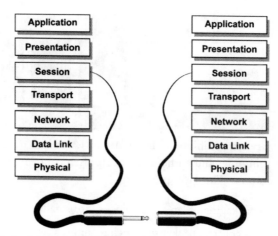

The lower layers deal with data loss or data integrity errors. The Session Layer is designed to deal with session errors by placing checkpoints in the data. A session is the logical connection between two network devices. The session layer provides:

- Dialog management.

    The session layer establishes the session, synchronizes conversations, and ends the session when it is no longer needed.

- Error correction.

    This layer is designed to handle problems, such as a printer going off-line or a hard drive running out of space during a file transfer.

- Logical address names.

    Support for logical names, such as machine names, allows you to give systems descriptive names.

OSI Presentation Layer

The Presentation Layer translates data from the Application Layer into a transmission format. This means that even though workstations may use different local data formats they can still communicate. Specific functions include:

- Data format translation

  Data is put into a transfer syntax for transmission. The receiving station will take this data and translate it into a format that is common across different platforms.

- Data encryption/decryption

  This allows the system to encrypt data before transmission and decrypt incoming data. Encrypted data is more secure because it cannot be read as easily by unauthorized sniffers on the wire.

- Data compression/expansion

  Whenever possible, data is compressed before transmission. It is then expanded by the receiving station.

OSI Application Layer

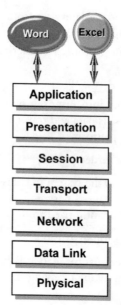

The Application layer provides a means for end-user applications to access the network. Services provided include:

- End-user interface
- Network management
- Directory services
- File access
- File transfer
- Mail services

SUMMARY

During this chapter you were introduced to some LAN basics. These included:

- The LAN heritage

  LANs can trace their heritage back to mainframe and minicomputer host systems. Each provides many of the same services.

- A comparison of LANs and WANs

  Though the industry has created a number of sometimes conflicting definitions, the primary difference is in size. LANs cover a small area, WANs a larger area.

- LAN features

  LANs allow users to share peripheral devices, storage space, and data files. They provide administrators or management personnel with the ability to implement centralized control over security and mechanisms to ensure improved data backup and integrity.

- Hardware and software component overview

  LANs are built from standard PCs with additional software and hardware that define their roles and allow them to communicate across the network.

- The OSI model

  Although it is considered a somewhat idealized model of network communications, the OSI model provides a standard set of terms and concepts to use when discussing network devices.

The next chapter continues the discussion of LAN basics with a more detailed look at the communication path, the cable plant, and network adapter.

Scenario

The president of Startup Personnel, Inc. has decided that the PCs in the accounting department should be connected to a LAN. He has asked you, the newly promoted network administrator, to determine the best LAN configuration.

There are ten employees in the department. They will need the ability to share files with each other. In addition, they will all need access to a printer. Due to the "mission critical" nature of the department, the president has demanded that the data be centrally managed to ensure system security.

Questions

The answers to these questions are in Appendix A at the end of this manual.

1. Which LAN configuration, client/server or peer-to-peer, is best for this situation?

    ....

    ....

2. Why?

    ....

    ....

POST-TEST QUESTIONS

The answers to these questions are in Appendix A at the end of this manual.

1. What is the correct term for a network connecting 20 workstations and one file server all located on the same floor?

    ....

    ....

2. What is the correct term for a configuration when two or more LANs are connected by means of a public carrier?

   ....

   ....

3. What is the name of the software component that turns a standard PC into a network server?

   ....

   ....

4. What is the term that describes the cable used for connections between the network nodes (servers and workstations)?

   ....

   ....

CHAPTER ②

LAN Concepts and Low-Level Devices

MAJOR TOPICS

OBJECTIVES

At the completion of this chapter, you will be able to:

- List common cable types and describe their characteristics.
- Identify common cable topologies and situations when they are used.
- List the cable type(s) used with selected protocols.
- Describe the characteristics of the following common LAN protocols:

    Ethernet

    Token Ring

    FDDI

- Compare and contrast broadcast communication methods.
- Describe the basic characteristics of:

    X.25

    Frame Relay

    ISDN

    ATM

    T1

- Identify common network adapter types.
- Describe concerns when installing and configuring a network adapter.
- Compare and contrast NDIS and ODI network drivers.

PRE-TEST QUESTIONS

The answers to these questions are in Appendix A at the end of this manual.

1. Which provides the least resistance to EMI: unshielded twisted pair, shielded twisted pair, or coaxial cable?

....

....

2. What is the access method used by Ethernet 802.3?

    ....

    ....

3. Ethernet 10Base2 supports up to _____ stations per segment.

    ....

    ....

4. Token Ring supports what cable connector types?

    ....

    ....

5. What IRQ is normally used by LPT2?

    ....

    ....

INTRODUCTION

The last chapter discussed basic LAN characteristics and the OSI model. This chapter discusses network components in greater detail. For much of this chapter, and the chapters that follow, you will work your way up through the OSI reference model.

The chapter starts at the bottom of the model with the cable that provides the communications path. A number of cable types, each matched to a particular configuration and protocol, are covered.

From here, the chapter jumps higher in the model with a look at protocols. This chapter specifically covers lower level protocols, often called Data Link, or access protocols, because they work primarily at that layer. These lower level protocols define the transmission characteristics across the cable.

The chapter next moves into a related subject, network adapter cards and drivers. Each network adapter is matched to a particular access protocol and supports that protocol only. Common types of adapter cards are introduced with guidelines for their installation.

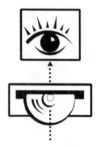

Stop now and view the following video presentation on the Interactive Learning CD-ROM:

Networking Essentials

Ethernet vs. Token Ring

LOW-LEVEL DEVICE OVERVIEW

This section provides a more detailed look at devices operating at the lowest levels of the OSI model. The following topics are discussed within this section:

- IEEE 802 Series Specifications
- The Physical Layer
- The Data Link Layer
- Transmission Media Overview
- Transmission Media Characteristics

The devices at this layer can often be pinpointed as the source of network problems. A good understanding will help you in your troubleshooting efforts.

IEEE 802 Series Specifications

The OSI Reference Model does not make explicit the actual specification of the 7 layers. The lower layers of the model have been *standardized* by organizations, such as the Institute of Electrical and Electronic Engineers (IEEE) committee, which has published a series of specifications for the OSI layers 1 and 2 (Physical and Data Link).

These specifications define the physical media popularly known as:

802.3	CSMA/CD (Ethernet)
802.4	Token Bus
802.5	Token Ring

Other IEEE Project Groups include:

802.0	Executive Committee
802.1	Higher Layer Interfaces
802.2	Logical Link Control (LLC)
802.6	Metropolitan Area Network (MAN)
802.7	Broadband LAN
802.8	Fiber Optic LAN
802.9	Integrated Voice and Data LAN
802.10	Standards for Interoperable LAN Security
802.11	Wireless Networks
802.12	Demand Priority Access LAN, 100BaseVG-AnyLAN

The Physical Layer

The OSI Physical Layer deals with the nuts and bolts of the network. It specifies the electrical characteristics of the media involved and how signals will be transmitted across the wire (or fiber).

In addition to describing the techniques for encoding bits on the wire, such as differential Manchester for Token Ring, the physical layer specifications also deal with practical matters, such as distance limitations. Thick Ethernet, for example, may be run in segments up to 500 meters. Up to four repeaters may be used to extend the reach of the network up to 2.5 Km, with certain restrictions.

The physical specifications may also go into great detail describing the criteria of the cabling and connectors (known as Multistation Access Units or MAUs) and their pin-outs.

The Data Link Layer

IEEE 802 specifications further divide the Data Link Layer into two sub-layers, the Logical Link Control (LLC) and Media Access Control (MAC) layers.   The LLC layer (802.2) is common to all of the 802 series of specifications. The MAC layer is defined separately for each of the physical implementations.

Transmission Media Overview

Transmission media refers to the physical connection that the computers have to one another. These pathways conduct electrical, radio, microwave, or light energy as waves or pulses. This energy from some part of the electromagnetic (EM) spectrum is used to transmit signals from one device to another.

EM energy is used to communicate, because it can:

- Originate from electrical currents.
- Be amplified and controlled by semiconductor equipment.
- Be used for binary communications.

Binary information is used almost exclusively in computer processing and high-speed networks. Binary implies that only two values are used, 0 and 1. Because computers store and process information in binary form, all computer network transmissions start and end in binary form. Although some media, such as a voice-grade telephone line, require use of an analog format, computers use that analog format to carry binary data.

Transmission Media Characteristics

Transmission media is classified as either cable (bounded) or wireless (unbounded). In the case of cable-based media, there is an actual set of copper wires, a fiber optic, or coaxial copper cable. In the case of wireless media there is no actual medium other than empty space. Thus, the signal energy is referred to as the "medium." For example, you might hear: "the medium is 'laser' or 'microwave'." Each medium has different characteristics, making it more suitable for some applications than others.

The capacity of a medium is usually stated as bandwidth. Bandwidth is the information carrying capacity of a communications channel. In the case of an analog signal (like an FM radio station), the bandwidth is the range of frequencies used. This range is measured in cycles per second or hertz (Hz). In binary communications, bandwidth is commonly measured as bits per second (bps).

The term baud is sometimes incorrectly used to refer to "bits per second" (bps). Phone lines are limited to 2400 baud, but modems operate at 28,800 bps or better.

The number of actual data bits that can be transported per second will always be lower than the bandwidth of the media, because that bandwidth is also used to send control signals. This is called overhead.

There is a limit to how far a given signal can travel on a given media and still be recognizable. Attenuation is a term used to describe the lessening or fading of electromagnetic signals over a given distance. The signal fades over distance just like a voice. The characteristics of the medium used will determine how much of the signal will be absorbed (or scattered) by the medium.

When electronic signals travel over metal wiring, some energy is radiated to the surrounding environment. The wiring can also act as an antenna to receive energy from the surrounding environment. The term electromagnetic interference (EMI) refers to external influences having an impact on the signal that is being transmitted over the media.

This causes problems whenever the interfering energy, called noise, is large compared to the energy of the desired signal. EMI can also be a security risk in secure environments, because eavesdropping devices can be used to pick up these emissions.

Each type of media varies in:

- Cost
- Ease of installation
- Bandwidth or capacity
- Attenuation or loss
- Resistance or immunity to EMI

Chapter Organization

It might be worthwhile to spend a little time talking about how the rest of this chapter is organized. The subject matter falls into three major categories:

- Bounded communications

    Wire- and fiber-based communications are covered first. This discussion is given the most emphasis since it is the type of media you will encounter most often. The discussion includes closely related subjects, such as network topologies, access protocols, and network adapter cards.

- Unbounded communications

    There is a short discussion of unbounded communications methods. While not commonly used at this time, the use of unbounded communications in both LAN and WAN technologies is increasing.

- Public carrier

    The chapter ends with a look at transmission methods used over public carriers. These methods are most commonly used in WAN implementations.

With each of these, the basic purpose remains the same, getting data from here to there.

BOUNDED COMMUNICATIONS

This section will present the devices that support bounded communication, that is, cable-based communication. This is by far the most commonly implemented option. The following are topics discussed within this section:

- Cable Media
- Twisted Pair (TP)
- Unshielded Twisted Pair (UTP)

- UTP Categories
- UTP Installation
- Shielded Twisted Pair (STP)
- Coaxial Cable
- Fiber Optic
- Topologies
- Bus Topology
- Ring Topologies
- Star Topology
- Mesh Topology
- Cellular Topology
- Wiring Guidelines
- Channel Access Methods
- CSMA/CD
- CSMA/CD Collisions
- Ethernet and 802.3
- Thin Ethernet 10Base2
- Twisted Pair 10BaseT
- Thick Ethernet 10Base5
- Ethernet Cable Connections
- Token Ring 802.5
- Token Passing
- Beaconing
- Token Ring Media

- MAUs
- IEEE 802.5 Cabling - IBM Cabling System
- Token Ring Cable Connectors
- Fiber Distributed Data Interface (FDDI)
- Network Adapter Cards
- Network Adapter Installation
- Combined Configuration List
- Adapter Drivers
- NDIS and ODI

A complete understanding of cable plant, transport protocol, and network adapter issues is critical to your ability to implement and support a network.

Cable Media

Cable media is the wire or fiber used to transmit light or electricity. The three main types of computer cabling are:

- Twisted pair
- Coaxial cable
- Fiber optic cable

Cable media selections will be tied closely to your access protocol implementations.

Twisted Pair (TP)

TP is made of insulated copper wires which have been twisted around each other to form wire pairs. Usually the wire is 22 to 26 gauge, and more than one pair can be carried in a single jacket or sheath. When working with twisted pair, note the difference between "wire" and "pair." A "two pair" cable has four wires.

Because wire carrying electricity transmits and receives electromagnetic energy, nearby pairs of wires carrying signals can interfere with each other. This is called crosstalk. To reduce crosstalk and other EMI, the wires are twisted. This causes any noise to be received more evenly by both wires in a pair. A voltage difference between the two wires carries the signal, so noise that is equal on both wires cancels itself.

Care must be taken when making twisted-pair wiring selections. This is especially true when selecting for high bit rate applications. The wire must meet specifications, such as gauge, how the wire is twisted, and number of twists. For example, Category 3 unshielded twisted pair has three twists per foot.

Twisted-pair wiring may or may not have an electromagnetic shield around the pairs. Therefore, it is classified as either:

- Unshielded Twisted Pair (UTP)
- Shielded Twisted Pair (STP)

Unshielded Twisted Pair (UTP)

UTP is a set of twisted pairs within a plastic sheath. The most common use for this type of cable is telephone wire. Different types of UTP cabling are suitable for different speed communications.

A number of wiring classification schemes are in use. The most common is the levels from Underwriter's Laboratory (UL) and categories from the Electrical Industries Association (EIA).

Category 3 and Category 5 UTP are used for most network cabling schemes. Category 5 (similar to Level 5) offers reduced noise levels by having more twists per foot and better insulation. It is suitable for rates of up to 100 Mbps.

The use of Category 5 cabling requires specific installation methods that raise the cost slightly when compared to the cost of slower UTP. For example, no more than one-half inch of the cable can be untwisted when connecting it to a device. Still, UTP is usually the least expensive of all the network transmission media types.

UTP Categories

The Electronic Industries Association created standards relating to UTP cable. These standards include the following five categories of UTP:

- Category 1

    Traditional telephone wire capable of carrying voice but not data.

- Category 2

    UTP cable containing four twisted pairs capable of data transmissions of up to 4 Mbps.

- Category 3

    UTP cable containing four twisted pairs capable of data transmissions of up to 10 Mbps.

- Category 4

    UTP cable containing four twisted pairs capable of data transmissions of up to 16 Mbps.

- Category 5

    UTP cable containing four twisted pairs of copper wire capable of data transmissions of up to 100 Mbps.

UTP Installation

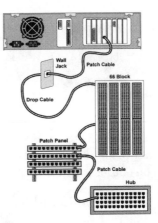

Hardware connectivity generally is accomplished by using an RJ-45 connector. These connectors are attached to a patch cable. One end of the patch cable is attached to the network device; the other end is attached to a wall jack. The wall jack is connected to a 66 punch-down block. The punch-down block, in turn, is connected to a patch panel that provides RJ-45, RS-232, or RS-449 jacks. Hubs, concentrators, and other network devices can then be attached to the patch panel using RJ-45 cables.

Cost	Low cost compared to other media.
Ease of Installation	Relatively inexpensive and easy.
Capacity	Data transfer rates from 1 to 100 Mbps, with 10 Mbps the most common.
Attenuation	Rapid attenuation, distance limited to hundreds of meters.
EMI Immunity	Very susceptible to EMI.

Shielded Twisted Pair (STP)

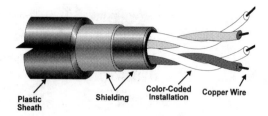

Plastic
Sheath   Shielding   Color-Coded   Copper Wire
                               Installation

STP includes a protective sheathing around the copper wire. The twisted pair is wrapped in foil to cut down on outside interference and electromagnetic radiation.

Cost	Moderately expensive.
Ease of Installation	The shield in STP cable must be grounded, making installation more difficult than UTP installation. Special connectors and installation techniques are also required. The use of a preconfigured cable and connectors makes this easier.
Capacity	With the reduction of external interference, greater transmission speeds (up to 500 Mbps) can be implemented. Some 155 Mbps cabling exists, but the most common transmission rate is 16 Mbps.
Attenuation	Similar to UTP. Distance is limited to 100 m for 500 Mbps, longer for lower speeds.
EMI Immunity	The foil shielding reduces both interference and EMI emissions. STP will still suffer from outside interference, but not as much as UTP.

Coaxial Cable

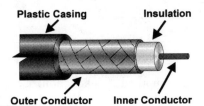

Coaxial cable is composed of two conductors that share the same axis. The center cable is insulated by plastic-foam, a second conductor, foil wrap, and an external plastic tube.

Common coaxial cable types include:

Use	Cable Type	Termination
10Base5 (Ethernet)	RG8 and RG11	50 ohm
10Base2 (Ethernet)	RG58	50 ohm
Cable TV	RG59	75 ohm
ARCnet	RG62	93 ohm

Advantages

- EMI resistance
- Resilience

Disadvantages

- Some EMI sensitivity
- Bulky installation
- Relatively expensive

Transmissions over coax may be either baseband or broadband. With baseband, the cables carry a single high-speed signal. This is the transmission method used by Ethernet. Broadband coax carries multiple signals, each at a different frequency. Broadband is sometimes used as a backbone cable.

Fiber Optic

Fiber optic cable is comprised of light-conducting glass on plastic fibers surrounded by a protective cladding and a durable outer sheath.

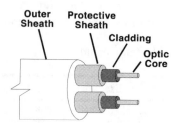

The bulk of the expense that characterizes fiber optic cabling systems can be attributed to the interface devices that convert computer signals to and from light pulses. The light pulses are generated by light emitting diodes (LEDs) or injection laser diodes (ILDs). Photo diodes reconvert the light pulses to electrical signals.

Data rates from 100 Mbps to over 2 Gbps are supported at distances from 2 to 25 Km.

Because it doesn't carry electricity, it is ideal for use in hazardous, high-voltage, or secure environments.

Common fiber optic cables are classified based on the diameter of their core. Thicker cores allow the signal to reflect from side-to-side and are referred to as multi-mode, while narrow core fiber cable is referred to as single-mode.

Most LAN fiber networks use 62.5-micron fiber cable.

Advantages

- Supports extremely high bandwidth
- EMI immunity
- Reliability and security
- High-bandwidth performance
- Extremely low attenuation

Disadvantages

- Relatively expensive component parts
- Installation relatively complex
- Somewhat fragile, requiring careful handling
- Tedious and expensive installation

Topologies

The transmission medium defines how the signal is being carried. The topology defines how the physical media links the network nodes. In early LAN development, the topology was always directly linked to the Data Link protocol. Now, some protocols can be implemented somewhat independent of cable topologies.

There are three types of topologies commonly used on LANs. These are:

- Bus
- Ring
- Star

Additional topologies have been developed for WAN connectivity, including point-to-point, multi-point, mesh networks, and clouds. Hybrid topologies are often found in a WAN. This is simply an implementation of multiple topologies.

Bus Topology

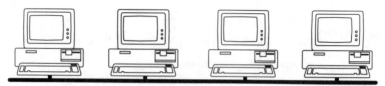

A bus topology consists of a linear transmission medium that is terminated at both ends. Nodes attach directly to the bus, making it difficult to troubleshoot. Difficulty in troubleshooting is considered the biggest drawback for this topology.

Although a bus is normally represented as a straight line in the picture, most bus networks represent cables that snake, weave, and wrap their way through building conduits and corridors. This results in the rapid growth of overall bus length. In addition, any break in the bus causes the entire network to become inoperable.

Bus topologies commonly use coaxial cable as their transmission medium. Traditionally, Ethernet has used a bus topology.

Bus topologies are often used for small, temporary installations.

Ring Topologies

A ring topology provides a closed-loop transmission medium. Repeaters at each node connection repeat the signals. This is done to minimize any signal degradation.

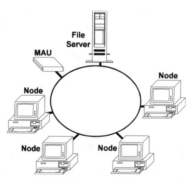

Traditional rings have the same failure risk as buses. Any break brings the entire network down. To prevent these failures, most ring implementations (such as Token Ring) are actually wired in a star topology with an out loop and a return loop from each workstation to the wiring hub.

The FDDI design specification calls for a dual fiber optic ring. Should a break occur in either ring, it automatically converts to a bus topology.

Star Topology

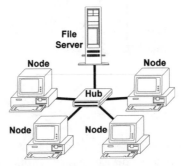

Star/hub networks connect the peripheral devices via point-to-point links to a central location. An Active Hub regenerates signals while a Passive Hub simply acts as a terminating point for the network. Star topologies provide architectural flexibility, but can require more cable than traditional bus and ring topologies.

Virtually all modern data networks are configured in a hub. This allows for simplified adds, moves, and changes. System failure from any individual segment break is minimized. Examples of hub configurations for traditional bus and ring topologies include:

Ethernet (traditional bus)	10baseT to wiring closet
	10base5 and 10baseT multi-port repeaters
Token Ring (traditional ring)	MAU hubs

A star may be wired with twisted pair or coax. Most current implementations use twisted pair.

Mesh Topology

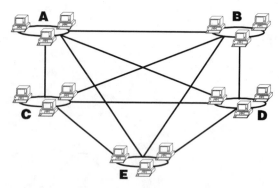

A mesh configuration consists of a network where each device has a point-to-point connection to every other device on the network. This provides the dedicated capacity of a point-to-point link to each device and significant fault tolerance. However, the complexity and cost make this configuration impractical for networks with a large number of devices. Also, much of the bandwidth available in mesh configurations is wasted.

For those reasons, mesh topologies are generally used for interconnecting only the most important sites with multiple links. This is called a hybrid mesh or partial mesh.

Advantages:

- Troubleshooting is easy.
- Isolation of network failures is easy.
- Fault tolerance is maximized by rerouting traffic around failed links.

Disadvantages:

- Difficult to install.
- Difficult to reconfigure.
- Expensive because of redundant connections and wasted bandwidth.

Cellular Topology

A cellular configuration breaks the area covered into *cells*. Each cell has a hub that covers the cell's area. These hubs are connected to other hubs using both point-to-point and multipoint topologies. The devices that are located within the cells communicate with the cell's hub, which interconnects to other hubs to provide communications within the entire network.

Because this is a wireless (unbounded) network, it does not rely on connection cables to link the devices. Cellular topologies use connectivity to wireless, centralized hubs to allow devices to physically relocate while maintaining a connection to the network.

Advantages:

- Easy to install.
- Easy to reconfigure.
- Easy to add new users and stations.
- Simple to troubleshoot.
- Simple to isolate failures.

Disadvantages:

- If the central hub fails, the devices attached to that hub are disconnected from the network.

- Can be very expensive to install.

Wiring Guidelines

There are some general guidelines to keep in mind when installing a cable plant. These include:

- Select the appropriate cable to match your protocol and topology.

- Stay within specified limitations.

- Properly group and terminate cables.

- For copper cable, avoid sources of excessive electronic noise.

- Do not route cable through electrical conduit.

- Plenum-sheathed cable is required in many areas, especially when wiring through suspended ceilings.

- Avoid routing cables through high traffic areas.

If the cable plant is installed by contractors, be sure to get a map of where the cable is routed. This will be helpful should problems occur in the future.

Channel Access Methods

Once the cable is in place, specifications are needed to define how systems will *talk* to each other.

There are three basic channel access methods:

- Contention

    Any network device may transmit whenever it wants.

    Protocol Example: CSMA–Carrier Sense Multiple Access

Contention

- Polling

    A primary or master device queries each of the other devices (referred to as secondaries) in a predetermined order. Secondaries can access the channel only after receiving a request from the primary. Polling is not commonly used in local area networks.

    Protocol Example: SDLC–Synchronous Data Link Control

Polling

- Token Passing

    A token is passed in an orderly fashion from one device to another. A device can access the channel by taking control of the token.

    Protocol Example: Token Ring, FDDI–Fiber Distributed Data Interface

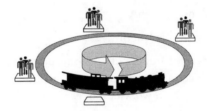

Token Passing

The IEEE has produced standards for the MAC layer which utilize these channel access methods.

CSMA/CD

Carrier Sense Multiple Access with Collision Detection (CSMA/CD) is the most common implementation of contention access.

- Carrier Sensing

    Listens for someone talking.

- Multiple Access

    All have concurrent access to the media.

- Collision Detection

    If two or more systems transmit at once, the system realizes the message didn't get through and repeats the message.

Transmission failures can be caused by:

- Bad cabling
- Improper termination
- Collisions
- Improper cable length

Collisions slow cable throughput. At some point in its growth, an Ethernet network may encounter a reduction in performance. When this occurs will depend on the amount of traffic generated by each workstation.

CSMA/CD Collisions

Any station may transmit when it senses that the carrier is free. If a collision is detected, each station will wait for a randomly determined interval before retransmitting.

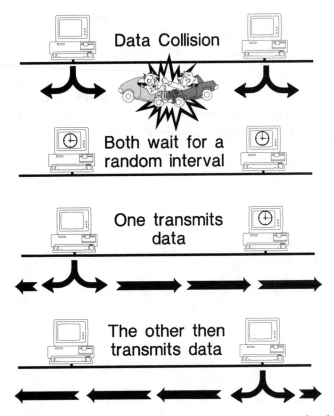

Most network operating systems track retransmissions, which are a good indication of the number of collisions occurring on the network.

Ethernet and 802.3

The terms Ethernet and 802.3 are often used interchangeably. There are some small differences, but both are CSMA/CD specifications.

Ethernet was originally developed by Xerox, Intel, and DEC in the late 1970s, with specifications first released in 1980. The IEEE 802.3 specification differs from Ethernet primarily with respect to the frame format.

An 802.3 frame contains a two-byte length field indicating the length of the frame. An Ethernet frame is fixed in length. Short frames are padded to fill them out. In the place of a length field is information on the type of higher layer protocol being used, such as TCP/IP or the Xerox Network System (XNS).

Other differences involve pinouts and the Signal Quality Error (SQE) signal, also known as a heartbeat.

These are three types of Ethernet cables:

- Thin Ethernet
- Twisted Pair
- Thick Ethernet

Thin Ethernet
10Base2

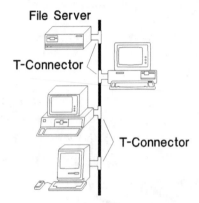

For many years, this was the most common Ethernet installation. 10Base2 features include:

- Linear bus topology.

- 0.25-in. (20 AWG) RG58A/U or TG58C/U 50-ohm cable.

- Thin Ethernet segments; maximum distance 185 m (607 ft) each.

- Maximum network length is five segments 925 m (3,035 ft).

- Repeaters connect segments, up to four repeaters per network.

- BNC T-connectors attach workstations to the cable.

- Minimum distance between T-connectors 0.5 m (1.6 ft).

- 30 stations maximum per segment.

- Often called "Cheapernet" or "Thinnet."

A thinnet network can have no more than 5 cable segments connected by 4 repeaters, with only 3 of the cable segments populated by workstations. This limitation is defined as the 5-4-3 rule: 5 cable segments, 4 repeaters, and 3 populated segments. The unpopulated segments are called inter-repeater links.

Twisted Pair 10BaseT

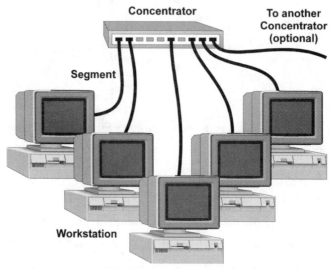

Currently, this is the most common choice for Ethernet installation. 10BaseT features include:

- Star topology.

- Number of stations set by number of concentrator ports.

- Concentrators may be linked together.

- Up to 1,024 stations per network.

- 24 AWG unshielded dual twisted pair.

- One network device attached to each cable.

- Maximum distance to concentrator < 100 m (328 ft).

- Minimum distance to concentrator > 0.6 m (2 ft).

- Auxiliary Unit Interface (AUI) attaches workstations to twisted pair cable via an RJ-45 connector.

Some Ethernet adapters now have a built-in RJ-45 connector.

Thick Ethernet
10Base5

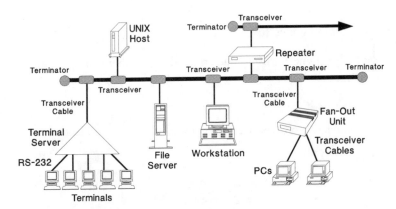

While not used as commonly as 10Base2 or 10BaseT, thick Ethernet is used in many networks, often as the backbone. 10Base5 features include:

- 0.4-in. (10 AWG) 50-ohm coaxial cable.

- Ethernet segments (trunk segment) maximum distance 500 m (1,640 ft) each (transceiver cable or AUI*).

- Maximum network length (network trunk) is 5 segments, 2,500 m (8,200 ft).

- Repeaters connect segments.

- Transceivers* attach workstations to the cable.

- Minimum distance between transceivers, 2.5 m (8 ft).

- Maximum transceiver cable length, 50 m.

- Maximum 100 nodes per segment.

- 1,024 maximum stations per network.

- Cables that are only grounded on one end.

          * Ethernet terminology

NOTE: *Ethernet terminology and IEEE 802.3/10Base5 terminology are not exactly the same.*

Ethernet Cable Connections

The cable connector used is determined by whether you are running 10Base2, 10Base5, or 10BaseT.

10Base2 - BNC

The standard BNC connector is considered a 2-pin connector.

Pin 1 is the inner wire and pin 2 is the tinned copper braid.

Pin #	Signal
1	Data signal (center conductor)
2	Ground (metal sheath)

10Base5 - AUI/DIX

The Attachment Unit Interface (AUI) connector is used for connecting to 10Base5 Thicknet transceivers. There are also transceivers available which connect through to 10BaseT concentrators.

Pin #	Signal
1	Control In Circuit Shield
2	Control In Circuit A
3	Data Out Circuit A
4	Data In Circuit Shield
5	Data In Circuit A
6	Voltage Common
7	Not Used
8	Control Out Circuit Shield
9	Control In Circuit B
10	Data Out Circuit B
11	Data Out Circuit Shield
12	Data In Circuit B
13	Voltage Plus
14	Voltage Shield
15	Not Used

The conductive shell of the connector is a protective ground. Under a variation of AUI called DIX (Digital, Intel, Xerox), pin 1 is connected to chassis ground.

10BaseT - RJ-45

For 10BaseT devices to communicate, there must be a crossover between the two devices. This means that the send signals at one end are connected to receive signals at the other end. This may occur at the device, transceiver, or wall plate, in which case a straight-through cable is used. Otherwise, a crossover cable is required.

In either case, the pin definitions for the RJ-45 are the same. The difference occurs in how the wires are routed between the RJ-45 connectors.

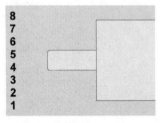

Pin #	Signal
1	Transmit +
2	Transmit -
3	Receive +
4	Not used
5	Not used
6	Receive -
7	Not used
8	Not used

Token Ring 802.5

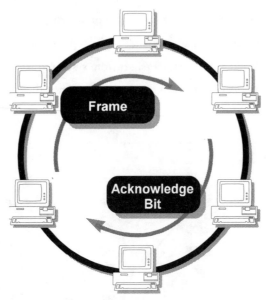

Token Ring was originally created by IBM. Over the last few years, it has steadily gained popularity. Token Ring features include:

- Logical ring usually wired as a physical star.
- Transfer rate of 4 to 16 Mbps.
- Unshielded twisted pair, shielded twisted pair, or fiber optic cable.
- Deterministic, it is possible to predict the passage of the token.

The predictability inherent in Token Ring makes it a popular choice for timing critical and control applications. The following statements describe token passing:

- There is only one active token on the ring at any time.

- Tokens travel at thousands of miles per second (fiber optic).

- A token (data frame) passes from system to system.

- A system can attach data to a token when the token is free (empty).

- Each system receives and regenerates the token.

Token Passing

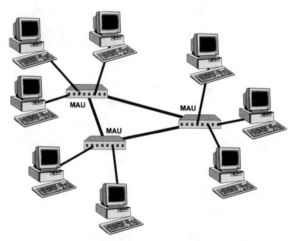

A token is a control signal that is passed from station-to-station between transfers of data. It consists of a starting delimiter, an access control field, and an ending delimiter. The token contains a single bit (the Token Bit) that indicates that the token is ready to accept information. If the node has data to send, it appends the data to the token. The token then becomes a frame. Only one token at a time is allowed to circulate around the ring.

A frame is a unit of data transmission and includes delimiters, control characters, information, and checking characters.

- When it wants to communicate, a station takes the token, flags it as busy (changes the token bit to 1), loads it with data, and passes it on.

- The frame makes its way through the network to the receiving station, which takes the data, marks the frame as received (by changing 2 sets of bits in the Frame Status (FS) byte), and passes it along.

- The frame returns to the sender, which sees the receipt (FS bits), removes the frame from the ring, and then releases a new token.

- An option called early token release allows a transmitting station to release a token after transmitting the ending delimiter of the frame.

- Each node acts as a repeater for the network.

- The first station that powers on and inserts on the ring becomes the active monitor. All other stations are capable of becoming the active monitor and are called standby monitors. If the active monitor fails or is removed from the network, the standby monitor with the highest address will become the active monitor.

- Every seven seconds or less, this active monitor will send a signal to the other nodes to identify itself as present.

The active monitor is responsible for verifying that the token is detected on the ring and generates a new token if it is missing. The active monitor will also remove continuously circulating frames.

Beaconing

When a station detects a hard error, it begins to transmit beacon frames. The beacon frame is used to define a failure domain. The failure domain includes the station reporting the failure, its nearest active upstream neighbor (NAUN), and everything in between. Once identified, the NAUN removes itself from the ring and begins a self test. If successful, the NAUN reattaches to the ring. If unsuccessful, it remains unattached. If the ring does not recover, the beaconing station assumes the NAUN has completed its self test and the beaconing station removes itself from the ring and begins self testing. If successful, it can reattach. If unsuccessful, it remains unattached. If the ring has not recovered at this point, manual intervention is required.

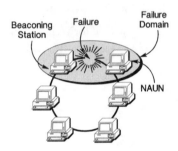

Token Ring Media

Token Ring can be installed using:

* Unshielded twisted pair in star or modified star at 4 Mbps.

* Shielded twisted pair in star or modified star configuration at 4 or 16 Mbps.

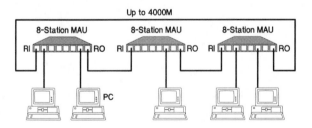

Typical Token Ring Network

Token Ring Wiring Options

- Multistation Access Unit supports up to 8 nodes.

- Maximum 12 MAUs per ring.

- Local Ring Hub allows four-node connections on one MAU port cable.

- 64 - 72 (max.) nodes recommended per ring for optimal performance.

Distances between:

Station to MAU	45 m
MAU to MAU	120 m
MAU to repeater	600 m
Maximum Network Length	750 m (Type 1 cabling)
MAU to Fiber Optic Repeater	1.5 Km (max. net. 4,000 m)

MAUs

Even though most token ring networks look like a star, they work as a ring. The Multistation Access Unit (MAU) makes this possible.

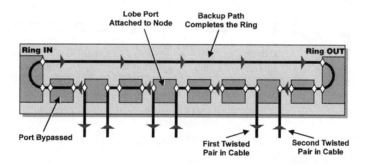

When a device connects to a MAU, a cable with two twisted pairs is used. One pair transmits from the device to the MAU, the other from the MAU to the device. As each device is connected and initialized, you can hear the *click* as the MAU makes a physical relay connection.

As you can see in the illustration above, the MAU is wired to provide a local loop through an internal backup path.

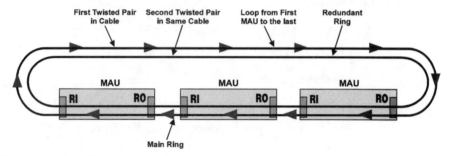

When multiple MAUs are used, the Ring Out of each is plugged into the Ring In of the next until the ring is completed.

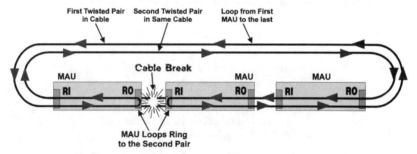

Two rings are actually completed. One is used for token passing between the devices. The second is a loop of all of the MAU backup paths. This is known as a redundant ring.

The redundant ring is used when there is a break in the cable. The MAUs on either side of the break will recognize it and set up a ring wrap connection. When the token gets to the last station in the ring, it is routed to the first station by way of the MAU's backup path.

IEEE 802.5 Cabling
IBM Cabling System

Since 802.5 Token Ring came from IBM, their cabling system has become the standard.

Type 1

- Braided cable shield around two twisted pairs of #22 American Wire Gauge (AWG) conductors for data communication.

- Suitable for 16 or 4 Mbps.

Type 2

- Same as Type 1 cable with four twisted pairs of #22 AWG telephone conductors.

- Unshielded pairs are available for phone service, RS-232 data, and so on.

Type 3

- Four solid Copper unshielded twisted pairs, 24 AWG; simply high quality phone wire.

- Recommended for 4 Mbps, not for most 16 Mbps rings.

Type 5

- Two fiber optic conductors, suitable for placement in underground conduit, indoor use, and aerial installations.

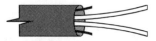

- Recommended for long distances, such as backbones, or between buildings.

Type 6

- Two shielded twisted pairs, 26 AWG. This is the cable recommended by Novell for both patch cables and adapter cables.

Token Ring Cable Connectors

Token Ring is supported through a wide variety of connectors. In each case, as with Ethernet 10BaseT, there must be a crossover between stations. If provided by either device or a connection block, a straight-through cable is used. Otherwise, a crossover cable is used.

The classic Token Ring cable has a DB-9 connector at one end and an IBM-Style hermaphroditic data connector at the other.

DB-9

Pin #	Signal
1	Receive +
2	Not used
3	Not used
4	Not used
5	Transmit -
6	Receive -
7	Not used
8	Not used
9	Transmit +

IBM Data Connector

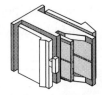

Pin #	Signal
1	Transmit -
2	Transmit +
3	Receive -
4	Receive +

When this connector is not in use, pin 1 grounds to pin 3 and pin 2 to pin 4, creating a current loop.

RJ-45

Modular connectors have become more popular due to their low cost, availability, and ease of use. Many Token Ring cards have a modular connector available on the card.

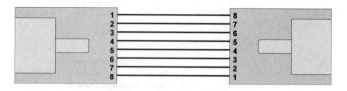

Pin #	Signal
1	Not Used
2	Ground
3	Transmit +
4	Receive +
5	Receive -
6	Recovery
7	Ground
8	Not used but set aside for future offerings.

RJ-11

There are two versions of the RJ-11 connector, 6-pin and 4-pin.

RJ-11 Connector

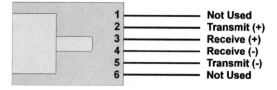

Pin #	Signal
1	Not used
2	Transmit +
3	Receive +
4	Receive -
5	Transmit -
6	Not used

RJ-11 Connector

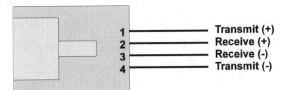

Pin #	Signal
1	Transmit +
2	Receive +
3	Receive -
4	Transmit -

Fiber Distributed Data Interface (FDDI)

The following are highlights of FDDI:

LAN Type:	FDDI ANSI X3T9.5
Access Method:	Token Passing
Topology:	Dual Counter-Rotating Rings
Medium:	Fiber Optics
Transmission Speed:	100 Mbps
Distance Limitation:	2 km between stations (1.3 miles) 200 km maximum length
Maximum Stations	1,000 stations

NOTE: Limitations are mutually exclusive. True maximums for redundant system are 500 stations and 100 Km.

Applications:

- High performance file transfer and bridging
- Security
- GOSIP
- High performance graphics communications
- Point-to-point digital imaging

Backbone network interface provisions include bridges, routers, and gateways. Direct station interfaces and concentrators are also defined.

Fault Tolerance

Dual attached stations require four strands of fiber to attach to both rings, so that in the event of a fiber break, the *wrap* feature will bypass the break by transferring data from the primary to the secondary ring. All stations must be dual attached, if this option is chosen.

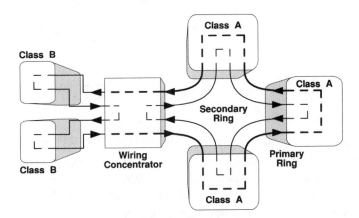

FDDI Star Configuration
Type A / Type B Stations

Class A stations maintain connections to both counter-rotating rings. Class B stations are connected to the primary ring via a wiring concentrator. In the event of a primary ring failure, only the dual-attached, Class A stations will participate in the ring reconfiguration process.

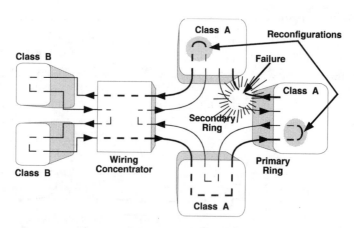

FDDI Star
Ring Failure Reconfiguration

When reconfiguration occurs, both the cable length and number of stations double. Both rings are used by each station. A single FDDI ring can include a maximum of 1,000 stations and a maximum cable length of 200 Km. If all stations on the ring are Class A stations, the maximum number of physical stations becomes 500, and the maximum cable length becomes 100 Km. Note that if a failure occurs, this ring would appear to be 1,000 stations, and 200 Km cable length.

Demand Priority Protocol - 100VG-AnyLAN

Demand Priority Protocol is a new, high speed 100-Mbps network technology, also called 100VG-AnyLAN. This LAN technology is defined with the IEEE 802.12 standard and requires 100VG-AnyLAN network adapters and 100VG-AnyLAN repeaters or hubs. An important benefit of this network technology is its ability to integrate, support, and allow for the continued use of existing LAN components. It also provides network connectivity with Category 3, 4, and 5 unshielded twisted-pair cable. It can be implemented with Token Ring and Ethernet on the same LAN and connect through existing bridges, routers, and switches. With appropriate drivers and NICs, it will support any existing NOS and application. This ability is based on the use of a frame format at the Data Link layer that supports the MAC (Media Access Control) and LLC (Logical Link Control) sublayers. The basic components of Demand Priority are end nodes and repeaters which are configured in a physical star topology.

100VG-AnyLAN uses a channel access method referred to as Demand Priority. It prioritizes packets with a deterministic request method to maximize efficiency and eliminate network collisions and token delays. The two priority levels are normal and high. This protocol assigns the priority after determining the type of packet. Repeaters will detect and/or determine packet priority. Packets are assigned a high priority if they are destined to a high priority repeater port, or if it is a time-sensitive transmission, such as video, sound, and other critical data. Normal priority traffic that has been waiting to transmit for over 200 ms will also be automatically promoted to high priority status. This protocol may also be less of a network security risk by instructing repeaters to not allow a station to run in promiscuous mode. Promiscuous mode is defined as a situation where a network card can monitor/view all network traffic that passes its port.

Demand Priority Protocol appears to offer many benefits; however, its implementation has been limited. To date, few vendors have established product platforms to support it.

Network Adapter Cards

Network adapter selections are determined by several factors:

* Access protocol

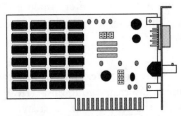

Each network adapter is matched to a particular access protocol and supports that low-level protocol only. If supporting multiple access methods, multiple card types will have to be supported, such as Ethernet, Token Ring, or FDDI.

- System bus

    The bus structure is another factor in selection. ISA bus systems support 8- and 16-bit cards, with 16-bit suggested for performance reasons. Both EISA and MCA can support 32-bit cards. Some manufacturers also have PCI bus cards available.

- Free slots

    The lack of an available expansion slot is not necessarily a limiting factor. Network adapters are available that plug into your system's parallel port.

- Cabling

    Select adapters that work with the type of cabling to be used. For example, Ethernet cards have traditionally had a BNC connector for Thinnet and an AUI connector for Thicknet. Many manufacturers now provide adapters with an RJ-45 for twisted pair.

Care must be taken to avoid conflicts with other devices during installation. Also, device drivers for your network adapter will be required by some network operating systems.

Network Adapter Installation

One of the most common failures after installing a new adapter is that it conflicts with an existing device. Conflicts can be located by checking settings for:

- IRQ

    With some limited exceptions (such as COM ports), each device must have a unique interrupt request line (IRQ). It is used as an attention signal between the processor and system devices. IRQ 3 and IRQ 5 are commonly used as default settings for network adapters.

- I/O Address

    The I/O address is used to pass commands and data to a device and receive data and status information from a device.

- DMA

    Some devices have the ability to directly address system memory. This process is managed through a DMA channel. ISA, EISA, and MCA systems each have 8 DMA channels available.

- ROM Address

  Many adapters have their own onboard ROM BIOS which must be given a unique memory address. Some adapters do not give you the ability to change this address, forcing you to reconfigure existing devices to *make room*.

IRQ, I/O address, DMA usage, and ROM addresses should be (but often are not) included as part of your system inventory for each computer on the network. If you can standardize how each of these is used on your systems, it will make them much easier to support.

Diagnostic programs, such as MSD (which ships with Windows v3.x and DOS v6.x) and WinMSD (which is included with Windows 95 and Windows NT), can provide you with information about device settings. However, some non-standard devices may generate inaccurate information.

Many new adapters are designed to the Plug and Play standard. The card will be configured automatically when installed in a system that has a Plug and Play BIOS and operating system (such as Windows 95).

Each network adapter, also called a Network Interface Card (NIC), has its own unique Media Access Control (MAC) address.

Combined Configuration List

The following is a combined list of common devices, showing IRQ, DMA, I/O Address, and Memory Address settings for PC/XT and AT systems.

Device	IRQ	DMA	I/O Address	Memory
System Timer	0			
Key Press	1		060 - 06F	
Real Time Clock	8		070 - 07F	
Math Coprocessor	13		0F0 - 0F8	
COM1	4		3F8 - 3FF	
COM2	3		2F8 - 2FF	
COM3	4		3E8 - 3EF	
COM4	3		2E8 - 2EF	
COM5	4		2F0 - 2F7	
COM6	3		2E8 - 2EF	
COM7	4		2E0 - 2E7	
COM8	3		260 - 267	
LPT1 (LPT3 not configured)	7		378 - 37F	
LPT1 (LPT3 configured)	7		3BC - 3BE	
LPT2 (LPT3 not configured)	5		278 - 27F	
LPT2 (LPT3 configured)	5		378 - 37A	
LPT3			278 - 27A	
Floppy controller	6		3F0 - 3F7	
XT Hard disk controller	5	3	320 - 32F	C8000-C8FFF
AT Hard disk controller	14		1F0 - 1F8	
Monochrome display adapter		0	3B0 - 3BF	B0000-B3FFF
CGA display adapter		0	3D0 - 3DF	B8000-BBFFF
EGA display adapter	2*	0	3C0 - 3CF	A0000-AFFFF
				B0000-BFFFF
				C0000-C3FFF

Device	IRQ	DMA	I/O Address	Memory
VGA display adapter	2/9	0	3C0 - 3DA	A0000-AFFFF
			3C0 - 3BA	C0000-C7FFF
Hercules Monochrome			3B4 - 3BF	B0000-B7FFF

*EGA will use IRQ 2, or none.

Adapter Drivers

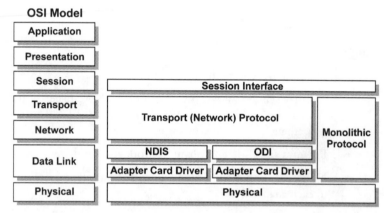

Earlier network operating systems used monolithic protocols. Monolithic protocols combined the network adapter card driver, access protocol, and transport protocol into one file. These included network operating system, network adapter card, and often, even DOS version-specific files. This frequently led to network management headaches.

To provide easier management, greater flexibility, and better support, the industry has moved away from this monolithic model. Instead, the elements are broken out into separate segments. This is done by using a separate network adapter card driver, an interface between the MAC (data link layer) and upper layers, and a separate transport protocol.

There are two common implementations of this model in the industry, known by their interface names. Network Device Interface Specification (NDIS) is an industry standard developed by Microsoft and 3Com Corporation. NDIS has been widely implemented. Open Datalink Interface is the Novell standard for the NetWare product. It performs the same function as NDIS, but is used only by Novell.

NDIS and ODI

Since both are layered models, there are a number of similarities in how the NDIS and ODI models work. The primary difference is that each has a different set of specifications for compliance, so that drivers for one will not work with the other.

NDIS

- Designed by Microsoft and 3Com.

- Industry standard used with Microsoft LAN Manager, Windows for Workgroups, Windows 95, Windows NT, IBM LAN Server, Banyan VINES, and others.

- Requires an NDIS compliant network adapter driver.

- NDIS 3.0 supports unlimited network adapters and unlimited protocols bound to each adapter.

- Allows network adapter drivers to communicate with upper level protocols.

- Associates NDIS compliant protocols with the adapter through a process called binding.

- Allows a single adapter to support multiple transport protocols.

ODI

- Unique to Novell NetWare.

- Requires an ODI compliant network adapter driver.

- Supports multiple ODI compliant network adapters and protocols.

- Allows network adapter drivers to communicate with upper level protocols.

- Associates ODI compliant protocols with the adapter through a process called binding.

- Allows a single adapter to support multiple transport protocols.

Even though NDIS and ODI support the same protocols, different protocol files are required due to differences in the interfaces.

Optional Exercise:
Exercise 2-1

This is an optional exercise. This exercise requires an operational system running DOS v6.x or with MSD.EXE available. It also requires a network adapter card and installation instructions for the cards showing how to set IRQ, I/O address, and ROM address information.

1. If not already started and running DOS, power on your system and boot DOS.

2. Type the following at the command prompt and press *ENTER*:

    MSD

3. After MSD launches, select memory to locate free blocks of upper memory. List the starting addresses of free blocks below.

4. Press *ENTER* to clear the memory summary.

5. Select **IRQ Status**. List free IRQs below. (These are identified with a "No" in the **Detected** column.)

6. Press *F3* to terminate MSD.

7. Turn off your system.

8. Using the tools, network adapter, and configuration instructions, install the network adapter. Use the values from steps 3 and 5 to determine proper IRQ and ROM address settings. Refer to your network card documentation for any other configuration values that you need.

UNBOUNDED COMMUNICATIONS

This section will present options for unbounded communication. The following topics are discussed within this section:

- Wireless Media
- Radio Frequency (RF)
- Single Frequency, Low-Power Devices
- Single Frequency, High-Power Devices
- Spread Spectrum Radio
- Microwave
- Infrared Systems

While less common, there may be situations where you need to support unbounded communications. If nothing else, you need to at least be aware of the options available.

Wireless Media

Wireless media is any media that does not use electrical or optical conductors to transmit and receive electromagnetic signals.

There are three types of energy used to signal over wireless media:

- Radio wave
- Microwave
- Infrared

Radio Frequency (RF)

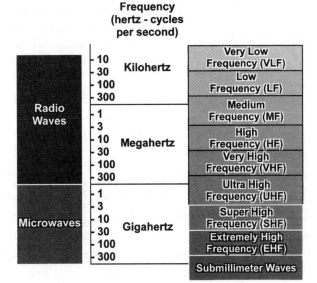

Radio Frequencies

Radio frequency, or RF, refers to broadcast systems that transport electromagnetic waves in the frequency ranges from 10 KHz to 1 GHz. Parts of this frequency range are used for the following signals:

- Shortwave radio

- Very High Frequency television (VHF)

- Frequency Modulation (FM) radio

- Ultra-high frequency radio and television (UHF)

Radio frequencies have been divided into two categories:

Regulated	Users in this category must receive a license from the regulating agency (in the US, the FCC) to maintain transmissions at the desired frequency. Having licensed frequencies guarantees clear transmissions. The licensing process can be cumbersome and costly. RF does not lend itself to flexibility.
Unregulated	These frequencies (902 to 928 MHz, 2.4 GHz and 5.72 to 5.85 GHz in the US) are not regulated through government agencies. Interference can be encountered on these frequencies. However, the equipment used for unregulated frequencies must operate with a limited power output. Thus the area covered by each system is small and unlikely to overlap others.

RF waves can either be broadcast in one direction (uni-directional) or all directions (omni-directional). The antenna and the associated transmitter will determine at which frequency the broadcast will be sent. Local systems generally use line-of-site systems, while global systems use shortwave.

There are three classes of radio transmissions:

- Single frequency, low-power
- Single frequency, high-power
- Spread spectrum

Single Frequency, Low-Power Devices

These devices generally are used for short distances and can only operate on a single frequency.

Even though low frequencies can pass through some material, the low power restricts these devices to requiring unobstructed pathways. Transmission rates are limited by the low power and frequencies used, but could be as high as that of cable-based networks. The transmission distance is limited and the cost of operation is often prohibitive.

Frequency Range	Can operate at any range. Networks generally operate in the GHz range.
Cost	Moderately priced, depending on the antennas and devices selected.

Ease of Installation	Depends on the type of equipment selected. Most equipment comes preconfigured and is simple to install.
Capacity	1 Mbps to 10 Mbps.
Attenuation	The lower the frequency and power, the higher the attenuation, so this type of signal has relatively high attenuation.
EMI Immunity	Extremely low EMI immunity.

Single Frequency, High-Power Devices

These devices are suitable for long-distance, outdoor use. The signals can either operate in a non-obstructed line of site topology or can be bounced off the earth's atmosphere. This flexibility makes these devices suitable for mobile stations.

Frequency Range	Can operate at any range. Networks generally operate in the GHz range.
Cost	The use of antenna towers, repeaters, and high-power transceivers can make this option moderately expensive.
Ease of Installation	These devices are typically complex and involve dangerously high voltage levels. The installation needs to be performed by qualified technicians. If not installed correctly, there can be safety or reliability problems.
Capacity	1 Mbps to 10 Mbps transmission speeds.
Attenuation	The high power provides relatively low attenuation.
EMI Immunity	Single-frequency transmissions are highly susceptible to EMI.

Spread Spectrum Radio

Spread spectrum radio transmissions use multiple frequencies simultaneously. There are two common methods used in selecting the frequencies to be used: direct sequence modulation and frequency hopping.

Direct Sequence Modulation

Direct sequence modulation is the most common form used. This technique encodes data as radio signals, known as chips, and carries them across a set of radio frequencies. Each frequency carries one part of each chip, simultaneously. The receiving station knows which band of signals to monitor and collects all valid signals, ignoring any spurious activity.

Frequency Hopping

This technique alternates rapidly between predefined radio frequencies. The sending and receiving stations must adhere to the same pattern of frequency hops.

Frequency Range	Can use the entire RF range. Typical installations use the unregulated frequencies in the 900 MHz and 2.4 GHz ranges.
Cost	Moderately priced, depending on the type of antennas and the receiving devices.
Ease of Installation	Most systems are purchased preconfigured. Installation can range from relatively easy to relatively difficult.
Capacity	Rates generally range from 2 to 6 Mbps.
Attenuation	Operating at low power levels, attenuation is high.
EMI Immunity	Fairly poor. However, the techniques used make it relatively easy to throw away unwanted signals.

Microwave

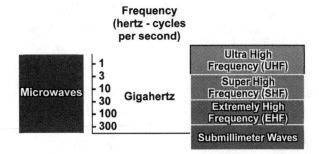

Microwave Frequencies

Terrestrial Microwave

Using terrestrial microwave requires the installation of directional line-of-sight parabolic antennas. This topology is used when cabling would be troublesome or impossible. Terrestrial microwave uses regulated frequencies that add time and expense to the installation. Omni-directional antennas can be used for microwave transmission inside buildings as well.

Frequency Range	Generally operates at either 4 to 6 or 21 to 23 GHz.
Cost	Depends on whether the network will be using short- or long-distance equipment. Long-distance equipment (including licensing fees) can be very expensive.
Ease of Installation	Very difficult and expensive to install because of the line-of-site limitation.
Capacity	Data rates range from less than 1 Mbps up to 10 Mbps.

| Attenuation | Long-distance systems will be affected by rain and fog. Short-distance systems are not affected. |
| EMI Immunity | All air transmitted systems are highly susceptible to EMI. Microwave is susceptible to atmospheric conditions as well. |

Satellite Microwave

Satellite microwave requires the installation of beamed line-of-sight parabolic antennas on the ground and on geosynchronous satellites. A basic system includes the antennas/ receiving devices located at source and destination sites plus a licensed frequency to an orbiting satellite.

Because the signal must travel to a satellite 22,300 miles above the earth and back, some time is required. This time is known as the propagation delay. In satellite systems, this delay can range from half of a second to five seconds or more.

Frequency Range	Generally operates between the 11- to 14-GHz range.
Cost	Relatively high cost.
Ease of Installation	Extremely difficult.
Capacity	Data rates for a single-frequency system generally range from less than 1 to 10 Mbps. Because of the distance traversed there will be noticeable propagation delays.
Attenuation	Atmospheric conditions affect the attenuation.
EMI Immunity	All air transmitted systems are highly susceptible to EMI. Microwave is susceptible to atmospheric conditions as well.

Infrared Systems

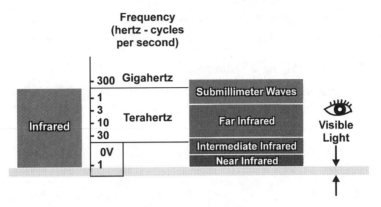

Infrared Frequencies

Infrared systems use light emitting diodes (LEDs) or injection laser diodes (ILDs) to transmit data between two sites. The light beams can be line-of-sight or can be reflected off walls or ceilings. The signals cannot penetrate either solid or opaque surfaces and are affected by strong light sources. High-frequency systems can be used to transmit data at high transmission rates. There are four types of infrared systems:

- Line-of-sight network

     The infrared signal's path between the transmitter and receiver must be unobstructed.

- Scatter infrared networks

     Transmissions are reflected by floors, walls and ceilings. One hundred feet is the limitation for this type of transmission.

- Reflective networks

     Optical transceivers pass the infrared beam to a location where it can be redirected to its destination.

- Broadband optical telepoint

    This broadband version of infrared can support cable quality multimedia presentation.

There are two infrared transmission technologies. A comparison follows.

Point-to-Point Infrared Systems

Infrared beams are tightly focused on a specific target. This decreases the effect of attenuation and eliminates eavesdropping.   This is the type of system used with TV remote controls and cordless mice.

Frequency Range	Generally operates in the 100-GHz to the 1,000-THz range.
Cost	High-quality systems can be very expensive, but consumer devices are inexpensive.
Ease of Installation	Requires exact installation and maintenance.
Capacity	Data rates are in the 115-Kbps to 16-Mbps range.
Attenuation	Depends on atmospheric conditions, intensity of beam, and any opaque material in the beam's path.
EMI Immunity	Fairly resistant to EMI.

Broadcast Infrared Systems

By relaxing the focus of the signal, this system is able to use a transceiver to transmit the signal to a multitude of receiving stations. This eliminates the need for aiming the infrared beam and can accommodate devices that move during operation. One infrared transmitter/receiver located on the ceiling can act as the hub for many users in open areas.

Frequency Range	Generally operates in the 100-GHz to the 1,000-THz range.
Cost	High-quality systems can be very expensive.
Ease of Installation	Relatively easy to install and reconfigure.
Capacity	Data rates generally are less that 1 Mbps.
Attenuation	Depends on atmospheric conditions, intensity of beam, and any opaque material in the beam's path.
EMI Immunity	Wide dispersion increases sensitivity to EMI.

PUBLIC CARRIERS

The remaining communications methods described in this chapter are used over public carriers. These are:

- X.25
- Frame Relay
- ISDN and B-ISDN
- ATM
- T1

X.25

The International Telecommunications Union (ITU, formerly the CCITT) first defined the X.25 standard as a way of physically attaching a computer to a packet-switched network. This protocol supports permanent virtual circuits (PVCs) and switched virtual circuits (SVCs). Connected devices can have multiple concurrent circuits and must provide end-to-end flow control and error control.

The main advantage of the X.25 standard is that, despite its relative slowness, it works well and is widely used in global telecommunications.

Each X.25 function is assigned to one of three levels, corresponding to the first three layers of the OSI model:

Level 1	This level includes all physical connectivity rules that have been based on communication protocols, such as the X.21, X.21bis and v.32.
Level 2	This level includes all mechanisms that are needed to create a connection-oriented path that is based on the ISO Link Access Procedures Balanced protocol (LAPB).

Level 3   This level includes the definitions of how the data packets
                       will be passed between the data terminal equipment
                       (DTE) devices, such as computers, and the data
                       communication equipment (DCE) devices, which are
                       X.25 network interface devices. Because switching and
                       routing algorithms are not part of the X.25 specifications,
                       each X.25 network service provider can select its own
                       method.

X.25 Compared to the OSI Model

OSI   X.25

| 7 Application |
| 6 Presentation |
| 5 Session |
| 4 Transport |
| 3 Network | X.25
| 2 Data Link | LAPB
| 1 Physical | X.21 and others

X.21   Physical Layer to provide point-to-point
                     connectivity on a physical mesh network
                     using synchronous communications.

LAPB   Data Link-LLC Layer to provide LLC flow
                     and error control services.

X.25   Network Layer to provide channel
                     addressing per connection and virtual circuit
                     packet switching, and Network Layer flow
                     and error control services.

Frame Relay

Frame relay addresses the same concerns as the X.25 series, except it assumes the
underlying network is reliable and has few errors. Because of this feature, frame relay
networks will perform fewer network connectivity services, but will operate at a faster rate
than X.25. Frame relay is ideal for public data networks and provides for efficient Data
Link Layer functions on permanent virtual circuit (PVC) networks.

Frame relay is commonly available at 56 Kbps to 1.544 Mbps in the U.S. and from 56 Kbps to 2.048 Mbps in Europe. When ordering frame felay services, it is customary to order a guaranteed throughput referred to as the Committed Information Rate (CIR). While the actual throughput can sometimes exceed the CIR, this extra data will be dropped by the network if it is busy. Below the CIR, all data typically will be delivered.

Frame relay has been recognized by the ITU (as 1.451/Q.931 and 1.922 specifications) and by ANSI. Frame relay is considered a WAN protocol.

Frame Relay Compared to the OSI Model

OSI　　　　　　　**Frame Relay**

| 7 Application |
| 6 Presentation |
| 5 Session |
| 4 Transport |
| 3 Network |
| 2 Data Link |
| 1 Physical |

Frame Relay

Frame Relay　　　　Works at the Physical Layer to provide point-to-point connectivity on a physical mesh network using virtual circuit packet switching communications, and at the Data Link-LLC Layer to provide LLC-level flow control and error detection (no error recovery is offered). Unlike X.25, frame relay does **not** provide Network Layer services.

Integrated Services Digital Network (ISDN) and Broadband-ISDN (B-ISDN)

ISDN is the ITU's standardized way of providing voice, data, and video transmission over the same telephone line. It uses data rates that are multiples of 64 Kbps. B-ISDN is the enhanced version offering higher data rates (multiples of 155 Mbps) over fiber optic lines. Both of these standards are generally used as WAN links.

ISDN requires the conversion of telephone networks into digital facilities so both the analog and the digital signals can be carried over the same media. Users access the digital channels through either circuit or packet switched connections known as bit pipes. These bit pipes have the following specifications:

Channel A	Runs at 4 KHz using analog signals.
Channel B	Runs at 64 Kbps using digital signals.
Channel C	Runs at 8 or 16 Kbps using digital signals. Generally used for out-of-band signaling.
Channel D	Runs at 16 or 64 Kbps using digital signals for out-of-band signals. Has the following subchannels:
	-sSubchannel for call setup and other signaling.
	-tSubchannel for telemetry like reading meters.
	-pSubchannel for low-speed packet data.
Channel E	Runs at 64 Kbps, using digital signaling for internal ISDN control.
Channel H	Runs at 384, 1536, and 1920 Kbps, using digital signals.

The ITU has also defined international services by combining the channels listed to provide particular services. The following service offerings are available for ISDN:

Basic Rate Interface (BRI)
> Two B channels at 64 Kbps and one D channel at 16 Kbps.

US and Japan Primary Rate Interface (PRI)
> Twenty-three B channels at 64 Kbps and one D channel at 64 Kbps.

Europe and Australia Primary Rate Interface (PRI)
> Thirty B channels at 64 Kbps and one D channel at 64 Kbps.

Hybrid
> One A channel at 4 KHz analog, and one C channel at 8 or 16 Kbps.

ISDN Compared to the OSI Model

OSI	ISDN
7 Application	
6 Presentation	
5 Session	
4 Transport	
3 Network	LAPD
2 Data Link	ISDN
1 Physical	

ISDN
> Works at the Physical Layer to provide time division multiplexing and at the Network Layer to provide packet or circuit switching.

LAPD
> Used with ISDN Channel D networks, works at the Data Link-MAC Layer to provide acknowledged, connectionless, fully-duplexed communications, and a physical device addressing service. Works at the Data Link-LLC Layer to provide frame sequencing and LLC flow control.

Asynchronous Transfer Modes (ATM)

This B-ISDN cell relay standard is currently being developed by the ITU-Telecommunications Standards Sector (ITU-TSS) committee and the ATM Forum. These governing bodies have defined a group of standards, Series I, that offers four classes upon which the upper-layer protocols can operate:

- Connectionless service.
- Connection-oriented service.
- Constant bit-rate service.
- Variable bit-rate service delivered with fixed delays.

These service classes are designed for different types of data. For example, computer networks would use the connectionless service, while the constant bit-rate service would be used for voice or video.

All ATM transmissions use a 53-byte long packet called a cell; 5 bytes are header information, and 48 bytes are data or payload.

ATM is generally considered a WAN protocol but has specifications for LANs and MANs.

ATM speeds range from 52 Mbps (OC-1) to 2.5 Gbps (OC-48). The most common channel speeds referenced by ATM products are 155 Mbps (OC-3) and 622 Mbps (OC-12).

ATM Compared to the OSI Model

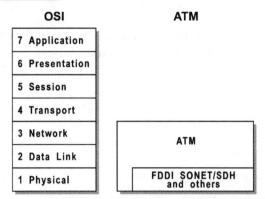

ATM works at the Data Link-LLC Layer to offer asynchronous communications and some error control and at the Network Layer to provide virtual circuit cell relay switching and static route selection services.

T1

T1 provides relatively high-speed remote connectivity. It supports digital transmissions at up to 1.554 Mbps. T1 operates over two 22-gauge twisted pairs. A regenerator is required at least every 6,000 feet. The available bandwidth can be used as a single channel or multiplexed as 24 separate channels. A regenerator is a digital device that not only amplifies the signal, but also improves signal quality. A repeater amplifies both the signal and any noise it has picked up during transmission.

SUMMARY

During this chapter, components and standards relating to the lowest levels of the OSI reference model were discussed. These included:

- Cable specifications
- Cable connectors by protocol and media type
- Access methods
- Access protocol comparisons
- Access protocol specifications
- Network adapters, drivers, NDIS and ODI

The next chapter moves up the OSI model to higher level protocols.

Scenario 1

Furry Hikers, Inc. provides dog walking services to the residents of a posh New York suburb. Due to the ever increasing need for accurate scheduling, record keeping, information sharing, etc., the 23 owner-employees have decided to install a network in their one-room office. In an effort to keep corporate costs to a minimum, each of the employees has agreed to provide his or her own PC. The server, printer, cables, and related hardware will be purchased by the company.

Questions

The answer to these questions are in Appendix A at the end of this manual.

1. Which topology should the employees of Furry Hikers, Inc. choose for their network? Why?

   ....

   ....

2. Which cable type should they use? Why?

   ....

   ....

Scenario 2

Your company is based in St. Louis. It has branch offices in Los Angeles and New York City. Each of the offices are networked internally. The networks were implemented three years ago and each is wired in a star topology that supports Ethernet 10-Mbps traffic.

Recently, your company has been developing projects that require resources from more than one office. Each office has some resources that the other offices do not. The project your company is working on requires all of these resources. As the WAN administrator, you must implement a networking solution which would offer WAN communications between all the sites. The WAN connection also needs to be able to continue operations even if one of the WAN links should fail.

Question

The answer to this question is in Appendix A at the end of this manual.

1. What topology and what type of lines will you use to connect the offices? Be specific.

    ....

    ....

POST-TEST QUESTIONS

The answers to these questions are in Appendix A at the end of this manual.

1. Which type of cable has two conductors sharing the same axis?

....

....

2. Which access protocols can be used on twisted pair cable?

....

....

3. Which cable type is least susceptible to EMI interference?

....

....

4. Token Ring is usually connected in a logical _____ topology, but a physical _____ topology.

....

....

CHAPTER 3

Protocol Suites

OBJECTIVES

At the completion of this chapter, you will be able to:

- Describe how higher-layer protocols and services relate to the OSI reference model.

- Compare and contrast popular transport protocols:

    NetBEUI

    IPX

    TCP/IP

    DLC

    AppleTalk

- Describe the relationship between TCP/IP and the Internet.

PRE-TEST QUESTIONS

The answers to these questions are in Appendix A at the end of this manual.

1. Which of the following are transport-layer or higher-layer protocols?

NetBEUI	TCP/IP
Ethernet	AppleTalk
IPX/SPX	NetBIOS

2. Which of the following are routable protocols?

    NetBEUI

    TCP/IP

    IPX/SPX

3. What is the protocol used for communication across the Internet?

    ....

    ....

4. Which provides better security, SLIP or PPP?

    ....

    ....

INTRODUCTION

Organizations such as the IEEE have prepared clearly defined specifications for devices operating at the lower levels of the OSI Reference Model. Moving through the higher levels of the model, specifications become less standardized. Different implementations are organized in a slightly different manner.

During this chapter, the protocols that operate at the network and transport layers of the OSI model will be covered. These include NetBEUI (the default protocol for LAN Manager), IPX (the default protocol for Novell's NetWare), and TCP/IP (the Internet protocol). The chapter will compare these protocols and discuss situations where each is used.

OSI Review

So far, the components and protocols that operate at the lowest two levels of the OSI model have been covered.

Our next set of protocols operates at the Network and Transport layers, managing higher-level communications activities. While each of the protocols format information in a slightly different manner, they all perform the same job.

....

....

....

....

It is important to remember that when using layered interface models, either NDIS or ODI, you have greater flexibility than with older monolithic protocol stacks. Higher-level protocols can be selected to meet organizational needs. You can even run multiple transport protocols on the same network adapter. As packets are received, they are identified according to their protocol and routed through the appropriate stack.

Network Protocols

This chapter looks at five protocols. These are:

- NetBEUI
- IPX/SPX
- TCP/IP
- DLC
- AppleTalk

Protocol selections will be determined by your NOS, organizational requirements, network size, and network configuration. Thanks to the flexibility built into modern networking products, use of a single solution within the network is not required. However, network management becomes simpler when fewer variables are involved.

TRANSPORT LAYER PROTOCOLS

This section introduces transport protocols, the *language* used when computers communicate. Key features of common LAN protocols are discussed. The following topics are discussed within this section:

- NetBEUI
- What About NetBIOS?
- IPX/SPX
- TCP/IP
- TCP/IP Suite
- TCP/IP and the Internet
- Off the Internet
- Sliding Windows
- Dial-up Connectivity

- SLIP vs. PPP
- DLC
- AppleTalk Protocol (ATP) Defined
- Network Names

A good understanding of protocols allows you to select the most appropriate protocol, or protocols, to meet your networking needs.

NetBEUI

NetBEUI (NetBIOS Extended User Interface) is a high-speed protocol first introduced by IBM.

- It was designed for use on small networks (20-200 nodes).

    Since it was designed for this environment, NetBEUI is very fast when used on small networks.

- It provides good error protection.

    NetBEUI has well-designed error detection and recovery routines.

- Tuning parameters are available to match network and organizational requirements.

    Parameters are provided to match both workstation and server configurations.

- There are limited memory overhead requirements.

    This is especially important for DOS workstations.

- It is not a routable protocol.

    Because of this, NetBEUI does not perform well on larger networks.

NetBEUI is especially suited to workgroup (peer-to-peer) network configurations, but also works well in smaller client/server networks. This was traditionally the default protocol in older LAN Manager-based network products.

What about NetBIOS?

It is not uncommon to see the term NetBIOS listed as a protocol or used in place of NetBEUI. NetBIOS (Network Basic Input/Output System) is actually an application interface operating at the session layer, rather than a protocol. NetBIOS:

- Allows applications to communicate with NetBIOS compliant protocols.

    Originally, this was limited to communication over NetBEUI, but NetBIOS applications can now be supported over TCP/IP and IPX.

- Manages communication sessions between computers.

    This is the session-level management required for a two-way interchange between computers.

- Tracks computers by computer name.

    Under NetBIOS, each system has a unique (up to) 15-character computer name that identifies it to NetBIOS sessions.

NetBIOS is supported over NetBEUI. It can be supported over other protocols, such as IPX/SPX and TCP/IP. Microsoft's implementation of NetBIOS over TCP/IP is called NBT.

IPX/SPX

IPX/SPX (Internetwork Packet Exchange/Sequenced Packet Exchange) is based on the Xerox XNS protocol. IPX runs at the Network Layer of the OSI model and SPX runs at the Transport Layer. The protocol set is commonly referred to as simply IPX.

- This is a Novell proprietary protocol.

    IPX is owned by Novell and runs almost exclusively on NetWare networks.

- IPX/SPX is available as monolithic or ODI-compliant.

    You may encounter the monolithic version of IPX on older networks. All recent drivers and IPX versions are based on Novell's ODI specification.

- IPX provides connectionless service.

    The IPX component provides high-speed communications between stations.

- SPX provides connection-oriented services.

    SPX is the portion of the protocol providing error checking, windowing, and flow control.

This is the default NetWare protocol. If you are supporting a network that includes NetWare servers, it is likely that you will need to support IPX/SPX.

IPX/SPX uses two different frame types (802.2 and 802.3). If a workstation and a server are both running IPX/SPX but are using different frame types, they will be unable to communicate.

Microsoft's implementation of IPX/SPX is called NWLink.

TCP/IP

In the last few years, TCP/IP has moved from being a specialty protocol used predominantly on UNIX-based minicomputers to the protocol of choice for many desktop computers. It is the current de facto standard for internetwork communications, a place it is likely to hold for the foreseeable future.

TCP/IP Suite

Core protocols, utilities, and services associated with the TCP/IP suite include:

- Internet Protocol (IP)

    IP provides connectionless delivery between computer systems. Since it is a connectionless protocol, there is no guarantee of proper sequencing or even arrival at the destination. Higher-lever protocols are required to ensure data integrity and proper sequencing.

- Transmission Control Protocol (TCP)

    TCP provides acknowledged, connection-oriented communications. It also provides guaranteed delivery, proper sequencing, and data integrity checks. Should errors occur during transmission, TCP is responsible for retransmitting the data.

- Internet Control Message Protocol (ICMP)

  ICMP is used to control and manage information transmitted using TCP/IP. It allows nodes to share status and error information. This information can be passed to higher-level protocols, informing transmitting stations of unreachable hosts and providing insight into the detection and resolution of transmission problems. ICMP also helps to re-route messages when a route is busy or has failed.

- Address Resolution Protocol/Reverse Address Resolution Protocol (ARP/RARP)

  ARP and RARP are maintenance protocols. They are used on Local Area Networks to enable hosts to translate IP addresses to the low-level MAC addresses that are needed to communicate at the Data Link layer.

  ARP is used to request a station's MAC (network adapter) address when only its IP address is known. Once obtained, this information is stored in the requesting system's ARP cache for later use. Since the information can be broadcast, it can also be used to update other systems. RARP is used when the MAC address is known, but not the IP address.

- User Datagram Protocol (UDP)

  UDP is designed for connectionless, unacknowledged communications. Using IP as its underlying protocol carrier, UDP adds information about the source and destination socket identifiers.

- TELNET

  TELNET may be more accurately described as a connectivity utility. It is a simple remote terminal emulation application, allowing one host to connect to and run a session on another.

- File Transfer Protocol (FTP)

  FTP supports file transport between dissimilar systems. Assuming sufficient rights, directory searches and file operations are supported.

- Simple Mail Transfer Protocol (SMTP)

  SMTP provides a mechanism for the exchange of mail information between systems. It is not concerned with the mail format, just the means by which it is transferred. SMTP is the most widely used service on the Internet.

- Domain Name System (DNS)

  Through DNS, a common naming convention is provided throughout the Internet. It is implemented as a distributed database supporting a hierarchical naming system.

- Network File Services (NFS)

    NFS is the industry standard for UNIX environment distributed file systems. It provides a common, transparent environment in which users can share files, regardless of their hardware platform.

TCP/IP and the Internet

Today's Internet is a collection of diverse networks, each connecting a range of systems together for a distinct purpose. There is an ever expanding list of systems connected to the Internet, including most major academic institutions throughout the world, the U.S. defense establishment, and a rapidly growing number of commercial organizations.

The common denominator between these networks is the use of TCP/IP. TCP/IP allows communication between different computer systems, even those using different communication methods. TCP/IP hides the computer types and communication methods from users on the Internet, allowing them to communicate on a peer-to-peer basis.

Each Internet user has access to a wealth of information, most supplied free by subscribers. TCP/IP shields the users from the mechanics involved in providing the information. It allows them to communicate seamlessly with available computer systems regardless of their type.

Off the Internet

Because TCP/IP is not owned by any one organization or corporation, but accepted by almost all computer systems, it has value beyond the Internet. It is widely becoming the protocol of choice due to its flexibility. Its performance is somewhat less than protocols such as IPX on small LANs, but the difference is usually not significant. TCP/IP has become the obvious first choice as an interconnectivity solution. The following is only a partial list of supported systems:

- MS-DOS PCs and compatibles
- Microsoft Windows-family PCs and compatibles (including Windows NT)
- OS/2 PCs and compatibles
- Apple Macintosh
- Novell NetWare
- Banyan VINES
- DEC VAX/VMS and ULTRIX
- IBM AS/400
- IBM VM or VMS mainframes
- UNIX-based systems

Though it may not meet all networking needs, TCP/IP fills most organizations' communication and connectivity requirements.

Sliding Windows

TCP uses the *sliding windows* concept to support transmission of multiple packets before receiving acknowledgement. On a reliable network, this can mean improved throughput on data transmissions. The first step is to set transmission parameters. During the initial handshake:

- The segment size is agreed upon, based on the maximum packet size of intermediate routers.
- Each system will send its receive buffer size.
- Each system will set its transmit buffer (send window) to the other's receive buffer size.

During data transfer, the sending system can send as many segments as will fit in the send window without waiting for acknowledgement. As each packet is sent, a retransmit timer is started. If acknowledgement is not received for that packet before the time expires, the packet is retransmitted.

The receiving system will send acknowledgement when:

- Two or more sequenced segments are received.

- The window has filled to 50%.

- When 50% of the window is freed by passing data to the client application.

- When acknowledgement is received for specific packets, those packets are removed from the send window (buffer). The window is then "slid" along the queue to include the next segments waiting to be transmitted. At that point, the only packets in the window are those waiting for acknowledgement or waiting for transmission. Those waiting for transmission are sent immediately, continuing until the entire data block is transmitted.

Dial-up Connectivity

When TCP/IP dial-up connectivity is needed, either to the Internet or to the corporate network, there are two popular protocols available. These protocols are SLIP (Serial Line Internet Protocol) and PPP (Point-to-Point Protocol).

SLIP vs. PPP

Both Serial Line Internet Protocol (SLIP) and Point-to-Point Protocol (PPP) provide a dial-up connection to the Internet. SLIP is the older protocol. It supports fewer features than PPP.

SLIP

- Established protocol
- Requires minimal overhead
- No compression
- No error checking or flow control
- No security provided by the protocol
- Supports TCP/IP only
- Uses static IP address

Once considered the de facto standard for serial (dial-up) connections, SLIP has lost popularity in recent years.

PPP

- Newer protocol
- Requires a small amount of overhead, though less than SLIP
- Supports compression
- Error checking and flow control are provided
- Security supports the use of encrypted passwords
- Supports TCP/IP, NWLink (IPX/SPX), and NetBEUI
- Allows DHCP dynamic IP addresses

DLC

Data Link Control is not used for general LAN communications, but is required for communications with other systems running the DLC protocol stack. Currently, there are only two applications where you are likely to see it used in a PC environment:

- IBM Mainframe connectivity

    The DLC transport protocol can be loaded to connect to an IBM mainframe.

- Network printers

    DLC is used to connect with HP (and compatible) printers directly attached to the network.

If you are not supporting either of these applications, there is no reason to install DLC transport protocol support.

AppleTalk Protocol (ATP) Defined

Apple created the AppleTalk protocol suite to offer networking capabilities for Macintosh computers. AppleTalk offers connectivity to a variety of computers, including IBM PCs running MS-DOS. AppleTalk Phase II offers increased maximum numbers of networked computers and interoperability with other protocols in large heterogeneous networks.

AppleTalk is a protocol suite, supporting:

LocalTalk (LLAP)

This Physical and Data Link layer protocol is a proprietary Carrier Sense Multiple Access/Collision Avoidance (CSMA/CA) protocol that is best used on small networks. It has a transmission rate of 230.4 Kbps and has a maximum of 32 devices (Phase II: 16,000,000 devices) spanning 300 meters.

These devices are self-addressing and will negotiate the network address with existing devices on the network. Apple refers to LocalTalk protocols using Ethernet cabling as EtherTalk, and LocalTalk protocols over Token Ring networks as TokenTalk.

AppleTalk Address Resolution Protocol (AARP)

This allows AppleTalk protocols to run over any Data Link Layer architecture using a mapping technique to associate logical and physical addresses.

Datagram Delivery Protocol (DDP)

> This protocol provides connectionless service between two sockets. Sockets can be assigned statically or dynamically. DDP performs route selection through an internetwork.

AppleTalk Data Stream Protocol (ADSP)

> ADSP provides a full-duplex connection-oriented service that runs on DDP. ADSP is a more conventional transport mechanism than the transaction-based ATP.

Routing Table Maintenance Protocol (RTMP)

> AppleTalk routing tables are established and maintained by this protocol.

Zone Information Protocol (ZIP)   ZIP maintains network-number-to-zone-name mappings in Zone Information Tables. Used primarily by routers, end nodes can also use ZIP to choose their zone and acquire internetwork zone information.

Name Binding Protocol (NBP)   NBP translates between AppleTalk names and dynamic node addressing.

AppleTalk Transaction Protocol (ATP)

> This protocol acknowledges delivery of information and initiates retransmission when data is unacknowledged for a given time. Unlike most transport protocols, ATP does not track a stream of data, but tracks a single transaction. A transaction is a single request-reply pair of transmissions.

AppleTalk Session Protocol (ASP)   This is a Session Layer protocol that establishes, maintains, and terminates network sessions.

Printer Access Protocol (PAP)   This Session Layer protocol is used to establish dialogue between the clients and ANY network service offered by the server, not just the printer services.

AppleTalk Filing Protocol (AFP)   This protocol provides for transparent access to network files.

The three primary services offered by the AppleTalk protocol suite are:

AppleShare File Services	This service offers remote access to networked files. AppleShare clients access AppleShare file servers.
AppleShare Print Services	This service offers communication to printers on the network.
AppleShare PC	This service offers file services that allow DOS-based computers access to AppleTalk files.

Network Names

One important area that needs to be discussed is network naming. At the lowest level, communications between machines is handled by the MAC address, a unique address coded on the network adapter. Upper-level protocols, such as TCP/IP, often use numeric or alphanumeric addressing to identify stations and the network on which they reside. The fundamental problem with both of these is that they are not very *human-friendly*.

As a way around this, most protocols support symbolic names, plain text names by which machines may be known. How names are managed is unique to the protocol and, somewhat, to the network operating system. As examples, let's look at how names are managed under TCP/IP and NetBEUI.

TCP/IP uses host names. In a Microsoft networking environment, these normally default to the machine name. Communicating with another host by its name under TCP/IP is an indirect process. The name must first be resolved, meaning that it must be mapped to a valid TCP/IP host (network and machine) address.

NetBEUI is tied very closely to NetBIOS and uses NetBIOS names. In a Microsoft networking environment, the machine name is used. Communications are resolved by name. Under NetBEUI, however, the machine must be in the same local subnetwork.

NetBIOS names are not limited to NetBEUI only. They can be supported under TCP/IP and IPX/SPX, but communication with systems on other subnetworks, requires resolution of the destination network address.

In a Microsoft networking environment, NetBIOS names can contain up to 15 alphanumeric characters with no embedded spaces. It is common usage to give machines names that are easily recognizable and if possible, give some clue as to the machine's location.

SUMMARY

This chapter included an introduction to:

- NetBEUI
- NetBIOS
- IPX/SPX
- TCP/IP
- SLIP
- PPP
- DLC
- AppleTalk

The next chapter introduces several LAN concepts and provides a look at additional LAN devices.

Scenario 1

Your network currently consists of 120 client computers and five servers. Some of the client computers are NetWare clients, some are Apple clients, and the rest are UNIX and Windows NT Workstations. Two servers run Microsoft Windows NT Server, and three servers run NetWare v3.12. Your company would like all users to be able to access all five servers. You have several printers with JetDirect cards attached directly to the network cable. Human Resources has expressed interest in an intranet to make policies and forms more easily available. You want to install the least number of protocols possible to optimize performance.

Question

The answer to this question is in Appendix A at the end of this manual.

1. Which protocol(s) would you choose in this situation? Why?

....

....

Scenario 2

Just-Us-Chickens, Inc. is a poultry company located in central Arkansas. It is primarily a Microsoft environment. However, the marketing department uses Macintosh computers for their desktop publishing, and the accounting department has several UNIX machines. Last year, the demands on the network grew to the point that Joe, the network administrator, was forced to install routers and create several subnetworks. At the same time, he brought up a new server and connected three new printers directly to the *wire*. That gave Just-Us-Chickens a grand total of three servers and five printers to meet the needs of all 120 employees. Unfortunately, Joe didn't know which protocols were required for this environment. He decided to cover all of the bases and install every protocol he could find. Joe installed TCP/IP, IPX, DLC, NetBEUI, and AppleTalk. This greatly affected computer performance because of the overhead required to run so many protocols.

Questions

The answers to these questions are in Appendix A at the end of this manual.

1. Which protocols should Joe remove? Why?

....

....

2. Why is each of the remaining protocols required?

....

....

POST-TEST QUESTIONS

The answers to these questions are in Appendix A at the end of this manual.

1. What protocol would you be most likely to use on a 25-node LAN Manager network?

....

....

2. What is the protocol used on the Internet?

....

....

3. Which Novell NetWare protocol component provides connectionless service?

....

....

4. What is the name of the protocol suite that offers networking capabilities for Macintosh computers?

....

....

LAN Concepts and Higher-Level Devices

OBJECTIVES

At the completion of this chapter, you will be able to:

- Describe the purpose and use of the following network devices:

    Repeater

    Bridge

    Router

    Brouter

    Gateway

- Identify at which layer of the OSI reference model selected network devices operate.

- Determine the most appropriate device to use, given a network connection scenario.

PRE-TEST QUESTIONS

The answers to these questions are in Appendix A at the end of this manual.

1. Between routers and bridges, which device typically has better throughput?

   ....

   ....

2. You want to divide your network into subnetworks to try to isolate traffic near servers. What type of device would you most likely use to connect the subnetworks?

   ....

   ....

3. Repeaters operate at which layer of the OSI model?

   ....

   ....

4. What type of device is used for connecting incompatible networks?

....

....

INTRODUCTION

The following communication devices are covered in this chapter:

* Repeaters
* Bridges
* Routers
* Brouters
* Gateways

Each device plays an important role in network management. These devices are covered in detail throughout the chapter, including what each device does and examples of situations in which each is appropriate.

Internetwork Devices

There are four different types of devices typically used to form internetworks:

* Repeaters
* Bridges
* Routers
* Gateways

On a technical level, these devices are distinguished by the OSI level at which they function:

Gateways	Level 1-7	All Layers
Routers	Level 3	Network
Bridges	Level 2	Data Link
Repeaters	Level 1	Physical

Another device, known as a Brouter, combines the characteristics of a Bridge and a Router.

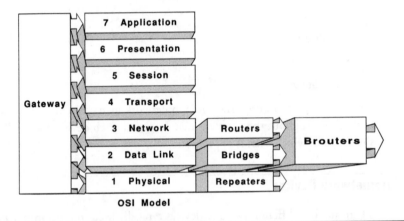

INTRODUCTION TO REPEATERS

Repeaters operate at the Physical Layer of the OSI Model. They allow you to physically extend network segments. The following topics will be covered in this section:

- Repeaters
- Repeaters and Their Role

Repeaters

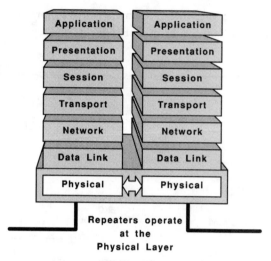

Repeaters operate
at the
Physical Layer

In simple terms, a repeater amplifies the electronic signal from one network cable segment and passes it to another. As an amplifier, a repeater connects network segments of similar media. It is not sensitive to higher-layer protocol attributes since it simply takes a signal from one side and amplifies it on the other side.

In addition to amplifying the signal, a repeater also amplifies noise. As a result, there will be a limit to the number of repeaters that may be used in a given network segment.

Intelligent repeaters regenerate the digital signal and are immune to the limitations of increasing attenuation over distance.

Repeaters extend baseband networks that use one signal. Broadbase networks support multiple signal transmissions simultaneously. An example of a broadbase network is cable TV. Broadbase networks use amplifiers to extend their signal transmissions.

Repeaters and Their Role

The earliest functional role of repeaters was to simply extend the physical length of a LAN. This is still one of the primary benefits of a repeater.

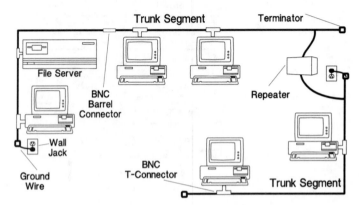

There are, however, several potential problem areas that are not addressed by repeaters. These include:

- Signal quality

  Most repeaters do nothing to filter noise out of the line, so it is amplified and sent on with the signal.

- Time delays

  Time delays can occur as signals are generated over greater distances. These delays may eventually generate timeout errors, keeping repeaters from being used for remote links.

- Network traffic

  Because they do not have the capacity to filter traffic, repeaters do nothing to reduce the network traffic load.

- Node limitations

  Repeaters are *invisible* to access protocols. All nodes added through a repeater count toward the total that can be supported in a subnet.

Repeaters are typically used on bus networks. To get the best signal quality, place a repeater so that the two segments connected are approximately the same length.

INTRODUCTION TO BRIDGES

This section introduces bridges. This includes a look at bridge functions and available options when implementing bridges. The following topics will be covered in this section:

- Bridges
- Heterogeneous (Translating) Bridges
- Encapsulating Bridge
- Flow Control In a Bridge
- Routing Management for Bridges
- A Learning (Transparent) Bridge
- Additional Filtering and Intelligence
- Local and Remote Bridges
- Layer 2 Switches

It is important that you understand each of the network connection devices, including bridges, to be able to select the correct device to meet network requirements. Bridges provide a way of segmenting network traffic and connecting different LAN types.

Bridges

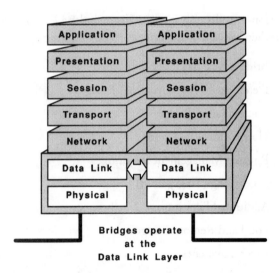

Bridges operate
at the
Data Link Layer

Bridges are more intelligent than repeaters. They can read the specific physical address of devices on one network and filter information before passing it on to another network segment.

Bridges operate at the Data Link Layer, or more precisely, at the Media Access Control (MAC) sublayer. They go beyond simply amplifying the signal and are able to regenerate it. Rather than passing on line noise, a clean signal is sent out. This allows bridges to expand a network beyond what is normally allowed with repeaters.

In general, bridges:

- Are transparent to higher-level protocols.

  Segments connected through a bridge remain part of the same logical network.

- Can filter traffic based on addresses.

  This allows a bridge to reduce traffic between segments. This feature can also be used to improve security by selecting the packets that can be passed.

There are a number of other terms and concepts relating to bridges and how they operate. The following presents detailed information on several of these.

Heterogeneous (Translating) Bridges

A bridge must read an actual MAC layer frame. Therefore, some bridges may be limited to linking similar MAC layer protocols.

In special cases where physical addressing is similar and the logical link services are identical, hybrid bridges can be developed to allow linkages between dissimilar MAC layer protocols.

Because a number of the 802 series of protocols share the common 802.2 Logical Link Control (LLC) layer, it is possible for bridges to interconnect different types of networks such as Ethernet and Token Ring. One example of this is the IBM Model 8209 Ethernet to Token Ring Bridge. Bridges of this type are also called translating bridges.

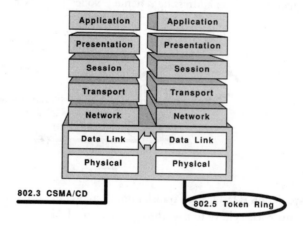

Encapsulating Bridge

In encapsulating mode, a bridge packages frames of one format in the format of the other. For example, Token Ring frames may be *encapsulated* in Ethernet frames and passed out onto the Ethernet network. Presumably, there would be another Ethernet-Token bridge which would de-encapsulate the packets and put them on a second Token Ring network where they would be read by a destination station.

To stations on the intermediate Ethernet, these *encapsulated* frames would be unrecognizable since there is no lower level address translation being performed by the bridge.

In the example below, Packets from LAN A could be read by nodes on LAN C because they share a common addressing scheme. Nodes on LAN B could not read the packets.

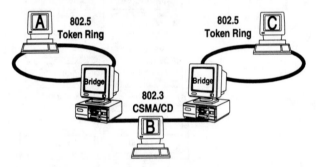

Encapsulation is faster than translation. It allows the LAN to pass data more quickly when the packets have to pass through multiple LANs.

Flow Control in a Bridge

In complex internetworks, any LAN segment may have multiple paths to reach a given destination. When such choices arise, two critical issues are confronted.

First, flow control information is necessary to know the relative capacities of each of the various bridge segments.

Second, some form of routing control is necessary to make sure that segments with multiple links do not reproduce and distribute the same information. In this case, it is possible that two bridged segments would transmit the same frame, leading to a redundant message arriving at the destination node. This can cause serious operational confusion in any network system.

Flow control is especially important on large, active networks; many studies suggest that 80% or more total traffic in a bridged network is local traffic. Less than 20% of the total traffic needs to be broadcast on the backbone.

Routing Management for Bridges

No aspect of bridging is more confusing than *routing* protocols that relate to bridges and not routers. The purpose of these routing protocols is to eliminate the possibility of duplicate frames that may be generated by having segments with multiple links that form loops in a bridged network. These loops could potentially allow packets to circulate within a segment of the network and ultimately clog the network.

Spanning Tree Routing Algorithm

Bridges that support the Spanning Tree Algorithm are able to communicate with each other and negotiate which bridge(s) will remain in a blocking mode (not forward packets) to prevent the formation of loops in the network. The bridges in the blocking mode continue to monitor the network. When they notice that another bridge has failed, they come back on-line and maintain the network connections.

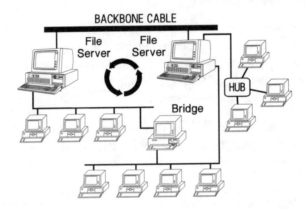

Source Routing Algorithm

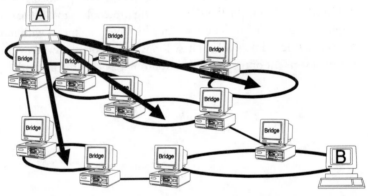

Source routing is found in IBM's Token Ring networks. In this environment, a workstation determines the routes to other workstations with which it wishes to communicate by transmitting an all-routes broadcast frame which propagates throughout the network. The second station's reply to the broadcast includes the route that the original frame took, and from that point on, that route is specified by the initial station (the source) for the duration of communications between the stations.

As a result, bridges in a Token Ring environment rely on the source to supply the routing information in order to be able to forward frames to other networks.

Source Routing Transparent bridges have been proposed by IBM which would forward other types of frames as well as those with source routing information.

A Learning (Transparent) Bridge

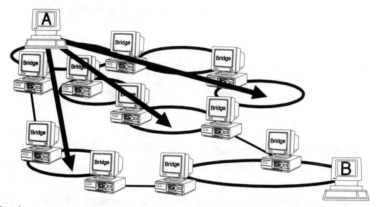

Modern bridges are usually referred to as learning bridges, because they are capable of automatically identifying devices on the segments they connect. A learning bridge listens to each of the attached cable segments and creates a table of addresses originating on each segment. It does this by listening to the replies. Until it knows where a destination station is, it forwards all of the packets for that station.

In the example shown, A's initial message to B may go out on the backbone, but B's reply teaches the bridge not to forward packets which are sent from A to B, or B to A. Similarly, a reply from C teaches the bridge C's location.

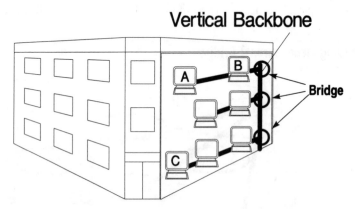

When a learning bridge receives a frame from Station A, it records A's source address as a node on LAN 1. The bridge does this for all frames coming from LAN 1. For any frame that comes from LAN 1, if the destination address is one of the addresses recorded on LAN 1, the frame will simply be discarded instead of being broadcast on the backbone. Only unrecognized frames from LAN 1 will be forwarded to the backbone.

This filtering process means that all local traffic from LAN 1 remains on LAN 1 and does not hit the backbone. A learning bridge's filtering effect on local traffic can be significant.

Additional Filtering and Intelligence

Many vendors have realized that the processor resources required to read frame addresses can be put to extended use and have thus created bridge filtering.

Bridge filtering consists of looking for other patterns within the frame to selectively control the frames which will be forwarded.

This additional capability in a bridge has raised confusion over the technical definition of a bridge. The standards-oriented technicians are inclined to say that looking at information within the frame envelope for such patterns is a higher-level service; which, indeed, it is. However, these services can be layered effectively in bridge devices.

> NOTE: *Given the ability to identify patterns within the frames, bridge filtering might be deployed to selectively bridge only certain protocols.*

Local and Remote Bridges

In addition to filtering and learning capabilities, bridges can also be categorized based on the linkage between the two network segments.

When a bridge has a LAN link directly attached on each side, it is referred to as a local bridge. Local bridges are characterized by comparable input and output channel capacities.

When a bridge must link a local network across a wide area segment, it is referred to as a remote bridge. The output channel from the remote bridge is usually of dramatically lower bandwidth capacity.

This difference in relative bandwidth capacity on the input and output channels makes remote bridges significantly more complex to design and manage. They must be able to buffer inbound traffic and manage timeout errors. It is also necessary to design your network to keep traffic requirements over the remote link to a minimum.

Layer 2 Switches

The term *Layer 2 Switch* (also known as a data switch) is generally a more modern term for multiport bridge. Like bridges, switches operate at the Data Link Layer of the OSI model. However, although their basic functionality is the same, switches often implement some more advanced filtering techniques to optimize performance. These filtering techniques are called Virtual LAN (VLAN) features. Although most VLAN filtering techniques have no universally accepted standard, they tend to fall into a few categories.

- Port-based grouping

    Certain ports can be assigned to a specific VLAN. Packets will be kept local to the VLAN.

- Address-based grouping

  Certain addresses can also be assigned to a specific VLAN. Packets will be forwarded only to the appropriate VLAN.

- Protocol-based grouping

  The switch can examine the access protocol and forward the packet accordingly. This is Level 3 switching.

- Subnet-based grouping

  If you are using TCP/IP, some switches may be able to identify the appropriate subnet and forward the packet accordingly. This is Level 3 switching.

INTRODUCTION TO ROUTERS

This section introduces routers and their appropriate use in a network environment. The following topics are discussed within this section:

- Routers
- About Routers
- Router Features
- Brouters

Routers allow you to build an internetwork computing environment and are a key element in wide area networking. Careful planning and proper implementation help to build an efficient communications environment.

Routers

As networks become more complex, simple bridging does not provide enough control of the flow of traffic. For example, broadcasts in a bridged network may propagate unnecessarily throughout the network. Routers allow for the segmentation of an extended internetwork into manageable, logical subnets.

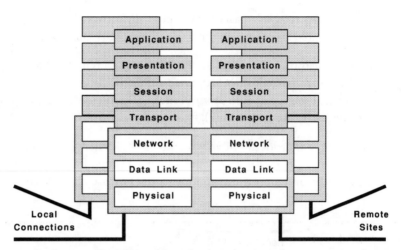

Routers are fundamentally different from bridges, because they operate at the Network Layer. This means that a router opens the MAC (Media Access Control) layer envelope and looks at the contents of the packet delivered at the MAC layer. The contents of the MAC layer envelope are used to make routing decisions. This also means that protocols must have Network Layer addressing to be routable.

Routers may not match the throughput of bridges. Router activities require more processor time, more memory, and multiple network connections. Current routers are typically fast enough to handle Ethernet and Token Ring traffic without dropping packets.

About Routers

Early routers often supported a single protocol, such as TCP/IP or XNS. Today, multiple protocol routers may support 15 to 20 protocols simultaneously. In some cases, routers may be integrated with a LAN operating system such as Novell's NetWare IPX routing or Banyan VINES (both of which are derivations of XNS). However, the rise of networks running multiple protocols on the same wire is leading to the increased use of third-party multiple protocol routers.

When a router receives a packet, it will generally forward it to the appropriate network based on a table maintained in the router. These tables may be either static or dynamic.

A static table is maintained by a system manager and is updated manually as the network is modified. A dynamic table is updated automatically as routers converse among themselves, using a common protocol such as Routing Information Protocol (RIP) or Open Shortest Path First (OSPF).

Bandwidth is dramatically cheaper on the LAN. Modern backbone networks are now migrating to 100 megabit speeds and above. The need for flow control, multiple path management, and routing decision rules arises primarily in wide area links.

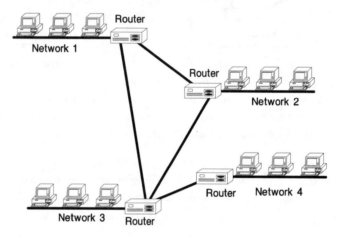

Wide-area connections generally require a routable protocol, such as TCP/IP or XNS. Each network segment is a separate logical network and may be administered independently. This also provides easier fault isolation.

The additional intelligence of routers allows for multiple (redundant) paths between locations, which provides both backup and the ability to do load balancing and makes full use of available bandwidth. With bridges, multiple paths have to be avoided. Spanning Tree, for example, shuts down redundant links until they are needed, which is a waste of bandwidth.

Offsetting the higher cost of managing and coordinating these more complex connections is the increased functionality that includes the ability to isolate individual workgroup networks as unique subnets. The router provides a port of entry that can control entrance and exit of traffic to and from the subnet. This segmentation is vital in organizations that rely on department-level network management. It also improves security and reduces congestion across the internetwork.

The programmable features of routers allow for effective management of remote links. Because these wide area connections are the most expensive components of the network, proper management and prioritization of traffic on these links is a vital concern for multi-site organizations.

Router Features

Processor/Memory/Storage

Routers are actually specialized microcomputers with highly tailored I/O capabilities. Memory is particularly important because it is used to buffer packets in times of congestion.

Routers are typically contained in a box the size of a PC. In some cases they may simply be a PC, as in the case of an external NetWare router or a Windows NT server with RIP for Internet or RIP for NWLink IPX. There is also a trend toward router cards used in hubs or wiring concentrators.

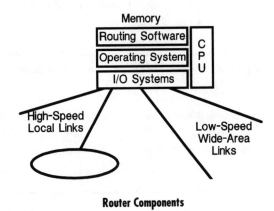

Router Components

Physical Interfaces (Ports) Supported

These may vary considerably from vendor to vendor. In some cases, the router may be a simple box with multiple ports from which two or three particular ports may be selected. Other boxes may be expanded through the addition of cards supporting particular interfaces.

On the LAN side, there may be the common Ethernet, Token Ring, or ARCnet interfaces. Connections to the wide area (telecommunications) network may include RS-232, V.35, and RS-442 interfaces. Other possible interfaces include FDDI and broadband.

Since hardware is similar for bridges, routers, and brouters, upgrades may simply require new software.

Protocols Supported

Multiprotocol routers typically support most of the common network protocols including, but not limited to, TCP/IP, Xerox XNS, other XNS-based protocols such as Ungermann-Bass, Banyan VINES, Novell's IPX, the ISO CLNS, DECnet, HP Advancenet, SDLC, and AppleTalk.

In the wide area, protocols to consider include X.25, Frame Relay, and Switched Multimegabit Data Services (SMDS) in addition to dedicated lines ranging up to 56 Kb or T1 speeds.

Protocols used between routers to communicate routing table information include RIP, OSPF, the End System-Intermediate System protocol (OSI ES-IS), and the Intermediate System-Intermediate System protocol (OSI IS-IS), as well as proprietary vendor protocols.

LAN Protocols	Router Protocols	WAN Protocols
TCP/IP	RIP	ATM
XNS	OSPF	X-25
IPX	OSI ES-IS	Frame Relay
AppleTalk	OSI IS-IS	SMDS
DECNet		
HP Advancenet		
many more...		

Configuration/Management (Open/Proprietary)

Most routers will have a simple (RS-232) serial port to provide terminal access to the router, either directly or by modem, if necessary. This provides a simple, generally character-oriented interface for configuring and managing the router. There may also be the possibility of connecting across the network to manage the router remotely.

Security with respect to managing the router may consist of simple password protection, but it may be possible to restrict access to particular network addresses or only the serial port. Many routers allow for the use of filters or access lists to limit access to or from a particular router. This feature makes it possible to isolate particular subnets or to restrict access to the wider network to particular users or stations.

Simple Network Management Protocol (SNMP) is a TCP/IP-based management protocol that may be implemented on routers. With SNMP, it may be possible to "SHOW" or "SET" various characteristics of a router to an SNMP-based management station. The difficulty with SNMP is that it does not provide for security, so the ability to "set" the parameters of routers using SNMP is avoided.

OSI standards for network management are expected to provide more in the way of security. Common Management Information Protocol (CMIP) is the OSI-based protocol expected to provide standard management of network devices in general. CMOT (CMIP over TCP/IP) is an implementation of CMIP using TCP/IP as a transport for use in managing TCP/IP networks specifically. Until CMIP is widely available, proprietary offerings may be the best alternatives where security is an issue.

Brouters

Brouters operate at both the Network Layer for routable protocols and at the Data Link Layer for non-routable protocols.

As networks continue to become more complex, a mix of routable and non-routable protocols has led to the need for the combined features of bridges and routers. Brouters handle both by acting as routers for routable protocols and bridges for non-routable protocols. Bridged protocols may propagate throughout the network, but techniques such as filtering and learning may be used to reduce potential congestion.

INTRODUCTION TO GATEWAYS

This section introduces gateways, which operate at all levels of the OSI Model. They provide a communications path between otherwise incompatible systems. The following are topics discussed within this section:

- Gateways
- Gateway Function
- Gateway Types

As with the other devices, gateways provide the most appropriate, and possibly, the only solution for certain network needs.

Gateways

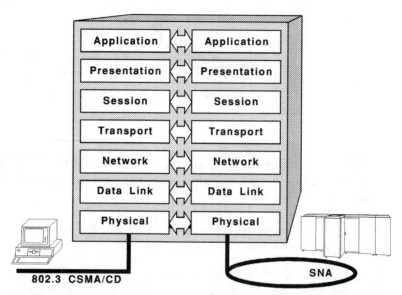

802.3 CSMA/CD

SNA

Gateways generally operate at all layers of the OSI Model. They may provide full content conversion between two environments, such as ASCII to EBCDIC, as well as other application and presentation layer conversions. In this role, they are the primary linkage between heterogeneous environments, such as PC-based LANs and host environments like SNA.

Other types of gateways include fax gateways, which may allow users to send and receive faxes from their workstations. These may also be integrated with mail service gateways which allow communications between users of different mail systems.

Gateway Function

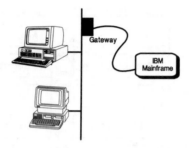

A gateway connects *incompatible* networks at the fourth through seventh layers of the OSI Model using protocol conversion and routing services. Gateways are comprised of both hardware and software.

Since they are designed to provide full application translation between two network types, a gateway examines the entire packet including the data portion.

Because of the overhead incurred by the protocol conversion process, gateways handle fewer concurrent devices and are much slower than repeaters, bridges, or routers.

Gateway Types

There are several different types of gateways, including:

Asynchronous	This gateway is used for communication with async host computers and bulletin boards.
X.25	This gateway allows connection to remote hosts through a PDN using a wide range of terminal emulation.
3270	This gateway is used for communication with IBM mainframe or compatible hosts.
5250	This gateway is used for communication with IBM System/3X series or IBM AS/400 minicomputers.
TCP/IP	This gateway links non-TCP/IP systems with TCP/IP systems.

Gateways can operate in both local and remote environments. 3270 gateways may establish a link from a workstation on a LAN to a cluster controller via coaxial cable on an Ethernet network, or through the placement of a cluster controller or Front-End Processor (FEP) in the ring of a Token Ring network.

Gateways can provide significant network savings because of the reduction in the number of required cables and computer parts, as opposed to each stand-alone microcomputer running gateway software.

Cost Comparison

Several factors should be considered when choosing a network connectivity device:

- Current needs

    Which device meets the needs of my current network environment?

- Future needs

    Will the current network be expanded? If so, should I purchase a device that will meet the current needs *and* allow for expansion?

- Cost

    How much money has been budgeted? Can I afford to plan for the future? Can I afford *not* to?

We have included this table to help summarize the key features and cost category of the most common network connectivity devices. This should help you decide which device fits within your budget. Please keep in mind that this table is to be used only as a guideline. The actual cost of these devices will depend on the manufacturer and additional features.

Device	Key Features	Cost
Repeaters	Amplifies the electronic signal from one network cable segment and passes it on to another.	Inexpensive
Bridges	More intelligent than repeaters. Can regenerate the original signal before passing it on to another network segment.	Inexpensive to Moderate
Routers	More complex than bridges. Allow for the segmentation of an extended internetwork into manageable, logical subnets.	Moderate
Brouters	Combination of bridges and routers. Act as routers for routable protocols and bridges for non-routable protocols.	Moderate to Expensive
Switches	Provides high speed connectivity to nodes, maximizing limited bandwidth.	Moderate to Expensive

Picking the Right Device

There can be some question as to the most appropriate device to use in a specific situation. Most of the issues have been covered during this chapter's discussion, but following summaries maybe helpful.

- Using Bridges

    Bridges allow you to segment directed (addressed) traffic and connect different low-level protocols as a single logical network. Through careful planning and adjusting the physical location of clients and servers, the overall network traffic can sometimes be reduced. A bridge can be used in these situations, but keep in mind that broadcasts are propagated through bridges and will add to the overall level of background traffic. Use a bridge for remote connections only if the remote site is to be treated as part of the local network.

- Using Routers

    Routers allow communication between different networks. Traffic is segmented by network. Only traffic destined for a network, or that must pass through the network to reach its final destination, is sent into the network. Non-routable traffic (such as NetBEUI) and broadcast messages (with the exception of DHCP, TCP/IP Dynamic Host Configuration Protocol messages) are not passed through routers. Routers allow traffic to be segmented by subnetwork and can reduce overall network traffic. Care must be taken, however, in placing servers and clients. Routers are commonly used when connecting remote LANs. They allow each subnetwork to be managed separately and typically help to minimize the traffic levels between the subnetworks, leaving a greater percentage of the bandwidth available for necessary transmissions.

- Using Gateways

    Gateways are used to connect dissimilar platforms where significant translation and other special support is required. The most common example is connecting network PCs to a mainframe or minicomputer host. There are, however, other uses. One use often encountered is the utilization of gateways to connect different mail systems, allowing them to pass messages.

One key point, especially when dealing with routers and bridges, is default packet sizes. When passing data from a segment that uses larger packet sizes to one that uses smaller packet sizes, the connection device is usually responsible for resizing the packets. It must break the data packets down into the smaller packet size, buffering the data until sent and verified. This can adversely effect performance during data transfers, such as when copying large files.

SUMMARY

This chapter continued the discussion of network devices and how they relate to the OSI reference model. These included:

- Network protocols
- Repeaters
- Bridges
- Routers
- Brouters
- Gateways

The next chapter moves on to system management fundamentals.

Scenario 1

Each of the accountants in Dollar Accounting has a workstation connected to an Ethernet network. The auditors, who work down the hall from the accountants, are also connected to an Ethernet network. All of the workstations are using NetBEUI as their transport protocol.

Questions

The answers to these questions are in Appendix A at the end of this manual.

1. Provided they have network software that supports peer-to-peer networking, can they share resources with each other?

   ....

   ....

2. What is the least expensive network device that can connect the accountant's network with the auditor's network?

   ....

   ....

Scenario 2

Fumble-Fingers Detective Agency has a server that the detectives use to store their case data. The detectives are connected to the server by an Ethernet network. They are using NetBEUI as their transport protocol. They are interested in combining their resources with Call Again Collections. Call Again Collections keeps their client database on a server attached to a Token Ring network. They are also using NetBEUI as their transport protocol.

Questions

The answers to these questions are in Appendix A at the end of this manual.

1. What will these companies need to change to share information?

    ....

    ....

2. Why?

    ....

    ....

Scenario 3

Earthbound Airlines has decided to connect their New York office with their Los Angeles office. Their Los Angeles office is using IPX/SPX as their transport protocol. Their New York office is using TCP/IP.

Question

The answer to this question is in Appendix A at the end of this manual.

1. What network device will allow them to connect their two offices together?

    ....

    ....

POST-TEST QUESTIONS

The answers to these questions are in Appendix A at the end of this manual.

1. A repeater operates at which layer of the OSI Model?

   ....

   ....

2. What type of device is used to connect incompatible networks?

   ....

   ....

3. What device is used to divide a network into logical subnets?

   ....

   ....

4. What is a bridge that can convert packets from one protocol to another (such as Ethernet to Token Ring) called?

   ....

   ....

5. When is a static router table updated?

   ....

   ....

6. What is the term for a device that combines features of a bridge and router?

    ....

    ....

7. What is the lowest-level device that can be used to filter network traffic, thereby reducing the communications load?

    ....

    ....

Network Management Fundamentals

OBJECTIVES

At the completion of this chapter, you will be able to:

*   Describe guidelines for proper user management.
*   Define key password guidelines.
*   Identify common fault tolerance features.
*   Describe the various network services.

PRE-TEST QUESTIONS

The answers to these questions are in Appendix A at the end of this manual.

1. What is the significance of using group definitions for user management?

    ....

    ....

2. Which security model provides more centralized control, user-level or resource-level?

    ....

    ....

3. What data is backed up by a differential backup?

    ....

    ....

4. On a small network (10-15 users), which would likely be less expensive to implement, client/server or peer-to-peer networking?

    ....

    ....

INTRODUCTION

The first four chapters covered the physical components of a network. This chapter covers another integral part of networking–network management. It begins with a section on system security. This will include user-management, as well as an overview of disaster recovery. The chapter will conclude with information pertaining to various networking services.

Although the overall concepts contained in this chapter apply to any network operating system, the text primarily covers the Microsoft Windows NT networking environment.

NETWORK SECURITY

This section takes a general look at network security with a special focus on the Windows family of products. The following topics will be covered in this section:

- User Management
- About Users
- A Word on Passwords
- Group Accounts
- Security Models

Security management is one of the most important tasks performed by network administrators. Users will let you know if you do not give them enough access, but you may not find out about security holes until it is too late.

User Management

Security is an important part of any network, and user definitions are the first line of defense. User account management is a common part of ongoing network management. It is appropriate, then, to examine user management.

The Windows NT security system is based on:

- User and group definitions.

  User names and passwords control primary access security and the logon process. Some security features can be more easily managed at a group level than at a user level.

- Domain-wide definitions.

  You can make domain wide definitions regarding password parameters and security policies.

- Rights assignments.

  Access to local and shared data files is determined according to rights assigned to a user or group.

- Security tracking.

  You have the ability to track security events such as logons and logoffs, and store them in a file for later viewing and analysis.

The real strength of a security system lies not in what is there, but in how it is used.

About Users

Users are the first, and perhaps the most vital link in the security chain. Some key points about user account definitions include:

- Create a user account for each user.

  Each user should have his or her own account for logons. If you use temporary personnel, create an account for each of them as well. Sharing accounts can lead to security problems, especially when trying to track down the source of unauthorized user access.

- Limit the number of users, especially administrators.

  Provide accounts for only those users who have a valid reason for access. Create administrator accounts only when no other account type can be used. Since administrators have nearly unlimited access to the system, each administrator account is a potential security risk.

- Limit the use of administrator accounts.

  Each administrator should also have a standard user account. Administrators should log on as administrator only when it is necessary to perform administrative or management functions. At all other times, they should log on as a standard user.

- Be cautious when assigning rights and permissions.

  Users will let you know if you do not assign the permissions they need. If you accidentally assign too many, you may not find out until it is too late.

- Enforce security through available tools.

  Set times and points of access according to user requirements. Use care in creating groups so that you do not give users rights or permissions you did not intend for them to have.

Proper user management can sometimes take up a significant amount of time, but this should be considered time well invested.

A Word on Passwords

An important issue in user management is the selection of good passwords. Since users in most cases set their own passwords, you need to provide them with guidelines that you hope will be followed.

- Always require passwords.

  By leaving a user name unprotected you are asking for trouble. You should give the user account an initial password when it is created and require the user to change the password after the first logon.

- Change passwords on a regular basis.

  It's normally suggested that passwords be changed every 30 to 60 days. More often than that can become inconvenient; less often, and you may be defeating the purpose of forcing password changes.

- Do not use easily guessed passwords.

  Children's names, spouse names, pet names, and such make bad passwords. If someone knows you well, it will not take long for them to guess your password.

- Use nonsense words and special characters.

    Common words with special characters leading, following, or embedded, are hard to guess. So are nonsense words or words that have been purposely misspelled.

- Do not leave passwords displayed in an obvious location.

    It is not uncommon to find passwords in desk drawers, taped under keyboards, even posted on display screens. Emphasize to your users the importance of keeping passwords secret. In some companies, disclosure of a password is grounds for termination.

Good passwords go a long way toward helping ensure access security.

Group Accounts

In many network operating systems, such as Windows NT, group account definitions are used to manage access permissions and user rights. Any rights and permissions granted to a group are granted to the group members. Security management is more efficient since you can make changes for sets of users, rather than managing each user separately.

Security Models

Network security is generally identified as following one of two general security models. These are:

- Share-level

    Access is defined by the resource (a directory or printer) when the resource is shared to the network. Access permissions are tied to passwords associated with the resource when it is shared out. Thus, the individual machine sharing the resource is responsible for access validation.

    This model is relatively easy to implement in a small network. Each user is given direct control over access security and is responsible for managing access permissions for resources shared from his or her workstation. This can, however, lead to inappropriate access permissions being assigned. Other drawbacks include:

    No Central Management.

    Users may have to remember multiple passwords, one per resource

    Share-level password are supported by Windows for Workgroups and Windows 95, but not by Windows NT

- User-level

    Rather than being based around passwords at the resource level, resource access is based around network users and groups. Network servers validate access security for all resources.

    This model gives tight, centralized control over resources, including resources shared by network workstations. Access validation is handled at the network server level for both network servers and peer servers (workstations). It does require a client/server network, normally either Windows NT Server or Novell NetWare.

The Windows family of products support both models. Windows for Workgroups and Windows 95 are designed to support share-level or user-level access. Windows NT Server, Windows NT Workstation, and Windows-family clients used in an NT Server domain or Novell NetWare environment, are configured around the user-level model.

BEING PREPARED FOR DISK FAILURES

This section discusses physical data security, focusing on disk fault-tolerance methods and the role of backups. The following topics will be covered in this section:

- Protecting Data With Windows NT
- NTFS
- Audit Policies
- Disaster Planning
- Disk Fault Tolerance
- Disk Mirroring
- Disk Duplexing
- Using Disk Mirroring/Duplexing
- Disk Striping With Parity
- About Disk Striping

- Using Stripe Sets

- Replication

- About Replication

- Backups

- UPS

Disk failures will occur. Your role is to minimize the resulting downtime and loss of data. The importance of protecting mission-critical data cannot be over-emphasized.

Protecting Data With Windows NT

Microsoft Windows NT provides an additional type of data protection. By implementing the New Technology File System (NTFS) and enabling event auditing, you can protect your system against another kind of threat–unauthorized user access.

Using the NTFS file system is one of the steps necessary to provide C2-level security. C2-level security is a United States Department of Defense definition.

C2-level requirements include:

- User point of access control through a unique user name and password.

- Resource access control with access limits set by user or group. Access control must be both inclusive and exclusive.

- Protected memory management restricting memory contents from access until released by the controlling process (program).

- Security event audits with access to audit contents restricted to administrators.

- A security audit, in which the identity of users performing actions is recorded.

- Protection against outside influence and tampering of operating system or system files.

The next few pages will provide an overview of NTFS and event auditing.

NTFS

The NTFS file system is new to, and designed for, Windows NT. It provides speed, reliability, additional data security, and support for very large disk volumes and data files.

- Operating system compatibility

  NTFS partitions can only be accessed locally while running Windows NT. The partitions are not available locally to either DOS, OS/2, or Windows 95. However, Windows NT allows users of other operating systems to access resources on the NTFS partition, provided they are shared to the network and the user has the appropriate permissions.

- File name formats

  File names of up to 255 characters are supported. When you create a long file name under NTFS, the operating system automatically creates a DOS/ Windows compatible file name.

- Fully recoverable

  NTFS is designed to have a fully recoverable directory structure. A log is kept of disk activities to "roll back" the disk in case of system failure. Windows NT also provides the AUTOCHK and CHKDSK utilities to repair a corrupted disk or in case automatic recovery fails.

- Secure

  With an NTFS partition, you can make full use of the Windows NT security system, including rights assignments and auditing.

Audit Policies

Windows NT uses auditing to track selected user events. Entries are placed in the Event Viewer's security log, which can only be viewed by an Administrator.

To establish Audit Policies on a Windows NT Server:

1. Launch User Manager for Domains.

2. Select **Audit** from the **Policies** menu. The Audit Policy dialog appears.

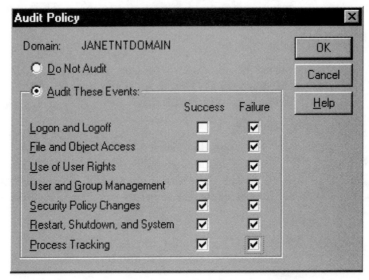

If the Audit These Events option is selected, the following categories can be included in the security log if the corresponding enabled for success or failure checkboxes are checked:

Logon and Logoff	An entry is generated each time a user logs on, logs off, or makes a network connection.
File and Object Access	This enables tracking of auditing events defined under Explorer and Print Manager.
Use of User Rights	Each use of user rights, except those relating to logon and logoff, generates an entry.

User and Group Management	An entry is generated any time a user or group account is created, changed, or deleted; when a user account is renamed, disabled, enabled; or when an account's password is set or changed.
Security Policy Changes	An entry is generated any time a change is made to User Rights or Audit policies.
Restart, Shutdown, and System	An entry is generated when the system is shut down or restarted when a system security event occurs, or when a security log event occurs.
Process Tracking	Generates entries for events such as program activation, selected handle duplications, indirect object accesses, and process exits.

Events can be set to generate entries on success, failure, or both.

Disaster Planning

Problems are going to occur. Hardware is going to fail. Networks are going to crash. The best thing is to plan for the inevitable, implement as many disaster avoidance mechanisms as possible, and be ready to react quickly when necessary. Some key points include:

- Plan for the worst.

    Look at worst case scenarios and determine what would be necessary for recovery. Identify critical systems, users, and resources. Determine how to get the network working again as quickly as possible. Document disaster plans and distribute them to everyone involved.

- Implement physical data security.

    Protect your data. Whenever possible, set up live redundant copies of the data. Back up all data on a regular basis, test backups to verify that they can be read, rotate backups, and keep a copy offsite whenever possible.

- Protect your critical systems.

    Implement physical security, keeping critical servers behind locked doors. Install UPS systems on critical servers and critical user stations.

While these will not avoid every possible disaster, they will help to make disaster recovery significantly easier. It also is recommended that disaster recovery drills be run to fully prepare for emergencies.

Disk Fault Tolerance

One of the best tools available on the modern network is implementation of Redundant Array of Inexpensive Disks (RAID) technology. Some documentation defines RAID as Redundant Array of Independent Disks. RAID is a set of specifications, describing hard disk fault tolerance configurations.

- Raid Level 0: Disk striping without parity

    Data is distributed across a series of drives. This is not recommended for file servers since failure of any drive in a level 0 array leads to the effective loss of all data on the array. Raid Level 0 does not provide fault tolerance. Its only benefit is that it increases the speed of disk I/O.

- Raid Level 1: Disk mirroring/duplexing

    Data is mirrored across two disk partitions. This can result in better overall performance than other RAID options. Mirroring a pair of disks reduces the total disk storage by one-half.

- Raid Level 2: Disk striping with Error Correction Code (ECC)

    Data is striped across the drives of an array at the bit level. This method was designed for large computers with disk controllers that are as smart as or smarter than a typical PC.

- Raid Level 3: ECC stored as parity

    Data is striped across a series of drives yielding high transfer rates. A single additional disk is used to store parity information. This type of system works well for workstations requiring fast sequential access to single large files, such as image processing systems. Not recommended for transaction processing systems or environments in which most I/O transactions are for small amounts of data.

- Raid Level 4: Disk striping with large blocks

    Clusters of data are placed across a series of drives enabling multiple reads. A single additional disk is used to store parity information. This allows a multitasking operating system to process independent read transactions for each data drive in the array.

- Raid Level 5: Disk striping with parity

    Data and parity blocks are spread across all drives in the array. This eliminates the dedicated parity drive and allows multiple read and write transactions to be performed in parallel. As more drives are added to the array, performance increases during disk reads.

Various manufacturers implement RAID at different levels. Disk units that support RAID 5 and are compatible with network operating systems are available, but they are often very expensive.

The fault-tolerance methods available with Windows NT are discussed on the following pages.

Disk Mirroring

Disk mirroring is an implementation of RAID Level 1. It uses two disk drives configured to have the same logical size that are connected to the same disk controller. During each data write, the same data is written to both disk partitions.

Disk mirroring features include:

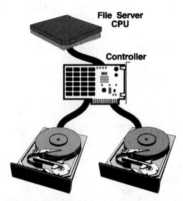

- Disk utilization is 50% of the dedicated storage space.
- All-around disk I/O performance is generally better than disk striping with parity.
- A mirrored pair can be split without loss of data.
- The boot partition (active system partition) can be mirrored.

Disk mirroring is designed to keep the system going in spite of disk errors or loss of a hard disk.

- Read error

    If an error occurs during a read, data from the other disk is used.

- Drive failure

    If one drive fails, the server will continue running, using the other drive.

Both Windows NT and NetWare support disk mirroring.

Disk Duplexing

Disk duplexing is an implementation of RAID Level 1 and is very similar to disk mirroring. It uses two disk drives configured to have the same logical size, and that are connected to separate disk controllers. During each data write, the same data is written to both disk partitions.

Disk duplexing features include:

- Disk utilization is 50% of the dedicated storage space.

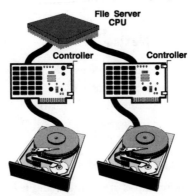

- All-around disk I/O performance is generally better than disk striping with parity and even better than disk mirroring during data reads.
- A mirrored pair can be split without loss of data.
- The boot partition (active system partition) can be duplexed.

Disk duplexing is designed to keep the system going in spite of disk errors or loss of a hard disk.

- Read error

    If an error occurs during a read, data from the other disk is used.

- Drive failure

    If one drive fails, the server will continue running, using the other drive.

Both Windows NT and NetWare support disk duplexing.   The term disk mirroring is often used to refer to both disk mirroring and disk duplexing.

Using Disk Mirroring/Duplexing

Disk mirroring and disk duplexing are normally used on peer-to-peer networks and smaller LANs to protect critical data files.   Due to the amount of storage lost through redundancy, it is not commonly used on larger LANs.

Use disk mirroring when:

- Data must be protected against drive failures.

- Hard disk resources are plentiful and will continue to be available as system requirements grow.

- Administrative resources are scarce, since the system continues to process read and write requests when a failure occurs.

Disk mirroring protects against the failure of any one drive.   Disk duplexing also protects in case of failure of a drive or disk controller.   With either, users can continue to work without interruption.

Disk Striping with Parity

Disk striping with Parity with parity is an implementation of RAID Level 5.   In essence, Windows NT Server is doing the same thing as commercial RAID drive arrays, but through software rather than hardware.   Between 3 and 32 (inclusive) disk drives may be included in a stripe set.   The disk space used on each drive will be approximately the same.   Windows NT Server will match the space selected to the smallest single partition when the stripe set with parity is created.

- Disk utilization is reduced by the size of one disk drive.

- Data and parity information is written across all drives.

- Performance on disk reads is improved.

- The boot partition (active system partition) cannot be included in a stripe set.

The system can continue working after the failure of any one disk drive. Performance before and after failure will be the same on disk writes, but will degrade on disk reads.

Windows NT server supports disk striping with parity. There is, however, a possibility of confusion. Windows NT also supports disk striping without parity, which does not provide any fault tolerance.

About Disk Striping With Parity

Data and parity are spread across all of the drives in a stripe set. As data is written, it passes through an algorithm to generate the information for the parity stripe. What might be lost in write performance, however, is more than made up in read performance and data security.

Disk Striping with Parity

Cluster1	Cluster2	Cluster3	Cluster4
Parity	Cluster5	Cluster6	Cluster7
Cluster8	Parity	Cluster9	Cluster10
Cluster11	Cluster12	Parity	Cluster13
Cluster14	Cluster15	Cluster16	Parity
Cluster17	Cluster18	Cluster19	Cluster20
Parity	Cluster21	Cluster22	Cluster23
Cluster24	Parity	Cluster25	Cluster26
Cluster27	Cluster28	Parity	Cluster29

Because of the way data clusters are organized, large data files tend to get written across multiple drives. By splitting read requests, the system can give excellent read performance.

Possibly more important is the data security. If a drive is lost, the system can recover any missing data by going through its calculations on the remaining data and parity stripes. Of course, read performance suffers when this happens. When the drive is replaced, all of its data can be recreated.

Using Stripe Sets

Disk striping with parity is normally used on larger networks where data integrity and minimized down time are critical concerns. While the amount of storage space lost can be significant, the percentage of space lost to parity becomes less as more drives are added.

Use disk striping with parity when:

- At least three hard disks are available.

- Optimal read performance is desired.

- Data integrity is a critical concern.

You are protected against the failure of any one drive. The failing drive should be replaced as soon as possible. Users can continue to work without interruption, but performance is degraded.

Replication

Replication is a feature somewhat specific to LAN Manager-based networking products, specifically Windows NT Server. It is also supported on Windows NTAS v3.1. Through replication, data is automatically copied from a source system (exporter) to a destination system (importer). This can be a one-to-one relationship, several exporters sending to one importer, or one exporter sending to several importers.

Only Windows NT Servers (including NT Advanced Server) and LAN Manager v2.x servers may act as exporters. An export directory is specified as the data source. Any number of direct subdirectories and up to 32 levels of subdirectories below the export directory are supported.

Windows NT Workstations, Windows NT Servers, and LAN Manager servers can act as importers. An importer does not have to be located in the same domain as the exporter with which it communicates.

Replication occurs when a file is modified, then closed. This gives you a near immediate backup of volatile data files, or allows you to propagates files as needed between network servers. Replication is a service that defaults to *off* but can be activated.

About Replication

Let's look as some key points about replication services.

- Replication runs as a background service, invisible to the station's use.

- Only subdirectories of the export directory are replicated.

- After any changes, files must be closed before they can be replicated.

- You can specify to replicate files immediately after a change or have the system wait a specified time after any changes occur in the subdirectory tree.

- Individual subdirectories may be locked, manually preventing replication of that subdirectory.

- An exporter can send files to one or more importers.

- An importer can receive files from one or more exporters.

- The import directory may be locked, manually preventing replication.

- A Windows NT Server may act as both an exporter and importer.

Suggested uses for replication include:

- Replication of logon scripts to all domain servers.

- Replication of mandatory user profiles.

- Replication of files to another location on the same server to provide separate master and working file sets.

- Replication of frequently used files across multiple servers to balance the server load.

As you work with directory replication, it is likely that you will find other uses.

Backups

No matter what type of disk management scheme you implement on your network, you must still have a way to back up and recover important data. You can choose from a wide range of storage media including magnetic tape, digital audio tapes (DAT), optical disks, or Write Once Read Many (WORM) drives. But regardless of which media you select, you should perform frequent backups and store a copy of the data off-site to protect it in the event of fire, flood, or any other unforeseeable disaster.

There are essentially three types of backups you can perform:

- Full backup

     This will back up all of the data on the server. Archive bits will be reset.

- Incremental backup

     This will back up any data that has changed since the last backup (full or incremental). Archive bits will be reset.

- Differential backup

     This will back up any data that has changed since the last *full* backup. Archive bits will not be reset.

Windows NT has a built-in tape backup utility. There are also a number of third-party backup products that are fully compatible with Windows NT.

UPS

The use of an Uninterruptible Power Supply (UPS) is strongly recommended. It keeps your system from going down unexpectedly due to line power loss.

A UPS uses a battery to supply power to the system. The computer is connected directly to the battery, which is connected to the outlet. A UPS also insulates the computer from spikes, surges, and other electrical inconsistencies, thus maintaining a consistent supply of power.

One newer innovation of UPS systems is the addition of a serial port. With a serial port, operating systems like OS/2 and Windows NT can utilize a monitoring system which will detect a power failure. When this occurs, a graceful shutdown will be initiated by the operating system.

When determining whether the backup power system will be powerful enough to maintain the computer in the event of a failure, watts and watt-hours need to be examined. The watt rating of the UPS should always be larger than the cumulative number of watts drawn by the equipment which will be plugged into the UPS.

Another issue to consider is the length of time that battery power is supplied. To determine maximum time relative to the computer system, check the rating of the batteries it uses. Most batteries are rated in ampere hours, which describes how much current they can deliver for how long. However, some of this power is consumed for the operation of the device, and the ratings are usually based on new batteries. In most cases, all the device needs to do is to allow several minutes for the computer to shut down gracefully. Five minutes is usually sufficient.

Servers and business-critical workstations should be protected by UPS.

NETWORK SERVICES

This section will discuss services provided by network operating systems and network servers. The following are topics discussed within this section:

- Network Services Defined
- File Services
- Print Services
- Messaging Services
- Network Service Implementation
- Centralized File Service
- Distributed File Service
- Specialized Servers
- Application Servers
- Database Services

It is important to know not only what capabilities are currently available for the network environment, but also those that may be implemented to improve support to network users.

Networking Services Defined

Another area that falls under the realm of network management is Networking Services.

Networking services allow computers to share data, processing power, and input/output devices to accomplish their computing tasks. The network services generally are combined into a Network Operating System (NOS). The trend has been for many of the network services to migrate to the local operating system.

However, the NOSs have been specifically designed to offer these services and generally perform them more efficiently. For instance, Server Message Block (SMB) is a protocol developed by IBM, Intel, and Microsoft. SMB defines how machines on a network communicate. SMB is the core of the Windows NT operating system. The redirector on an NT network workstation packages network control blocks (NCB) which contain SMBs to send to the destination device. When the NCB is received, the data portion of the SMB request is stripped away so the local machine can fulfill the request. The local operating system is installed on a single computer and controls the resources of that machine. Network operating systems can be distributed on machines throughout the network.

Some common network services offered by the NOS include:

- File services
- Print services
- Messaging services

There are also a number of specialized services that can be provided by network servers.

File Services

File service applications are used to store, retrieve, and pass data between devices. They perform the read, write, access control, and data management functions for the NOS. File services allow you to:

- Move files from environment to environment.

- Take full advantage of network storage devices.

- Keep track of several copies of the same file.

- Allow backup of critical files.

File services are one of the primary services offered by networks. These can be subdivided into the following categories:

- File transfer

     File transfer is any activity that saves, retrieves, or moves a file for a network client. File transfers can be performed regardless of the size of the file or the distance to be traversed. While this service will not increase an organization's efficiency, it will make corporate data and information readily available to those who need it. For organizations that maintain a high level of security, the file servers can also offer access control for the individual files. This control can take the form of password protection or data encryption.

- File storage and migration

  Because of the massive amount of data that is accessed by clients on the network, the industry has been forced into creating numerous online, near-line, and offline storage devices. Online means the media is mounted and always available, as in a hard drive. Near-line means the media may not always be mounted, but can be automatically mounted without human intervention. An example of near-line storage is a jukebox containing multiple CD-ROM volumes. Offline means the media is not usually mounted and human intervention is required to mount it, such as a floppy disk or tape. Some of the popular storage media today are:

  Magnetic or optical disks.

  Diskettes.

  Tapes.

  Each of these storage media offers unique capabilities and management requirements. Sometimes the savings in physical space can help justify the purchase of high-density storage media. All networked clients can take advantage of the storage devices depending on their needs. As data ages it can be migrated to less expensive, slower storage media.

  Copies of critical data can be stored off site as an added security measure.

  Moving data from one storage media to another is referred to as data migration. Data might be migrated based on any of the following:

  Who owns the data.

  How long the data has been on the storage device.

  How large the file is.

- File synchronization

  If the server that stores information is available all the time, it is simple to keep track of the most recent copy of the file. Remote users connected over unreliable links and occasionally connected laptop computers make this more challenging. Having multiple users accessing the same files offline can cause the user to retrieve information that is not the latest. File-update synchronization deals with this challenge.

  By offering synchronization services, the system will not allow users to retrieve out-of-date information. The synchronization process will use a time stamp system to track file updates. The synchronization services will check the time stamp and determine which of the corresponding dates are the most current. Using this information, the server will update all copies of the file in the order in which they have been changed.

- File backup

    It is often important to make a copy of your data to guard against loss, just as you might keep a photostat copy of an important document. For computers, this process is called backup or archival. The data can be stored on magnetic tape or some other type of offline storage media. This archival process will keep one copy of the file on the on-line retrieval system and keep a dated copy in permanent storage. These file storage devices can be connected to the network to allow system administrators to perform remote backups.

Print Services

Print services allow applications to share output devices including printers and fax servers. Print services accept the print job, interpret the format and configuration, manage the print queue, and interact with the networked printers and fax equipment.

Some of the advantages of using print services are:

- Minimizing the number of printers within a company.
- Providing convenient physical locations for printers.
- Using print queues to reduce the time computers spend handling a print job.
- Sharing specialized or expensive printers.

Print service functions fall into the following categories:

- Offering access to devices using limited interfaces.

    Some printers offer multiple ports for connecting to other devices. However, to connect the printer to the network, only one port is necessary. All networked computers will be able to use this one connection to send their print jobs. Multiple clients can be served more efficiently. One of the major uses of computer networks today is providing this printer sharing.

- Eliminating distance limitations.

    The type of interface used on the printer determines the distance limitation. Networking the printers avoids these limitations, allowing companies to place the printers in strategic locations.

- Queuing facilitates acceptance of multiple jobs per printer.

    Print servers are used primarily as *traffic cops*. However, they can also receive multiple print jobs and hold them in a queue for the printer. This capability frees up the computer to perform other tasks. The print server agent will keep track of the job, often notifying the client when the job has been printed. The client's applications believe that they are sending the output directly to a printer. It is the network operating system's print service that captures the job and queues it for the printer.

- Sharing specialized or expensive equipment.

    There is often specialized equipment that needs to be shared on the network. Examples are fax servers, high-speed printers, and color printers. This equipment can be expensive and infrequently used. This is where economy of scale in networking comes into play. These devices can be offered to multiple clients, thus reducing the need to purchase multiple devices.

    An example of this is the use of fax servers. Fax servers are used to accept and send copies of documents in an electronic format, thus eliminating the *paper* phase of the fax process. Advanced fax servers can route incoming faxes directly to the client workstation for user viewing or editing.

Messaging Services

Messaging services offer similar services to those found in file services. Instead of dealing with just the storage of information, messaging services deal with the communications between users, their applications, network applications, and individual documents.

The messaging services not only store data, but transport it between the devices and notify users that they have a message. The *user* of the messaging service may be a person or other software.

Messaging services allow the user to:

- Exchange electronic notes and files.
- Use electronic mail packages with voice mail systems.
- Access objects distributed throughout the network using object-oriented software.
- Share corporate data using both work flow and linked-object applications.
- Centralize and maintain user messaging directories.

Messaging services fall into these categories:

- Electronic Mail

    Electronic mail, or e-mail, is a set of applications that allows the transfer of information between two or more networked users. While early versions of e-mail allowed the transfer of text-based messages, today's e-mail allows for a wide variety of data formats and for automation of routing and delivery decisions.

    Today's e-mail allows the attachment and translation of multiple data formats in one *message*. E-mail has become so standard that many companies use it as a primary means of communications over their global networks.

- E-Mail and Voice Mail Integration

    Voice mail servers use specialized computer hardware with associated software components to answer telephone signals and record voice messages in a digital format. Because these systems are wholly contained, they can be easily integrated into the network and interfaced with e-mail applications.

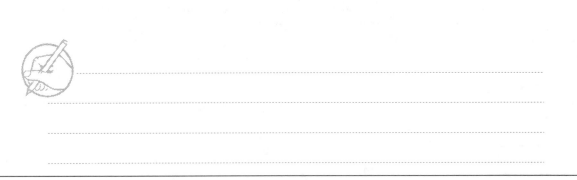

- Object-Oriented Design Applications

    Object-oriented applications are constructed of multiple, limited-function application modules.   Each module has certain characteristics, defining both data types and instructions.   These modules are used to construct larger, more complex application modules.   Applications that have been created using object-oriented designs are merely a set of smaller applications that perform specific tasks bundled into applications that perform more complex tasks.

    Messaging applications that are object-oriented can provide message servicing by acting as the application module's object agent.   By using the agent as an intermediary, the individual modules do not need to interact with each other.   Individual modules communicate with the agent, and it is the agent's responsibility to communicate the message to the receiving module.   Each application module does not need to know how to communicate with other application modules or entities, only how to communicate with the object agent.

- Workgroup Applications

    Workgroup applications are a class of applications that work on the message server's platform.   There are two major types of these applications:

    Workflow Management

    For multi-user business applications, workflow managers act as intelligent routers to deliver forms, notices, and other documents to users on the network.   For example, a form that needs to be processed by three employees can be automatically routed from one to the next.   The messaging servers will ultimately be responsible for the routing and delivery of the workflow management information.

    If properly implemented, workflow management can provide cost and time savings.   This is especially true if it can replace paper-based systems.   The workflow management services eliminate most of the time involved in moving paper from one place to another.   Instead, the information flows over the network at electronic speeds.

Dynamically Linked Object Applications

The linked-object model is becoming a standard for client workstation compound documents. A compound document is one that can contain links to graphics, audio, video, databases, spreadsheets, and programs. Applications that handle these compound documents incorporate independent data objects into a larger document. This allows the applications to take text and integrate it with graphics, voice, and video components. Each object has the intelligence to act as the messaging agent to the other objects to which it is linked.

•   Directory Services

All messaging servers must maintain directories so they can keep track of the source and destination of messages. Messaging servers identify the entities in a workgroup and keep current address information on these entities. Messaging servers also communicate any changes in local directories to other messaging servers on the network.

This process of creating, maintaining, and updating directories is called directory synchronization. By using this process, the messaging server's clients do not need to know the exact address of other clients on the network. They can rely on the directory services to perform this task.

Network Service Implementation

After the system administrator chooses the types of network services to offer, he or she must also choose whether the services will be centralized or distributed. Network services can be offered using peer-to-peer computing environments, but most services are combined into a server-centric NOS. Service distribution decisions should be based on the following criteria:

- Control of Resources

    The decision of who controls the devices that offer the services is often political in nature. The least complicated means of controlling service hardware is to centralize the responsibility into one dedicated group that can monitor all activity.

    By centralizing this process, it is easy to track which computer is offering which service. If this process is distributed, it may become difficult to track faulty equipment if there is a failure. However, a centralized support group may be less responsive than a more local group.

- Server Specialization

    Some tasks are best performed by specialized servers. The need for server specialization depends on the resources required to complete a particular task. It is necessary to determine how powerful the computer acting as the server needs to be. In small LANs, the file server usually offers all necessary services for that particular network. The use of specialized servers implies a degree of centralization.

- Network Operating System

    How many of the services can be distributed will depend on the network operating systems chosen. In today's market, most vendors are attempting to make their software as flexible as possible. Historically, NOSs have been either server-centric or peer-to-peer. Today these definitions are blurring as server-centric and peer-to-peer methods are used on the same networks and by the same clients.

    The NOS chosen will determine which services are offered. As the vendors become more standard, organizations should be able to choose different systems to perform multiple services all on the same network.

    File services are greatly affected by the decision to centralize or distribute the network services. If the network clients need to access the same files, it becomes the responsibility of the network servers to keep track of the shared files and the storage media.

Centralized File Service

Centralized file services are normally provided by a network file server. A file server operates on a single computer on the network. The file server tracks all requests for reads and writes to the files and controls the storage media.

The advantages of using centralized file servers are:

- Storage, retrieval, and file swapping are accomplished rapidly and efficiently.

- Cost of purchasing and maintaining the file server is spread among all users.

- File server administrators control resources including maintenance and data protection.

The disadvantages of using centralized file servers are:

- Server failure can bring down the network.

- Non-archived data can be irretrievably lost.

- File retrieval times across a network are often much slower than the retrieval from a local workstation's hard drive.

Centralized file services normally use the user-level validation module.

Distributed File Service

With distributed file services, the file services are provided by multiple computers for both their own applications and for others on the network. Each computer provides the necessary data and/or resources for their peers within the network framework, making each station approximately equal. This type of service networking is commonly referred to as peer-to-peer.

The advantages of using peer-to-peer are:

- Failure of one peer computer does not bring down the system.
- Local file retrieval times are quicker because they are coming from the client workstation's primary storage.
- Often less expensive to install because a dedicated server is not required.

The disadvantages of using peer-to-peer are:

- Complex security issues arise regarding file accessibility.
- Specialized services can become slow and less reliable.
- High-performance equipment becomes expensive because more units are required.

Depending on the peer operating systems and network configuration, this can be supported through user-level or share-level security.

Specialized Servers

Specialized application servers use high-end equipment to provide the following capabilities:

- Increased throughput
- Increased data integrity
- Increased security

The typical application server has much more processing power than the client workstations that access it. Clients can use the application servers to perform tasks that are beyond their local capabilities.

An example of a specialized server is a mainframe or host computer that can perform data storage and retrieval tasks for personal computers. The data and processing that are used by many people can be on the host computer, while the data and processing appropriate for a single user can be on the desktop.

A Private Branch eXchange (PBX) system is another example of a specialized server that can be joined to a network. When this occurs the client will be able to request telecommunication services from their workstations.

Application Servers

Care must be taken when discussing applications servers to make it clear about what type of system you are discussing. The term is sometimes used to refer to a server on which end-user applications are stored. This is generally considered a misuse of the term, since this is simply a file server that happens to contain executable files.

An application server is a network resource, normally thought of as the server end of a client/server application. The application server is responsible for a share, often a large share, of application processing. It works with a client application running at the end-user workstation which provides the user interface and is normally responsible for preparing server requests and formatting returned results. Server system requirements can sometimes be significant, with the client requirements somewhat less.

This makes for an efficient model, letting you optimize machines to their role. In many cases, it means that pieces are somewhat interchangeable. You will often have a choice of client applications as long as your selections are compatible with the server application. In many cases, upgrades to the server application do not necessarily mean you need to upgrade your client applications. This reduces the long term costs of supporting the application.

One of the most common applications of this model is through database servers.

Database Services

Database servers are machines that store and retrieve data. Database servers differ from file servers in that certain search functions and some processing of the data can be performed on the server. A special term is used to describe the interaction between the clients and database servers: client/server database management.

Typically, the client software will formulate the request and process the responses, while the server database software will evaluate the requests and return any required data. It is this division of labor that is the mark of a client/server database system.

Network database services provide the following:

- Optimization of the computer running the database application for storing, searching, and retrieving database records.

- Controlling where in the network the database is physically stored.

- Logical organization of the data.

- Directory security.

- Fast access time.

Network database servers must also offer:

- Distributed Data Coordination

    Most companies distribute the responsibility for controlling and updating information. When using a common database, ownership and control of the data becomes an issue. To address this, we can use distributed data coordination services. Using this tactic, the different portions of the data are assigned to individual departmental computers for storage. This offers seamless data retrieval by allowing the database server to act as the database manager, retrieving and updating the data when necessary.

- Replication of the Database

    Keeping more than one copy of information might make sense if we want to have a local copy of distant information. When multiple copies of the database exist, we run the risk of basing decisions on outdated information. Replicating the database and synchronizing it across the network cuts down on retrieving faulty data.

    Currently there are two methods for replicating the database.

    The first method uses a master database to store all additions and changes. The database server will be responsible for updating both the master and copying the master to the portions of the database that are stored in the individual departments.

    The second method distributes the responsibility for additions and changes to the local database engines. This second method also makes the local database servers responsible for updating any copies of the database across the network.

    The first method is easier to implement, but the second method may be needed for networks that include unreliable links and portable computers.

Scenario 1

Your company is a medium-sized insurance firm which leases two floors in an office park. The claims department is located on one floor and the accounting department is located on the other. The claims department is networked with a coaxial bus that ties their 386- and 486-based computers together in a peer-to-peer network. The accounting department has a conglomeration of PC-compatibles. These computers are not networked.

The owner of the company would like to network all of the computers for the accounting department and connect the accounting department to the claims department network. You must decide whether to implement a peer-to-peer network or a server-based network. The network must accommodate all the computers used by the accounting department staff and the claims department staff. You want to have a reasonable level of security on the network. You also want to be able to expand the network in the future.

Question

The answer to this question is in Appendix A at the end of this manual.

1. Which LAN configuration, client/server or peer-to-peer, is the best for this situation?

   ....

   ....

Scenario 2

The primary file server on your network contains several GB worth of data. You have four 8-GB hard drives. The amount of data is likely to grow and you want to maximize your available storage space. Although the system is backed up every day, a crash would be catastrophic because of lost productivity while the data was being restored, and the system was being brought back online. You need to ensure down-time is kept to a bare minimum while at the same time ensuring no data is lost in the event of a crash, even if the crash occurs before you have backed up the drive.

Question

The answer to this question is in Appendix A at the end of this manual.

1. What should you implement to ensure minimum down-time due to server disk failure?

    ....

    ....

SUMMARY

During this chapter various aspects of network management were covered. This included:

- Limiting access to data
- Protecting the data in the event of a system failure
- Various network services

In the next chapter, the focus turns to domain-based and enterprise networks.

POST-TEST QUESTIONS

The answers to these questions are in Appendix A at the end of this manual.

1. The name of your pet makes a good password.

    A. True

    B. False

2. Which RAID level provides disk striping with parity?

    ....

    ....

3. Which hardware component provides time for proper system shutdown in the event of a power loss?

    ....

    ....

4. Which type of backup saves a copy of all the data on a server?

    ....

    ....

Domain and Enterprise Networking

OBJECTIVES

At the completion of this chapter, you will be able to:

- Compare and contrast features of LANs and WANs.

- List common network device types.

- Describe the ways in which routes may be configured for a router.

- List and describe major features of Windows NT Server.

- Describe how Windows NT Server domains are organized.

- Explain the significance of primary and backup domain controllers.

- Describe the purpose and use of DHCP.

- Explain why BOOTP routers are important when supporting remote DHCP users (users not on a subnet with the DHCP server).

- List and describe the name resolution methods supported under Windows NT.

- Describe the features and benefits of the Remote Access Server service.

PRE-TEST QUESTIONS

The answers to these questions are in Appendix A at the end of this manual.

1. What type of device is typically used to connect subnetworks into a Wide Area Network?

   ....

   ....

2. What Windows NT Server service provides automated NetBIOS name resolution?

   ....

   ....

3. What Windows NT service supports remote dial-in connectivity?

   ....

   ....

4. What are the three network server roles for which Windows NT Server can be configured during installation?

....

....

INTRODUCTION

Network design, implementation, and support are seldom easy. There is no such thing as a *one-size-fits-all* network environment. The day of the single vendor network, if there ever was such a time, is long past. Decisions are frequently made to accommodate the exceptions rather than being based on predetermined rules.

The chapter starts by looking at network environments in general. It discusses networking concepts and compares local and Wide Area Network environments. From there, it moves into a more focused discussion about Windows NT and TCP/IP support. While the discussion focuses on Windows NT, much of the information provided in this chapter applies to most network operating systems.

NETWORK COMPONENTS

This section takes a look at practical considerations when setting up a network. Decisions must be made regarding what type of network you need, performance requirements, server requirements and so on. Special attention is given to network solutions based around the Windows family of products. The following topics will be covered in this section:

- Network Environment
- Design and Implementation Issues
- Network Performance
- Optimizing Routes

....

....

....

....

- Network Capacity
- Bridges vs. Routers
- Network Reliability
- Implementing Windows NT
- Windows NT Features
- Windows NT Server Features
- Where Does It Fit?
- Domain Organization
- Primary/Backup Domain Controllers
- Additional Server
- Security IDs
- Working With Domain Servers

Planning is key to successful network implementation. This means that you need to understand the options available and how they relate to one another in a network environment.

Network Environment

One of the potential problems is defining what, exactly, constitutes an enterprise. In general usage, an enterprise refers to all corporate computers and support devices as a whole. This means that each organization's specific definition of an enterprise is going to be slightly different.

There are some general expectations which, though they may not be present in all environments, are common to many modern networks.

- Mixed network clients

    You are likely to encounter a mix of MS-DOS, Windows, Windows 95, and Windows NT clients on a network. Also, you will often find it necessary to support a mix of Macintosh clients.

- Mixed network servers

    You will seldom find a *pure* environment. It is common to have to support NT Server domains on the same network as Novell NetWare, or NT Servers implemented as part of a NetWare network. You may also have a need to support other platforms as well, including minicomputer or mainframe connections.

- Multiple LANs

  Usually, it is more accurate to refer to these as multiple subnetworks. As a network grows, divisions often must be imposed for performance, geographic, or security reasons.

- Multiple domains

  When supporting an NT Server network environment, you may find it advantageous, or physically necessary, to break the network into multiple domains. The exact configuration will depend on a number of factors, including security requirements and, to some extent, physical system locations.

- Remote access requirements

  This covers a wide range of areas. Physically separated networks require a means to communicate. Often, mobile employees need a way of attaching to a home network. In addition, the Internet is quickly becoming a vital part of how companies do business.

This chapter addresses these and other support and management issues.

Design and Implementation Issues

Start by looking at your current network, if any. This will give a starting point as to the systems, operating system, and applications that need to be supported. Before making any changes, it is necessary to determine which systems or applications, if any, will have to be upgraded or replaced.

Another early concern is going to be network security. This includes logon security, resource access, assigned management responsibility, and security tracking. You will want to build security into your network design from the beginning. Keep in mind that if you initially set the security too tight, you can always loosen it later, as necessary. If you set security too loose, you may not find out until after critical data has been lost or compromised.

An area of special interest to end users is performance. When looking at network performance and potential bottlenecks, you have to look beyond your local LAN or subnet. You need to consider the network as a whole, especially in large WAN configurations. Tuning considerations include:

- Network performance
- Network capacity
- Network reliability

Careful consideration and tuning of these factors will help you maximize use of the available bandwidth, allowing for information to be streamed. This refers to the ability to transmit data continuously without having to wait for acknowledgments or retransmissions. Network optimization is discussed in some detail later in this course. An area deserving special mention now, however, is working with routers and optimizing routes.

Network Performance

There may be little that can be done about overall performance. Large Wide Area Networks often include a combination of link types and line speeds. Local connections typically have high speed links: 10 Mbps for Ethernet, 16 Mbps for Token Ring, or 100 Mbps for FDDI. Wide area links are significantly slower, typically in the 64-Kbps range. Low-speed links, such as X.25 and standard modem links, provide the poorest performance.

Any time traffic has to travel across one of the lower speed links, performance suffers. Performance can sometimes be improved through careful routing. Of course, if there is only one route to a destination, there is nothing you can do to adjust the route taken.

Optimizing Routes

Overall performance can sometimes be improved by routing your heaviest traffic requirements across your fastest links. Static routers must be configured manually. The router table containing all of the route information must be edited to make any changes. The router table on dynamic routers is updated automatically. Updates are either through Router Information Protocol (RIP) or Open Shortest Path First (OSPF) update packets coming across the network.

- Static routers

    You set the routes on static routers through router table entries. When supporting large amounts of traffic, use the speed of the intermediate routes rather than the number of hops as a guideline. Keep in mind that static routers cannot compensate if the route becomes congested.

- Dynamic routers (RIP)

    If a router uses RIP, all routes are determined by lowest hop count. Some routes can be adjusted by giving them a higher apparent cost. You also have the restriction that routes will not dynamically readjust if a route becomes congested. Windows NT 4.0 supports RIP when it is configured as a router.

- Dynamic routers (OSPF)

    The best solution in this situation is OSPF routers. Routes are calculated based on real performance and are dynamically adjusted if a route becomes congested.

In all situations, but especially when working with manual routes, regular performance tests and careful documentation are critical.

Network Capacity

The speed at which data is transmitted across a network link directly affects the amount of data the link can carry. If the capacity of the link is overloaded, packets must be buffered, and may end up out of sequence, or they can end up lost completely. This leads to retransmissions, which in turn increases the level of traffic. Careful network design can help minimize this problem:

- Physical subnets

    Divide the network into physical subnets linked by routers. Design the subnets so that most of the resources the workstations need are available locally. This ensures that most traffic is across the local, high-speed link and traffic routed out of the subnet is kept to a minimum.

- Balance loads

    Use routers to help balance the load across subnet links. Whenever possible, keep the majority of the traffic on higher speed links.

- Application planning

    The locations of applications and data files are significant. If possible, install applications on the local hard disk. Data files can be kept on network servers.

This is a situation where it is much easier to plan around a problem than to try to correct the problem after the network is in place.

Bridges vs. Routers

Routers should be given preference over bridges when designing and configuring WANs. Bridges, by design, can escalate a transient reliability problem into a serious network failure.

Frequently, a host will use broadcast transmissions if there is an unexplained loss of contact with another host. Typically, these broadcasts are not propagated by routers.

Remote bridges, on the other hand, pass on all broadcasts. Every host receiving the broadcast must process it, if only to reject it. As broadcasts go above a certain level, the performance loss due to broadcast can lead to further broadcasts. This can lead to a broadcast storm, which can result in a complete breakdown of network communications.

Network Reliability

Network reliability problems can result in lost packets and retransmissions, generating artificially high traffic levels. The problem can come from marginal transmission media (cable), bad WAN links, and so forth. It can be further aggravated by failing hardware or environmental factors. Packet fragmentation and congestion also affect reliability.

One of the first steps is to make sure that the network hardware is all working properly. Replace or repair marginal hardware. Replace marginal transmission media whenever possible. Make sure that all cabling is installed within accepted specifications.

Another potential problem area is the physical connection between locations. Most remote connection methods have a limited bandwidth in comparison to local connections. You will want to minimize traffic across these links.

Implementing Windows NT

Windows NT was designed with network environments in mind. It can be implemented as the basis around which you establish your network or added to an existing network environment.

Careful planning is a critical part of the implementation process. However, before you make any decisions, you need to know:

- Windows NT features
- Windows NT domain characteristics
- Server roles
- Security fundamentals
- Restrictions on moving servers between domains

Windows NT Features

Windows NT Workstation and Windows NT Server share a number of common features. These include:

- 32-bit operating system

    Windows NT is a true 32-bit operating system. Your system starts up and runs in Windows NT.

- Hardware platform support

    You have the choice of selecting the hardware platform to best meet your operational requirements. Windows NT supports x86-based and RISC-based platforms.

- Preemptive multitasking

    The operating system retains control over system activity, sharing available processor time between the processes running.

- Security

    Windows NT meets C2 security specifications. A valid username and password is required for logon and resource access. Permissions can be set on a user-by-user basis or by groups of users.

- Application support

    In addition to native applications written to the Win32 API set, Windows NT supports a wide variety of 16-bit Windows and MS-DOS applications.

- Network support

    Windows NT can be used to build your network or as a powerful addition to an existing network environment.

- Internet/Intranet support

    Windows NT ships with Microsoft's Internet Explorer and other Internet support tools. This simplifies the implementation of a corporate intranet.

- Microsoft Exchange

    Microsoft Exchange client installs during Windows NT setup. It provides support for both Microsoft Mail and Internet Mail.

In addition, many of the familiar utilities have been improved and enhanced with this latest release.

Windows NT Server Features

There are some features that are specific to Windows NT Server. These include:

- Microsoft Networking

  Windows NT Server includes a fully integrated network operating system. The network model is based on the concepts developed over years of experience with LAN Manager and earlier Windows NT releases.

- NetWare support

  Windows NT supports utilities specifically designed to support existing NetWare networks. Gateway Service for NetWare lets an NT Server act as a gateway between Microsoft clients and NetWare servers. The NetWare Migration utility lets you migrate users and data from one or more NetWare servers to one or more NT Servers. Additional services that may be purchased for use with NT Server include File and Print Services for NetWare and NetWare Directory Services. File and Print sharing for NetWare gives NetWare clients access to NT Server resources. NetWare Directory Services gives you a way of managing your NetWare servers from a central location.

- Advanced fault tolerance

  Windows NT Server provides support for disk mirroring, disk duplexing, and disk striping with parity. This gives you the ability to not only protect your data, but also to allow users to keep working (often uninterrupted) when a disk failure occurs.

- Internet and TCP/IP Support

  The TCP/IP support utilities have been improved and enhanced. Windows NT now includes support for a Domain Naming System (DNS) server. Microsoft Internet Information Server (IIS) can be installed at the same time as NT Server, or later, after installation. Windows NT Server also ships with Microsoft's FrontPage, an easy-to-use HTML page editor.

Windows NT Server can be used both as a base around which to build a network or as an addition to an exiting network.

Where Does it Fit?

It is a good idea to spend some time planning where you are going to implement Windows-family products in your organization. It is unlikely that you would install Windows NT Workstation for all of your end users. Despite its intuitive interface, it is unlikely that you would provide Windows NT Server at any individual's desktop, except for a few very special cases. So, how do they all fit together?

Use Windows 95 or Windows NT Workstation to support *average* end users. They will meet application support and network access requirements for most users.

Use Windows NT Workstation:

- As a stable, powerful platform for power users.

- As a means of sharing a workstation between users while providing a custom environment matched to individual needs.

- As a secure workstation for sensitive applications and data files.

- To provide additional resources to an existing network.

Use Windows NT Server:

- As a base for resource-intensive client/server applications.

- As a platform for building a stable, secure LAN.

- To provide shared resources to users while maintaining centralized control over access permissions.

- To enhance existing networks.

- As a base for Internet/Intranet implementation.

These are, of course, just general suggestions. Where Windows-family products fit for your specific situation will depend on your business requirements.

Domain Organization

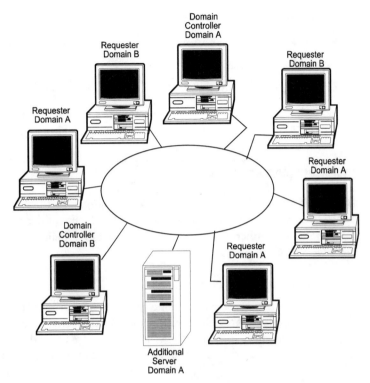

Windows NT Server is based around a domain model. A small network may contain only one domain to which all of the stations in the network belong. A larger network may contain many domains, which may or may not be set up to share resources with each other.

A domain is a logical, rather than physical, organization. Domain members do not need to be physically grouped together. In fact, they can reside in different cities, or even countries, as long as they have a means to communicate.

So what makes a group of systems a domain? Systems become part of a domain by being identified as domain members. Valid domain members include:

- Primary Domain Controller
- Backup Domain Controller
- Additional Servers
- Client Workstations

As members of the same domain, the systems work together. When a user logs on from any workstation, all of the domain servers become available as a group.

Primary/Backup Domain Controllers

Most servers are installed as either primary or backup domain controllers. Either, once defined, will remain a member of that domain for the life of the server. The only way to change domain membership for a primary or backup domain controller is to reinstall Windows NT Server.

- Primary domain controller

  Each domain will have one, and only one, primary domain controller. The primary domain controller holds the domain accounts database, the user and group database. Any time changes are made through User Manager for Domains, they are automatically made to the primary domain controller.

- Backup domain controller

  Each backup domain controller contains a backup copy of the domain accounts database. As changes are made to the database at the primary domain controller, these are replicated to any backup domain controllers in the domain.

  It is normally suggested that at least one server in a domain be installed as a backup domain controller. A backup domain controller can help handle user account validation and can, should the need arise, be promoted to take the place of the primary domain controller.

If you have a domain that includes wide area links, you should install at least one backup domain controller at each remote location. That will allow for local processing of logon requests and help to reduce traffic across the link.

Additional Server

Specialty servers are sometimes set up as additional servers, also called member servers. An additional server is a machine that is running Windows NT Server, but not acting as a primary or backup domain controller.

If integrated into a domain as a domain member, a member server can grant access to resources through the use of group memberships. The member server does not contain a copy of the domain accounts database, so it cannot be used to validate domain logon attempts. Instead, it will contain its own local list of users and groups.

Possible uses of member servers include:

- Time-critical or resource-intensive tasks

    If installed as servers, the machines do not assist in user logon validation. This means that there is not an additional strain placed on system resources for this, or for updating the account database through replication.

- Separate management requirements

    Specialized servers, such as SQL servers, are often managed separately from the rest of the domain. By setting up a specialized system as a server, you can assign management duties to the appropriate administrator without giving them unnecessary access to domain controllers.

- *Mobile* server

    If there is a chance that the server will be moved to a different domain in the future, it should be installed as a member server rather than as a domain controller. Member servers can be moved between domains simply by setting up a machine account in the domain and specifying a different domain name at the member server.

Security IDs

Windows NT Server tracks account objects, users, groups, and servers through Security IDs (SIDs) rather than by their textual names.

The two instances where references to the SID are likely to be encountered are when working with domain servers and with users.

- Domain SID

    The domain SID is generated when the domain controller is installed. This ID is then used with the account database for all accounts in the domain, including member systems, additional servers, users, and groups.

- Account SID

    This is created whenever a user or group account is created on a Windows NT workstation. It is used for tracking access permissions. The domain SID is used in generating each account SID, identifying the domain to which the account belongs.

The use of security IDs, especially the domain SID, helps to determine what you can and cannot do when changing domain definitions.

Working With Domain Servers

Because of the use of the domain SID, there are restrictions placed on changes that can be made to the domain and its members.

- Changing computer names

    Use the Control Panel Network utility to change computer names. You must reset the system for the change to take effect.

- Changing domain names

    Use the Control Panel Network utility to change the domain name. Change the name at the primary domain controller first, then the backup domain controller, then at each of the additional servers, then at the member workstations. You must reset the system for the change to take effect.

- Moving primary/backup domain controllers

  Primary or backup domain controllers cannot be moved to a different domain due to the different domain SID. Because the SID is assigned to a machine when it is installed, you must reinstall Windows NT Server to move a primary or backup domain controller.

- Moving additional servers

  Use the Control Panel Network utility to change the domain name for an additional server. You must provide an administrator name and password so that an account can be created for the machine, or create an account at the primary domain controller using the Server Manager utility.

NOTE: *To change an additional server's role to that of backup or primary domain controller, you must reinstall Windows NT Server.*

- Moving accounts

  To move a user or group account between domains, you must delete the account record from the old domain and recreate it in the new domain. User rights, permissions, and group memberships must be redefined.

As you can see, careful network planning and design will pay off in the long run with easier management.

CHOOSING A NETWORK PROTOCOL

This section will present information on the types of adapters and protocols that are supported by Windows NT. The following are topics discussed within this section:

- TCP/IP at the Desktop
- Multihomed Adapters
- DHCP
- BOOTP Routing
- LMHOSTS, WINS, and DNS

- LMHOSTS

- WINS

- Database Updates

- Supporting Large Networks

- WINS Proxy Agents

- Domain Name System (DNS)

- DNS Manager

- Additional DNS Manager Features

- Remote Access Service

- Supported Protocols

Select your protocol, and optional services, to meet your specific network needs. This may, in some cases, mean implementing multiple protocols.

TCP/IP at the Desktop

TCP/IP is accepted as the standard for internetwork communications. Its popularity at the desktop continues to grow. However, TCP/IP was never designed for use with PCs. In fact, PCs didn't exist when TCP/IP was developed. This has led to some potential problems.

- Population size

    TCP/IP was designed for use with a limited population: mainframes and minicomputers. The large number of PCs in modern networks leads to problems in allocation of unique IP addresses and may eventually create an address shortage.

- Portability

    PCs, by design, are portable. They can move easily between different physical locations. This also means that they can be moved between logical subnets. This means having to reconfigure IP addresses, or the need for dynamic address management.

- End users

    The average PC user lacks the sophistication required to fully understand IP address and subnetting concerns. This can sometimes lead to errors in address and configuration parameters.

Manufacturers, including Microsoft, have developed products and procedures to help work around these problems and simplify TCP/IP management.

Multihomed Adapters

A computer supporting multiple IP addresses is referred to as a multihomed device. In a Windows NT networking environment, the machine will have a single machine (NetBIOS) name no matter how many addresses it supports.

One reason it is important to realize this is that the same name may show up with different addresses under management and communication utilities. This is a normal situation when supporting multihomed devices.

Situations where you might want to have multihomed devices include:

- Routing

    A system must be configured as a multihomed device before it can be configured as a router. Typically, the machine will have multiple network adapters with a unique address defined on each.

- Multiple subnetworks on a physical network

    By defining multiple addresses on a single adapter, you have the ability to create multiple logical subnetworks on a single physical network. Though they share the same cable, each is treated as a separate, unique network.

- Internet Information Server (IIS) support

    Microsoft's IIS has the ability to support virtual servers. This lets it look as if there are multiple Internet servers when, in fact, they are all being supported by the same server.

It is possible that you may find other situations where it will be appropriate to set up a machine as multihomed.

DHCP

It is more convenient to use Dynamic Host Configuration Protocol (DHCP) to manage IP addressing parameters for the majority of your network stations. With DHCP, a system is issued an address for a specified period of time. Before this lease period expires, the system will attempt to renew for the same period. If the system does not attempt to renew its lease, the DHCP server assumes that the IP address is available for reassignment to another system.

DHCP is especially well suited to PC-based network environments, given the inherently mobile nature of PCs. Even for a desktop system, it is not that difficult to move the machine to another office. This could mean that the machine has moved to a different subnetwork, which would require assignment of a new IP address. Manual address assignment and tracking could quickly become tedious.

Not all systems can be configured as DHCP clients, however. Machines that need a static, known address, must be configured manually. These include:

- DHCP servers
- WINS servers
- DNS servers
- Gateways (routers)

This is not a complete list of all machines and situations that may require a static IP address.

BOOTP Routing

It is possible to configure a DHCP server to provide support for multiple subnetworks. There is, however, a requirement. All routers between the client system and the DHCP server must comply with Bootstrap Protocol (BOOTP).

Initially, and to some extent now, BOOTP was used to boot and configure diskless workstations. DHCP was created to be an extension to the BOOTP. Originally BOOTP was defined in RFC 951. Currently, the BOOTP RFC is RFC 1542 which includes DHCP support.

A workstation needs a variety of configuration parameters, including an IP address and default gateway. A default gateway is the node (IP) address that will receive forwarded packets that have been determined to be remote to a node's network address. The subnet mask is used to calculate whether an IP address is local or remote. The subnet mask marks which portions of an IP address are used for the network ID and the host ID. This use of messaging to configure workstation(s) paved the way for DHCP as an extension.

BOOTP and DHCP message formats are nearly identical; however, some fields are used by DHCP differently and DHCP has new fields that are not included in BOOTP. The major advantage of DHCP using the same messaging format as BOOTP is that DHCP messages can be relayed between two subnets by existing routers that act as BOOTP (RFC 1542) relay agents. This makes it possible to have IP addresses and configuration information for systems on both subnets configured on a single DHCP Server.

LMHOSTS, WINS, and DNS

Windows NT 4.0 supports resolution of machine (Host) names and IP addresses through LMHOSTS, WINS, and DNS. HOSTS resolution is also supported, but not commonly used in Microsoft networking. Name resolution using a HOSTS file is not discussed in this course.

LMHOSTS is a static file that is used to locate remote computers for Microsoft networks by mapping NetBIOS (machine) names to IP addresses. LMHOSTS may be used in conjunction with DHCP, but this is not normally suggested since a station's IP address may change, making the LMHOSTS entry invalid. If you plan to use LMHOSTS, it is safer to limit file entries to stations with permanent, manually configured IP addresses.

Primary uses include the support of printing, remote access, browsing, replication, and domain services logon. The major drawback of using LMHOSTS is that the administrator must manually update the LMHOSTS file and distribute it to each workstation or update a master copy that is available to each machine.

While LMHOSTS must be manually updated, WINS provides a dynamic solution to NetBIOS name resolution. On a network, you can set up one or more WINS Servers configured to collect all of the computer names and their IP addresses in the WINS database. Each WINS server will have its own database, but mapping entries can be replicated between WINS servers so that each contains the same list. When a WINS client needs to communicate with another host (machine operating in a TCP/IP network), it can contact the WINS database for these mappings. This helps to reduce broadcast traffic on the network.

Using WINS to track name and IP address mappings eliminates the need for LMHOSTS. WINS can be used in conjunction with DHCP. DNS can use WINS for name resolution.

DNS is used primarily when connecting to the Internet. DNS uses a hierarchical naming system for resolving computer names in a distributed database. The naming scheme used by DNS is very structured and must be closely followed. DNS does not directly support DHCP because the relationship between the host name and IP address will not change dynamically. You can, however, configure the DNS server to query a WINS server for unresolved names, giving you a way to support dynamic addressing needs.

LMHOSTS

LMHOSTS address resolution is a modified B-node resolution method. It uses a combination of B-node name query broadcasts and the contents of one or more LMHOSTS files.

During address resolution with LMHOSTS support enabled:

- The name is checked to see if it is a local name (assigned to the local computer).
- The local LMHOSTS cache is checked.
- A name query broadcast is issued.
- All LMHOSTS files are checked for the name.

If these methods fail, an error is returned stating that the network name was not found.

WINS

Windows Internet Name Service, or WINS, is an automated way of supporting NetBIOS address resolution. It is a modification to NetBIOS Name Service (NBNS), using dynamic name registration. As each WINS client system starts up, it registers itself with a WINS server.

WINS uses H-node for address resolution. When a client issues a command to a NetBIOS name, the client will try the following:

- Check to see if the name is on the local machine.
- Check the local cache of remote NetBIOS names.
- Query the WINS server for address resolution.
- Issue a local name query broadcast.
- Parse the LMHOSTS file, if LMHOSTS support is configured at the client.
- Parse the HOSTS file, if one exists.
- Query DNS, if supported.

Each of the above will be attempted until address resolution occurs.

While troubleshooting name resolution, if you are able to ping an IP address but not a NetBIOS name, check your WINS Server configuration or LMHOSTS file.

Database Updates

WINS clients will automatically update the WINS database with their names. You may, however, need to add static mappings to the database. For example, if you are using an NT system as an IP router between multiple subnets, you will have to configure it as a multihomed static mapping. Static mappings are also required to provide address resolution to systems that do not recognize WINS servers.

Supporting Large Networks

Supporting WINS over medium- to large-sized networks carries its own special problems. You will often need to support multiple WINS servers to provide redundancy, reliability, and performance. Some special concerns include:

- Replication

  When supporting multiple WINS servers, replication provides a way of passing names between servers, so that a name registered on one server can be queried on another.

- Browsing and trusts

  In a large network with multiple subnets and multiple domains, maintaining browse lists and trust relationships can be a significant concern.

WINS Proxy Agents

Not all systems running NetBIOS over TCP/IP can be configured to use WINS servers. They can, however, be given access to WINS server databases through the use of proxy agents.

Windows NT, Windows for Workgroups, and Windows 95 stations can be configured as WINS proxy agents, provided they are not WINS servers. If a system is configured as a WINS server, it cannot also act as a WINS proxy agent.

WINS proxy agents provide indirect access to the WINS database. When a system broadcasts a name query:

- A WINS proxy agent intercepts the broadcast.
- The broadcast is answered, if possible, from the local cache or a WINS server query.

There is a possibility of a strain being placed on the WINS proxy agent, depending on the number of name query broadcasts occurring. Only a limited number of WINS proxy agents should be defined on each domain, preferably systems that are not already supporting resource-intensive tasks.

Domain Name System (DNS)

The Domain Name System (DNS) allows users to access information across UNIX-based systems, the Internet, and Intranet. Administrators can easily configure and manage name-to-IP address mapping by using a graphical administration tool. Before the GUI utility, administrators would manually edit an ASCII file named HOSTS to resolve domain names to the appropriate IP address. This was tedious and error prone. A DNS name server is a subtree of a DNS database that is administered as a single separate entity, also called a zone. A zone can consist of a single domain or a domain with subdomains. One or more name servers can be set up for the zone.

While troubleshooting name resolution, if you are able to ping an IP address but not a domain name, check your DNS server configuration or HOSTS file.

DNS Manager

The Windows NT 4.0 DNS Manager allows you to:

*   Add a new server

    Run **New Server** from the **DNS** menu to add a DNS Server. You will be prompted for the name or IP address of the DNS server. The server must be running and accessible. An icon with the name or the IP Address will appear under the Server List.

    You can also add a new server by clicking with mouse button 2 on the Server list, then running **New Server** from the pop-up menu.

NOTE: *If a red X is drawn through the icon, it indicates that the DNS Manager was unable to connect to the specified server.*

- Add a new zone

    A primary zone has a Start of Authority (SOA) resource record associated with it and is also known as the zone root domain. A world icon in the DNS Manager Server List represents the primary zone(s). A secondary zone is a read-only copy of an existing zone.

    Select the DNS Server and run **New Zone** from the **DNS** menu. The default is to add a primary zone. Click on **Next**. Type in the zone name. You can type in the zone file name or leave the name at default. Click on **Next**, then on **Finish**.

Additional DNS Manager Features

The DNS Manager also has the following choices:

- Pause Zone

    To pause a zone, highlight the zone, then either use the **DNS** menu or right-click on the highlighted zone and choose **Pause Zone**. This effectively takes the zone offline. The zone world icon will have two bars across it showing that it has been paused.

- New Domain

    To add a new domain to the zone, highlight the zone, then either use the **DNS** menu or right-click on the highlighted zone and choose **New Domain**. In the Domain Name box enter a name for the new domain for that zone, then click on the **OK** button.

- New Host

    To add a new host to the zone, highlight the zone, then either use the **DNS** menu or right-click on the highlighted zone and choose **New Host**. In the Host Name box, enter a name for the host, then enter an IP Address in the Host IP Address box. Click on the **Add Host** button. The new host will be added to the Zone Info. Click on the **Done** button.

- New record

    A New Record can be added to either a zone or a domain. There are several different records that may be added.

- Delete

    Delete is used to remove any item that the administrator may have added. To delete an item, highlight the item and choose **Delete** from the **DNS** menu or press *DELETE*. You will be prompted to verify your action.

- Update server Data Files

    Choosing to **Update Server Data Files** from the **DNS** menu will broadcast any updated or new information about the DNS server to the network(s).

DNS Client Configuration

Typically, you will need to provide one or more of the following when configuring DNS clients:

- Host Name

    This is used to identify your computer on the network. By default, this is the Windows NT computer's machine name.

- Domain

    This is used to enter the name of the domain to which your computer belongs.

- DNS Service Search Order

    This provides name resolution by allowing you to specify the IP addresses of the DNS servers. The query is done in the order in which the server's IP addresses are listed.

- Domain Suffix Search Order

    This allows you to append DNS domain suffixes to host names during
    name resolution. There can be up to six domain suffixes and they will
    append in the order listed. A domain suffix is a name that identifies your
    computer on the Internet; for example ".com" is the suffix used to identify a
    company.

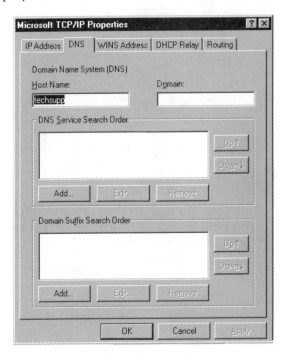

Remote Access Service

Most clients are connected directly to the network. In some cases, however, you are going
to need to provide remote connections for your users. Microsoft provides Remote Access
Service (RAS) to let you set up and configure client access.

Users connecting to a RAS server can be limited to accessing that server only or can be
given access to the network. Effectively, this is the same as a local connection to the
network, except that any type of data transfers run significantly slower. It is important to
select connection options appropriate to your access requirements, available support, and
budgetary constraints.

You can select from:

- Modem

  A modem allows connection over a standard phone line. Though transfer rates are limited, this allows connection by nearly any type of client and from nearly any location. Windows NT supports nearly 200 modems. You can also manually configure unsupported modems.

- Null Modem

  A null modem is a direct serial connection between systems. A null modem connection is made by running a cable between serial ports on the server and client.

- ISDN

  Integrated Services Digital Network provides a moderate-speed connection (typically 64 Kbps to 128 Kbps) between stationary remote sites. ISDN requires special digital telephone lines and connection equipment.

- X.25

  A standard packet-switching communication protocol, X.25 is designed to support WAN connectivity. Normally, connection requires Packet Assemblers/Disassemblers (PADs) and X.25 smart cards. Some carriers provide support through standard modems.

In most cases, the best option for connecting a mobile user is through a modem connection. RAS also supports multi-link connections, combining two or more serial lines (such as modems) into one communication path and thereby increasing throughput.

Supported Protocols

RAS supports the following protocol options:

- TCP/IP

    For TCP/IP connection, you must provide IP addresses for your clients. IP addresses can be managed through a static range at the server. You may also need to provide a name resolution method.

- IPX

    You can integrate RAS servers and clients into an existing IPX-based network. This allows for easy integration with existing NetWare networks. The RAS server can also act as an IPX router for RAS clients. The RAS server can automatically generate IPX network numbers for RAS clients.

- NetBEUI

    The NetBEUI client protocol and NetBIOS gateway are installed by default on all RAS servers and most clients. NetBEUI is required for MS-DOS and MS-DOS based clients, including Windows for Workgroups clients.

- Microsoft RAS

    This is a proprietary protocol supported on older RAS versions and legacy RAS clients. Microsoft RAS provides support for NetBIOS. Older clients must be running NetBEUI, but the RAS server can act as a gateway to networks running other protocols.

RAS server continues to support NetBIOS gateway services. This allows a client to connect using NetBEUI, and then be routed to an IPX or TCP/IP network. The client can then access shared resources, but applications that require IPX or TCP/IP at the client are not supported.

In addition to these, Microsoft Windows NT v4.0 supports connectivity through SLIP, PPP, and PPTP.

Both Serial Line Internet Protocol (SLIP) and Point-to-Point Protocol (PPP) provide a dial-up connection to the Internet. SLIP is the older protocol, and supports fewer features. The newest protocol Point-to-Point Tunneling Protocol (PPTP) provides a higher standard of security and adaptability than either SLIP or PPP.

- SLIP

  Established protocol

  Requires minimal overhead

  No compression

  No error checking or flow control

  No security provided by the protocol

  Supports TCP/IP only

Once considered the de facto standard for serial (dial-up) connections, SLIP has lost popularity in recent years.

- PPP

  Newer protocol

  Requires a small amount of overhead, even less than SLIP

  Supports compression

  Error checking and flow control are provided

  Security supports the use of encrypted passwords

  Supports TCP/IP, NWLink (IPX/SPX), and NetBIOS

  Supported by DHCP

- PPTP

  The Point-to-Point Tunneling Protocol provides secure client connections over the Internet. Through multiprotocol Virtual Private Networks (VPNs), secure communications are supported over standard Internet connections.

Your protocol selections will be determined by application requirements and client capabilities.

SUMMARY

The following were introduced during this chapter:

- Network environments
- LANs and WANs
- Optimizing routers
- Windows NT features
- Domain organization
- TCP/IP implementation
- TCP/IP name resolution
- Using RAS

POST-TEST QUESTIONS

The answers to these questions are in Appendix A at the end of this manual.

1. What type or types of routers can automatically compensate for changes in network traffic patterns?

   ....

   ....

2. A Windows NT Server domain can have up to how many primary domain controllers?

   ....

   ....

3. Of TCP/IP, NWLink, and NetBEUI, which are not routable protocols?

    ....

    ....

4. What service provides for automatic configuration of TCP/IP clients?

    ....

    ....

Ongoing Management

OBJECTIVES

At the completion of this chapter, you will be able to:

- Describe ways to improve overall network performance.
- Describe the purpose and use of Windows NT Performance Monitor.
- List common diagnostic tools and when they should be used.
- Describe logical troubleshooting steps.
- List common bottlenecks that can degrade server performance.

PRE-TEST QUESTIONS

The answers to these questions are in Appendix A at the end of this manual.

1. Name the three most common server bottlenecks.

   ....

   ....

2. What types of cable checks can you make using a volt/ohmmeter?

   ....

   ....

3. What type of test device would you most likely use to analyze network packet contents?

   ....

   ....

INTRODUCTION

During this final chapter, a number of subjects relating to the ongoing management, maintenance, and support of a network will be covered.

The chapter begins with a discussion of network performance factors. These are general concepts that will help you optimize your network. From there, the discussion moves into troubleshooting. This will include some basic guidelines for problem isolation, as well as an overview of the more common diagnostic tools. Finally, the chapter concludes with a look at several of the most common network failures and how to resolve them.

Network Performance

Network performance becomes a factor whenever workstations interact with network servers. File transfer rates can become a limiting factor for data-intensive applications (database applications, for example). Server-based applications communicating with client front ends have become very popular, but can put a great deal of strain on network servers and the network in general.

All of workstations are affected to some extent by network performance. While not the only area where optimization is a concern, it is an important part of the overall performance picture.

It would be difficult to discuss specific tuning parameters. Each network operating system handles these parameters differently. Some NOSs can have over a hundred tuning parameters available. However, reviewing some general performance guidelines is helpful.

PERFORMANCE GUIDELINES

This section looks at network performance factors and performance tuning. The following topics are discussed within this section:

- Performance Factors
- Performance Monitoring
- Server Hardware
- Server Configuration
- Network Configuration
- Monitoring Performance with Windows NT
- Performance Monitor
- Resolving Bottlenecks
- Processor Bottlenecks
- Disk Bottlenecks
- Memory Bottlenecks

By understanding the tools available, you can locate performance bottlenecks. You can then balance performance against the costs involved to determine an appropriate solution.

Performance Factors

Some general performance issues include:

- Performance monitoring

    Performance monitoring can help to locate bottlenecks and test to determine if you have corrected them. It can also help you to determine if the problem actually is at the server end, or if it lies elsewhere.

- Server hardware configuration

    A server's performance is directly tied to its capabilities. Faster PCs make faster servers. How fast a server needs to be depends on what services it provides.

- Server configuration

    How a server is set up can also make a difference in how well it runs. Also, the number of servers in a network can impact performance.

- Network configuration

    In light of all of the other variables, it can be easy to forget about the basic network. Since this is the path over which all data travels, it is an important part of your performance equation.

It is also important to remember that complaints about network speed are just that, complaints. There are those users who will never be happy with network performance.

Performance Monitoring

Most network operating systems have some type of tracking and error logging built in. There are also a number of third-party tracking programs available that let you record data about specific performance factors. Areas to watch include:

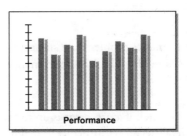

- CPU usage

    If CPU usage holds at high levels, the server is probably working at its maximum potential. The solution may be to replace it with a more powerful system, or to install other servers and off-load some of its duties.

- Memory usage

    If memory usage remains high, or if memory overcommit situations occur, you need more memory in the server. If problems continue, keep a close watch on CPU usage and data transmission errors.

- Collisions

    This problem only occurs on Ethernet networks. Some collisions are inevitable. As the percentage of collisions versus overall traffic increases, you may need to isolate network segments or switch to a different protocol. Isolating segments is usually the least expensive of the two.

- Lost packets/rebroadcasts

    Undelivered packets and negative acknowledgments can be due to media problems, but may also be due to performance issues. The server is not able to keep up with all of the traffic in these cases.

You may want to keep an eye on other items as well, depending on your NOS and the protocols that you are using.

Server Hardware

When server performance problems are suspected, most people start their search at the hardware level. Quite often, limited performance is due to limited hardware resources.

- CPU

    You can tell if a processor is up to the load by monitoring CPU statistics. Overall server performance is tied directly to the CPU type and speed. Many NOSs support multiprocessor systems which provide a significantly larger CPU throughput.

- Memory

    Monitor memory statistics to see if the server has enough memory. Optimum memory is required for optimum performance. Performance can sometimes be improved by allocating additional memory to caching operations, but it is possible to create such large data caches that they actually slow the system.

- Disk drives

    Disk drive access speed will directly affect file-intensive applications. Higher-speed drives, spreading data across multiple drives, and special drive configurations (such as disk striping or disk duplexing) can help.

If possible, it is best to start by collecting performance data before randomly changing server hardware. You may also find it cheaper to replace a system rather than to try to upgrade it.

Server Configuration

Server configuration includes a number of different factors:

- Tuning parameters

    Nearly all network operating systems have tuning parameters you can adjust to match server performance to the particulars of your network environment. Use caution when adjusting these because it is possible to degrade server performance.

- Dedicated vs. non-dedicated servers

    Dedicated servers, those that perform no other function, usually provide the best performance. However, this is not always an option. Many NOSs support a non-dedicated configuration only, where the server can potentially be used as a workstation as well.

- Multiple servers

    Multiple servers allow the load to be balanced so that no one server is being pushed beyond capacity. In a domain-based NOS, such as LAN Manager or Windows NT, there is an added advantage that any server in the domain can verify user logons.

- Specialty servers

    You may want to dedicate some servers to performing only specialty tasks, such as database servers or print servers. That allows you to tune that server for optimum performance in that task.

Select a server configuration that best meets your current and immediate growth needs. From there, monitor server performance so that it is apparent when the network needs to be reconfigured or expanded.

Network Configuration

Media quality affects performance, but so does network organization.

- Protocols

   Different protocols do better in different situations. Ethernet can be a problem in larger, more active networks due to collisions. NetBEUI is extremely fast in a LAN, but is not routable and slows wide area communications.

- Media

   Do not try to extend media past specification limits. This will cause transmission problems requiring rebroadcasts. Use care in media routing to avoid interference sources.

- Traffic levels

   Whenever appropriate, use bridges or routers to divide users into logical groups. This will help to keep most of the traffic confined to that subgroup and reduce traffic across the network.

- LAN vs. WAN

   WAN connections traditionally have slower transfer rates than LANs. You can improve performance by keeping as many resources as possible local to the network and thereby reducing WAN transfers.

Set up your network to best meet your needs, but keep future growth and expansion in mind.

Monitoring Performance with Windows NT

Performance monitoring is an important part of system administration and ongoing support. It is normally categorized as error monitoring, status monitoring, and performance monitoring.

One way of monitoring errors and some status conditions is through system messages. These are also recorded in the system event logs, which can be accessed through the Event Viewer.

The primary tool for monitoring system performance in a Windows NT environment is the Performance Monitor. This tool lets you view realtime data or record performance counters for later review. It is commonly used in locating performance bottlenecks.

NT's Performance Monitor has four views:

- Chart

    Provides a realtime graphical representation of the selected counters.

- Report

    Provides a realtime textual representation of the selected counters.

- Log

    Allows monitoring of long term trends.

- Alert

    Allows you to set thresholds for critical system counters and send alert messages when the thresholds are exceeded.

Performance Monitor

The Performance Monitor is often used to locate and help resolve performance bottlenecks. This is, however, a powerful and flexible utility, and should not be limited to that use only. Performance Monitor can be used to:

- Check performance of system objects.
- Compare the performance of different systems.
- Gather data for more detailed analysis.
- Set alerts to occur when selected object parameters hit specified levels.
- Run executable commands or batch files when alerts occur.
- Create report screens displaying exact values in a timely manner.

Windows NT Server installs a common set of performance counters for objects such as the memory cache, disk usage, processor, processes, and threads. Network counters are installed according to the network software running at the system. Some applications, such as SQL Server or Microsoft Exchange, install their own counters.

As a special note, SNMP must be installed to monitor TCP/IP-specific counters.

Resolving Bottlenecks

Nearly all computers have at least one bottleneck. If it's something minor, or occurs very intermittently, it may not be noticed. Then again, it might affect performance to the point that nothing gets done.

These bottlenecks often occur in common areas:

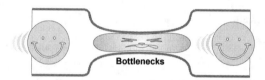

Bottlenecks

- Processor
- Disk
- Memory

The key lies in being able to recognize bottlenecks when they occur, and then removing the source, if possible. Often, finding the real source requires some detective work. One bottleneck may hide another. Bottlenecks will likely occur only at certain times, so it is critical to know when to catch them.

Do not make too many changes at a time. Make one change, check the results, then go on to the next. Also, record everything, or time will be wasted repeating actions.

Processor Bottlenecks

The simplest test for a processor bottleneck is processor utilization. If this counter goes to 100% and holds there, then it is apparent that the processor is a limiting factor. It also helps to monitor active processes, or even active threads, to determine which are placing the greatest load on the processor. The processor queue is also a good indicator of how well the processor is managing the load.

Solutions are somewhat limited for a processor bottleneck. Some are obvious, such as running fewer applications or upgrading to a more powerful processor. If 8-bit adapter cards for network or disk drive access are used, upgrading to 16- or 32-bit cards will help improve performance. If the system board will support it, the size of the processor cache (secondary cache) can be increased.

While adding memory can help improve performance, increasing RAM without increasing the size of the processor cache may reduce performance.

Disk Bottlenecks

If a number of disk-intensive applications are run, the hard disk is an obvious place to look for a bottleneck. In this case, looking at both instantaneous values and averages over a period of time is desirable. Neither by itself gives a complete picture of disk performance. Some results may need to be compared. For example, to get the average transfer rate, divide the Average Disk Transfer Bytes per transfer by the Average Disk Seconds per Transfer.

There are a number of options for correcting disk bottlenecks. If there are multiple physical drives, check the performance on each. Performance may be improved by moving a few files around to balance the load. Ensuring that the drive is set at the correct interleave is also necessary.

Another way to balance the load is to use disk striping. This can be done through software using the Windows NT Disk Administrator, or by installing a hardware RAID drive array. Whichever method is selected, the most significant performance increases are seen when working with large data files.

Other options, unfortunately, require investing in additional hardware. Obviously, faster hard disks will improve performance. So will selecting a controller that uses the widest data path available on your system bus. If the controller supports Direct Memory Access (DMA), this will also help to improve performance, since the controller can write directly to memory.

Memory Bottlenecks

In many cases, memory bottlenecks can be resolved by either of the following:

- Installing more memory.
- Running fewer simultaneous processes.
- Avoiding programs that use excessive memory.

Memory problems often appear to be other types of problems.

Insufficient memory adversely affects disk performance. Disk usage goes up significantly since the system is unable to cache disk data.

Memory is a relatively common cause of poor performance. This is somewhat aggravated in Windows NT due to the operating system's memory requirements. The problem becomes especially evident when the system starts paging out to virtual memory: not only is there time lost while data is moved between RAM and the paging file, but you are also adding to the burden on the hard disk. This is one reason a memory bottleneck may first appear as a disk bottleneck, depending on which you check first.

There are really only two ways to correct a memory bottleneck. The first is to run fewer simultaneous processes. Only launch those programs that you are actively using, and exit them when you are finished. The other option is to install additional memory.

One area of special concern is the size of the virtual memory paging file. Having to increase the size of this file *on-the-fly* can be somewhat resource intensive. If the file regularly grows beyond the initial size, it should be reset to the higher value.

TROUBLESHOOTING GUIDELINES

This section will present some guidelines for troubleshooting network problems. The following topics are discussed within this section:

- Troubleshooting
- General Troubleshooting Guidelines
- Gathering Information

- Troubleshooting Steps
- Diagnostic Tools
- Troubleshooting Network Problems

Downtime is costly. A little research and advance planning in advance can help keep failures and the resulting downtime to a minimum.

Troubleshooting

Everything breaks sooner or later. Most of the time, things seem to pick the most inopportune times to do so. Printers go out during quarterly reports, networks during the busiest day of the year.

Caught up with day-to-day firefighting and dodging user complaints, it is easy to lose track of the primary objective:

Fix the business problem first!

On the following pages, some general guidelines for network troubleshooting will be reviewed, as well as some specific instructions for problems that may be encountered. Troubleshooting becomes much easier with the correct background information, the proper logical procedures, and the right attitude.

General Troubleshooting Guidelines

While this list is in no way complete, here are some general items to keep in mind when troubleshooting any system.

- Backup, backup, backup

  Good, reliable, and recent backups are your best guarantee of recovering critical files.

- Look for the obvious

  Check for obvious possibilities like loose cables and systems not plugged in.

- Transparent changes usually are not obvious

  If anything has changed recently (new expansion cards, replacement cards, software upgrades, and so on) that is where you should start looking.

- Ask the user

  You should ask the user if there have been any ongoing minor problems, or if they have done anything to the system, no matter how slight. Be sure to phrase your questions in a non-threatening manner.

- Trust your sense of DLR

  Most people involved with troubleshooting have a fine-tuned sense of *Doesn't look right,* where you think something might be wrong, but you cannot quite put your finger on the problem. Trust your instincts.

- Keep it simple

  During troubleshooting, change only one variable at a time, and change it back before going on to the next.

Another guideline that could be added to the list is DON'T PANIC! Often, simple problems become more complicated by things we introduce when we do not think through our actions.

Gathering Information

An important part of both ongoing management and troubleshooting is information. You need to keep information about each of the systems you are supporting. When problems occur, gather as much information about the failure as possible.

- System inventory

  Keep a complete inventory of all systems, including make and model, disk capacity, memory, BIOS type and version, expansion hardware, operating system type and version, and any installed software.

- System files

  If possible, keep a current backup of each PC's critical system files.

- Error messages

  Train users to record any error messages they receive.

- User observations

  Even though they may not realize it, users can often give you a lot of useful information.

In addition, you will probably want to keep some third-party tools on hand, such as reliable hardware diagnostic and test programs.

Troubleshooting Steps

Most troubleshooting is a process of elimination. In other words, find what is not broken, and whatever is left over, is.

- Determine the nature of the problem—whether it is a user or system error.
- Start troubleshooting by asking the user for problem symptoms and for any error messages.
- Correct the user's operating procedures for user errors.

- Look for obvious problems first, such as disconnected cables.

- If a component is suspected, change that component and test it. If the problem does not change, return the original component.

- If you are having trouble pinpointing the problem, try to isolate it to a major subsystem first, then go on from there.

- Begin a detailed diagnosis of system errors by viewing the system log and eliminating components unrelated to the problem.

- If the system log is inconclusive, test the physical components.

- Network card and cables can be tested by replacing suspected units and checking whether the problem still exists.

- If the problem is rectified by such a procedure, that particular component was the fault of the problem.

- Once a system problem has been verified (whether it is hardware or software), confirm the status with the user and contact management to obtain direction regarding further disposition.

- Be prepared to fix the problem when such authority has been given.

- Track all problems using a database that lists problems and their resolution. This will allow you to determine high failure areas, find ways to avoid these failures, and track trends for future strategic planning.

Diagnostic Tools

No matter how well you understand the concepts of logical troubleshooting, diagnostic tools are needed to solve difficult network problems. There are several common hardware and software diagnostic tools from which to choose.

Voltmeter/Ohmmeter (Multimeter)

A multimeter is a well-known device used to measure voltage, resistance, and continuity. It is frequently used when troubleshooting computer hardware problems. However, few people realize how valuable it can be when isolating network cable problems.

A voltmeter can be used to check:

- Cable continuity

  This will help you determine if the cable segment has an open (break) or short.

- Terminator resistance

    This will help you determine if the terminator is working properly. For example, a resistance reading on a 50-ohm terminator should measure 50 ohms of resistance.

Other than the terminator resistance reading, the two most common readings you will most likely encounter are zero resistance and infinite resistance.

- Zero resistance

    This is the reading you will look for when testing the continuity of a wire. If attempting to read the terminator on a coaxial cable, this value indicates that the cable has a short.

- Infinite resistance

    This is the reading received if a wire has an open (break). If attempting to read the terminator on a coaxial cable, the terminator may not be connected, or the cable or terminator may have an open.

Time Domain Reflectometer

From a technical standpoint, a Time Domain Reflectometer (TDR) is a highly sophisticated line test device. In most cases, however, modern TDRs have been designed as small, easy-to-use devices that many technicians consider an invaluable troubleshooting tool.

A TDR works by sending out a signal and looking at the characteristics of the return signal. With most modern devices, you do not need to concern yourself with the way the device works, but with the information it provides.

Typically, a TDR can tell you:

- If your cable has a short or open.
- The distance to a short.
- The distance to an open.

- Overall cable length.
- Termination value.
- Line impedance.

While useful in troubleshooting any type of cable, a TDR is often critical for locating and resolving coaxial cable faults.

Cable Testers

Cable testers can be used to check the condition of the cable. They can also be used to monitor network traffic. Traffic to or from a specific computer can be monitored as well.

A cable tester can also be used to:

- Check for excessive collisions
- Check for beaconing
- Locate bad cable segments
- Locate bad network adapter cards

Network Monitors

A network monitor is a software tool that tracks network transmissions. One of the most popular network monitors is Microsoft Network Monitor.

Microsoft Network Monitor provides administrators with the means to detect and troubleshoot problems with the network. Administrators can capture and display packets (or frames) directly from the network. Traffic to or from a specific computer can be captured as well. The captured frames can even be edited and transmitted across the network to aid in troubleshooting.

A network monitor can be an indispensable tool that will help you do such things as:

- Monitor collisions
- Analyze bad packets
- Evaluate short frames
- Isolate failing network adapter cards
- Locate faulty network communication devices

- Resolve network bottlenecks
- Isolate the source of excessive traffic
- Monitor trends such as peak traffic times
- Monitor bandwidth usage

Protocol Analyzers

Another tool that can capture network data is the protocol analyzer. A protocol analyzer is similar to a network monitor. However, it is usually a hardware device rather than a software tool. Analyzers can range from an add-on circuit board (and companion software) to an actual computer. In addition, analyzers almost always contain a built-in time-domain reflectometer.

Protocol analyzers can be used to:

- Locate bad cable segments
- Isolate failing network adapter cards
- Track down faulty communication devices
- Resolve network bottlenecks
- Isolate the source of excessive traffic
- Monitor trends such as peak traffic times
- Analyze bad packets
- Evaluate short frames

Troubleshooting Network Problems

When troubleshooting network problems, try to isolate an event or series of events that may have adversely affected the network. Always start by asking a few questions such as:

- What changes were made to the network before the trouble began?
- Were any computers added to the network?

- Were any new connectivity devices installed?

- Has anyone installed a different network protocol or removed an existing one?

- Is anyone using a new network application?

- Has anyone attempted to optimize the network?

Once you have eliminated the obvious, use diagnostic tools to help narrow the search. Look for *tell-tale* signs such as excessive collisions or broadcast storms. An extremely high collision rate could point toward a failing hardware component. It may also be an indication that it is simply time to expand the network.

Try to isolate the source of the problem to a specific subnet, connectivity device, cable segment, or computer.

Once the source of the network trouble has been located, it is necessary to determine why it is causing the problem. For example, the problem may have been tracked to a particular cable segment, but it is critical to know why the cable is not functioning properly. The following table is intended as a guideline to help you resolve the situation in a timely and efficient manner.

Source of Problem	Troubleshooting Guidelines	Comments
Cables	Reseat cables to eliminate loose connections.	Vibration and temperature changes can cause cables to work loose.
	Check for crimps or damaged areas.	Check behind desks and near employee work areas.
	Check cable continuity.	A bad cable does not always have visible damage.
	Make sure segments do not exceed the specified length.	Also make sure that the maximum number of segments has not been exceeded.
	Verify that the number of nodes is within specification.	
	Check coaxial terminators for proper resistance.	A bad terminator can cause many different problems.
	Make sure the cable is properly grounded.	
	Check for interference from external sources such as electrical motors or other cables.	You may need to reroute the cable or use a cable type that is not susceptible to interference.

Source of Problem	Troubleshooting Guidelines	Comments
Connectivity devices	Make sure that power has been applied to the device.	Almost every technician falls victim to this problem.
	Verify that the ports are functioning properly.	A port problem can appear to be a cable problem and vice versa.
	Check routing tables.	
	Reseat cables.	
Computer	Reset or replace suspect network interface cards.	Before replacing, check for conflicts with I/O or IRQ address.
	Verify that the proper protocol is being used.	The protocol installed must be the same as the protocol that is being used on the network.
	Check binding order.	The most frequently used bindings should be listed first.
	Look for network-intensive applications.	Consider moving the application to the local hard drive.
Broadcast storms	A broadcast storm is caused by an overabundance of broadcast messages on the network. This can generate so much traffic that the network will "crash."	To resolve a broadcast storm, use a protocol analyzer to isolate the source of the broadcast message. If one computer is causing the problem, look for faulty hardware such as a failing network card. If the problem is being caused by the sheer number of devices connected to the network rather than a particular computer, consider installing routers to alleviate the storms. Routers do not forward broadcast messages.

Scenario 1 (Part 1)

Ray, the network administrator at Simply Riveting Sheet Metal, Inc., has been receiving complaints that the network is slow. The network consists of a 10Base5 backbone with four subnets that are also using 10Base5 cabling. Ray has noticed that almost all of the complaints have come from users on one particular subnet.

Question

The answer to this question is in Appendix A at the end of this manual.

1. Name some of the things that Ray can do to help isolate the cause of the problem.

    ....

    ....

Scenario 1 (Part 2)

After several hours of troubleshooting, Ray believes that the aforementioned problem is being caused by a cable segment on the subnet. Ray's diagnostic equipment consists of a voltmeter and a TDR.

Questions

The answer to these questions are in Appendix A at the end of this manual.

1. Is there anything Ray can try before using the diagnostic equipment?

    ....

    ....

2. What things can Ray test with the voltmeter?

    ....

    ....

3. What things can Ray test with the TDR?

    ....

    ....

Scenario 2

You are concerned with the problem of attenuation and broadcast storms on your Ethernet TCP/IP network. As more and more computers are added to your network, the problem is becoming worse. You need to choose a type of connectivity device that will not only regenerate signals to expand the distance of a network segment but also reduce traffic bottlenecks resulting from an excessive number of attached computers. You also want to prohibit broadcast storms.

Question

The answer to this question is in Appendix A at the end of this manual.

1. What type of device do you use?

    ....

    ....

SUMMARY

The following were discussed during this chapter:

- Network Performance
- Network Monitoring
- Resolution of bottlenecks

Troubleshooting was covered during the last part of the chapter. This included basic troubleshooting guidelines, common diagnostic tools and software, and a look at common network failures and how to resolve them.

POST-TEST QUESTIONS

The answers to these questions are in Appendix A at the end of this manual.

1. All of your workstations are affected to some extent by network performance.

    A. True

    B. False

2. What procedure allows you to detect bottlenecks and test to determine if you have corrected them?

    ....

    ....

3. Disk drive access speed will directly affect _____.

    ....

    ....

4. When troubleshooting a network failure, you should look for obvious problems first.

    A. True

    B. False

Appendix A — Answers to Pre-Test and Post-Test Questions

CHAPTER 1

Pre-Test Answers

1. Physical Layer
2. Client/Server
3. Workstation shell (requester or redirector component)
4. The Logical Link Control (LLC) and Media Access Control (MAC) layers
5. Public

Scenario Answers

1. Client/Server
2. The small number of PCs would work well in a peer-to-peer environment. The employees would have the ability to share files, and a printer could be attached to one of the PCs and then shared to the rest of the group. However, the need to centrally manage the data requires a client/server environment.

Post-Test Answers

1. A Local Area Network (LAN) or a Client/Server LAN
2. A Wide Area Network (WAN)
3. The Network Operating System (NOS)
4. Cable plant

CHAPTER 2

Pre-Test Answers

1. Unshielded twisted pair
2. CSMA/CD
3. 30
4. DB-9, RJ-45, RJ-11, and IBM data connector
5. 5

Scenario 1 Answers

1. Bus topology. Generally, bus topologies are less expensive than star or ring topologies which require the purchase of additional components such as active hubs or media access units (MAUs).

2. Thin Ethernet. Thin Ethernet, also known as *cheaper-net,* works well in a small network environment. The 30-node per segment limitation should not cause a problem for the 23 employees. However, if the need for network connections grows beyond 30, a repeater and another cable segment can be added.

Scenario 2 Answer

You should us a T1 link at each site because it can carry both voice and data simultaneously. Three connections will link the three sites together, hence a mesh topology. With this topology redundancy is built into the design. If any one link fails, each site can communicate with any other site by going through an intermediate site.

Post-Test Answers

1. Coax
2. Token Ring, and Ethernet (10BaseT)
3. Fiber optic
4. Ring, Star

CHAPTER 3

Pre-Test Answers

1. NetBEUI, TCP/IP, AppleTalk, and IPX/SPX
2. TCP/IP and IPX/SPX
3. TCP/IP
4. PPP

Scenario 1 Answer

- TCP/IP

  TCP/IP is routable and provides compatibility for the UNIX clients. Although NetWare computers generally run IPX/SPX, they can run TCP/IP. This allows you to use TCP/IP for connectivity with the NetWare computers. An added bonus is that when Human Resources is ready to implement the intranet, TCP/IP will already be installed.

- AppleTalk

  AppleTalk is required for the Apple computers.

- DLC

  DLC is required for the network printers.

Scenario 2 Answers

1. IPX—not a Novell environment and NetBEUI—not a routable protocol
2. TCP/IP is routable and provides compatibility with the UNIX environment; DLC is required for the printers that are connected directly to the network; and AppleTalk is required for the Macintosh computers.

Post-Test Answers

1. NetBEUI
2. TCP/IP
3. IPX
4. AppleTalk

CHAPTER 4

Pre-Test Answers

1. Bridges

2. Routers

3. Physical Layer

4. Gateway

Scenario 1 Answers

1. Yes. Provided the auditors and the accountants are willing to be a part of the same network, they can share resources with each other.

2. A repeater can be used to boost the signal so that it will travel over the distance between them.

Scenario 2 Answers

1. Since the companies are connecting two separate networks, they will need to use a router. The companies will need to change their transport protocol to one that is routable.

2. NetBEUI is not a routable protocol.

Scenario 3 Answer

1. Earthbound Airlines can use gateways to connect their Los Angeles office with their New York office.

Post-Test Answers

1. Physical Layer (layer 1)

2. Gateway

3. Router

4. Heterogeneous or Translating Bridge

5. When the administrator manually updates the table

6. Brouter

7. Bridge

CHAPTER 5

Pre-Test Answers

1. Groups simplify user management by letting you make changes for all group members at one time.

2. User-level

3. Any data that has changed since the last full backup

4. Peer-to-peer

Scenario 1 Answer

A peer-to-peer network will only be appropriate if there are fewer than ten users and the users are all located in the same general area. If not, a server-based network should be implemented. Because you want to be able to expand the network in the future, you should choose a server-based network. A server-based network should also be implemented if security is an issue.

Scenario 2 Answer

Implement RAID level 5. In this situation, RAID level 5 (disk striping with parity) will provide the best fault tolerance and the best available disk space. It is clear that you need a fault tolerant configuration to ensure that there is no downtime. This means either disk mirroring (or duplexing) or disk striping with parity. If you mirror the disks, half of your disk space would be used for fault tolerance. If you stripe the disks with parity, only 1/3 of the space is used for fault tolerance when you stripe 3 disks; 1/4 of the space when you stripe 4 disks, etc. This means that as your data grows and you add hard disks, you will use a smaller percentage for redundancy.

Post-Test Answers

1. B. False

2. RAID Level 5

3. UPS

4. Full backup

CHAPTER 6

Pre-Test Answers

1. Router

2. WINS

3. Remote Access Service (RAS)

4. Primary domain controller, backup domain controller, and additional server

Post-Test Answers

1. OSPF

2. One

3. NetBEUI

4. DHCP

CHAPTER 7

Pre-Test Answers

1. Processor, disk, and memory

2. Cable continuity and terminator resistance.

3. Network Monitor

Scenario 1 (Part 1) Answer

Because the problem seems to only involve one subnet, that is where Ray should focus his attention. Examples of things Ray can do include the following:

- Check server performance. Look for bottlenecks involving CPUs, hard drives, and memory.

- Watch for excessive collisions.

- Check for an excessive amount of lost packets and rebroadcasts.

- Verify that only the required protocols are in use.

- Make sure that no one is playing games across the network.

Scenario 1 (Part 2) Answers

1. Ray can try to resolve the problem by reseating all of the cable connections. He should also make sure that the cable length and number of nodes do not exceed 10Base5 cable specifications.

2. Ray can check the terminators for proper resistance. He can also check cable continuity and verify that the cable is properly grounded.

3. Cable continuity, distance to an open or short, overall cable length, and termination values.

Scenario 2 Answer

- Router

    Routers interconnect networks and provide filtering functions. They work at the network layer to route packets across multiple networks based on specific network addresses. Because routers only read addresses of network packets, they will not allow bad data to be passed on to the network. Routers can be used to prohibit broadcast storms because broadcasts are not forwarded.

Post-Test Answers

1. A. True

2. Performance monitoring

3. Disk-intensive applications

4. A. True

Appendix B — Frame Types

ETHERNET FRAME FORMATS

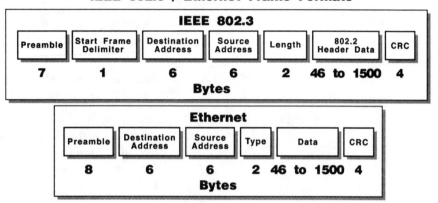

IEEE 802.3 / Ethernet Frame Formats

Preamble		Sent at the head of all frames, all seven bytes contain the binary pattern 10101010. The function of the preamble is to achieve bit synchronization before the actual data is received.
SFD		The binary pattern 10101011 follows the preamble and is used to signal the start of the actual frame contents.

Source and Destination Address	Each Ethernet card is assigned a 48-bit integer known as its Ethernet address, physical address, or hardware address. IEEE manages and assigns Ethernet addresses.

The 48-bit address can be one of three types:

Unicast	The physical address of one network interface.
Multicast	An address recognized by a logically related group of interfaces.
Broadcast	(all 1s) Sends to all stations simultaneously.

Length of Data	Reports the number of bytes of data that follow before the Frame Check Sequence. If this value is less than the minimum frame size, a sequence of bytes is added, known as **padding**.

Maximum Frame Size   1,518 Bytes

Minimum Frame Size   64 Bytes

Data	Contains the frames data from higher levels and padding when fewer than the minimum data bytes are to be transmitted. The receiver will discard frames of less than 64 Bytes.
Frame Check Sequence	The results of a CRC are placed in this 4-byte field. The receiver will also compute a CRC and discard any frame in which the two values do not match.

TOKEN RING FRAME FIELD FUNCTION

IEEE 802.5 Frame Format

SD = Start Delimiter   SA = Source Address
AC = Access Control   FCS = Frame Check Sequence
FC = Frame Control   ED = Ending Delimiter
DA = Destination Address   FS = Frame Status

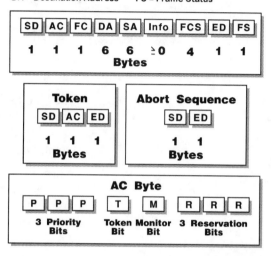

Start Delimiter

All frames begin with a unique Start Delimiter (SD) which is one byte in size and must be exactly as shown below:

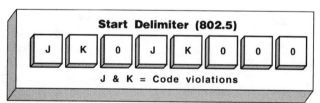

J and K represent positive and negative Differential Manchester code violations. These code violations are used at the beginning and end of the frame to ensure their uniqueness from the rest of the frame. Any initial frame sequence other than the above is considered invalid.

Access Control Field

A single byte with the following format:

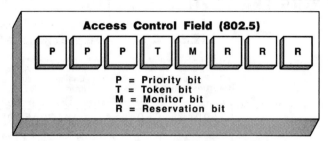

In a Token, T is set to 0; in a data/command frame, T is set to 1.

The Monitor bit is set to 0 in every transmitted frame. When the ACTIVE MONITOR repeats the frame, it sets the monitor bit to 1.

When the active monitor sees a frame with M=1, it assumes the frame has completely circled the ring. The active monitor removes the frame and originates a new token.

Priority and Reservation bits: In a multiple-priority system, each station is assigned an allowed access priority. A station can capture a token at a priority less-than or equal-to its allowed access priority. After transmitting a frame, the transmitting station will release a token with priority 0 if no reservation bits are set. When a higher priority station wants to transmit, it can request a high priority token be released by changing the reservation bits to a value equal-to or less-than its own priority.

Frame Control Field

Indicates whether the frame contains data or control information. Control information can be used to check for duplicate addresses, attempt to become active monitor, initialize the ring, etc.

Destination address	Identifies the stations that are to copy the frame. The address may be broadcast (everyone), multicast (group), or unicast (single station).
Source Address	Identifies the station that originated the frame.
Information Field	Variable length field which contains the actual data that will be sent to higher-level protocols. Each station has only a limited amount of time to transmit data (hold the token) before it is required to transmit a new token. For a typical IBM Token Ring network, the holding time is on the order of 10 milliseconds. The maximum frame size a station can transmit is limited by this holding time. In a normal Token Ring environment, the maximum frame size will be approximately 18 KB.
Frame Check Sequence	A 4-byte cyclic redundancy check (CRC) covering the FC field, DA, SA, INFO field, and the frame check sequence itself. Other fields can change after transmission and are therefore not included in this check. The receiving station recalculates the CRC and, if the two values differ, an error is assumed.
End Delimiter	Unique sequence to indicate the end of the token or frame.

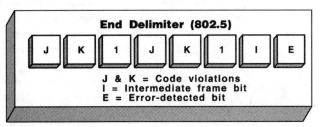

The first six bits must be as shown, indicating Differential Manchester Code violations similar to the start delimiter.

The Intermediate frame bit is set to 1 for the first frame of a multiple-frame transmission using a single token. It is set to 0 for the last frame of a multiple-frame transmission or for a single-frame transmission.

The Error bit is set to 0 by the transmitting station. If an error is detected, the receiving station sets the bit to 1 and sends the frame on to the transmitting station. The transmitting station may then retransmit the frame.

Frame Status Byte

The frame status byte has the following format:

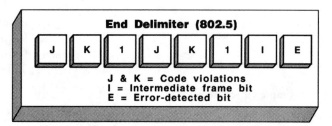

The A and C bits occur twice because this field is not protected by the Frame Check Sequence. Both values of A and both values of C must be the same if the bits are to be considered valid.

The transmitting station sets the A and C bit to zero. If the receiving station recognizes the address as its own, it sets the A bit to 1. If the receiving station copies the frame to its receive buffer, it changes the C bit to 1. Upon receiving the frame back, the transmitting station can now determine that:

The destination address is non-existent (A=0).

The destination address exists, but did not copy the data (A=1 C=0).

The frame was copied (A=1 C=1).

ARCNET

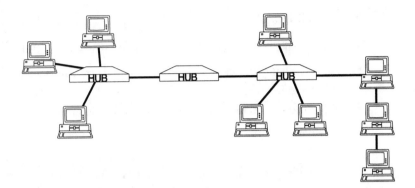

Typical ARCnet Network

ARCnet, a product of Datapoint Corporation, was developed before the IEEE 802 standards. It is similar to 802.4, the standard for Token Bus.

Token Passing Access Method

- Token is passed sequentially by node address, regardless of physical network layout.

- Handshake is a short data transmission that broadcasts a query to check the receive status and location of the designated workstation.

- Each station knows only the address of the workstation to which it forwards the token.

- Automatic Reconfiguration updates network changes.

- Owned and Developed by Datapoint.

- Deterministic.

- Star/Bus Topology.

- 2.5 Mbps/20 Mbps.

- RG62/U Coaxial Cable, Twisted Pair, Fiber Optics.

ARCnet holds a spot in a competitive market by remaining relatively inexpensive, easy to install, and easy to maintain.

ARCnet Token Passing

What this means is ...

- A node takes the invitation to transmit and issues a Free Buffer Inquiry.

- After receiving an Acknowledgment, the node transmits a data packet and waits for another ACK.

- When through transmitting, it passes on the invitation to transmit.

- The network must reconfigure itself each time a node is added or removed from service.

- NIC addresses are assigned with an 8-position DIP switch on the interface card.

Media Selection (common choices):

- 3270 Coax (RG62/U), usually in star or modified star.

- Twisted pair, usually in star or modified star.

One reason for ARCnet's popularity is that 3270 coax is often already in place and available without running new cable.

ARCnet Frame Types

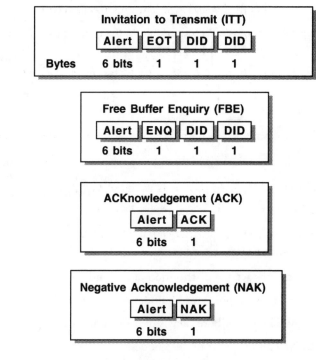

ARCnet Frame Types

Invitation to Transmit (ITT)

Alert	EOT	DID	DID

Bytes   6 bits   1   1   1

Free Buffer Enquiry (FBE)

Alert	ENQ	DID	DID

6 bits   1   1   1

ACKnowledgement (ACK)

Alert	ACK

6 bits   1

Negative Acknowledgement (NAK)

Alert	NAK

6 bits   1

Data (PAC)

Alert	SOH	SID	DID	DID	Count	Data	CRC

6 bits   1   1   1   1   1 - 2   1 - 508   2

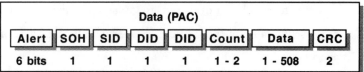

EOT - End of Transmission
DID - Destination Identification
SOH - Start of Header
SID - Source Identification

ARCnet Wiring Options

Typical ARCnet Network

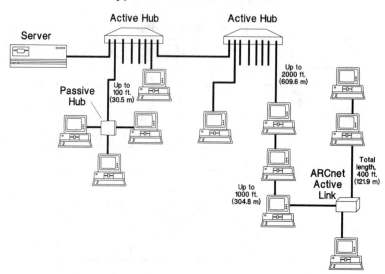

- Active Hubs act as a distribution device and signal amplifier.
- Active Hubs support up to 8 nodes.
- Passive Hubs distribute signals over short distances.
- Passive Hubs support up to 3 nodes.
- Maximum number of stations is 256 per 2.5-Mbps network.
- Maximum number of stations is 2,048 per 20-Mbps network.

Distances between:

Workstation-to-passive hub	50 feet
Workstation-to-active hub	2,000 feet
Active hub-to-active hub	2,000 feet
End-to-end passive hub connection	100 feet
Network end-to-end	20,000 feet

ARCnet only uses a single pair of twisted pair: one for receive, and the other for transmit.

FDDI TOKEN-PASSING PROCEDURES

The FDDI token-passing process is very similar to that of 802.4 and 802.5, with the exception that a new token is released at the end of a station's transmitted frames. Because of the high-speed nature of FDDI, there may be multiple frames on the network at a given time. However, there remains only one token on the network at all times.

FDDI Encoding	FDDI uses a 4-bit of 5-bit (4B/5B) encoding scheme that incorporates a 4-bit chunk of data into a symbol consisting of five cells. NRZ-I encoding is then used to transport the data.

FDDI Frame Format

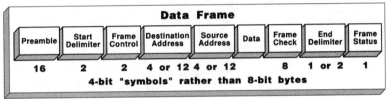

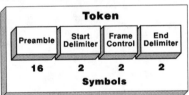

Preamble	At least sixteen 5-bit symbols (all 1s) which separate frames.
Start Delimiter	Alerts the receiver to the start of a frame. Consists of two symbols: J (start1) and K (start2).
Frame Control	Indicates frame type, data or command frame, and type of command.
Destination and Source Addresses	16- or 48-bit addresses.
Information	Data conveyed by the frame.

Frame Check Sequence	CRC check.
End Delimiter	The symbol T. One T for data/command frames, two Ts for tokens.
Frame Status	Three symbols which inform the source of frame's disposition. If the symbols are unchanged, the source assumes the receiver is not on the ring. If modified, it tells the source that the frame was either acceptable or unacceptable.

Glossary

Abbreviated addressing	In packet-switched networks) Addressing in which a simple mnemonic code is used in lieu of the complete addressing information. The reference to the complete address is stored in the PAD.
ABR	Autobaud, Automatic Baud Rate Detection. A process by which a receiving device determines the speed, code level, and stop bits of incoming data by examining the first character, usually a pre-selected sign-on character. ABR allows the receiving device to accept data from a variety of transmitting devices operating at different speeds without needing to establish data rates in advance.
Abstract syntax	A description of a data structure that is independent of machine-oriented structures and encodings.
Access Control List (ACL)	1. A list of trustees who have been granted rights to an object or rights to the properties of an object. Each object in the NDS contains an Access Control List.
	2. Under Windows NT, the Access Control List contains user and group Access Control Entries.
Access method	1. In IBM environments, it is a host program managing the movement of data between the main storage and an input/output device of a computer system. BTAM,TCAM, and VTAM are common data communications access methods.
	2. In LAN technology, it is a means to allow stations to gain access to make use of the network's transmission medium, which is classified as a shared access or discrete access method.
Access time	Access time is a measurement of the average time it takes from when the PC issues a command, to get data from a disk drive. This is a combination of several factors. The major determining factor is drive seek time. Moving the read/write heads is the slowest single operation for a hard disk. The faster it can move the head array during seek time, the faster the disk access time.
Access unit	The electronic mail component responsible for transferring messages between dissimilar mail systems.
Account SID	A unique value identifying a Windows NT or NT Server user, group account, or object.

Accounting	In networking, a method of allocating space, time, and costs to users. In NetWare, user accounts are created by using the SYSCON supervisor option. The accounts keep track of connection time, logins, and network use. They also calculate and apply charges, and withdraw charge privileges, when necessary.
Accunet	AT&T data-oriented digital services, including the following: Accunet T1.5 terrestrial wideband at 1.544 megabits per second used primarily for video teleconferencing applications, Accunet packet-switching services, and Accunet Dataphone digital services (DDS).
Acknowledgment (ACK)	A response by the receiver of a communications message indicating the message was received correctly.
Adaptive Bridge	Sometimes referred to as a "learning bridge" because it learns the node address of workstations on the LAN. This type of bridge builds its own table of address which frees the administrator or installer of this task.
Address	A unique designation for the location of data, the identity of an intelligent device, or a logical network address. An address allows each device on a single communications line to respond to its own message.
Address mask	A bit mask used to select bits from an Internet (TCP/IP) address for subnet addressing. The mask is 32 bits long and selects the network portion of the Internet address and two or more bits of the local portion. It is sometimes called subnet mask.
Address resolution	A means for mapping logical addresses to physical addresses.

Address Resolution Protocol

A protocol used between routers and nodes to determine the MAC or OSI physical layer address when the Network layer (IP) address is known.

Administration Management Domain (ADMD)

An X.400 Message Handling System public service carrier. Examples: MCImail and ATTmail in the U.S., British Telecom Gold 400mail in the U.K. The ADMDs in all countries worldwide together provide the X.400 backbone.

Administrative Domain (AD)

This is a single NetWare administrative unit that has authority over hosts, links, and networks.

Advanced Program-to-Program Communications (APPC)

An Application Program Interface (API) developed by IBM for its Systems Network Architecture (SNA).

AFP Server Object	An AFP Server Object represents an AppleTalk Filing Protocol file server on the network.

AFP.NLM	The AFP.NLM is the NetWare Loadable Module loaded on the file server to provide AppleTalk Filing Protocol (AFP) services.
Agent	In the client server model, the part of the system that performs information preparation and exchange on behalf of a client or server application.

American Standard Code for Information Interchange (ASCII)

The American Standard Code for Information Interchange (ASCII) character set is used to translate a byte into a character or number. Devised in 1968, ASCII is used for the purpose of standardizing the transmission of data to achieve hardware and software compatibility.

ASCII has 128 Characters and uses seven of the eight bits to form these characters. The eighth bit is used for error checking.

IBM developed the Extended Character Set, which contains 256 characters. In this character set, the eighth bit is used for special symbols, such as bullet points, fractions, and copyright or trademark symbols.

American National Standards Institute (ANSI)

A group of committees formed to establish voluntary commercial and government standards. The committee responsible for computing, data processing, and information technology is ANSI-X3, formerly named USASI (United States of America Standards Institute). ANSI is a member of International Standards Organization (ISO).

American Wire Gauge (AWG)

A standard for determining wire diameter. The diameter varies inversely to the gauge number.

Amplitude modulation	A method of encoding enabling the frequency of the carrier wave to remain constant while the information it carries changes in strength. This system changes the strength (size) of an analog signal (wave) from the zero line to a positive peak, and then to an equal negative peak. The stronger the voltage, the higher the wave. Often abbreviated as AM.
Analog	The representation of a continuously changing physical variable (sound, for example) by another physical variable (such as electrical current).
Analog signal	A smoothly varying value of voltage or current. The signal varies continuously in amplitude and time.
ANSI character set	The American National Standards Institute 8-bit character set containing 256 characters.
AppleShare	The software that allows a Macintosh computer to share file system resources with other networked Macs. This is also the name of the extension (utilized by the Chooser) that allows a Mac to connect to other shared file system resources via AppleTalk.

AppleShare software	A Macintosh computer can function as a file server in an AppleTalk network using this networking software. As Macintosh workstation software, it allows access to an AppleShare server.
AppleTalk	Protocols for a network of Macintosh computers.
	AppleTalk is based on the ISO/OSI Reference Model and incorporates the SPX protocol. AppleTalk networks may be configured in Ethernet and token ring topologies. AppleTalk networks use various kinds of cables. The AppleTalk Filing Protocol (AFP), for client server architecture, runs on VAX and other non- Macintosh servers. AppleTalk and AFP are compatible with NetWare and are available as VAPs (v2.x) and NLMs (v3.x) in NetWare for Macintosh.

AppleTalk Data Stream Protocol (ADSP)

ADSP is responsible for providing a simple transport method for data across the network.

AppleTalk Echo Protocol (AEP)

AEP is responsible for checking for communications between different nodes on the network.

AppleTalk Filing Protocol (AFP)

This is the AppleTalk protocol that allows communication and data transmission between file servers and clients in an AppleShare network. If AFP.NLM is loaded on a NetWare server that is running NetWare for Macintosh, the AFP lets Macintosh users share files by interacting directly with the NetWare file system. It operates on the same level as NetWare Core Protocol (NCP).

AppleTalk Phase I	AppleTalk Phase I networks are limited to one network number per cable segment as well as 256 nodes.
AppleTalk Phase II	AppleTalk Phase II networks exceed the 254 device limitation by allowing the assignment of multiple network numbers on the same network segment. Phase II networks allow the creation of larger, more open networks with the introduction of TokenTalk and EtherTalk.

AppleTalk Session Protocol (ASP)

ASP is responsible for maintaining all sessions between the workstation and the file server. Some of these tasks may include: session initiation, maintenance, and termination.

AppleTalk Transaction Protocol (ATP)

ATP is responsible for handling network messaging. Unlike DDPm, ATP requires an acknowledgement of delivery.

Application	The use to which an information processing system is put. For example, a payroll application, an airline reservation application, or a network application.

Application layer   OSI Layer 7 providing an interface with user or application programs.

Application Program Interface (API)

Used where proprietary application programs have to talk to communications software or conform to protocols from another vendor's product. API also provides a standardized method of "vertical" communications. Apple Macintosh was the first computer to use the API concept.

Architecture

The specific design and construction of a computer. Architecture usually refers to the hardware makeup of the central processing unit and the size of the byte or set of bytes it processes, such as 8-bit, 16-bit, or 32-bit architecture.

ARCnet

The Attached Resource Computing Network (ARCnet) is a token-passing network that can utilize both star and bus topologies. ARCnet is not an IEEE standard, but was developed by the Datapoint corporation in 1977.

Although generally considered old technology, ARCnet originally used coaxial cable and transmitted at 2.5 Mbps.

Several vendors announced ARCnet Plus, a 20 Mbps version compatible with the 2.5 Mbps ARCnet standard. Both versions can run on the same LAN. Each node advertises its capabilities, and faster nodes slow their speed to communicate with slower nodes.

Some of the newer ARCnet cards operating at speeds of 100 Mbps, and use twisted pair or fiber optic cable.

With ARCnet, active hubs can support cable lengths up to 2,000 feet.

ARCnet is a reliable system that is not as susceptible to failure as coaxial-cabled Ethernet. If a cable is cut or comes loose, only the workstation goes down, not entire network. The token-passing protocol requires that every transaction be acknowledged, so there is little chance for errors.

The trade-off is that ARCnet data throughput is much slower than with other networking schemes.

ASCII terminal

A terminal that uses ASCII. Usually synonymous with asynchronous terminal and dumb terminal.

Asia and Oceania Workshop (AOW)

One of the three regional OSI Implementors Workshops, and is equivalent to OIW and EWOS.

Association Control Service Element (ACSE)

The method used in OSI for establishing a call between two applications. Checks the identities and contexts of the application entities, and could apply an authentication security check.

Asymmetric Multiprocessing (ASMP)
Multiprocessor management method where one processor supports the operating system and any additional processors support process threads.

Asynchronous
A form of communication where each transmitted character is preceded by a start bit and followed by a stop bit. This eliminates the need for a particular spacing or timing scheme between characters. Personal computers communicate asynchronously via a serial port.

Asynchronous modem
A modem which cannot supply timing signals and requires all the timing information to be supplied by the associated data terminal equipment (DTE).

Asynchronous Transfer Mode (ATM)
ATM is a high-speed (155 - 162 Mbps) communications transport facility capable of carrying voice, data, and video signaling. ATM forms the backbone for broadband ISDN networks.

In ASCII, where eight bits form a character or byte, ten bits must be sent for each character. Asynchronous transmission is sometimes known as start-stop transmission.

Asynchronous transmission In computer communications, data (binary digits) can be transmitted in asynchronous mode or synchronous mode. When the mode is asynchronous, the binary digits are not orderly, meaning they are out of synchronization and sent at irregular intervals in characters, words, or blocks. To ensure that the receiving device is ready, a special "start bit" is sent ahead of each character and a "stop bit" at the end of each character, a process which continues until the final character is sent.

In ASCII, where eight bits form a character or byte, ten bits must be sent for each character. Asynchronous transmission is sometimes known as start-stop transmission.

ATCON
A NetWare utility that allows the network manager to monitor AppleTalk routing on the MultiProtocol Router product.

ATPS.NLM
The ATPS.NLM is the NetWare Loadable Module which is loaded on the file server to provide print services to an Apple LaserWriter.

Attachment User Interface (AUI)
Standard Ethernet connector.

Attribute
A characteristic describing or distinguishing a piece of hardware or software, such as security attributes or database field character types.

Autonomous System
Internet (TCP/IP) terminology for a collection of gateways (routers) that fall under one administrative entity and cooperate using a common Interior Gateway Protocol (IGP).

Average access time
The average time between the instant of request and the delivery from a storage device.

Backbone	The primary connectivity mechanism of a hierarchical distributed system. All systems which have connectivity to an intermediate system on the backbone are assured connectivity to each other. This does not prevent systems from setting up private arrangements with each other to bypass the backbone for reasons of cost, performance, or security.
Backup	1. Pertaining to a system, device, file, or facility that can be used to recover data in the event of a malfunction or loss of data.
	2. To copy information, usually onto diskette or tape, for safekeeping.
Balanced transmission	A transmission mode in which signals are transmitted as a current that travels down one conductor and returns on the other. For digital signals, this technique is known as differential signaling, with the binary value depending on the voltage difference.
Baseband	Characteristic of any network technology that uses a single carrier frequency and requires all stations attached to the network to participate in every transmission.

Basic Encoding Rules (BER)

Standard rules for encoding data units described in ASN.1. Sometimes incorrectly lumped under the term ASN.1, which properly refers only to the abstract syntax description language, not the encoding technique.

Basic Input/Output System (BIOS)

Software or firmware embedded in chips on the circuit board which determines compatibility. Examples of these are IBM, Compaq, AMI, Award, and Phoenix.

Basic Telecommunications Access Method (BTAM)

An IBM software routine; the basic access method for 3270 data communications controls.

Batch	A method of computer job processing where input is collected and run through the processing programs all at once and outputs produced in the form of files and reports. Batch is the opposite of interactive job processing, in which an operator at a terminal interacts with the processing program directly during data entry. Most personal computers employ interactive processing. Mainframes use batch processing.
Baud	1. Abbreviation for Baudot, which gets its name from J. M. Emile Baudot (1845-1903), who invented the code. The Baudot code is a special set of binary characters using five bits per character to form 32 combinations. The number of combinations was increased to 62 through the use of two special shift characters. The Baudot code was mainly used to handle telex messages by common communications carriers such as Western Union. The main disadvantage of the Baudot code is its lack of an error-checking bit.
	2. Used commonly to refer to transfer rates on dial-up lines.

Baud Rate	The data transmission speed setting of a serial device. Typical rates include 300, 1200, and 2400. Higher speeds, 9600, 19200, 38400, and 57600 baud, are achieved through data compression. Sometimes referred to simply as baud.
Beacon	Sent when Token Ring failure occurs. Used to identify ring failures.
Bell 103	An AT&T, 0-300 bps modem providing asynchronous transmission with originate/answer capability; also, often used to describe any Bell 103-compatible modem.
Bell 113	An AT&T, 0-300 bps modem providing asynchronous transmission with originate/answer capability (but not both). Also, often used to describe any Bell 113-compatible modem.
Bell 201	An AT&T, 2400 bps modem providing synchronous transmission; Bell 201 B was designed for leased-line applications; Bell 201 C was designed for public telephone network applications. Also, often used to describe any Bell 201-compatible modem.
Bell 202	An AT&T, 1800 bps modem providing asynchronous transmission that requires a 4-wire circuit for full-duplex operation. Also, often used to describe any Bell 202-compatible modem.
Bell 208	An AT&T, 4800 bps modem providing synchronous transmission; Bell 208 A was designed for leased-line applications; Bell 208 B was designed for public telephone network applications. Also, often used to describe any Bell 208-compatible modem.
Bell 209	An AT&T, 9600 bps modem providing synchronous transmission. Also, often used to describe any Bell 209-compatible modem.
Bell 212	An AT&T, 1200 bps full-duplex modem providing asynchronous transmission or asynchronous transmission for use on the public telephone network. Also, often used to describe any Bell 212-compatible modem.
Bell 43401	Bell Publication which defines requirements for transmission over telco-supplied circuits have DC continuity (that are metallic).

Bell Operating Company (BOC)

> More commonly referred to as RBOC for Regional Bell Operating Company. The local telephone company in each of the seven U.S. regions.

Berkeley Software Distribution (BSD)

> A term used when describing different versions of the Berkeley UNIX software, as in "4.3BSD UNIX."

Binary Synchronous Communications (BSC)

A type of synchronous communications control procedure set up by IBM as a line control procedure in which the sending and receiving stations are synchronized before a message is sent. The synchronization is checked and adjusted during the transmission, using a defined set of control characters.

Big-endian

A format for storing or transmitting binary data in which the most significant bit (or byte) comes first. The reverse convention is called little-endian.

Binary

Having two components or possible states. Usually represented by a code of zeros and ones.

BIND

A NetWare v3.x and v4.x console command that links an installed network board's communication protocol to its LAN driver loaded in the file server. It is used to bind one or several protocols to a board, or a protocol to one or several boards.

Bindery

In NetWare 3, the bindery stores information about users, groups, file servers, print servers, and other logical and physical entities on the network. Network information, such as passwords, account balances, and trustee assignments, are also kept in the bindery.

The bindery files, NET$OBJ.SYS, NET$PROP.SYS, and NET$VAL.SYS, are stored in the SYSTEM directory on the SYS volume. The files are system files and do not appear in a normal directory search.

BINDFIX is a utility that rebuilds the bindery files, purges deleted users and groups, and then removes their mail directories and trustee rights. The original bindery files are copied to NET$OBJ.OLD, NET$PROP.OLD, and NET$VAL.OLD.

BINDFIX runs without other parameters. One should be logged in as SUPERVISOR and have SYS:SYSTEM as the default directory before running the utility. Insure there is no other activity on the system before running BINDFIX.

BINDREST is a utility used to restore the original bindery files should BINDFIX fail for any reason. BINDREST runs without additional parameters.

Binding

The process by which an object's type library is located.

bis

A suffix to CCITT v.xx standard numbers. Whenever a CCITT V.xx standard is followed by the bis extension, it indicates that modifications have been made to the original CCITT standard.

Bit	Abbreviation for binary digit. A bit is the fundamental unit of information and is either a zero or a one; the basic unit for storing data in primary storage (zero for "off," one for "on"). Groups of bits are needed to represent other symbols such as letters of the alphabet.
Bitmap	A group of bits (binary digits) representing an image stored in a computer's memory as a pattern of dots.
BITNET address	This is a mail address for the BITNET network made up of a user name and host name. BITNET hosts are accessed from the Internet by adding the suffix ".bitnet" to a BITNET address.
Bits per second (bps)	Usually the number of bits (binary digits) which can be transmitted or transferred each second.
Boot	To start or restart your computer, loading the operating system from a disk drive.
Break	An interruption in program execution or data transmission; a loss of communication between sender and receiver. Also a keyboard key that enables the interruption.
Bridge	Bridges are network devices that are more intelligent than repeaters, in that they can read the specific physical address of devices on one network and filter information before passing it on to another network segment. The connection is made at the Data Link Layer of the OSI model.

British Naval Connector (BNC)

A connector for coaxial cable.

Broadband	A technique for transmitting analog signals along a medium, such as a radio wave, also called wideband. Broadband signaling works the way radio and television work, by splitting up the available frequencies into different channels. The data is transmitted simultaneously and is represented by changes in amplitude, frequency, or phase of the signal.
	Broadband transmission can be used to transmit different combinations of data, voice, and video information along one physical cable with multiple communication channels of different frequencies. In LAN technology, broadband is a system in which multiple channels access a medium, usually coaxial cable, that has a large bandwidth (50 Mbps is typical) using radio-frequency modems.
Broadcast	1. A transmission of a message intended for general reception rather than for a specific station.
	2. In LAN technology, a transmission method used in bus topology networks that sends all messages to all stations even though the messages are addressed to specific stations.
	3. A NetWare console command that transmits a message to all network nodes or list of nodes.

Buffer	A temporary storage place for information. Many times it is a device used to compensate for a difference in either the rate of data flow or the time of occurrence of events in transmission from one device to another.
Bulletin Board System (BBS)	A popular PC network that allows users to dial into a central point and read group messages, copy public-domain information, and leave messages for other users.
Burst Mode	A NetWare utility that allows a protocol window for higher performance.
Bursty	An adjective used to describe data transmission. Data sent in large packets requiring all available bandwidth, but which is quickly gone is a "bursty" transmission.
Bus	1. A pathway on which data travels. Examples of buses in a typical Macintosh computer include the expansion bus (NuBus or PCI), Apple Desktop Bus (ADB), and SCSI bus.

2. LAN data pathway based on a single cable terminated at both ends. |
Byte	Short for "binary digit eight." A unit of information consisting of usually eight bits. A file's size is measured in bytes or potential storage capacity is measured in bytes, but when dealing with very large numbers, the terms kilobyte, megabyte, or gigabyte are used.
Bytes per second (Bps)	Usually the number of bytes which can be transmitted or transferred each second.
Cache	An area of computer memory set aside for frequently used data to speed operations. Some caches are general purpose, while others are for specific operations. A disk cache is an area of system memory reserved for caching disk reads and writes. A CPU cache is a dedicated, high-speed memory array used to cache pending instructions.
CALLMGR	A NetWare v3.11 utility that allows the network manager to manually call other networks from the MultiProtocol Router product.
CAPTURE	A NetWare command-line utility that sends an application's print job to a network print queue in cases where the application can direct the job only to a station's LPT port. CAPTURE can also be used to send data to a file and print screen displays.
Carrier Sense Multiple Access (CSMA)	A contention method of operating a network, where multiple nodes "sense" the communications medium and transmit when the medium is free from transmissions. This technology greatly reduces the chance that two stations will try to use the channel at the same time. However, in networks with a large number of stations, another node will likely transmit at the same time and two messages will collide.

Carrier Sense Multiple Access with Collision Avoidance (CSMA/CA)

In a LAN (Local Area Network), when a single resource is to be used by multiple entities, some control method is required to regulate the use of the resources. There are several methods for each station to gain access to the LAN when it needs to send a message. The three main categories of LAN access methods are token passing, contention access, and time slot. CSMA/CA tries to avoid collisions by reserving specific time slots for each of the stations during which they may transmit without threat of collision. This works well for small networks with few stations. However, performance is quickly degraded as the network size and station number increase. A more widely used contention access method is CSMA/CD, where emphasis is on fast detection and recovery of collisions.

Carrier Sense Multiple Access with Collision Detection (CSMA/CD)

Carrier Sense Multiple Access with Collision Detection (CSMA/CD) is the most common implementation of contention access. It is Carrier Sensing in that it listens for systems to transmit. Multiple Access indicates that all systems have concurrent access to the network media. If two or more systems transmit at once, the systems realizes the message didn't get through and repeat the messages at different time intervals, thus providing Collision Detection. Collisions slow cable throughput.

Transmission failures can be caused by collisions or bad cabling. It can happen due to improper termination or cable length.

At some point in its growth, an Ethernet network may encounter a reduction in performance. The time when this will occur depends on the amount of traffic generated by each workstation.

Catenet

A network in which hosts are connected to networks with varying characteristics, and the networks are interconnected by gateways (routers). The Internet is an example of a catenet.

CCITT

Comite Consultatif Internationale de Telegraphie et Telephonie. An international consultative committee that sets international communications standards. It develops interface, modem, and data network recommendations. Membership includes PTT's scientific and trade associations, and private companies. CCITT is part of the International Telecommunications Union (a United Nations treaty organization in Geneva).

Central Processing Unit (CPU)

A highly complex set of electrical circuits that execute stored program instructions. The CPU consists of the control unit and the arithmetic/logic unit (ALU). In a personal computer, the CPU is typically a single, powerful microprocessor chip. CPUs can be measured by the amount of data they can read from memory in one access, the number of operations per second, the total amount of memory supported, and whether more than one job can be run at one time. Sophisticated computer systems can have more than one CPU operating within the same system.

Character set

A set of acceptable and recognizable characters used by a particular computer system or software package. Character sets are binary-coded, and often follow a standard such as ASCII, ANSI, or EBCDIC.

Characters per second (cps)

Cps is used as one measure of print speed.

Checksum

Used in data communications to monitor the number of bits being transmitted between communications devices by means of a simple mathematical algorithm. The checksum is used to ensure that the full complement of bits is received successfully by the receiving device.

Chooser

The Macintosh OS desk accessory (DA) that provides access to shared network drives and printers via AppleTalk.

Circuit

1. In data communications, a circuit is a means of bidirectional communication between two points, consisting of transmit and receive channels.

2. In electronic design, a circuit is one or more components that act together to perform one or more functions.

Claim Token

Used by a station to become the active monitor when no active monitor is present on a Token Ring network.

Client

1. A client is a workstation that requests services of another computer (server).

2. The portion of a client/server application providing the end-user interface (front-end).

Client/Server Model

The client/server model concerns networking and provides for distributed processing. Applications and data files are stored on the file server. The files are downloaded to intelligent workstations (the clients) for processing. The results of the processing are uploaded to the server for storage. The server may provide additional services to the client such as printing or communications support.

Most high-level network operating systems use the client/server model. Novell's NetWare and Microsoft Windows NT Server operate in a client/server environment.

The terms client and server are also used when discussing interprocess communication. It is important to keep the term usage in this context separate from describing a network environment. In interprocess communications, the terms server and client refer only to the function of the process within the context of a transaction. When involved in a different transaction, the roles could be reversed.

In interprocess communications, the server is the process that provides information to another process, or creates an object that is used by another process. For example, you may have a process that is responsible for gathering data from a spreadsheet and provides it to a presentation program. In this case, the data-gathering process would be referred to as the server.

The client is the process that accepts information from another process, or uses an object that was created by another process. In the previous example, the data-gathering process would be the client of the spreadsheet, and, at the same time it is the server to the presentation program. The presentation program would be the client of the data-gathering process.

Closed-Circuit Television (CCTV)
One of the many services often found on broadband networks.

Cluster control unit
Also called cluster controller; a device that can control the input-output operations of more than one device connected to it. A cluster control unit may be controlled by a program stored and executed in the unit.

CMOS RAM
This memory stores system configuration data, for example the number of drives, types of drives, and amount of memory. It is battery-powered, so it can retain the data, time, and other information that must be stored when the computer is turned off.

CMOT (CMIP Over TCP)
An effort to use the OSI network management protocol to manage TCP/IP networks.

Coaxial Cable	Coaxial cable is composed of two conductors that share the same axis. The center cable is insulated by plastic-foam. The plastic foam is wrapped with a second conductor, usually foil. All is covered with an external plastic casing.

Coaxial Cable

Coaxial Cable Connectors and Installation

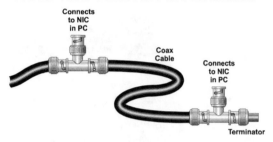

Common coaxial cable types include 10Base5 (Thick Ethernet), 10Base2 (Thin Ethernet), ARCnet, and Cable TV.

Coaxial cable is resistant to Electro-Magnetic Interference.

Transmissions over coax may be either baseband or broadband. With baseband, the cables carry a single high-speed signal. This is the transmission method used by Ethernet. Broadband coax carries multiple signals, each at a different frequency. Broadband transmission is sometimes used for backbone cables.

Code	A set of rules that specify the way data is represented, such as ASCII or EBCDIC. Code is also used to describe lines of instructions for the computer, as in program code.
Coder-decoder (Codec)	An assembly comprising an encoder and a decoder in the same equipment. Also, a device that performs the dual function of encoding two-way analog data into digital data and two-way digital data into analog data.

Collisions

In some networking schemes, any station may transmit when it senses that the carrier is free. A collision occurs when two stations transmit simultaneously. If a collision is detected, each station will wait for a randomly determined interval before retransmitting the data.

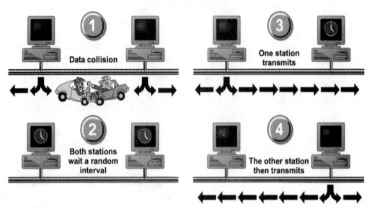

Collisions

Most network operating systems track retransmissions, which is a good indication of the number of collisions occurring on the network.

COM port

A connection on the computer where the cable for a serial device is attached. The serial device could be a printer, network interface card, modem, or other device. COM ports are often called serial ports. COM ports are numbered, and generally COM1 through COM4 are supported on most personal computers. It is possible to have more or less than four COM ports.

Common carrier

In the U.S., a private business or corporation that offers general communication services to the public such as telephone, teletype, or intercomputer communications. All common carriers operate under FCC guidelines and all services offered are subject to tariff schedules filed with and approved by the FCC.

Communication protocols

Rules used by a program or operating system to communication between two or more points. It allows information to be packaged, sent, and delivered.

Communications rate

Also called the transfer rate or the transmission rate. The communications rate cannot exceed the maximum rate that both devices can handle.

Communications Software

To communicate with the modem, communications software is required. The software helps control the modem and specifies what data should be sent where. Communication software is required at both the sending and receiving computers.

Community Antenna Television (CATV)

CATV cable is used for broadband local networks and broadcast TV distribution.

Complementary Metal Oxide Semiconductor (CMOS)

A specialized memory chip, powered by a small battery, that stores basic system configuration information.

Component

Hardware or software that is part of a functional unit.

Computer Science Network (CSNET)

CSNET was a large computer network located mostly in the United States, but with some international connections. CSNET sites included universities, research labs, and some commercial companies. It was merged with BITNET to form CREN.

Concentration

Collection of data at an intermediate point from several low- and medium-speed lines for transmission across one high-speed line.

Concentrator

A small programmable device which acts as a communications control unit used to maintain control over a communications network by handling a variety of functions such as converting code. Concentrators are also used for combining signals from many terminals and then retransmitting these signals over a single channel; also for directing communications traffic, buffering, multiplexing, and polling.

Connection Oriented Network Protocol (CONP)

The layer 3 (routed) connection-oriented protocol used between host nodes in an OSI network.

Connection-oriented

The model of interconnection in which communication proceeds through three well-defined phases: connection establishment, data transfer, connection release. Examples include X.25, Internet TCP and OSI TP4, ordinary telephone calls.

Connectionless

The model of interconnection in which communication takes place without first establishing a connection. Sometimes called datagram. Examples: LANs, Internet IP and OSI CLNP, UDP, ordinary postcards.

ConnectionLess Network Protocol (CLNP)

The layer 3 (routed) connectionless protocol used between host nodes in an OSI network.

ConnectionLess Transport Protocol (CLTP)

Provides for end-to-end Transport data addressing (via Transport selector) and error control (via checksum), but cannot guarantee delivery or provide flow control. The OSI equivalent of UDP.

Context switch	The immediate switching from one program to another without first closing the files, allowing users to operate several programs concurrently, such as a graphics program and a word processing program. With context switching, unlike multitasking, when one program is being used the other halts. Advantages of context switching are rapid switching, exchange of clipboard files, and fast data transfer. In a multiple loading operating system such as Macintosh, the programs are held in random access memory.
Control character	Any one of 32 special hardware control characters and symbols available in ASCII which are used to control a communications process or a peripheral device such as a printer. Control characters may be used to instruct the printer to advance paper, or move one line; also can be used to signify the start and finish of a data transmission.
Control Panel	1. On a Macintosh, the Control Panel is a system software utility stored in the Control Panels folder (found in the System Folder). Panels are used to configure various services such as AppleTalk and user preferences such as desktop patterns and wallpaper.
	2. Windows-family utility containing management tools.
Control Unit (CU)	In the processor, the CU is the part that retrieves instructions in proper sequence, interprets each instruction, and applies the proper signals to the arithmetic logic unit and other parts in accordance with this interpretation.
	Also, one of two parts of the Central Processing Unit (CPU) containing circuits that, with electrical signals, direct and coordinate the entire computer system.
Cooperation for Open Systems Interconnection Networking in Europe (COSINE)	
	A program sponsored by the European Commission, aimed at using OSI to tie together European research networks.
Cooperative multitasking	A multitasking method where an application must release the processor before the next application may be given processor time.
Coprocessor	An auxiliary processor designed to relieve the demand on the main processor by performing a few specific tasks such as floating point math or graphics calculations. In general, coprocessors handle tasks that would be performed more slowly by the main processor.
Core gateway	One of a set of gateways (routers) operated by the Internet Network Operations Center (NOC) at BBN. The core gateway system forms a central part of Internet routing in that all groups must advertise paths to their networks from a core gateway using the Exterior Gateway Protocol (EGP).

Corporation for Open Systems (COS)
:   A vendor and user group for conformance testing, certification, and promotion of OSI products.

Crosstalk
:   The disturbance caused in a circuit by an unwanted transfer of energy from another circuit. Also, interference which occurs when cables are too close to each other, resulting in loss or corruption of data.

Customer Information Control System (CISC)
:   An IBM program and mainframe operating environment designed to enable transactions entered at remote terminals to be processed concurrently by user-written application programs. CICS includes facilities for building and maintaining databases.

Current loop
:   1. (Single-current signaling, used in U.S.A.) Methods of interconnecting Teletype terminals and transmitting signals that represent a mark by current on the line and a space by the absence of current.

    2. (Double-current signaling, used everywhere else.) A mark is represented by current in one direction and a space by current in the other direction.

Cyclic Redundancy Check
:   A redundancy check in which the check key is generated by a cyclic algorithm. Also, a system checking or error checking performed at both the sending and receiving station after a block check character has been accumulated.

Daemon program
:   Slang for a program not used explicitly, but normally loaded when the system is started, and lies dormant in the background awaiting the occurrence of some condition or conditions.

Data communication
:   The transfer of data from one device to another via direct cabling: telecommunication links involving modems, a telephone network, or other connection methods. Transfer of information between functional units by means of data transmission according to a protocol.

Data file
:   A collection of related data records organized in a specific manner, such as a payroll file or an inventory file.

Data integrity
:   The data quality that exists as long as accidental or malicious destruction, alteration, or loss of data does not occur.

Data Link Control (DLC)
:   A protocol used for communication with mainframe systems and printers directly attached to a network.

Data Link Layer
:   OSI Layer 2, the OSI layer that is responsible for data transfer across a single physical connection, or series of bridged connections, between two Network entities.

Data set (DS)	The major unit of data storage and retrieval, consisting of a collection of data in one of several prescribed arrangements and described by control information to which the system has access.
Data stream	All data transmitted through a data channel in a single read or write operation. Also, a continuous stream of data elements being transmitted, or intended for transmission, in character or binary-digit form, using a defined format.
Data Transfer Rate	The data transfer rate determines how fast a drive or other peripheral can transfer data with its controller. The data transfer rate is a key measurement in drive performance.
Data-over-voice	A FDM technique which combines data and voice on the same line by assigning a portion of the unused bandwidth to the data; usually implemented on the twisted-pair cables used for in-house telephone system wiring.
Database	A collection of interrelated data stored together that is fundamental to a system or enterprise. A data structure for accepting, storing, and providing on-demand data for multiple independent users.
Datagram	A message transmitted in a network, requiring no response or acknowledgment.
DECnet	Trademark for DEC's communications network architecture that permits interconnection of DEC computers using DDCMP.
Default	One of a set of operating conditions that is automatically used when a device such as a printer or computer is turned on or reset. Pertaining to an attribute, value, or option when none is explicitly specified.
Default Zone	Usually the first defined zone within a zone list.
Defense Advanced Research Projects Agency (DARPA)	The U.S. government agency that funded the ARPANET.
Defense Communications Agency (DCA)	The government agency responsible for the Defense Data Network (DDN).
Defense Data Network (DDN)	This is a collection of networks, including MILNET, portions of the Internet, and classified networks used for military purposes. DDN is managed by the Defense Information Systems Agency (DISA).
Demodulation	The decoding of modulated analog signals after being received from a carrier wave, so they can be converted back to digital signals. For example, the demodulation or extraction in a television receiver of a video signal from a UHF carrier.
Demultiplexing	Dividing one or more information streams into a larger number of streams.

Dependent service	A service that will not run unless a prerequisite service is loaded.
Desk Accessory	DAs are Macintosh system accessories such as the Calculator, Find File, AppleCD Audio Player, Note Pad, and Scrapbook. NetWare for Macintosh provides a desk accessory called the NetWare Desk Accessory (NetWare DA).
Desktop	Most Graphical User Interfaces (GUIs) refer to the work area on the computer screen as the desktop. All window items appear and are moved around on this desktop area.
Device	Any computer peripheral or hardware component (such as printer, mouse, monitor, or disk drive) capable of receiving and/or sending data, generally through the use of a device driver.
Device driver	Hardware-specific software that acts as an interface between the operating system and the hardware attached to a computer. Device drivers allow applications to communicate with hardware in a controlled and orderly fashion. A device driver is installed when the system is initialized, either by the operating system or through an installable device driver. Some examples of installable device drivers are mouse, graphical/video monitor, communications port, printer, and network interface card.
Dial network	Synonymous with public telephone network.
Digital	Devices that represent data in the form of digits, based on the binary system where the binary digits (bits) are zero or one. Also, pertaining to data that consists of digits.
Digital data	Data represented by digits, perhaps together with special characters and the space character.
Digital, Intel, Xerox (DIX)	A type of AUI Ethernet connector.
Digital Multiplexed Interface	One of two voice/data PABX standards for using T1 transmission that involves T1-to-64 Kbps conversion prior to connection to the computer bus; represents a move toward an open architecture.
Digital switch	A star topology local network. Usually refers to a system that handles only data, but not voice.
Digital to Analog Converter (DAC)	DAC chips are found on analog adapters. Because the PC operates digitally, it sends digitized information to the adapter. If the device accepts analog input only, the DAC on the adapter must convert the digital data into analog instructions for the device.
Digital transmission	The transfer of encoded information using on and off pulses; unlike analog transmission which uses a continuous wave form and carries more than one channel at a time.

Direct Memory Access	Direct Memory Access (DMA) channels allow devices to communicate directly with memory. This is generally used with add-in boards or devices that transfer large amounts of data. Examples include are network interface cards, CD ROMs, and sound cards.

IBM XT-style systems have four available DMA channels (0 through 3). ISA/AT, MCA, and EISA systems have eight DMA channels (0 through 7).

Each device that uses DMA must have its own unique DMA channel. Channel 0 is available in ISA/AT-type systems and above. Channel 1 is used for the disk controller in XT systems, but is available for AT-style systems and above. DMA channel 2 is used for the floppy disk controller. Channels 3 through 7 are available for use.

For some devices, use of a DMA channel may be optional, but will normally result in improved performance.

Directory

1. Part of a structure for organizing files on a disk. A directory can contain files and subdirectories. The structure of directories and subdirectories on a disk is called a directory tree. The top-level directory in a directory tree is the root directory.

2. In NetWare, the highest organizational level is the file server. Each server's main directory is called a VOLUME, and subdirectories are called directories.

Directory Server Postoffice Primary postoffice Microsoft Mail directory synchronization containing the global address list.

Directory Synchronization A process for automatically transferring user list changes and updates between Microsoft Mail postoffices.

Directory System Agent (DSA)

The software that provides the X.500 Directory Service for a portion of the directory information base. Generally, each DSA is responsible for the directory information for a single organization or organizational unit.

Directory User Agent (DUA)

The software that accesses the X.500 Directory Service on behalf of the directory user. The directory user may be a person or another software element.

Discrete access

An access method used in star LANs; each station has a separate (discrete) connection through which it makes use of the LAN's switching capability.

Disk

A circular object with a magnetic surface used to store files (programs and documents) on a computer. For example, a floppy or hard disk.

Disk drive

A magnetic or optical device used to store files and folders. Types of disk drives include fixed (hard) disks, floppy disks, and removable media such as Syquest, Jaz, Zip, and magneto-optical (MO) disks.

Disk Duplexing

Disk duplexing is an implementation of Redundant Arrays of Independent Disks (RAID) Level 1 and is similar to disk mirroring. It uses two disk drives that are configured to have the same logical size. Both drives are connected to separate disk controllers. During each data write, the same data is written to both disks.

Disk Duplexing

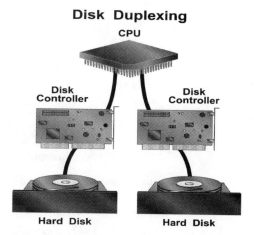

Disk I/O performance is generally better than when using disk striping with parity. Performance is better during data reads than with disk mirroring.

The boot partition (active system partition) can be duplexed.

Disk duplexing is designed to keep a network going in spite of disk errors or the loss of a hard disk. If a read error occurs, data from the other disk is used.

If one drive or controller fails, the server will continue running by using the other drive and controller. Users can continue to work without interruption.

Disk duplexing is normally used on peer-to-peer networks and smaller LANs for the protection of critical data files. Due to the amount of storage lost through redundancy, it is not commonly used on larger LANs.

Disk Mirroring	Disk mirroring is an implementation of Redundant Arrays of Independent Disks (RAID) Level 1. It uses two disk drives configured with equal sized partitions, and connected to the same disk controller. During each data write, the same data is written to both disk partitions.

Disk Mirroring

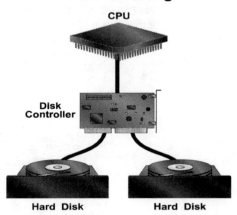

With disk mirroring, disk utilization is 50% of the dedicated storage space. I/O performance is generally better than when using disk striping with parity. A mirrored pair can be split without loss of data.

Disk mirroring is designed to keep the computer operational in spite of disk errors or loss of a hard disk. If a read error occurs, data from the other disk is used. If one drive fails, the server will continue running by using the other drive.

Use disk mirroring when data must be protected against drive failures, and hard disk resources are and will be plentiful as system requirements grow.

Disk mirroring is normally used on peer-to-peer networks and smaller LANs to protect critical data files. Due to the amount of storage lost through redundancy, it is not commonly used on larger LANs.

Disk Operating System	The software programs that control the operation of the computer and the movement of information throughout the computer system.
	DOS is the medium by which the user communicates with the computer system and manipulates data.
Disk Striping	A method of spreading data evenly across multiple physical hard disks.
Disk Striping with Parity	Disk striping is an implementation of Redundant Arrays of Independent Disks (RAID) Level 5. Microsoft Windows NT Server does the same thing as commercial RAID drive arrays, but through software rather than hardware.

Between 3 and 32 disk drives may be included in an NT Server stripe set. The disk space used on each drive will be approximately the same. NT Server will match the space selected to the smallest single partition when the stripe set is created.

Disk striping provides improved performance on disk reads. Disk utilization is reduced by the size of one disk drive.

Data and parity is spread across all of the drives in a stripe set. As data is written, it passes through an algorithm to generate the information for the parity stripe.

Disk Striping with Parity

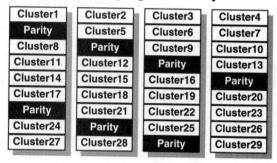

The way data clusters are organized, large data files tend to get written across multiple drives. There is a loss in write performance, however, this is made up by splitting read requests, giving excellent read performance and improved data security.

Possibly more important is the data security aspect. If a drive is lost, the system can recover any missing data by going through its calculations on the remaining data and parity stripes. When this happens, read performance suffers. All of the data can be recreated when the drive is replaced.

When implementing disk striping without parity, data is written to the drives in much the same manner. The major difference is that the stripe used here for parity is instead used for additional data storage.

One thing to remember is that the boot partition (active system partition) cannot be a stripe set.

Disk striping with parity is normally used on large networks where data integrity and minimized down time are critical concerns. While the amount of storage space lost can be significant, as more drives are added, the percentage of space lost to parity becomes less.

Use disk striping with parity when multiple hard disks are available, optimal read performance is desired, and data integrity is a critical concern. You are protected against the failure of any one drive. A failing drive should be replaced as soon as possible, even though the users can continue working after the failure. Performance will be the same on disk writes, but will degrade on disk reads.

When performance is the overriding concern and budget constraints allow, you should install a RAID disk subsystem rather than configuring discrete hard disks through disk striping with parity. A RAID disk subsystem, though more expensive, will provide significantly better performance.

Dispatch Program Microsoft Mail program controlling directory synchronization.

Distributed architecture A LAN that uses a shared communications medium. Uses shared access methods; used on bus or ring LANs.

Distributed computing The name of the trend to move computing resources such as minicomputers, microcomputers, or personal computers closer to individual workstations.

Distributed Computing Environment (DCE)
An architecture of standard programming interfaces, conventions, and server functionalities (e.g., naming, distributed file system, remote procedure call) for distributing applications transparently across networks of heterogeneous computers. Promoted and controlled by the Open Software Foundation (OSF), a consortium led by HP, DEC, and IBM.

Distributed Data Management Architecture (DDM)
Allows transparent record-level access to files on remote machines.

Distributed processing A technique for implementing a set of information processing functions within multiple physically separate physical devices.

Domain 1. A logical grouping for file servers within a network, managed as an integrated whole.

2. In NetWare DOMAIN is used as a console command that will create a protected operating system domain for running untested NLMs in Ring 3. This prevents a module from interferring with the core operating system.

3. In the Internet, a domain is a part of the naming hierarchy. The domain name is a sequence of names (separated by periods) that identify host sites. For example: galenp@mail.msen.com

Domain Controller Server within a domain and storage point for domain-wide security information.

Domain Model   A method of organizing Windows NT Server domains for security and management.

Domain Name System (DNS)

The Domain Name System (DNS) is a hierarchical, distributed method of organizing system and network names on the Internet. DNS administratively groups hosts (systems) into a hierarchy of authority that allows addressing and other information to be widely distributed and maintained. A big advantage of DNS is that using it eliminates dependence on a centrally maintained file that maps host names to addresses.

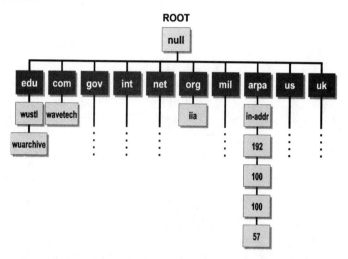

The diagram above shows the hierarchical organization of domain names. The bottom level of the tree structure contains the names of companies or even machines within a company. For example, consider wuarchive.wustl.edu. The bottom of the tree is wuarchive. This is the name of a particular piece of equipment within the wustl domain, which is under the edu domain.

The name of a particular domain is read from the bottom of the tree up to the root. The root is unnamed and is represented with just a period. For example, wavetech is a particular domain. If we were to give the fully qualified domain name (FQDN), we would include the unnamed root, so it would be written as "wavetech.com". The final period at the end of the name specifies the root of the tree. The root must always be specified for the host equipment. To make it easy, most software will convert a domain name to an FQDN for the user, by appending any missing domain names all the way to the root.

The top of the tree lists the top-level-domains. These are reserved names. Every domain will have a top-level domain by type or country.

Some of the types are com (commercial), edu (educational), gov (governmental), mil (military), net (network provider), org (non-profit organization), and int (international).

The two-letter country top-level-domains identify the country of a particular Internet site. Most of the countries have formed a similar structure for categorizing site types under the country domains. There is a two-letter country domain for every country. Examples include uk (United Kingdom), za (South Africa), us (United States), de (Germany), fr (France), hk (Hong Kong), jp (Japan), br (Brazil), and mx (Mexico).

When a domain name is registered with InterNIC, it is added to the tree under a particular top-level-domain. The company registering the name is given control over the sub-domain they've registered. Because control of the sub-domains is given over to the individual registries, they must provide a DNS Server for their own domains. The DNS Server provides the domain name to TCP/IP address resolution. When an Internet user refers to a particular host on the Internet by name, there must be a mapping made between the name entered and the TCP/IP address required for creation of the data packets.

Domain SID	Unique value imbedded in the SID for all domain servers, workstations, users, and groups. The Domain SID identifies domain ownership of objects.
DOS ODI	Novell Open Data Link Interface software that allows various network protocols to be used on a single network board and forms a logical network board that emulates various protocol configurations on the installed board. The logical network board operates as if physical boards were being used.
DOS Requester	Software which enables a DOS workstation to communicate on a network.
Dots per inch (dpi)	A measurement (dpi) of the resolution of a video display monitor, printer or other output device.
Dotted decimal notation	The syntactic representation for a 32-bit integer that consists of four 8-bit numbers written in base 10 with periods (dots) separating them. Used to represent IP addresses in the Internet as in 192.67.67.20.
Download	A process where a file is transferred from a host computer to a user's computer. Download is the opposite of upload.
Downloadable font	Also known as soft font, an electronically represented printer font (a graphic design of characters and symbols) which must be installed on the computer and sent to a printer before it can be printed.

Drive Type	The drive type number is placed in a table stored in the computer's CMOS memory. The table identifies the drive and its characteristics (number of read/write heads, storage capacity, number of cylinders, number of sectors per track, etc.) so that the operating system knows how to access the drive.
Drop	Individual connections (sometimes called nodes) on a multipoint (also called multidrop) circuit.
Dumb terminal	A workstation consisting of keyboard and monitor. A dumb terminal is used to put data into the computer or receive information from the computer. Dumb terminals were originally developed to be connected to computers running a multiuser operating system so that users could communicate directly with them. All processing is done at and by the computer, not the dumb terminal.

In contrast, a smart terminal contains processing circuits which can receive data from the host computer and later carry out independent processing operations. |
Dump Devices	SQL Server devices defined to receive data during a dynamic dump.
Duplex transmission	A method of transmitting information over a communications channel in which signals may be sent in both directions. Other methods of transmission include half duplex, full duplex, and simplex.
Dynamic Backup	Process of backing up active databases and logs. Also called a Dynamic Dump.
Dynamic Drive	Dynamic attach and release of network drives under Microsoft Mail.
Dynamic Dump	Process of backing up active databases and logs. Also called a Dynamic Backup.
Dynamic link library (DLL)	A module that is linked at load time or run time.
Dynamic linking	Using an update command to ensure that all data changed in one program is automatically changed in another program, thereby keeping the data consistent. Dynamic linking is particularly useful in database management.
Dynamic priority	The priority assigned to a thread in response to how the user interacts with it.
Echo	The reflection of transmitted data back to its source. Also a phenomenon in voice circuits.
Echoplex	An asynchronous communications protocol in which the information sent to the receiving station is echoed to the sender, or transmitter, to acknowledge correct receipt of data. Also, low-speed data transmission usually used between a keyboard unit and the computer. When a key is struck on the keyboard, a character is sent over the line and echoed back to the sending unit, where it is shown on a screen or printed.

Electronic Mail (e-mail)	Electronic mail (e-mail) is the most popular Internet application, and the driving force behind the Internet's rapid growth. While controlling another computer remotely or transferring files from one computer to another may be useful, neither is as exciting as being able to communicate with millions of Internet users around the globe. Many users join the Internet just for e-mail access.
	Fortunately, it is possible to exchange e-mail with people that are not directly part of the Internet. For example, by using gateways to other public e-mail networks, Internet e-mail can reach users with commercial service provider accounts such as CompuServe, BITNET, America Online, Prodigy, and the Microsoft Network.
	E-mail can also reach users who work at companies that get their mail access from corporate network providers such as, MCImail, Applelink, and uuNet.
	E-mail is popular because it works very quickly. Traditional mail can take a day or two to cross town or weeks to reach an international destination. E-mail can travel from sender to receiver within hours (sometimes minutes), despite the distance between them. If the network is extremely busy, or if an administrator configures a user's system to send e-mail once a day (as opposed to every few minutes), the email may take a little longer to arrive. In general, however, e-mail moves around the world at a rapid pace. It is possible for a person in the U.S. to send a message to West Africa, receive a response, and send another message, all in the space of an hour.
	E-mail is also very flexible. Users can attach different types of files to their e-mail messages. Marketing can embed audio and video clips within text messages, co-workers can transfer spreadsheets or project updates, families can share pictures and birthday messages.
Embedded object	Information created in one document and inserted into another document. The two documents usually were created in different applications.
Emulation	The imitation of all or part of one system by another. This can be accomplished either in hardware or software. The imitating system accepts the same data, executes the same programs, and achieves the same results as the imitated system.
	Products such as SoftWindows and Virtual PC allow Macintosh computers to emulate the Windows or Windows 95 operating system and an Intel-based PC.
	Apple designed the "68K" emulator for the PowerPC processor in order to allow Power Macintosh computers to run older 680x0-specific software.

Encapsulation	In object-oriented programming (OOP), encapsulation defines a data structure of attributes and a group of member functions as a single unit called an object. In networking, encapsulation is the process of enclosing packets of one type of protocol by another.
End system	An OSI system which contains application processes capable of communicating through all seven layers of OSI protocols. Equivalent to Internet host.

End System-Intermediate System (ES-IS)

The routing protocol used between routers and end nodes to assist in finding each other.

Enhanced Connectivity Facilities (ECF)

A set of micro-to-mainframe programs used for file-transfer, printer-sharing, virtual disk, and virtual file services.

Enhanced IDE (EIDE)	An enhanced version of IDE. IDE (Integrated device electronics) is a disk-drive interface. A separate adapter card is not necessary because the controller electronics reside on the drive itself.

Enhanced Industry Standard Architecture (ESDI)

ESDI was introduced in 1988 and is a 32-bit bus design for x86-based computers.

Enhanced mode	One of two modes of operation for Windows v3.1. If a computer has the minimum configuration, Windows automatically runs in the Enhanced mode.
ENQ/ACK protocol	A Hewlett-Packard communications protocol. The HP3000 computer follows each transmission block with ENQ to determine if the destination terminal is ready to receive more data; the destination terminal indicates its readiness by responding with ACK.
Entity	1. OSI terminology for a layer protocol machine. An entity within a layer performs the functions of the layer within a single computer system, accessing the layer entity below and providing services to the layer entity above at local service access points.
	2. A definable object during database definition.
Entity Integrity	The process by which each database entity is identified as unique within a database.

Entity-Relationship Modeling

Identifying the important subjects about which information will be stored, their attributes, and the relationships among these entities. Also known as "entity modeling."

Environmental variables	Environmental information such as drive, path, or filename which is associated with a symbolic name that can be used by an operating system.

Error control	An arrangement that combines error detection and error correction.
Error correction	A method used to correct erroneous data produced during data transmission, transfer, or storage.
Error log	A data set or file in a product or system where error information is stored for later access.
Error rate	The ratio of the total number of errors detected to the total amount of data transmitted or transferred.
Error-detecting code	A code in which each coded representation conforms to specific rules of construction so that their violation indicates the presence of errors.
Ethernet	Ethernet is a Carrier Sense, Multiple Access with Collision Detection (CSMA/CD) specification.
	Ethernet was originally developed by Xerox, Intel, and Digital Equipment Corporation in the late 1970s, with specifications first released in 1980. The standard defines the cabling, connectors, and other characteristics for the transmission of data, voice, and video over local area networks at 10 Mbps. Recent improvements have increased the speed to 100 Mbps.
	There are four types of Ethernet frames defined: 802.2, 802.3, Ethernet_SNAP, and Ethernet II. These are similar, but incompatible.
	The types of Ethernet cables are Thin Ethernet (Thinnet), Thick Ethernet (Thicknet), Twisted Pair, and Fiber Optic.
EtherTalk	A name used to describe the AppleTalk protocol suite running over an Ethernet network.
European Academic and Research Network (EARN)	A network begun in 1983 as a backbone connecting European academic and research institutions with electronic mail and file transfer services.
European Workshop for Open Systems (EWOS)	The OSI Implementors Workshop for Europe.
Event Handlers	Open Data Services events requested by clients on a regular basis.
Exclusive Lock	A lock set command at the start of a read operation preventing read or write access.
Expansion Slots	Electrical connectors on the system board that allows additional hardware to be added to the computer. PCs can include 8- or 16-bit ISA, EISA, MCA, Vesa LocalBus, or PCI slots, or a mixture of ISA and any other slot type. Macintosh computers provide either NuBus or PCI slots.
Exporter	System acting as a replication source.

Extended Binary-Coded Decimal Interchange Code (EBCDIC)
> A coding scheme established by IBM providing 256 letters, numbers, and symbols, using eight bits per character. EBCDIC is used mainly on IBM mainframes and minicomputers, whereas ASCII is used in a desktop microcomputer environment.

Exterior Gateway Protocol (EGP)
> EGP is a reachability routing protocol used by gateways in a two-level Internet. EGP is used as part of the Internet's core system.

External Data Representation (XDR)
> A standard for machine-independent data structures developed by Sun Microsystems. Similar to ASN.1.

External Program
> Microsoft Mail MTA element.

Family Applications Program Interface
> A standard environment under MS-DOS versions 2.x and 3.x, and OS/2. The programmer can use the Family API to create an application that uses a subset of OS/2 functions (but a superset of MS-DOS 3.x functions), and that runs in a binary-compatible fashion under MS-DOS versions 2.x and 3.x, and OS/2.

Fault tolerance
> Operating systems feature designed to accommodate failures, therefore improving disk reliability. Related terms are Disk Mirroring, Disk Duplexing, and Disk Striping with Parity.

Federal Communications Commission (FCC)
> A U.S. government board of seven presidential appointees (established by the Communications Act of 1934) that has the power to regulate all U.S. interstate communications systems, as well as all international communications systems that originate or terminate in the U.S.

Federal Information Processing Standard (FIPS)
> A publication (FIPS PUB) issued by the U.S. National Bureau of Standards which serves as the official source of information in the U.S. federal government regarding standards issued by NBS.

Federal Networking Council (FNC)
> The body responsible for coordinating networking needs among U.S. Federal agencies.

Federal Research Internet Coordinating Committee (FRICC)
> Now replaced by the FNC.

Fiber Distributed Data Interface (FDDI)
> A LAN (Local Area Network) specification from ANSI X3T9.5 committee on computer input/output interface standards. FDDI uses fiber optic cables with token-passing access in a ring topology and transmits at 100 megabits per second across a cable length of up to 62.1 miles with up to 1.24 miles between nodes.

Fiber optics	Transmission of data in the form of light pulses produced by a laser or light-emitting diode (LED) through glass fiber, plastic, or other electrically non-conductive material. Fiber optics provide high-speed, long-distance transmission at low power.
File	A sequence of bytes stored on a secondary storage medium such as a floppy disk or hard disk. Generally, a computer file contains either a program or data.
	Program files contain instructions or commands which are to be executed by the computer. Data files which contain only ASCII characters are text files; while files containing binary data, i.e., data other than ASCII characters, are called binary files. Bytes that comprise a file are not necessarily stored on contiguous disk blocks and may be scattered across a disk due to fragmentation.
	Macintosh files generally consist of a Data Fork (the file contents) and a Resource Fork (a pointer to the application that created the file.)
File Format API (FFA PI)	API set supporting message transfer between Microsoft Mail and foreign mail systems.
File lock	A file lock prevents more than one user from using a file at the same time. Locks can be put into place for security purposes, or to prevent users from making changes to a file simultaneously. A lock can be placed on part of a file if it is supported in the application being used.
File server	A computer that stores files and provides access to them from workstations. File servers generally contain large hard disks and high amounts of memory.
	If a computer is used exclusively as a file server, it is a dedicated file server. If a computer is used as a workstation and a file server simultaneously, it is a non-dedicated file server.
	The NOS (Network Operating System) runs on the file server and controls access to files, printers, and other network resources.
File server protocol	A communications protocol that allows application programs to share files.
File Sharing	1. The ability for more than one person to use the same file at the same time.
	2. The process of making a file or directory available for network client access.
File system name space	Names that have the format of filenames. All such names will eventually represent data or special disk files.

File Transfer Protocol (FTP)

The File Transfer Protocol (FTP) is a part of the TCP/IP suite that is used to transfer files between any two computers, provided they support FTP. The two computers do not have to be running the same operating system.

In general, people use FTP to move files from one account or machine to another, or to perform what is called an "anonymous FTP." For example, if storage space on a particular machine is low, the user can free up storage space by using FTP to move the files to a machine with more space. Another reason to move a file to a different account is to print a file to a particular printer. If the file is on a machine that cannot access the desired printer, it must be moved to a machine that does have access.

Whatever the reason for the transfer, FTP requires the user to know the proper login name and the password for both computers to move files between them.

While an anonymous FTP also moves from one computer to another, it has two main differences. An anonymous FTP session usually involves gathering files that a user does not have. Anonymous FTP does not require the user to know a login name and password to access the remote computer.

The Internet has many anonymous FTP sites. Each site consists of an FTP server, a large number of files, and guest login names such as "anonymous" or "FTP." This allows any user to visit these systems and copy files from the FTP site to their personal computer. With the appropriate authority, users can copy files from their system to an anonymous FTP site.

Despite the variety of FTP servers and clients on the Internet and the different operating systems they use, FTP servers and clients generally support the same basic commands. This standard command set allows users to accomplish tasks such as looking at a list of files in the current directory of the remote system, regardless of the operating system in use. Other common commands allow users to change directories, get specific file information, copy files to a local machine, and change parameters.

Graphical Web browsers transform the traditional character-based, command-line FTP interface into a point-and-click environment. The only way a user may know that they are in the middle of an FTP session is that the Universal Resources Locator (URL) box in the browser will change from an address that begins with "http://..." to "ftp://...".

File Transfer, Access, and Management (FTAM)
: The OSI remote file service and protocol.

Fill pattern
: In a Token Ring network, a specified bit pattern that a transmitting data station sends before or after frames, tokens, or abort sequences to avoid what would otherwise be interpreted as an inactive or indeterminate transmitter state.

Filter
: A device or program that separates data, signals, or material in accordance with specified criteria.

Finder
: The system software that controls the Macintosh Desktop and is used for file and application management tasks.

Flag
: A variable indicating that a certain condition holds.

Flame
: Originally, flame meant to carry forth in a passionate manner in the spirit of honorable disagreement. It most often involves the use of flowery language.

: More recently, flame has come to refer to any kind of electronic mail message with a derogatory comment. A flame may be used to tell the recipient in strong words ("shouted" in all capital letters) there has been a breach of netiquette (Internet etiquette).

FLeX/IP
: A Novell NetWare Loadable Module that adds FTP server capability to a NetWare file server.

Font
: In typography, a complete set of characters of one particular size, style, and weight, including punctuation marks, symbols, and numbers. The term font is often confused with typeface, which refers to a particular style of character, or type family to which the font belongs.

Foreign Key
: A key used to establish a link between two tables, with the foreign key in one table referencing values in the primary key of the second.

Foreign Mail System
: Under Microsoft Mail usage, any electronic mail system other than Microsoft Mail.

Fragment
: Part of an IP message.

Fragmentation
: The process in which an IP datagram is broken into smaller pieces to fit the requirements of a given physical network. The reverse process is termed reassembly.

Frame
: In IEEE (Institute of Electrical and Electronics Engineers) terminology, the unit of data transferred at the OSI (Open Systems Interconnection) data link layer.

Frame Check Sequence (FCS)
: The error check portion of a LAN data frame.

Frame relay	Commonly referred to as "bandwidth on demand." Unlike other transmission protocols or processes, frame relay offers users significant benefits over other transmission services, such as T1, by eliminating the processing overhead associated with packets of data moving between packet-forwarding devices.
Frequency	The number of times one complete incident or function occurs. In electronics, frequency usually refers to the number of waveforms that are repeated per second, measured in Hertz.
Frequency Modulation (FM)	
	The modification of the frequency of a carrier wave so that it carries information. A frequency is the number of waveforms that are repeated per second, and is measured in hertz.
Front end	As in processor (IBM FEP) which is a stand-alone intelligent device which executes the transfer of data or the protocols for the host machine.
Front End Processor (FEP)	Usually a minicomputer that is connected to a larger host computer in order to handle all the communications requirements independently, thereby leaving the host computer free to concentrate on internal data processing.
Full-duplex transmission	A method of transmitting information over an asynchronous communications channel, in which signals may be sent in both directions simultaneously. This technique makes the best use of line time but substantially increases the amount of logic required in the primary and secondary stations.
Gateway	Gateways are the primary linkage between mixed environments such as PC-based LANs and host environments such as SNA.
	Gateways generally operate at all seven layers of the OSI Reference Model. They may provide full content conversion between two environments, such as ASCII to EBCDIC, as well as other application and presentation layer conversions.

Gateway Functionality

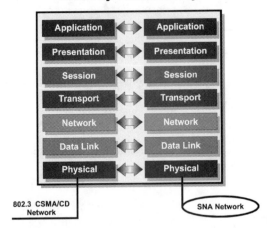

Other types of gateways include fax gateways, which allow users to send and receive faxes from their workstations. These may also be integrated with mail service gateways, which allow communications between users of different mail systems.

Gateway List	List of Microsoft Mail gateways available to a local postoffice.
Global Account	A Windows NT Server user account authorized interactive logon in its own and trusting domains.
Global Address List	Combined user list including users from all postoffices taking part in directory synchronization.
Global data segment	A data segment that is shared among all instances of a dynlink routine. In other words, a single segment that is accessible to all processes that call a particular dynlink routine.
Global Group	A group definition allowing permission assignments to local machines or other domains through local group membership of the global group.
Global Naming	A naming convention which allows users to view and access resources anywhere on a network. The users do not need to become concerned with the physical location of a resource because they can simply browse and choose a resource from a list.
Government OSI Profile (GOSIP)	A U.S. Government procurement specification for OSI protocols.
Guard band	The unused bandwidth separating channels to prevent crosstalk in an FDM, (Frequency Division Multiplexing) system.

Half-duplex (HDX)	Transmission link that allows two-way communication, although transmission is possible only one way at a time. When the communications device at one end has completed its transmission, it must advise the device at the other end that it has finished and is ready to receive. Half-duplex transmission is analogous to a single-lane bridge on a two-way road.
Handshake	Used in communications technology to define the exchange of data when connection is achieved.
Handshaking	Before data is transmitted serially, certain communications conditions, or protocols, must be met. Handshaking allows both the sending and receiving computers to understand the required signals, i.e. the method of transmission.
Hard disk	A peripheral mass-storage device which uses sealed, rotating, non-flexible, magnetically coated disks to store data and program files. Hard disk types include SCSI, IDE, and EIDE.
Hard Disk Controller	The board that communicates with and controls the hard (fixed) disk drive.
Hard Disk Interface	The communication device which allows the hard disk drive to interact with the hard disk controller. There are many different types which will affect the speed of data transfers. Examples of hard disk interfaces are ST506, SCSI, ESDI, and IDE.
Hardcopy	Sending computer data out to the printer and printing the information on paper is referred to as producing hardcopy, or a copy on paper which can be physically handled.
Hardware	All electronic components of a computer system, including peripherals, circuit boards, and input and output devices. Hardware is the physical equipment, as opposed to software consisting of programs, data procedures, rules, and associated documentation.
Hayes	The company, Hayes Microcomputer Products, developed a special synchronizing compression technique to allow fast line turn-around making a half-duplex modem simulate full-duplex transmission speeds. Hayes patented their method and allow other vendors to utilize the method through licensing fees and royalties. Hayes and Hayes-compatible modems are the de facto standard for PC communications.
Hertz (Hz)	The International System of Units measure of frequency. Hertz was named for German physicist Heinrich Hertz and was often abbreviated as hz. One hertz is one complete cycle per second. A cycle may relate to light, heat, radio waves, or other vibrations.

High Capacity Storage System (HCSS)

> A component of NetWare, it is a data storage system which extends the storage capacity of a NetWare server by allowing an optical disk library, or jukebox, to become a part of the NetWare file system.

High Performance File System (HPFS)

> This is the native file system for OS/2.

High-level Data Link Control (HDLC)A data link control protocol developed by ISO (International Organization for Standardization) in response to IBM's SDLC (Synchronous Data Link Control), which is a subset of HDLC.

Hive files

Component files making up the Windows NT Registry.

Home directory

On Local Area Networks, a directory which belongs to a single user for storage of data. Normally, the user is the only person with access to this directory. On most networks, the Supervisor or Administrator can also access any user's home directory.

Home folder

The NetWare for Macintosh's equivalent of a Home directory.

Hot Fix redirection

In NetWare, a method to prevent data from being written to bad data blocks on a hard disk. When data is saved to the hard disk, the NetWare operating system verifies the save's accuracy by comparing the disk and RAM versions. If the two versions aren't identical, the disk version is moved to a disk address known as the HotFix redirection area.

Hub

1. In disk drives, the hub is the central mechanism within the drive that causes the disk to rotate and keeps it centered during the rotation. On floppy diskettes, the hub fits into the hole in the center of the diskette to keep it level and balanced during rotation.

2. In networking, a central connecting point for network wiring.

I/O

I/O (Input/Output) refers to the sending and receiving of data from the central processing unit (CPU) to other peripheral devices such as disk drives. The input/output channel carries out all the transfer of data so as to free up the CPU. The keyboard is the most common input device and the monitor is the most common output device.

I/O address

I/O address is space used to access I/O hardware such as I/O adapters, buses, and special registers used by I/O devices known as control status registers (CSR). I/O address space is one of two equal parts of primary memory, or addressable memory. The other equal part is memory address space.

IBM PC network

A CSMA/CD network introduced by IBM in 1984 that uses a star or bus topology. It was originally a broadband network using coaxial cable, but lower-cost twisted-pair wire was subsequently introduced by IBM.

IBM Token Ring network	A baseband star-wired ring network developed by IBM, using the token-passing access method and running at 4 or 16 megabits per second (Mbps).
Icon	A graphical picture used to represent an application, folder, file, disk drive, or printer.
Importer	System receiving data during replication.
INETCFG	A NetWare utility that allows the network manager to control the MultiProtocol Router product.
Initialization files	Files with the extension .INI that contain information that define your setup and various other parameters which are needed by a program. This is used extensively in Microsoft Windows and OS/2 for storing environmental or other device information.

Institute of Electrical and Electronics Engineers (IEEE)

A professional ANSI-accredited body of scientists and engineers based in the U.S. IEEE promotes standardization, and consults to the American National Standards Institute on matters relating to electrical and electronic development. The IEEE 802 Standards Committee is the leading official standard organization for LAN (Local Area Networks).

Integrated Device Electronics (IDE)

Integrated device electronics is a disk-drive interface. A separate adapter card is not necessary because the controller electronics reside on the drive itself.

Integrated Login Security	Validation method where members of a Windows NT domain are automatically logged in for SQL Server access.

Integrated Services Digital Network (ISDN)

A special kind of telecommunications network designed to handle more than just data. Using existing telephone lines and computer networks, integrated networks can handle video, text, voice, data, facsimile images, graphics, etc.

Interactive	The term interactive pertains to the exchange of information and control between the user and a computer process.
	Interactive also refers to time-dependent (real-time) data communications. Typically communications in which a user enters data and then waits for a response message from the destination before continuing.
Interface	1. A shared boundary between two functional units, defined by functional characteristics, signal characteristics, and other characteristics, as appropriate. Also, any of the electrical and logical devices that permit computers and peripherals to be interconnected.
	2. A contract between an object and its users.

Interior Gateway Protocol (IGP)

IGP is the protocol used to exchange routing information between collaborating routers in the Internet. Router Information Protocol (RIP) and Open Shortest Path First (OSPF) are examples of IGPs.

Intermediate system

An OSI system which is not an end system, but which serves instead to relay communications between end systems.

Intermediate System-Intermediate System (IS-IS)

The routing protocol used by routers to share network information in an OSI network.

Internal Organization of the Network Layer (IONL)

The OSI standard for the detailed architecture of the Network Layer. Basically, it partitions the Network layer into subnetworks interconnected by convergence protocols (equivalent to internetworking protocols), creating what Internet calls a catenet or internet).

International Standards Organization (ISO)

Founded in 1946, ISO promotes the development of international standards for the computer, communications, and other fields. ISO members are the standards organizations of 89 countries. The United States representative is the American National Standards Institute (ANSI).

Internet

An international computer network of networks that connect government, academic and business institutions. Networks on the Internet include MILNET, NSFnet, and other backbone networks, as well as mid-level networks and stub (local) networks.

Internet networks communicate using TCP/IP (Transmission Control Protocol/Internet Protocol). The Internet connects colleges, universities, military organizations and contractors, corporations, government research laboratories, and individuals.

Although parts of the Internet operate under single administrative domains, the Internet as a whole reaches around the globe, connects computers from personal computers to supercomputers, and is not administered by any single authority. The Internet in July of 1995 roughly connected 60,000 independent networks into a vast global Internet.

Used as a descriptive term, an Internet is a collection of interconnected packet-switching networks. Any time you connect two or more networks together, you have an Internet—as in inter-national or inter-state.

Internet Activities Board (IAB)

> The IAB is the technical body that oversees the development of the Internet suite of protocols commonly referred to as "TCP/IP." It has two task forces, the IRTF and the IETF, each charged with investigating a particular area.

Internet Address

> A 32-bit value written or displayed in numbers that specify a particular network and node on that network.

Internet Control Message Protocol (ICMP)

> ICMP is used for error reporting and recovery, and is a required component of any IP implementation.

Internet Engineering Steering Group (IESG)

> The IESG is the executive committee of the Internet Engineering Task Force (IETF).

Internet Engineering Task Force (IETF)

> One of the task forces of the IAB, the IETF is responsible for solving short-term engineering needs of the Internet. It has over 40 Working Groups.

Internet Gateway Routing Protocol (IGRP)

> The Internet Gateway Routing Protocol is a proprietary IGP used by Cisco System's routers.

Internet Protocol (IP)

> IP is the OSI layer 3 routed protocol used to transmit packetized information on a TCP/IP network.

Internet Research Task Force (IRTF)

> The Internet Research Task Force is one of the task forces of the Internet Activities Board (IAB) that is responsible for research and development of the Internet protocol suite.

Internetwork

> Two or more networks connected by a router.

Internetwork Packet Exchange (IPX)

> IPX is used with SPX as the resident protocol in NetWare. A router with IPX routing can interconnect local area networks (LANs) so that Novell NetWare clients and servers can communicate.

> In v3.x of NetWare, IPX is the name of the command line utility used to see the versions and options of IPX.COM. This was used prior to the introduction of ODI drivers.

Internetwork Packet Exchange Open Data-Link Interface (IPXODI)

> This is a module that takes the workstation requests determined to be for the network by the NetWare DOS Requester and packages them with transmission information (such as their destination), then transfers them to the Link Support Layer (LSL). IPXODI requires each packet have an initialized header specifying information targeting network delivery and announcing from where the packet came, where it is going, and what happens after delivery.

Interoperability Technology Association for Information Processing (INTAP)

> The technical organization which has the official charter to develop Japanese OSI profiles and conformance tests.

Interprocess communication

> The exchange of information between processes by means of messages.

Interrupt Request Lines (IRQ)

> Interrupt Request Lines are normally referred to as IRQ lines, and each line requires a separate IRQ number. Many PC add-in boards and devices require a unique dedicated IRQ line. Some IRQs are assigned to system devices.
>
> The original IBM PC was an 8-bit system with eight available IRQ lines numbered 0 through 7. These lines support the system timer, keyboard, COM and LPT ports, and the floppy disk controller.
>
> With the 16-bit IBM AT came eight additional IRQ lines which "cascade" through IRQ2. These IRQ lines support the Real Time Clock, hard disk controller, math coprocessor, and other devices. Examples of devices that use these IRQ lines are VGA and network adapters, CD-ROM drives, and SCSI controllers.
>
> Some COM ports share IRQ lines. All odd numbered COM ports (COM1, COM3, etc.) share IRQ 4, while all even numbered COM ports share IRQ 3.

IP datagram

> The IP datagram is the fundamental unit of information passed across the Internet. It contains source and destination addresses, along with data and a number of fields which define the length of the datagram, the header checksum, and flags to indicate whether the datagram can be (or has been) fragmented.

IPXODI.COM

> A NetWare file containing the IPX and SPX protocol stacks for use with the Open Data Link Interface. It allows workstations to communicate with NetWare file servers.

IPXS

> NetWare v3.x and v4.x loadable module for use with other modules, such as CLIB, that require the STREAMS IPX module services.

ISO Development Environment (ISODE)

A popular implementation of the upper layers of OSI. Pronounced eye-so-dee-eee.

ISOCON

A NetWare v3.11 utility that allows the network manager to monitor and control OSI routing on the MultiProtocol Router product.

Joint Academic Network (JANET)

A university network in the U.K.

KA9Q

A popular implementation of TCP/IP and associated protocols for amateur packet radio systems.

Kermit

A popular file transfer and terminal emulation program.

Kernel

A set of essential operating routines used by the operating system (usually hidden from the user) to perform important system tasks such as managing the system memory or controlling disk operations.

Kernel Mode

Lower level Windows NT or Windows 95 operating system functions.

Keyboard

The device which allows the user to input data into the computer or to execute commands. Most keyboards resemble a typewriter. The standard is a 101-key keyboard.

Kilobit (Kb)

In computing, it refers to 1024 bits. (A bit is the basic unit for storing data in primary storage.) Kilobit is used mainly to express the speed of data transmission.

Kilobits per second (Kbps) Thousands of bits per second.

Kilobyte (KB)

In computing, it refers to 1024 bytes. (A byte is a unit of information consisting of 8 bits.) Kilobyte is mainly used to express the capacity of primary storage.

Kilobytes per second (KBps)

Thousands of bytes per second.

LAN Adapter and Protocol Support (LAPS)

This is the program that provides LAN adapter and protocol device drivers for OS/2.

LAN driver

Software that establishes communication between a file server's network board and the NetWare operating system.

LAN Requester

The term used to refer to a workstation on a LAN Server network. It is also the name of LAN Server's primary management utility.

Leased-line

A telephone line reserved for the exclusive use of leasing customers, without interexchange switching arrangements. Also called a Private Line.

Library

A group of programs in a file.

Link Access Protocol Balanced (LAPB)

An alternative protocol developed after LAP. LAPB allows the DTE/ DCE interface to operate in "balanced mode."

Link Support Layer (LSL)   A component of the Open Data Link Interface (ODI) software implementation on a workstation. Link Support Layer functions between the LAN driver and IPX, TCP/IP, or other communications protocol. LSL.COM is a NetWare program file used for communication between the device driver (LAN DRIVER) and IPX or other protocol on the client workstation.

Little-endian

A format for storage or transmission of binary data in which the least significant byte (bit) comes first.

Local Access and Transport Area (LATA)

Within a LATA, a local exchange common carrier provides connections, service, and a dial tone to all telephone subscribers. A LATA typically includes all of the local exchanges and inter-office trunks and toll offices required to service a metropolitan area which may include several small cities and towns. The U.S. has been divided into more than two hundred Local Access and Transport Areas, in order to define areas of responsibility.

Local Account

A Windows NT Server user account not authorized interactive logon, but supporting resource access.

Local Area Network (LAN)

A Local Area Network (LAN) is a group of computers running specialized communications software, and joined through an external data path.

A LAN will cover a small geographic area, usually no larger than a single building. The computers have a direct high-speed connection between all workstations and servers, and share hardware resources and data files. A LAN has centralized management of resources and network security.

PC-based networks can trace their heritage back to what are now often referred to as legacy systems. These systems were mainframe and minicomputer hosts accessed through dumb terminals.

There are a number of similarities between LANs and these legacy systems, such as centralized storage and backup, access security, and central management of resources. There are, however, a number of differences.

Traditional host systems are characterized by centralized processing, dumb terminals, custom applications, high expansion costs and management overhead. LANs are characterized by distributed processing, intelligent workstations (PCs), and off-the-shelf applications. LANs are modular, inexpensive to expand, and have more moderate management costs.

Local Caching
Storage of a copy of a user's personal profile on a local hard disk.

Local Group
When discussing Windows NT Server Domains, it is a group definition supporting local domain resource management. When discussing Workstations, it is a group definition supporting local management of a Windows NT workstation.

Local printer
A printer directly connected to one of the ports on the computer. The opposite is one connected through a network, which would be a remote printer.

Local Profile
User profile stored on and specific to a particular Windows NT workstation.

LocalTalk Link Access Protocol (LLAP)
LLAP provides the physical connection of LocalTalk and to various hardware including EtherTalk (ELAP) and TokenTalk (TLAP).

Locked files
1. Files protected against user access.

2. Files that were in use during an installation or software removal. The files will be processed the next time the system is restarted.

Logical Unit (LU)
The element within a network based on IBM's System Network Architecture (SNA) by which a user (terminal or program) attaches to the network. LUs are described by type to indicate their functional capabilities. LU2, for example, is a 3270-type device.

Login
The act of entering into a computer system, usually requiring a password.

LOGIN is also the NetWare command line utility whose execution will log a user into the network. The login process includes a defined set of commands called the login script.

LOGOUT
A NetWare v3.x, v4.x, and Portable NetWare command-line utility that is used to close communication with one or more file servers.

Low Entry Networking (LEN)
A form of IBM's System Network Architecture (SNA) that permits PCs and minicomputers to communicate when a network does not contain an IBM mainframe.

Low priority category
A classification of processes that consists of processes that get CPU time only when no other thread in other categories needs it. This category is lower in priority than the general priority category.

LPT port	The LPT port is also known as a parallel port. It is a connection on the computer, usually LPT1, where the cable for a parallel printer is connected. Generally, LPT1 through LPT3 can exist on a personal computer. Special equipment can be added to extend this capability.
LS	Determines the number of link stations for a Token Ring driver. This parameter may be required on a Novell network in the SHELL.CFG file depending on the network interface card.
LU6.2	A peer-to-peer communication protocol that serves as the architectural base for implementing Advanced Program-to-Program Communications (APPC) for IBM or non-IBM computers.
Mail exploder	Part of an electronic mail delivery system which allows a message to be delivered to a list of addressees. Mail exploders are used to implement mailing lists. Users send messages to a single address (e.g., hacks@somehost.edu) and the mail exploder takes care of delivery to the individual mailboxes in the list.
Mail gateway	A machine that connects to two or more electronic mail systems, including those on different networks, and transfers mail messages among them.
Mailbox	An area on a computer used to receive and store electronic mail messages.
Management Information Base (MIB)	A collection of objects that can be accessed via a network management protocol.
Mandatory Profile	A server-based profile defined for the user by the domain administrator. Users cannot store changes made to a mandatory profile.
Manufacturing Automation Protocol (MAP)	A token-passing bus designed for factory environments by General Motors; standard IEEE 802.4 is nearly identical to MAP.
Mapping	1. Mapping is the transferring of data between a disk and a computer's RAM.
	2. Attaching to a server-based directory using the local drive ID.
Martian	Humorous term applied to packets that turn up unexpectedly on the wrong network because of bogus routing entries. Also used as a name for a packet which has an altogether bogus (non-registered or ill-formed) Internet address.
Master	An instance where the highest privileges reside in a device (usually a computer) where they have control of other devices, or servers.
Master Database	SQL Server database controlling all user databases and the SQL Server program.

Master Domain Model	Windows NT Server domain model when one domain provides user and global group management for a set of trusting domains. Resources and local groups are managed individually at the trusting domains.
Math Co-Processor	A specialized chip that supplements the mathematical operations of the CPU or microprocessor. Older systems had a separate chip for this purpose, while newer systems incorporate it into the microprocessor.

Maximum Transmission Unit (MTU)
>The largest possible unit of data that can be sent on a given physical medium. Example: The MTU of Ethernet is 1500 bytes.

Media	Media is a generic term for the medium that is used to record data. Media can be a floppy diskette, a hard disk, or other similar recording surface (an audio tape for instance).

Media Access Control Sublayer (MAC)
>The level of the IEEE 802 data station that controls and mediates access to media.

Megabit (Mb)	1,048,576 bits.

Megabits per second (Mbps)
>Millions of bits per second (bps).

Megabyte (MB)	1,048,576 bytes.

Megabytes per second (MBps)
>Millions of bytes per second (Bps).

Megahertz (MHz)	A million cycles per second. A CPU that operates at 200 Mhz uses a clock oscillator that runs at 200 million cycles per second.
Memory	A hardware component of a computer system that can store information and applications for later retrieval. Types of memory are RAM (Random Access Memory), ROM (Read Only Memory), conventional, expanded, and extended memory.
Memory manager	The section of an operating system that allocates both physical memory and virtual memory.
Memory overcommit	Allocating more memory to the running program than physically exists.
Memory suballocation	An operating system facility that allocates pieces of memory from within an application's segment.
Menu	1. A displayed list of items from which a user can make a selection.
	2. A NetWare menu utility in v3.x that allows for the use of customized menus created as ASCII text files.

Message Handling System (MHS)

The system of message user agents, message transfer agents, message stores, and access units which together provide OSI electronic mail. MHS is specified in the CCITT X.400 series of Recommendations.

Message Store

A server component of an electronic mail system. The Postoffice is the message store under Microsoft Mail.

Message Transfer Agent (MTA)

Electronic mail component which transfers messages between message stores. The external program is the MTA for Microsoft Mail.

Messaging API (MAPI)

One of the primary ways that people use the computer to communicate with each other. This is accomplished by sending messages and documents to each other via an electronic mail system.

Most companies are using at least one type of electronic mail system. Unfortunately, many companies are not using a single unified mail system for all their employees and other companies need interconnectivity with users who work for different companies.

Traditionally, corporations have installed gateways to get around this problem. However, gateways are highly specialized and can only be used to connect a particular pair of mail systems. Corporations often need a number of gateways to handle the different combinations of mail systems used by their employees and other contacts.

To resolve this problem, an API was developed which allowed for connectivity between various mail service providers and mail-aware/ mail-enabled client applications. The result was the Messaging API, otherwise known as MAPI.

MAPI has a layered architecture that allows various client applications to communicate with multiple messaging systems. The main components are the client application, the MAPI subsystem, the MAP spooler, service providers, and the messaging system.

The client application is a front-end application that makes MAPI calls.

The MAPI subsystem, also known as the messaging subsystem, handles the client application's calls and provides standard user interface objects, such as dialog boxes and forms.

The MAPI spooler is responsible for forwarding the message to the appropriate transport service provider.

Service providers are responsible for translating MAPI methods to a format the messaging system can understand.

The messaging system is a back-end application that is responsible for routing messages over the network or across phone lines. Messaging systems currently available include Microsoft Mail, cc:Mail, IBM PROFS, X.400, and Novell MHS.

Metropolitan Area Network (MAN)

A complete communications network set up by a local telephone company. This network services customers in regional locations, providing them with microwave and satellite relay stations, fiber optics, and cellular radio services with a 50-kilometer range operating at speeds from 1 megabit per second to 200 megabits per second.

A MAN is larger than a LAN (Local Area Network), but smaller than a WAN (Wide Area Network). A MAN may be made up of several LANs. MANs provide an integrated set of services for real-time voice, data, and image transmission.

Micro-to-mainframe link The connection of personal computers to mainframe-based networks.

Military Network (MILNET)

Originally part of the ARPANET, MILNET was split off in 1984 to make it possible for military installations to have reliable network service, while ARPANET continued to be used for research.

Million Instructions Per Second (MIPS)

A measure of the speed of execution of a computer's central processsing unit.

Milliseconds (ms) A thousandth of a second. Access rates are expressed in milliseconds.

Modem Modem is an abbreviation for modulator/demodulator. A modem is a peripheral device that permits a personal computer, microcomputer, or mainframe to receive and transmit data in digital format across voice-oriented communications links such as telephone lines.

Modem eliminator Also known as a modem emulator, it is a device used to connect a local terminal and a computer port in lieu of the pair of modems that would be expected to connect these. Allows DTE-to-DTE data and control signal connections otherwise not easily achieved by standard cables or connectors. Modified cables (crossover cables) or connectors (adapters) can also perform this function.

Modulation The process of changing the amplitude, frequency, or phase of a carrier wave in a periodic or intermittent way from a digital signal to an analog signal for the purpose of transmitting information.

MS-DOS MS-DOS is Microsoft's version of the DOS operating system.

MTA Electronic mail component which transfers messages between message stores. The external program is the MTA for Microsoft Mail.

Multi-homed host	A computer connected to more than one physical data link. The data links may or may not be attached to the same network.
Multicast	A special form of broadcast where copies of the packet are delivered to only a subset of all possible destinations.
Multidrop	Referring to a circuit in a communications line which is a multipoint link where the telephone company "drops" several sets of local-loops into various customer sites at secondary stations. Multidrop is in contrast to a standard multipoint link where there is only one set of local-loop connections at each end of the telephone network.
Multimedia	In computing, multimedia refers to the presentation of information using sound, graphics, animation, and text.

Multiple Master Domain Model

Windows NT Server domain model when multiple trusted domains provide user and global group administration for a set of trusting domains. Resources and local groups are managed individually at the trusting domains.

Multiplexer	A device that takes several input signals and combines them into a single output signal in such a manner that each of the input signals can be recovered.
	A device used to transmit information more efficiently and economically across a network. A multiplexer combines a number of low-speed inputs into a smaller number of high-speed outputs. Some multiplexers temporarily store information in buffers, so all of the information can be sent at once when the line becomes free.
Multiplexing	In data transmission, a function that permits two or more data sources to share a common transmission medium in such a way that each data source has its own channel.
Multipoint line	A circuit established between one primary station and multiple secondary stations simultaneously. This type of network groups devices together so they can share the same communications line.
Multiprogramming	A mode of operation that provides for the interleaved execution of two or more computer programs by a single processor.

Multistation Access Unit (MAU)

The central hub where drop cables attach to the Token Ring network. MAUs are typically located in central locations, such as a wiring closet.

Multitasking	A mode of operation that provides for the concurrent performance or interleaved execution of two or more tasks.
Multiuser	The ability of a computer to support several interactive terminals at the same time.

Musical Instrument Digital Interface (MIDI)

> The Musical Instrument Digital Interface is a standard communications protocol for the connection of a computer to a musical synthesizer. MIDI enables musicians to compose complex music on a piano-style keyboard and then capture that information using a computer which can be used to automatically write the score.

Name Binding Protocol (NBP)

> NBP is reponsible for resolving naming schemes contained within network addresses.

Name resolution

> The process of mapping a node name into the corresponding network address.

Named pipe

> An Application Program Interface which allows an unlimited number of sessions on the network. Named pipe is a much higher-level interface than NetBIOS (Network Basic Input/Output System). A single named pipe function is equal to many NetBIOS calls.

National Institute of Standards and Technology (NIST)

> U.S. governmental agency that assists in developing standards. Formerly the National Bureau of Standards.

National Science Foundation (NSF)

> The National Science Foundation is a U.S. government agency that promotes the advancement of science.

> This foundation funded NSFnet, a high-speed network connecting supercomputing and research facilities in the United States. NFSnet also has connections to Canada, Mexico, Europe, and other geographic locations.

> NSFnet is part of the Internet.

National Science Foundation Network (NSFnet)

> NSFnet is an Internet backbone that began as a project with the National Science Foundation in cooperation with corporate partners IBM, MCI, and the Michigan Strategic Fund. It is now owned by America Online.

> NSFnet was established to enable researchers and scientists working on complex problems to instantaneously access library resources, supercomputer computation, and databases as well as exchange information with colleagues worldwide.

NSFnet links regional networks to each other and to the NSF-sponsored supercomputer networks. These other networks include BARRNET (Stanford University), NCAR/USAN (National Center for Atmospheric Research), NorthWestNet (University of Washington), SDSCNET (San Diego Supercomputer Center), Sesquinet (Rice University), Westnet (Colorado State University), MIDnet (University of Nebraska-Lincoln), NDSA/UIUC (University of Illinois, CNSF (Cornell Theory Center), JvNC (John von Neumann Supercomputer Center), NYSERNet (Syracuse, New York), PSCnet (Pittsburgh Supercomputing Center), and SURAnet (University of Maryland). These networks are based on TCP/IP and are part of the Internet.

Native SQL	The SQL dialect used by a particular DBMS.
Natural join	An equijoin in which one of the two columns used in the join is deleted from the result table (removes the redundancy).
NBACKUP	NetWare menu utility that backs up and restores MS-DOS and Macintosh files on file servers and local drives. NBACKUP is also used to change the current file server attachments. Up to eight file servers can be attached, and only attached servers can be backed up or act as backups.
NBF	Windows NT enhanced implementation of NetBEUI.
NETADMIN	A text-based utility in NetWare v4.x which is used to create and manage objects, properties, and rights.
NetBIOS	Standard programming interface for the development of distributed applications.

NetBIOS Extended User Interface (NetBEUI)

This is a non-routable transport protocol written to the NetBIOS interface.

NetWare Control Center (NCC)

NetWare for Macintosh utility which allows the management of users and security via a Macintosh client.

NetWare Desk Accessory (NetWare DA)

NetWare for Macintosh utility which allows a Macintosh user to view print jobs, send messages, and set rights.

NetWare Directory Services (NDS)

The NetWare Directory Services (NDS) is a database containing all network information, such as users, printers, and servers. It is important to divorce the concept of individual printers, servers, and users being on a particular server. NDS maintains these objects globally for the whole network, and not on a server basis.

Each server on the network "looks" to the global NDS for information on objects. Therefore, all servers and clients have access to the same information. When a network administrator makes any changes to the NDS, it is made once, and all servers "see" the new information.

This is sometimes referred to as the Directory Tree.

NetWare for Macintosh   A version of NetWare that allows Apple Macintosh computers to run on NetWare networks. NetWare for Macintosh consists of software for the Macintosh Desktop and for the NetWare file server.

NetWare for UNIX   A version of NetWare for use with UNIX and other non-DOS operating systems. In UNIX systems, the Portable NetWare file server runs as a set of processes on the host computer, rather than on a dedicated file server.

NetWare Loadable Modules

NetWare Loadable Modules (NLMs) link disk drivers, LAN drivers, and other file server management utilities and enhancements with the NetWare operating system. NLMs may be loaded (linked) from a DOS drive on the file server through entries in the AUTOEXEC.NCF file.

Available NLMs include disk drivers, which control communications with the hard disk(s). This NLM type is identified by a .DSK extension.

NLMs also include LAN drivers, which control communications with the network interface card(s). This type of NLM is identified by a .LAN extension.

NetWare Loadable Modules with an .NLM extension identify server files such as utilities and server applications. These can be both Novell and third-party files. For example, some files bundled with NetWare are the INSTALL.NLM installation utility, the MONITOR.NLM monitor program, and the VREPAIR.NLM disk test utility program.

All NLMs, with the exception of VREPAIR, can be loaded dynamically, used as necessary, and unloaded to free server memory for other tasks. Volumes must be unmounted to use the VREPAIR NLM.

Name Space NLM Modules allow non-DOS names to be stored in the directory system. This type of NLM is identified by an .NAM extension.

NetWare Name Service (NNS)

NetWare global naming of directory service product allowing the network to handle requests for services. NetWare Name Service permits creation of a domain of a file server and resources, so that logging into one server in the domain makes all its servers and resources available. NetWare Name Service consists of a program and utilities that are loaded on top of the NetWare operating system. This product was the predecessor to the NDS in NetWare v4.x.

NetWare UAM	Allows the use of password encryption.
Network	A group of computers and other devices connected together so they can communicate with each other.

Network Administrator (NWADMIN)
A Windows-based utility in NetWare v4.x which can be used to create and manage objects, properties, and rights.

Network File System (NFS) Software developed by Sun Microsystems that allows you to use files on another computer or network as if they were on your local computer.

Network Interface Card (NIC)
Workstations communicate with each other and the network server via this circuit board which is installed in each computer. It can also be referred to as an NIC, LAN card, or network card.

Network Layer	The OSI layer that is responsible for routing, switching, and subnetwork access across the entire OSI environment.

Network Management Station (NMS)
The system responsible for managing a (portion of a) network. The NMS talks to network management agents, which reside in the managed nodes, via a network management protocol.

Network Operations Center (NOC)
The authority for monitoring network or Internet operations. Each Internet service provider (organization providing Internet connections) maintains its own network operations center and is responsible for users connectivity.

Network printer	A printer shared by multiple computers over a network.
Network server	A network node that provides file management, printing, or other services to other nodes or workstations. A node can function as a file server exclusively, or as both a file server and a workstation.

Network Service Access Point (NSAP)
The point at which the OSI Network Service is made available to a Transport entity. The NSAPs are identified by OSI Network Addresses.

Node	A device at a physical location that performs a control function and influences the flow of data in a network. Node can also refer to the points of connection in the links of a network. Any single computer connected to a network.
Noise	In data transmission, any unwanted electrical signal which interferes with a communications channel. Noise is often a random transmission of varying frequency, amplitude, and phase. Such noise may radiate from fluorescent lights and electric motors, and can also be caused by static, temperature changes, electric or magnetic fields, or from the sun and the stars.

Non-Priority Scheme	A Token Ring can be used on a priority or non-priority basis. When a station receives a free token it transmits the data units it needs to send. Opposite of Priority Scheme.
Non-Resident Attribute	An attribute that is not stored in the NTFS directory entry, but elsewhere on the hard disk.
Non-trusted Connection	SQL Server connection by an IPC method other than named pipes, such as IPX/SPX or TCP/IP sockets.
Non-Windows application	An application designed to run with DOS, but not specifically with Microsoft Windows. The application may not be able to take full advantage of all Windows features, such as memory management.
NTFS	This is the native file system for Windows NT.
Null modem	A device that connects two DTE devices directly by emulating the physical connections of a DCE device.

Object Linking and Embedding (OLE)
Microsoft's specification which allows applications to transfer and share data.

Octet	A set of 8 bits or one byte.
One-Way Trust	A trust relationship where trust exists in one direction only.
Open Data Services	An API set which extends the capabilities of SQL Server.

Open Datalink Interface (ODI)
NetWare software used in open systems. ODI allows one network board, LAN driver, and cabling system to support multiple connections to communications protocols such as AppleTalk, IPX/SPX, and TCP/IP, and use them interchangeably.

Open Network Computing (ONC)
A distributed applications architecture promoted and controlled by a consortium led by Sun Microsystems.

Open Shortest Path First (OSPF)
A "Proposed Standard" IGP for the Internet.

Open Systems Interconnection (OSI)
To support international standardization of network terminology and protocols, the International Standards Organization (ISO) proposed a reference model of open systems interconnection. Currently under development, OSI ensures that any open system will communicate with any other OSI-compliant system.

Open Token Foundation	A private nonprofit organization composed of users and vendors of Token Ring products who are dedicated to expanding the interoperability of multivendor Token Ring products and broadening their use. Founded in 1988 by such companies as: 3Com, Memorex Telex, Madge Networks LTD., Proteon Corp., NCR, Texas Instruments.
Optical fiber	A thin filament of glass or other transparent material through which a signal-encoded light beam may be transmitted by means of total internal reflection.
OSI layer 1	OSI layer 1 is the Physical Layer. It is the lowest of the seven defined layers of the generalized network architecture. It defines the transmission of bits over a communication channel, ensuring that 1s and 0s are recognized as such. The physical layer accepts and transmits a bit stream without recognizing or defining any structure or meaning.
OSI layer 2	OSI layer 2 is the Data Link Layer. It provides methodologies for transforming the new physical layer link into a channel that appears free of errors to the network layer (the next higher layer). The data link layer accomplishes this by splitting the input or data stream provided in the physical layer into data frames that are transmitted sequentially as messages, and by processing the acknowledgment (ACK) frames sent back over the channel by the receiver.
OSI layer 3	OSI layer 3 is the Network Layer. It accepts messages of data frames from the transmitting host, converts the messages to packets, and routes the packets to their destination.
OSI layer 4	OSI layer 4 is the Transport Layer. It accepts data from the session layer (the next layer up, which is the human user's interface to the network), splits this data into smaller units, passes these units down to the network layer, and ensures that all the pieces arrive at the destination in the correct order. The transport layer is a true end-to-end process. A program on the source transmitter carries on a conversation with a similar program at the end receiver. This end-to-end consideration in layers 4 to 7 is different from the protocols in layers 1 to 3, which regulates subnetworks at intermediate stages of a true end-to-end transmission.
OSI layer 5	OSI layer 5 is the Session Layer. It is the user's interface into the network through which the user establishes a connection with a process on another distant machine. Once the connection is established, the session layer manages the end-to-end dialog in an orderly manner, supplementing the application-oriented user functions to the data units provided by the transport layer. The session layer connection is typically a multistep operation involving addressing the host, authenticating password access, stating communications options to be used, and billing arrangements. Once the session is underway, the session layer manages the interaction.

OSI layer 6	The Presentation Layer protocols format the data to meet the needs of different computers, terminals, or presentation media in the user's end-to-end communications. The protocols at this layer may also provide data encryption for security purposes in transmission over networks, or data compression for efficiency and economy.
OSI layer 7	OSI layer 7 is the Application Layer. It specifies the protocols for the user's intended interaction with the distant computer, including such applications as database access, document interchange, or financial transactions. Certain industry-specific end-to-end application protocols, such as in banking or airline reservations, enable computers and terminals of connection created by a physical link.
OSI Network Address	The address, consisting of up to 20 octets, used to locate an OSI Transport entity. The address is formatted into an Initial Domain Part which is standardized for each of several addressing domains, and a Domain Specific Part which is the responsibility of the addressing authority for that domain.
OSI Presentation Address	The address used to locate an OSI Application entity. It consists of an OSI Network Address and up to three selectors, one each for use by the Transport, Session, and Presentation entities.
Pacing	A technique by which a receiving station controls the rate of transmission of a sending station to prevent overrun.
Packet	A unit of data transmitted at the OSI network layer; or any addressed segment of data transmitted on a network.
Packet Assembler/Disassembler (PAD)	
	A translating computer that provides access for asynchronous character-at-a-time terminals to a synchronous packet switching network.
Packet internet groper (Ping)	
	A program used to test reachability of destinations by sending them an ICMP echo request and waiting for a reply. The term is used as a verb: "Ping host X to see if it is operational!"
Packet Switch Node (PSN)	A computer that accepts, routes, and forwards packets in a packet switching network.
Packet-switching network	A communications network that breaks a message into small units called packets, in order to transmit data from one computer to another. Each packet contains destination (header) information and a part of the message. The packets are routed from the sending computer to the receiving computer through switching points, where each of the switches (nodes) is a computer capable of recognizing the address information and routing the packet to its destination.

The Packet Switching Nodes can dynamically select the best route for each packet so that later packets may arrive prior to earlier packets. The switch at the receiving end reassembles the packets in the proper order.

Packet-switching networks do not establish a real connection between transmitter and receiver, but instead create a virtual circuit that emulates the connection created by a physical link.

Page	1. A basic SQL Server I/O unit, 2 KB in size.
	2. A Web "page" isn't literally a page, but an entire document, however long. A home page (often called "home.html" or "index.html") is the first page called up when you enter a Web site, or if the URL doesn't give a filename.
pages per minute (ppm)	Ppm is a term used to describe the output speed of printers.
Paging File	Dedicated hard disk space used to emulate RAM for virtual memory.
Parallel interface	A connection between a parallel device, such as a printer, and a computer. The computer sends multiple bits of information to the device simultaneously. This is also known as a Centronics interface.
Parallel multitasking	The process whereby programs execute simultaneously.
Parallel Ports	In a parallel interface, eight bits of data are sent at the same time, in parallel, on eight separate wires. Therefore, parallel transmissions are faster than serial transmissions.
	Parallel ports, also called LPT ports, were originally used to connect line printers and terminals. Most systems have at least 1 parallel port, which is called LPT1.
	There are two parallel standards: Bi-Tronics and Centronics (IEEE 1284). Centronics cables support a higher data rate. The Centronics connector is a 25-pin D-shell connector and is considered the standard.
	Printers generally use parallel communications, as do some early notebook PC network adapters. Devices are available which allow the connection of SCSI devices to a parallel port.
Parallel transmission	In computer communications, parallel transmission is the transmission of data (binary digits) simultaneously (in parallel with each other) using separate lines. In contrast, serial transmission sends only one bit after the other using only one communications line.
Parameter	A variable that is given a constant value for a specified application and that may denote the application; or a variable that is given a constant value for a specific document processing program instruction.
Parity bit	A check bit which is added to each byte to signal the computer that the bits in a byte have transmitted correctly.

Parity check	A technique used to quickly check the integrity of data received after a transmission, or from memory. Parity checking can apply to bytes, words, longwords, and other units of information.
Partition	1. An area of storage on a fixed disk that contains a particular operating system or a logical drive where data and programs can be stored.
	2. The NetWare Directory database is divided into these logical divisions. A partition represents a distinct unit of data in the Directory tree that can store and replicate Directory information. Each Directory partition has a container object. All objects and data about the objects are contained in it. Directory partitions do not include any information about the file system, directories, or files located therein.
Pass-through validation	A process where a logon attempt that cannot be validated by the local domain is passed to trusted domains for validation.
Password	A word or set of letters and numbers allowing access to a facility, computer, or network. A password may be accompanied by some other unique identifier before the user is allowed to login.
Path	1. In hierarchical data structures, such as operating system directories, the path is the chain from a root directory, as in MS-DOS, or volume, as in NetWare, to a specific subdirectory or file.
	2. In data communications, the path is the transmission route from sending node to receiving node.
PC-DOS	PC-DOS is IBM's version of the DOS operating system.
Peer-to-peer	Communication in which two communications systems communicate as equal partners sharing the processing and control of the exchange, as opposed to host-terminal communication in which the host does most of the processing and controls the exchange.
Permanent Virtual Circuit (PVC)	
	The permanent virtual circuit provides for a fixed logical connection between two network subscribers by reserving buffer space in the switching nodes. A connection between two subscribers can be established by either a virtual call or a permanent virtual circuit. The permanent virtual circuit is established by prior arrangement between the network subscribers and the network provider. On a permanent virtual circuit, the network is aware of the fixed association between two stations. Permanent logical channel numbers are assigned exclusively to the permanent circuit.
Personal Address List	User-specific private address list.
Personal Profile	The server-based, user-specific profile applied when a user logs in from any domain workstation. Users are allowed to make changes to local profiles.

Phase modulation	The time difference between two identical wave forms which are delayed (phased) to represent the binary digits 0 and 1.
Physical Layer	OSI Layer 1, it is the OSI layer that provides the means to activate and use physical connections for bit transmission. In plain terms, the Physical Layer provides the procedures for transferring a single bit across a Physical Media.
Physical Media	Any means in the physical world for transferring signals between OSI systems. Considered to be outside the OSI Model, and therefore sometimes referred to as "Layer 0." The physical connector to the media can be considered as defining the bottom interface of the Physical Layer, i.e., the bottom of the OSI Reference Model.
Physical Unit (PU)	An input-output unit identified by its actual label or number.
Pipe	To start execution of an instruction sequence before the previous instruction sequence is completed to increase processing speed.
Plain Old Telephone Service (POTS)	A term used by the telecom industry to denote the service has not been upgraded to support higher-level data transmissions.
Point-to-point	Data communications links are divided into two main categories, depending on how the line is structured: either point-to-point or multipoint. Point-to-point describes a channel that is established between two, and only two, stations. The link may be a dedicated or a dial-up line connecting a processor and a terminal, two processors, or two terminals.
Point-to-Point Protocol (PPP)	The successor to the SLIP protocol, PPP allows a computer to use a regular telephone line and a modem to make IP connections. PPP can also carry other routable protocols such as IPX.
Polling	The process by which a computer periodically asks each terminal or device on a LAN if it has a message to send, and then allows each to send data in turn. On a multipoint connection or a point-to-point connection, polling is the process whereby data stations are invited one at a time to transmit.
Port	1. A memory address that identifies the physical circuit used to transfer information between a microprocessor and a peripheral.

2. On the Internet, "port" often refers to a number that is part of a URL, appearing after a colon (:), immediately after the domain name. Every service on an Internet server "listens" on a particular port number on that server. Most services have standard port numbers. Web servers normally listen on port 80. Services can also listen on non-standard ports, in which case the port number must be specified in a URL when accessing the server. You might see a URL of the form: gopher:// peg.cwis.uci.edu:7000/ which shows a gopher server running on a non-standard port (the standard gopher port is 70).

3. Port also refers to translating a piece of software from one type of computer system to another, for example, to translate a Windows program so that will run on a Macintosh.

Portable NetWare	A version of NetWare for use with UNIX and other non-DOS operating systems. In UNIX systems, the Portable NetWare file server runs as a set of processes on the host computer rather than on a dedicated file server.
Postoffice	Microsoft Mail message store element.
Postoffice Address List	Local users at a Microsoft Mail postoffice.
Postoffice Network List	External postoffice list.
PostScript	PostScript is a registered trademark of Adobe Corporation, and is the accepted language standard for high resolution printing on laser printers. PostScript is a language used to tell the printer how to print a character on the page. PostScript uses vector information to define graphics. Some printers, such as Apple LaserWriter printers, are true PostScript printers. Some printers use PostScript emulation, either at the system or in the printer.
Power Supply	A PC's power supply is a device that takes the AC (alternating current) electric current from the wall and converts it into the DC (direct current) current required by the computer.
	The power supply outputs four discreet voltages: +5 VDC, -5 VDC, +12 VDC, and -12 VDC. Spikes are smoothed out with capacitors connected across the power supply leads.
	For a list of power supply manufacturers and their home pages, see www.yahoo.com/Business_and_Economy/Companies/Computers/ Hardware/Components/Power_Supplies.
Preemptive multitasking	A multitasking method where the operating system allocates processor time to tasks according to their relative priority.
Presentation Layer	The Presentation layer is OSI Layer 6. It is the OSI layer that determines how application information is represented (i.e., encoded) while in transit between two end systems.

Primary Key	In database terminology, the purpose of the primary key is to insure that each row in a table is unique. The primary key will contain one or more columns defining a unique value. Normally, you will want to protect the column(s) defining the key so that a value cannot be changed after it is entered.
Print server	A network computer, either dedicated or nondedicated, used to handle the printing needs of workstations.
Printer Access Protocol (PAP)	PAP is responsible for handling all print requests/transactions on the network.
Printer driver	A program that translates the file that is printed into the language the printer understands. A printer cannot be used unless the correct driver is installed.
Printer fonts	Fonts which are built into the printer. They may also be downloadable soft fonts.
Printer languages	In addition to simple control characters, more advanced printers (such as laser printers) support a command and control language, which allows for even greater application support. PCL (Hewlett-Packard) and PostScript (Adobe) are two primary, de facto industry standards for printer languages.
Priority	Sometimes abbreviated as PRI, PRIO, or PRTY; a rank assigned to a task that determines its precedence in receiving system resources.
Priority Scheme	A Token Ring can be used on a priority or non-priority basis. When a station receives a free token, it compares the priority value with the priority of any data unit it has to transmit. If the data units priority is equal or higher than the token priority, the data unit is transmitted. If the data unit's priority is lower than that of the token, the data unit is not transmitted.
Private Branch Exchange (PBX)	A telephone exchange on the user's premises. Provides a switching facility for telephones on extension lines within the building and access to the public telephone network. May be manual (PMBX) or automatic (PABX). A digital PBX that also handles data devices without modems is called a CBX.
Private Management Domain (PRMD)	An X.400 Message Handling System private organization mail system. Example: NASAmail.
Problem determination	The process of identifying the source of a problem, such as machine failure, power loss, or user error.

Procedure	1. A block of program code with or without formal parameters (the execution of which is invoked by means of a procedure call).
	2. A set of executable Visual Basic program steps.
Procedure Cache	Memory allocated to running compiled procedures under SQL Server.
Process	To perform operations on data in a process; or a course of events defined by its purpose or by its effect, achieved under given conditions. A course of events occurring according to an intended purpose or effect.
Processor	In a computer the processor, or Central Processing Unit (CPU), is a functional unit that interprets and executes instructions. A processor contains at least an instruction control unit and an arithmetic and logic unit.

Promoting Conference for OSI (POSI)

The OSI arm in Japan. Consists of executives from the six major Japanese computer manufacturers and Nippon Telephone and Telegraph. They set policies and commit resources to promote OSI.

Protocol	1. A set of strict rules (usually developed by a standards committee) that govern the exchange of information between computer devices. Also, a set of semantic and syntactic rules that determine the behavior of hardware and software in achieving communication.
	2. PROTOCOL is also a NetWare v3.x console command that displays the protocols registered on a file server, along with the names of their frame types and protocol identification numbers as included by the LAN driver when it is installed.

Protocol Control Information (PCI)

The protocol information added by an OSI entity to the service data unit passed down from the layer above, all together forming a Protocol Data Unit (PDU).

Protocol Data Unit (PDU)	This is OSI terminology for "packet." A PDU is a data object exchanged by protocol machines (entities) within a given layer. PDUs consist of both Protocol Control Information (PCI) and user data.
Proxy	1. Proxy is the mechanism whereby one system "fronts for" another system in responding to protocol requests. Proxy systems are used in network management to avoid implementing full protocol stacks in simple devices, such as modems.
	A copy of an out-of process component's interfaces. Their role is to marshal method and property calls across process boundaries.
Proxy ARP	Proxy ARP is the technique in which one machine, usually a router, answers ARP requests intended for another machine. By "faking" its identity, the router accepts responsibility for routing packets to the "real" destination.

	Proxy ARP allows a site to use a single IP address with two physical networks. Subnetting is normally a better solution.
Public Switched Network	Any switching communications system—such as Telex, TWX or public telephone networks—that provides circuit switched connections to many customers.

Pulse code modulation (PCM)

> A technique used by the coder-decoder to convert an analog signal into a digital bit stream. The amplitude of the analog signal is sampled and a digital code is selected to represent the sampled value. The digital code is transmitted to the receiving end, which uses it to generate an analog output signal. Encoding techniques may be used to reduce the amount of data that is transmitted between the sender and the receiver.

Pulse dialing	Older form of phone dialing, utilizing breaks in DC current to indicate the number being dialed.
Query	1. The process where a master station asks a slave station to identify itself and to give its status.
	2. In interactive systems, query is an operation at a terminal that elicits a response from the system.
	3. In another usage of the term, a query specifies the criteria to be used to find database objects. When the query is executed, the objects that match the criteria of the query will be displayed in the Query Results window.
Queue	A holding area in which items are removed in a first in, first out (FIFO) manner. In contrast, a stack removes items in a last in, first out (LIFO) manner.
RAM disk drive	A RAM drive is also known as a virtual drive. A portion of memory used as if it were a hard disk drive. RAM drives are faster than hard disks because the memory access time is much faster than the access time of a hard disk. Information on a RAM drive is lost when the computer is turned off.
RAM semaphore	A kind of semaphore that is based in memory accessible to a thread; fast, but with limited functionality.

Random Access Memory (RAM)

> RAM is the computer's storage area to write, store, and retrieve information and program instructions so they can be used by the central processing unit. The contents of RAM are not permanent.

RAS programs	Reliability, Availability, and Serviceability programs. These programs monitor the operating system and facilitate problem determination.

Read-Only Memory (ROM)

Read-Only Memory is used to store permanent instructions for the computer's general housekeeping operations. A user can read and use, but not change, the data stored in the computer's ROM. ROM is stored on a non-volatile memory chip enabling the information to be retained, even after the computer's power has been turned off.

The Apple Macintosh ROMs contain a large portion of the operating functionality in permanent storage on the system board. Macintosh clone vendors must license these ROMs in order to build Mac-compatible computer systems.

Redundancy check

A check made with redundant hardware or information that can provide an indication that certain errors have occurred.

Redundant Array of Independent Disks (RAID)

A Redundant Array of Independent Disks is usually referred to as a RAID system. The "I" originally stood for Inexpensive, but was changed to Independent because RAID systems are typically expensive.

A RAID system is composed of multiple hard disks that can either act independently or emulate one large disk. A RAID disk system allows increased capacity, speed, and reliability.

RAID was defined in nine levels by to the RAID Advisory Board. Each level provides a different amount of reliability and fault tolerance. The level numbers do not indicate that one level is superior to another.

For an online RAID Guide, see www.invincible.com/rguide.htm.

Reentrant

The attribute of a program or routine that allows the same copy of a program or routine to be used concurrently by two or more tasks.

Referential Integrity

The process by which critical data remains accurate and usable as a database changes.

Registry

Windows NT and Windows 95 configuration database.

Reliable Transfer Service Element (RTSE)

A lightweight OSI application service used above X.25 networks to handshake application PDUs across the Session Service and TP0. Not needed with TP4, and not recommended for use in the U.S. except when talking to X.400 ADMDs.

Remote Access Server (RAS)

In most networks, clients are connected directly to the network. In some cases, however, remote connections are needed for your users. Microsoft provides Remote Access Service (RAS) to let you set up and configure client access.

Users connecting to a RAS server, generally through a modem, can be limited to accessing only that server, or can be given access to the entire network. Effectively, this is the same as a local connection to the network, except that any type of data transfer runs significantly slower. You will need to select connection options appropriate to your access requirements, available support, and budgetary constraints.

Remote Client Remote Microsoft Mail user.

Remote File System (RFS) A distributed file system, similar to NFS, developed by AT&T and distributed with their UNIX System V operating system.

Remote Management Use of a remote console by a network supervisor or by a remote console operator to perform file server tasks.

Remote Operations Service Element (ROSE)

A lightweight RPC protocol, used in OSI Message Handling, Directory, and Network Management application protocols.

Remote Procedure Call (RPC)

A protocol that standardizes initiation and control processes on remote computers.

Repeaters The earliest functional role of repeaters was to extend the physical length of a LAN. This is still the primary benefit of a repeater.

There are, however, several potential problem areas that are not addressed by repeaters. These include signal quality, time delays, network traffic, and node limitations.

Most repeaters do nothing to filter noise out of the line, so it is amplified and sent on with the signal.

Time delays can occur as signals are generated over greater distances. These delays may eventually generate timeout errors. This is why repeaters are not used for remote links.

Repeaters do nothing to reduce the network traffic load, because they don't have any capacity for filtering traffic. Repeaters are "invisible" to access protocols. All nodes added through a repeater count toward the total that can be supported in a subnet.

Repeaters are typically used on bus networks. To get the best signal quality, place the repeater so that the two connected segments are approximately the same length.

Replication 1. Process whereby data directories are dynamically copied between selected file servers.

2. Process whereby transactions are applied to copies of database tables.

Request For Comments (RFC)

RFC is the name of the result and process for creating a standard on the Internet. New standards are proposed and published on line, as a Request For Comments.

The Internet Engineering Task Force is a consensus-building body that facilitates discussion, and new standards. When a new standard is established, the reference number/name for the standard retains the acronym "RFC." For example, the official standard for e-mail is RFC 822.

Requester

NetWare program on the REQUESTER diskette that allows a workstation running under OS/2 to communicate through a NetWare network by attaching to a file server.

Requester Postoffice

Postoffice participating in directory synchronization.

Reseaux Associes pour la Recherche Europeenne (RARE)

European association of research networks.

Reseaux IP Europeenne (RIPE)

European continental TCP/IP network operated by EUnet.

Resident Attribute

Attribute that is stored in the NTFS directory entry.

Restore

To bring back computer data or files that have been lost through tampering or other corruption or through hardware malfunction. Files should be backed up frequently to protect against such loss.

Reverse Address Resolution Protocol (RARP)

The Reverse Address Resolution Protocol (RARP) is used to map the MAC, or hardware address, to a host's IP, or software address.

If the only thing a station knows at initialization is its own MAC address (usually from configuration information supplied by the manufacturer), how can it learn its IP address? The RARP protocol serves this purpose.

RARP allows a station to send out a broadcast request in the form of a datagram that asks, "Who am I?" or "What is my IP address?" Another host (typically a RARP server) must be prepared to do the inverse of ARP. For example, taking the MAC address and mapping it into an IP network and node number. This only happens at startup. RARP is not run again until the next time the device is reset or restarted.

A value of 0x8035 in the Ethernet Type field indicates that the datagram is a RARP datagram. There must be a RARP server on each segment because broadcasting is used, and broadcasts are not normally forwarded by IP routers. All machines on the network receive the request, but only those authorized to supply the RARP service will process the request and send a reply. Such machines are known as RARP servers.

REVOKE	A NetWare command-line utility used to revoke specific rights of a user or group in a directory or file.
Ring Insertion and Exit	In Token Ring networks, insertion is accomplished by the network station applying voltage to its cable which activates a relay in the MAU and electrically includes the station in the ring. Exit is accomplished by removing voltage from the cable, thereby closing the relay in the MAU.
Rlogin	A service offered by Berkeley UNIX which allows users of one machine to log into other UNIX systems across a network (for which they are authorized) and interact as if their terminals were connected directly. Similar to Telnet.
Round robin scheduling	A method of allocating CPU time in a multi-user environment, with each user being allocated a certain amount of quantum or processor time. Once a user has exhausted his quantum, control passes to the next user.
Router	1. A connection between two networks that specifies message paths and may perform other functions, such as data compression.
	2. In early versions of NetWare, the term bridge was sometimes used interchangeably with the term router.
Router Information Protocol (RIP)	1. This protocol allows routers to exchange routing details on a NetWare internetwork. Using RIP, NetWare routers can crate and maintain a database, or routing table, of current information. Workstations can query the nearest router to determine the fastest route to a distant network by broadcasting a RIP request packet. Routers send periodic RIP broadcast packets with current information to keep all routers on the internetwork synchronized. They also send RIP update broadcasts when a change is detected in the internetwork configuration.
	2. An Internet standard IGP (Interior Gateway Protocol) supplied with Berkeley UNIX. It is based on distance-vector algorithms that measure the shortest path between two points on a network.
Routing Table Maintenance Protocol (RTMP)	The routing protocol used by routers to share network information in an AppleTalk network. RTMP is responsible for maintaining routing table information. This information is received from broadcasts from other networks and routers on the network.
RS-232-C	A low-speed serial interface used to connect data communications equipment (such as modems and terminals) defined as a standard by the Electronic Industries Association. All standards recommended by the EIA have an RS prefix.

RSPX	A NetWare v3.x, v4.x, and Portable NetWare loadable module that contains the SPX driver, which allows a workstation to function as a remote console.
Scheduler	Also known as a dispatcher. The part of the operating system that determines which thread should run and the relative priority of each executing thread.
Segment	1. A self-contained portion of a computer program that may be executed without the entire computer program necessarily being maintained in internal storage at any one time.
	2. In computer graphics, a segment is a collection of display elements that can be manipulated as a unit. A segment may consist of several and separate dots, line segments, or other display elements.
	3. In TCP/IP, a segment is a message block.
Selector	The identifier used by an OSI entity to distinguish among multiple SAPs at which it provides services to the layer above.
Semaphore	An object that limits access to a particular number of threads.
Sequenced Packet Exchange (SPX)	
	A Novell protocol used as the resident protocol in NetWare, along with IPX.
Serial interface	A connection point through which information is transferred one digital bit at a time. The term serial interface is sometimes applied to interfaces in which the data is transferred serially via one path, but some control signals can be transferred simultaneously via parallel paths.
Serial Line IP (SLIP)	SLIP is an Internet protocol used to run IP to connect two systems over serial lines such as telephone circuits or RS-232 cables. SLIP is now being replaced by PPP.
Serial multitasking	The process by which multiple programs execute, but only one at a time.
Serial Port	In a serial interface bits of information are sent in a series, one at a time. Data bits are typically surrounded by starting and ending flags which provide synchronization.
	Serial ports are also called communications (COM) ports and referenced by number; COM1 is serial port 1. Most systems come with two COM ports.
	The standard serial port connector is a 9-pin D-shell connector, but some systems still have older 25-pin D-shell connectors. Adapters are available to convert between the two standard connectors. With either connector, only 9 connector pins are soldered to 9 wires inside the cable.
	Most serial cables are no longer than 50 feet. Use of longer cables can result in transmission errors.

Modems, serial printers, and serial mice use serial communications.

A new bus type, the Universal Serial Bus (USB), will become more prevalent in the future. The concept behind the USB is to consolidate all desktop peripherals into a single high-speed (12 Mbps) access route.

The USB allows up to 64 devices to be daisy-chained together. The single USB connector type will support many devices, including some that in the past used the serial, parallel, keyboard, mouse, or game ports.

The USB will usher in a new set of hardware peripherals and accessories, including products such as digital cameras and virtual-reality gloves.

More information about USB can be found at the Universal Bus Implementers Forum Home Page: www.usb.org

Serial transmission

Transmission in which data (binary digits) can be transmitted only one bit at a time using only one communications line. In contrast, parallel transmission sends each byte simultaneously using separate lines. Connections exceeding one meter in distance typically use serial transmission.

Server

A computer or a software package that provides services to client software running on other computers on a network. Possible services include file sharing, printer sharing, or communications services.

Server Manager

In Windows NT Server, the Server Manager lets you manage domain members, and provides a quick way of viewing information about your domain. With Server Manager, you can view system properties, or view and manage shared directories and services running on Windows NT Workstations and Servers. It will also allow you to add member systems to, or remove member systems from the domain, promote a backup domain controller into the role of domain controller, and broadcast messages to the domain. You can also view and manage trusting domains.

DOS, Windows v3.x, and Windows for Workgroups stations will be listed while active on the domain, but are not registered as domain members.

Server Requester Programming Interface (SRPI)
A subset of APPC.

Server-based Profile

A user profile that is stored on a domain server.

Service Access Point (SAP)

The point at which the services of an OSI layer are made available to the next higher layer. The SAP is named according to the layer providing the services: e.g., Transport services are provided at a Transport SAP (TSAP) at the top of the Transport Layer.

Service Access Point Stations (SAPS)
> Number of service access point stations for Token Ring. This parameter may be required on a Novell network in the shell.cfg file depending on the network interface card.

Service Advertising Protocol (SAP)
> The protocol used by NetWare service providers such as file server, print server, etc., to notify network elements of services provided on the network.

Session
> 1. That group of processes or tasks associated with an application.
>
> 2. A NetWare v3.1x menu utility used to change a user's environment while logged into the server. It can be used to change file servers, logout, view a list of network groups or users, or send a message to a group or user. It can display, add, delete, or modify drive mappings.

Session Layer
> OSI Layer 5, it is the OSI layer that provides means for dialogue control between end systems.

Session manager
> A system utility that manages screen group switching. The session manager is used only in the absence of the presentation manager. The presentation manager replaces the session manager.

Shared Lock
> Lock set at the start of a read operation allowing further read access to the page, but no write access.

Shared memory
> The use of the same portion of memory by two distinct processes, or the memory so shared. Shared memory is used for interprocess communication and for purposes that lead to compactness of memory, such as common subroutines.

Shell
> A portion of a program that responds to user commands, also called user interface. The shell is loaded as a terminate and stay resident program (TSR).

Short-haul modem
> A signal converter which conditions a digital signal to ensure reliable transmission over DC continuous private-line metallic circuits without interfering with adjacent pairs in the same telephone cable.

SID
> Unique identifier value used in Windows NT and NT Server security management.

Signaling
> Using semaphores to notify threads that certain events or activities have taken place.

Signals
> Notification mechanisms implemented in software that operate in a fashion analogous to hardware interrupts.

Simple Gateway Management Protocol (SGMP)
> SGMP is the predecessor to SNMP.

Simple Mail Transfer Protocol (SMTP)

    The Internet standard protocol for transferring electronic mail messages between computers.

Simple Network Management Protocol (SNMP)

    The Simple Network Management Protocol (SNMP) is one of the most comprehensive tools available for TCP/IP network management. It operates through conversations between SNMP agents and management systems. Through these conversations, the SNMP management systems can collect statistics from and modify configuration parameters on agents.

    The agents are any component running the SNMP agent service, and which is capable of being managed remotely. Agents can include mini-computers, mainframes, workstations, servers, bridges, routers, gateways, terminal servers, and wiring hubs.

    Management stations are typically more powerful workstations. Common implementations are Windows NT or UNIX stations running a product such as HP OpenView, IBM Systemview/6000, or Cabletron Spectrum. The software provides a graphic representation of the network, allowing you move through network hierarchy to the individual device level.

    There are three basic commands used in SNMP conversations: GET, SET, and TRAP.

    The GET command is used by the management station to retrieve a specific parameter value from an SNMP agent. If a combination of parameters is grouped together on an agent, GET-NEXT retrieves the next item in a group. For example, a management system's graphic representation of a hub includes the state of all status lights. This information is gathered through GET and GET-NEXT.

    The management system uses SET to change a selected parameter on an SNMP agent. For example, SET would be used by the management system to disable a failing port on a hub.

    SNMP agents send TRAP packets to the management system in response to extraordinary events, such as a line failure on a hub. When the hub status light goes red on the management systems representation, it is in response to a TRAP.

    An SNMP management station generates GET and SET commands. Agents are able to respond to SET and GET and to generate TRAP commands.

Simplex transmission   Data transmission in one direction only.

Single Domain Model   Simplest Windows NT Server domain model where only one domain exists on the network.

Slave   Opposite of master. The device which is controlled by the master.

Small Computer System Interface (SCSI)
                                   Small Computer System Interface is a high-speed parallel interface used
                                   for connecting microcomputers to peripheral devices, such as hard disks
                                   and printers.

Smart   Containing microprocessor intelligence. A modem or adapter is smart if
                                   it has its own computer chip. A dumb device is limited in functions and
                                   features, and takes processing power from a high-level system.

SMODE   Abbreviation for Search MODE, it is a NetWare command-line utility
                                   that defines a program's method of looking for a data file. Eight search
                                   modes are possible.

Software   A computer program, or a set of instructions written in a specific
                                   language that commands the computer to perform various operations on
                                   data contained in the program or supplied by the user.

SPXS   SPXS is a NetWare v3.x and v4.x loadable module that provides SPX
                                   protocol services under the STREAMS loadable module.

ST506   ST506 is an old standard interface for connecting standard disk drives to
                                   PCs.

Standard Login Security   Term referring to SQL Server validation of login attempts.

Standards Promotion and Application Group (SPAG)
                                   A group of European OSI manufacturers which chooses option subsets
                                   and publishes these in a "Guide to the Use of Standards" (GUS).

Star Topology	Star/hub networks connect the peripheral devices via point-to-point links to a central location. An Active Hub regenerates signals while Passive Hubs simply act as a terminating point for the network. Star topologies provide architectural flexibility, but can require more cable than traditional bus and ring topologies.

Star Network

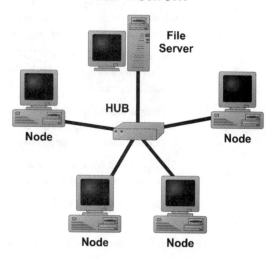

Most modern data networks are configured with hubs. This allows for simplified adds, moves, and changes. System failure from any individual segment break is minimized. Examples of hub configurations for traditional bus and ring topologies include the use of the wiring closet in Ethernet 10BaseT networks, or multi-port repeaters in both Ethernet 10BaseT and 10Base5 networks. The use of MAU hubs in Token Ring networks is another example.

A star may be wired with twisted pair or coax cabling. Most current implementations use twisted pair.

Start/stop bits	Additional bits inserted to mark the beginning and the end of transmitted characters. Start bits and stop bits are used in asynchronous communications.
Statistical multiplexor	An apparatus that serves as a time division multiplexor and contains a microprocessor control unit for allocating the available bandwidth dynamically, to improve the utilization of the channel.
Storage dump	The copying of all or a portion of a storage.
Storage Management Services (SMS)	
	A combination of services which allows data to be stored and retrieved.

STREAMS

A NetWare v3.x and v4.x loadable module that acts as an interface between NetWare and the network's transport protocols, such as IPX/SPX. STREAMS requires that the CLIB, IPXS, SPXS, and TLI modules are loaded.

Structure of Management Information (SMI)

The rules used to define the objects that can be accessed via a network management protocol.

Structured Query Language (SQL)

An ISO data definition and data manipulation language for relational databases. Variations of SQL are offered by most major vendors for their relational database products. SQL is consistent with IBM's Systems Application Architecture and has been standardized by the American National Standards Institute (ANSI).

Subnet Mask

A filter which separates subnetted addresses into network and local entities. Local systems have subnet masks so they can restrict the broadcast to be received on the local network only.

Subnetting

When a complex network is recognized as a single address from outside of the network.

Subnetwork

A collection of OSI end systems and intermediate systems under the control of a single administrative domain and utilizing a single network access protocol. For example, private X.25 networks amd a collection of bridged LANs.

Suspend

An action that causes an active program to become temporarily inactive. In effect, the suspended program is waiting for the user to reactivate it.

Switched line

A communications link for which the physical path may vary with each usage, such as the public telephone network.

Switched Multimegabit Data Service (SMDS)

SMDS is a high-speed packet switching application that enables users (primarily businesses) to communicate at speeds ranging from 1.5 Mbps to as high as 155 Mbps. This type of service is most beneficial to organizations distributed in regional, national, and/or international configurations, often with separate local area networks at each end.

Symmetric Multiprocessing (SMP)

In an SMP operating system such as Windows NT, the operating system can run on any processor, or share tasks between several processors. User and applications threads can also be shared between processors, making best use of processor time and reducing bottlenecks.

Synchronization

1. Replica synchronization is a way to ensure that replicas of a NetWare Directory partition have the same information as other replicas of the same partition. Time synchronization is a way to ensure all servers in a NetWare Directory tree register the same time.

2. Under SQL Server replication, this is the process of copying database schema and data from a publishing server to a subscription server.

3. When discussing the Internet, it is the process of setting the same clock or data rate in the receiving terminal as in the sending terminal. This is a requirement to enable the receiving device to read the incoming bits and to translate them into characters. Synchronization, accomplished by a signal from the sending terminal, enables the receiving band to recognize any single bit and to identify which group of bits belong in which characters. Once the first bit of a character is recognized, the receiver can count off the required number of bits and identify each character if it learns the number of bits in the character, and the speed at which the bits are coming. Two common approaches to synchronized transmission between devices are synchronous transmission and asynchronous transmission.

Synchronous	Pertaining to two or more processes that depend upon the occurrence of a specific event such as a common timing signal.

Synchronous Data Link Control (SDLC)

A data transmission protocol used in networks conforming to IBM's SNA.

Synchronous modem	Modem that carries timing information with data.
Synchronous terminal	A data terminal that operates at a fixed rate with transmitter and receiver in synchronization.
Synchronous transmission	Process of sending blocks of data characters without any pause between the characters. The source and receiving terminals establish synchronization (the rate of data transmission) at the beginning of each block of data. The synchronization is generally accomplished by having the source terminal send at least two synchronizing characters (SYN characters) preceding each block of data. The receiver is designed to recognize the SYN characters. Synchronous transmission is generally done with buffers in which the blocks are held until sent, and is more efficient than asynchronous transmission.
System configuration	A process that specifies the devices and programs that form a particular data processing system.
System Default Profile	A Windows NT profile defining background color, screen saver, and wallpaper settings when no user is logged on.
System dump	A dump of all active programs and their associated data after an error stops the system.
System Procedures	Predefined procedures provided with SQL Server.

System Network Architecture (SNA)

A proprietary network that links IBM and non-IBM devices together. Introduced in 1974 before the OSI reference model was defined, SNA was originally a mainframe-centered hierarchical network architecture. SNA is an architecture or design specification which defines the data communications facilities, functions, and procedures that are distributed throughout the network. It also defines the formats and protocols used to support communication between programs, device operators, storage media, and workstations which may be located anywhere in the network. Before SNA, there were no formalized architecture standards or guidelines for computer-based online data processing systems.

SYSTEM.INI

An initialization file used by Microsoft Windows. It contains hardware- and setup-specific information used for the operation of Windows. It includes printer driver references and other device driver information.

Systems Application Architecture (SAA)

SAA was created by IBM in 1987 to help developers standardize applications so that software can function in different operating environments with minimal program modifications and retraining of users. SAA provides a common programming interface, common user access, and a common communications support for IBM operating systems.

T1

A leased-line connection capable of carrying data at 1,544,000 bps. At maximum theoretical capacity, a T1 line could move a megabyte in less than 10 seconds. That is still not fast enough for full-screen, full-motion video, for which you need at least 10,000,000 bps. T1 is the fastest speed commonly used to connect networks to the Internet.

T2

A leased-line connection capable of carrying data at 6,312,000 bps.

T3

A leased-line connection capable of carrying data at 45,000,000 bps. This is more than enough to do full-screen, full-motion video.

T4

An AT&T term for a digital circuit capable of supporting transmissions at a rate of up to 274.176 Mbps.

TBC

Transmit buffer count for Token Ring. This parameter may be required on a Novell network in the NET.CFG file depending on the network interface card.

TBZ

Transmit buffer size for Token Ring. This parameter may be required on a Novell network in the NET.CFG file, depending on the network interface card.

Teletex

A means of medium- to high-speed text transmission, from keyboard to printer, over public switched data networks. Teletex permits a more extensive character set than telex, and permits line and paragraph formatting as in normal correspondence. Teletex was expected to replace telex by 1990 but has so far had limited market acceptance.

Teletext

A non-interactive information system that preceded the videotex. Teletext terminals consist of a specially modified television set and keypad to provide 24 lines of 40-column color text and graphics. Connection is made to teletext systems by specially assigned television broadcast channels, hence the need to use a television set.

Teletypewriter Exchange Service (TWX)

A teletypewriter dial network owned by Western Union. ASCII coded machines are used.

Teletypewriter Exchange Service (TNX)

A network of teleprinters connected over a North American public switched network which uses ASCII code.

Telex

Teleprinter Exchange. A teleprinter dial network offered by Western Union and the International Record Carriers. Uses baud code.

Telnet

1. The Telnet protocol is a part of the TCP/IP protocol suite. Many Internet nodes support Telnet, which is similar to UNIX's rlogin program. Telnet lets users log into any other computer on the Internet, provided that the target computer allows Telnet logins, and the user has a valid login name and password. The computers do not have to be of the same type to Telnet between them.

Some systems expect external access and a special software package is set up to handle outside calls. This eliminates the need to "log in" once a user reaches the remote host.

The most popular reason to log into a remote computer is to run software that is available only on the remote computer. Another reason is when a user's computer is incompatible with a particular program, operating system, available memory, or have the necessary processing power.

People with several Internet accounts can use Telnet to switch from one account to the other without logging out of any of the accounts.

Users can use Telnet as an information-gathering tool by searching databases for information. These databases include LOCIS (the Library of Congress Information System), CARL (Colorado Association of Research Libraries), ERIC (Educational Resources Information Center) and CIJE (Current Index to Journals in Education).

2. An Internet standard user-level protocol that allows a user's remote terminal to login to computer systems on the Internet. To connect to a computer using Telnet, the user types Telnet and the address of the site or host computer.

Terminal emulation

The use of hardware and software on a personal computer to duplicate the operation of a terminal device at both the operator and communications interface sides of the connection, so that a mainframe computer capable of supporting the emulated terminal will also support the PC.

Terminate and Stay Resident program (TSR)

A program that is loaded into memory and remains available even when another application is active.

Termination

Placement of a load on the ends of a cable. For example, both SCSI and Ethernet bus cabling required termination.

Thread

The object of a process that is responsible for executing a block of code. A process can have one or multiple threads.

Three-way-handshake

The process whereby two protocol entities synchronize during connection establishment.

Time Out

When two computers are talking and, for whatever reason, one of the computer fails to respond.

Time sharing

The interleaved use of time on a computer system enabling two or more users to execute computer programs concurrently. Also, a mode of operation of a data processing system that provides for the interleaving in time of two or more processes in one processor.

Time slice

An interval of time on the processing unit allocated for use in performing a task. After the interval has expired, processing unit time is allocated to another task. Therefore, a task cannot monopolize processing unit time beyond a fixed limit. In systems with time sharing, time slice is a segment of time allocated to a terminal job.

Time-critical priority

A classification of processes that may be interactive or noninteractive, in the foreground or background screen group, which have a higher priority than any non-time critical thread in the system.

Time-Division Multiplexor (TDM)

A device that accepts multiple channels on a single transmission line by connecting terminals, one at a time, at regular intervals; interleaving bits (Bit TDM) or characters (character TDM) from each terminal.

Token

In a LAN (Local Area Network), the symbol of authority which is passed successively from one data station to another to indicate the station temporarily in control of the transmission medium. Each data station has an opportunity to acquire and use the token to control the medium.

Token Bus	A form of network, usually a local area network (LAN), in which access to the transmission medium is controlled by a token. The token is passed from station-to-station in a sequence. A station wishing to transmit will do so by removing the token from the bus and replacing it with the data to be transmitted. When transmission is complete, the transmitting station will re-initiate the token passing process.
Token Ring	IBM originally created Token Ring (IEEE 802.5). Over the last few years, it has steadily gained popularity.
	It is a network that runs as a logical ring, but is usually wired as a physical star. It has a 4 Mbps or 16 Mbps transfer rate, and runs on Unshielded Twisted Pair, Shielded Twisted Pair, or Fiber Optic cabling.
	A Token (data frame) passes from system to system. A system can attach data to a token if the token is free (empty). In turn, each system on the ring receives, regenerates, and passes the token.

Token Passing in a Token Ring Network

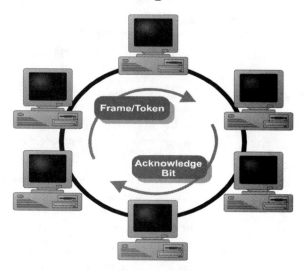

With Token Ring, it is possible to predict the passage of the token. The predictability inherent in Token Ring makes it a popular choice for timing-critical and control applications.

Token Rotation Time	The elapsed time for a token to rotate around the ring network.
TokenTalk	The name used to describe the AppleTalk communications protocol suite operating over a Token Ring network.
TP0	OSI Transport Protocol Class 0 (Simple Class). This is the simplest OSI Transport Protocol, useful only on top of an X.25 network (or other network that does not lose or damage data).

TP4	OSI Transport Protocol Class 4 (Error Detection and Recovery Class). This is the most powerful OSI Transport Protocol, useful on top of any type of network. TP4 is the OSI equivalent to TCP.
Transaction	A series of SQL statements and procedures that are completed as a unit.
Transaction Log	SQL database log file that tracks all transaction activity for a database.

Transaction Tracking System (TTS)

A NetWare v3.x and v4.x protection system for bindery files and other database files. TTS monitors transactions and backs out (or rolls back transactions) that are incomplete because of hardware or software failure, error, or user preference.

Transceiver	A terminal device that can transmit and receive information signals. Transceiver is an contraction of transmitter-receiver.

Transmission Control Protcol (TCP)

The reliable connection-oriented protocol used by DARPA (Defense Advanced Research Projects Agency) for their internetworking research. TCP uses a three-way handshake with a clock-based sequence number selection to synchronize connecting entities and to minimize the chance of erroneous connections due to delayed messages. TCP is usually used with IP (Internet Protocol), the combination being known as TCP/IP.

Transmission Control Protocol/Internet Protocol (TCP/IP)

Originally designed for WANs (Wide Area Networks), TCP/IP was developed in the 1970's to link the research center of the U.S. Government's Defense Advanced Research Projects Agency. TCP/IP is a protocol that enables communication between the same or different types of computers on a network. TCP/IP can be carried over a wide range of communication channels. The Transmission Control Protocol is connection-oriented and monitors the correct transfer of data between computers. The Internet Protocol is stream-oriented and breaks data into packets.

Transmission rate	The transmission rate is stated in baud or bps. If the connection cannot be made at the selected transmission rate, most modems and communications software will automatically attempt to connect at a slower speed.
Transmit	To send data from one place for reception elsewhere. Also, to move an entity from one place to another, as in broadcasting radio waves, dispatching data via a transmission medium, or transferring data from one data station to another via a line.
Transport Layer	OSI Layer 4, it is the OSI layer responsible for reliable end-to-end data transfer between end systems.

Transport Layer Interface (TLI)
> NetWare v3.11 loadable module that provides TLI communication services as part of the STREAMS system, which provides communication between NetWare and the network's transport protocols, such as IPX/SPX. In addition to the STREAMS AND TLI modules, the CLIB, IPX, and SPX modules must be loaded.

Trigger
> A trigger is used to set off an alert when specified conditions are detected.

TrueType fonts (TTF)
> Fonts conforming to a specification developed by Microsoft and Apple. TrueType fonts can be scaled to any height, and will print exactly as they appear on the screen, to the highest resolution available to the output device. The fonts may be generated as bitmaps or soft fonts, depending on the output device's capabilities.

Trunk
> A signal route to which several items of a computer system may be connected in parallel so that signals can be passed between them. Signals on a trunk may be only of a particular kind, or they may be intermixed. There are a number of widely used proprietary trunk systems. A trunk is also called a bus, and in the U.K., the term used is "highway."

Trunk Coupling Unit
> The generic name for a MAU.

Trust Relationships
> Trust relationships are only significant in a multiple domain environment. A trust relationship is a one-way logical relationship established between two Windows NT Server domains. Once established, the domains are referred to as the trusted domain and the trusting domain.
>
> The trusted domain can be assigned rights and permissions in the trusting domain. In other words, the trusting domain says, "I trust you to access my resources." This is a One-Way Trust Relationship.
>
> The trusted domain does not automatically receive rights or permissions in the trusting domain. These must be explicitly assigned. The trust relationship makes it possible for these assignments to be made.
>
> You can also have Two-Way Trust Relationships, which is a mutual trust between domains. This is established as two one-way trusts, one in each direction.

Trusted Connection
> SQL Server named pipe connection.

Trusted Domain
> A domain receiving security rights and permissions from another (trusting) domain.

Trusted Users
> Users from a trusted domain.

| Trustee | In NetWare, a user or group eligible to be granted rights in a directory or file. For any specific directory or file, the trustee can be granted all, some, or none of the rights available. Trustee rights in a directory or file are called trustee assignments. |

Trusting Domain — The domain granting security rights and permissions to another (trusted) domain.

Twisted-Pair Cabling — Twisted Pair (TP) is made of insulated, copper wires that have been twisted around each other to form wire pairs. Usually the wire is 22 to 26 gauge, and more than one pair can be carried in a single jacket or sheath. When working with twisted pair, note the difference between "wire" and "pair." A "two pair" cable has four wires.

Because any wire carrying electricity transmits and receives electromagnetic energy, nearby pairs of wires carrying signals can interfere with each other. This is called crosstalk. To reduce crosstalk and other Electro-Magnetic Interference (EMI), the wires are twisted. This causes any noise to be received more evenly by both wires in a pair. A voltage difference between the two wires carries the signal, so noise that is equal on both wires cancels itself.

Twisted pair wiring may or may not have an electromagnetic shield around the pairs. It is therefore classed into one of two types: Unshielded Twisted Pair (UTP), and Shielded Twisted Pair (STP). Unshielded Twisted Pair is a set of twisted wire pairs within a plastic sheath. The most common use for this type of cable is telephone wire. Different types of UTP cabling are suitable for different speed communications.

UTP is usually the least expensive of all the network transmission media types.

Shielded Twisted Pair includes a protective sheathing around the conductors. This cuts down on outside interference.

Twisted-Pair Cables

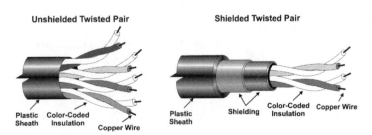

Two-Way Trust — A trust relationship where there is mutual trust between two domains.

Tymnet	The U.S. public packet-switching carrier that developed from Tymshare Inc.'s internal terminal network used by their public time-sharing service.
Uninet	A common carrier offering an X.25 PDN.
Uninterruptible Power Supply (UPS)	If power loss, surges or drops (brownouts) are a significant concern, an Uninterruptible Power Supply (UPS) may be your best option. With a UPS, line voltage is fed into a battery keeping it constantly charged. The computer is, in turn, powered from the battery. Because the computer is already running from the battery, there is no switching time if power is lost. UPS systems supply protection against power events more effectively than most other devices. Uninterruptible Power Supplies are considered essential for network servers. If normal power is lost or interrupted, the UPS allows time to safely shut down the file server. Many UPSs can alert network users to warn when the system is going down.
	When selecting a UPS, examine the software and hardware available for the UPS. Options and features vary greatly.
Unique Index	An index which does not allow duplicate entries.
UNIX	UNIX is a computer operating system originally developed at AT&T's Bell Research Laboratories and later at the University of California Berkeley. It is implemented in a growing number of minicomputer and microcomputer systems.
	UNIX is "multi-user" because it is designed to be used by many people at the same time and has TCP/IP built into the operating system. It is the most common operating system for servers on the Internet.
UNIX-to-UNIX Copy Program (UUCP)	UUCP is a software program that facilitates file transfer from one UNIX system to another via dial-up phone lines. The UUCP protocol also describes the international network used to transfer USENET News and electronic mail.
Upstream Neighbor Address	In Token Ring networks, it is the address of the network station that is physically and immediately upstream from another specific node. The upstream neighbor is the location from which the signal is being received.
User	An individual permitted to access a computer, network, or other system.
User Agent (UA)	An OSI application process that represents a human user or organization in the X.400 Message Handling System. Creates, submits, and takes delivery of messages on the user's behalf.

User Datagram Protocol (UDP)

A transport protocol in the Internet suite of protocols. UDP, like TCP, uses IP for delivery. However, unlike TCP, UDP provides for exchange of datagrams without acknowledgements or guaranteed delivery.

User Manager

A Windows NT user and group administration utility.

User Manager for Domains

User Manager for Domains is a utility installed on all NT Server systems. On additional servers it is operationally identical to the Windows NT Workstation version of the utility, User Manager. The utility is also installed as part of the NT Server remote management tools.

When User Manager for Domains is started, the current domain users and groups are displayed. Domain Administrators and Account Operators can view and modify users and groups by selecting the appropriate account and running "Properties" from the "User" menu, or by double-clicking on the account. Administrators can manage any account.

Additional menu selections let you create and manage accounts, select the sort order for account names, manage domain policies, and establish trust relationships.

User Mode

Higher level Windows NT or Windows 95 operating system functions. The user mode includes the protected subsystems and application sessions.

User Profile

Environment configuration settings applied when a user logs on from a Windows NT workstation to Windows NT Server domain. Each user is given either a personal or a mandatory profile. See also Local Profile, Default Profile, Personal Profile, and Mandatory Profile.

User Program

A program that resides and runs in the outside of the operating system kernel.

Utilities

In NetWare, utilities are programs that add functions to the operating system by being added to the file server, workstation, or router. Utilities can be in the form of console commands, including screen commands, installation, maintenance, and configuration commands.

Utility

The capability of a system, program, or device to perform the functions for which it is designed.

V.10

A CCITT interface recommendation; electrically similar to RS-423.

V.11

A CCITT interface recommendation; electrically similar to RS-422.

V.21

A CCITT modem recommendation; similar to Bell 103.

V.22

A CCITT modem recommendation; similar to Bell 212.

V.23	A CCITT modem recommendation; similar to Bell 202.
V.24	A CCITT interface recommendation that defines interchange circuits; similar to and operationally compatible with RS-232.
V.26	A CCITT modem recommendation; similar to Bell 201.
V.27	A CITT modem recommendation; similar to Bell 208.
V.28	A CCITT interface recommendation that defines electrical characteristics for the interchange circuits defined by V.24; similar to and operationally compatible with RS-232.
V.29	A CCITT modem recommendation; similar to Bell 209.
Vector font	Generally used to refer to any font that is defined mathematically, and which supports scaling to any size. Vector fonts provide a smooth appearance at large font sizes.

Vertical Redundancy Check (VRC)

An error-detection scheme in which the parity bit of each character is set to "1" or "0," so that the total number of "1" bits in the character is odd or even.

Very Large-Scale Integration (VLSI)

A chip technology with 20,000 to 900,000 logic gates per chip. The flow of electrons in chips is controlled by the transistors which form switches or logic gates. Chips are categorized by the number of logic gates available.

Videotex	An interactive information system also known as videotext and viewdata. The system can be used for public access, or broadcast to a select user/subscriber, making large volumes of information available to an authorized audience. Videotex systems usually operate over switched telephone lines and allow 40 columns by 24 lines of color text and graphics to be displayed on the screen. Information is arranged in pages.
View	A method of creating custom presentation of data stored in database tables.

Virtual DOS Machine (VDM)

Emulated DOS machine used to support DOS and WOW under Windows NT.

Virtual Loadable Module (VLM)

VLMs are a series of executable programs that run at a DOS workstation and enable communication with the NetWare server.

Virtual machine	The Windows technique used to execute an application. Virtual machines include a virtual address space, processor registers, and privileges.

Virtual Memory	Some operating systems have the ability to increase the apparent physical system memory through virtual memory. Virtual memory is a file on the hard disk that emulates physical Random Access Memory (RAM). This file is called a swap file.

With virtual memory, a portion of the program and data is kept in RAM at all times, with the remainder stored on the disk. This is normally referred to as "swapping" the information to the disk. When an attempt is made to access code or data on the disk, it is swapped back into RAM, and if necessary, other code or data will be swapped out to make room available. The swapping process is controlled by the VMM (Virtual Memory Manager).

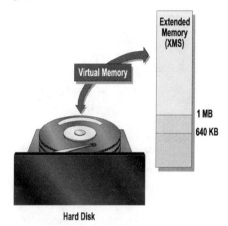

Except for a loss of performance when swapping occurs, virtual memory is transparent to the user and application.

Virtual memory gives you more memory, providing the ability to launch more concurrent applications and work with larger data files. The system's capabilities are increased, but at a small performance decrease. Adding more physical memory will still provide better system performance.

Voice-frequency	Frequency in part of the audio frequency range essential for the transmission of commercial quality speech.
Voice-Grade-Line	A channel that is capable of carrying voice frequency signals.
Volume	A NetWare name for amount of named storage space on a hard disk. This space is allocated when the network is installed.

Wide Area Networks (WANs)

Wide Area Networks (WANs) expand the basic LAN model by linking Local Area Networks (LANs), and allowing them to communicate with each other. By traditional definition, a LAN becomes a WAN when it crosses a public right-of-way, requiring a public carrier for data transmission. More current usage of the term usually includes any situations where a network expands beyond one location/building. A WAN is characterized by low- to high-speed communication links, and usually covers a wide geographic area. The remote links may be operational LANs or only groups of workstations. With the exception of a WAN's wider area of operation, the benefits and features of LANs and WANs are the same.

Wide Area Telephone Service (WATS)

A service provided by telephone companies in the United States that permits a customer to make calls to or from telephones in specific zones for a flat monthly charge. The monthly charges are based on the size of the zone instead of the number of calls.

Wideband

A communications channel used to transmit over 230,000 bps, for direct data transfer from one computer to another.

WIN.INI file

An initialization file used by Microsoft Windows. The file contains settings used to customize the Windows environment. Windows applications will sometimes store initialization information in the WIN.INI file.

Windowing

In routing terms, windowing refers to flow control technique to send multiple message packets before requiring an acknowledgment from the receiver.

Windows (Microsoft)

A graphical shell operating environment which runs on top of DOS. It contains many accessories and features which access DOS functions such as file, program, and printer management. Windows is referred to as a GUI (Graphical User Interface).

Workgroup

A defined set of Windows for Workgroups, Windows 95, or NT stations that are able to communicate and share file and print resources.

Workgroup manager

The person appointed by a NetWare network supervisor to manage data and users belonging to a group.

Workshop for Implementors of OSI (OIW)

Frequently called NIST OIW or the NIST Workshop, this is the North American regional forum at which OSI implementation agreements are decided. It is equivalent to EWOS in Europe and AOW in the Pacific.

WOW

Term used to describe DOS Windows running under Windows NT.

X Recommendations	The CCITT documents that describe data communication network standards. Well-known ones include: X.25 Packet Switching standard, X.400 Message Handling System, and X.500 Directory Services.
X Window System™	A popular window system developed by MIT and implemented on a number of workstations.
X-ON/X-OFF	An abbreviation for Transmitter On/Transmitter Off. These are control characters used for flow control. They instruct a terminal to start transmission (X-ON) and end transmission (X-OFF).
X.21	A CCITT recommendation that defines the most popular physical interface for X.25; it is equivalent to RS-232 and V.24.
X.21 bis	A CCITT recommendation that defines the most popular physical interface for X.25; it is equivalent to RS-232 and V.24.
X.25	A data communications interface specification that describes how data pass into and out of packet switching networks. The CCITT and International Standards Organization (ISO) approved protocol suite defines the origination, termination, and use of virtual circuits that connect host computers and terminals across the network.
X.25 Pad	A device that permits communication between non-X.25 devices and the devices in an X.25 network.
X.28	A CCITT recommendation that defines the interchange of commands and responses between a PAD and its attached asynchronous terminals. Supplementary packet-switched protocol.
X.29	A CCITT recommendation that defines the use of packets to exchange data for control of remote PADs.
X.3	A CCITT recommendation that defines the parameters that determine the behavior of the interface between a PAD and its attached asynchronous terminals.
X.75	Supplementary packet-switched protocol.
X/Open	A group of computer manufacturers that promotes the development of portable applications based on UNIX. They publish a document called the X/Open Portability Guide.
x86	Term used to refer to Intel family processors, such as the 80386 and 80486.

XMODEM	A communications protocol developed in the late 1970s to perform error checking on data sent between two data transmission devices. Xmodem protocol adds a checksum to each block of data at transmission. The sum is recalculated when the block is received and the new number is compared with the received checksum. If there is a difference, this reflects an error and the last block of data is retransmitted. Xmodem is sometimes referred to as Christensen Protocol, after its designer.
Zone	A grouping of logical devices on one or more networks.
Zone Information Protocol (ZIP)	
	ZIP is responsible for linking users and resources on the network with the appropriate zone.
Zone List	A list of zones (up to 255).

ACRONYMS

-A-

AAL	ATM Adaptation Layer
Abend	Abnormal end
ABR	Automatic Baud Rate Detection
ACDI	Asynchronous Communications Device Interface
ACE	Access Control Entry
ACF/VTAM	Advanced Communications Function/Virtual Telecommunications Access Method
ACK	Acknowledgement
ACL	Access Control List
ACSE	Association Control Service Element
AD	Administrative Domain
ADB	Apple Desktop Bus
ADMD	Administration Management Domain
ADSP	AppleTalk Data Stream Protocol
AEP	AppleTalk Echo Protocol
AFP	AppleTalk Filing Protocol
AIFF	Audio Interchange File Format
ANI	Automatic Number Identification
ANSI	American National Standards Institute
AOW	Asia and Oceania Workshop
APA	All Points Addressable
API	Application Program Interface
APPC	Advanced Program-to-Program Communications
ARA	AppleTalk Remote Access
ARP	Address Resolution Protocol
ARPA	Advanced Research Project Agency
ARPANET	Advanced Research Projects Agency Network
ARQ	Automatic Request for Retransmission
ASCII	American Standard Code for Information Interchange

ASMP	Asymmetric Multiprocessing
ASN.1	Abstract Syntax Notation One
ASP	AppleTalk Session Protocol
ATM	Asynchronous Transfer Mode
ATP	AppleTalk Transaction Protocol
AUP	Acceptable Use Policy
AUI	Attachment Unit Interface
AWG	American Wire Gauge
-B-	
BBS	Bulletin Board System
bcp	Bulk Copy Program
BDC	Backup Domain Controller
BER	Basic Encoding Rules
BIOS	Basic Input/Output System
BISDN	Broadband ISDN
bit	Binary Digit
BITNET	Because It's Time Network
BNC	British Naval Connector
BOC	Bell Operating Company
Bps	Bytes per second
bps	Bits per second
BRI	Basic Rate Interface
BSC	Binary Synchronous Communications
BSD	Berkeley Software Distribution
BTAM	Basic Telecommunications Access Method
-C-	
CAP	Competitive Access Provider
CATV	Community Antenna Television
CBR	Constant Bit Rate
CBT	Computer-Based Training
CCITT	International Consultative Committee for Telegraphy and Telephony
CCL	Common command language

CCR	Commitment, Concurrency, and Recovery
CCTV	Closed-Circuit Television
CD-ROM	Compact Disc Read-only Memory
CERN	European Laboratory for Particle Physics
CERT	Computer Emergency Response Team
CGA	Color Graphics Adapter
CGI	Common Gateway Interface
CICS	Customer Information Control System
CIR	Commited Information Rate
CISC	Complex Instruction Set Computer
CIX	Commercial Internet Exchange
CLNP	ConnectionLess Network Protocol
CLTP	Connectionless Transport Protocol
CMIP	Common Management Information Protocol
CMOS	Complementary Metal Oxide Semiconductor
CMOT	CMIP Over TCP
CN	Common Name
CO	Central Office
Codec	Coder-decoder
CONP	Connection Oriented Network Protocol
COS	Corporation for Open Systems
COSINE	Cooperation for Open Systems Interconnection Networking in Europe
CPE	Customer Premise Equipment
CPI	Common Programming Interface
cps	Characters per second
CPU	Central Processing Unit
CRC	Cyclic Redundancy Check
CREN	Corporation for Research and Educational Networking
CRT	Cathode Ray Tube
CSMA	Carrier Sense Multiple Access
CSMA/CA	Carrier Sense Multiple Access with Collision Avoidance
CSMA/CD	Carrier Sense Multiple Access with Collision Detection

CSNET	Computer Science Network
CSU	Customer Service Unit
CU	Control Unit
-D-	
DAC	Digital to Analog Converter
DACS	Digital Access Cross Connects
DARPA	Defense Advanced Research Projects Agency
DAV	Digital Audio Video
DB2	IBM Data Base 2
DBCS	Double Byte Character String
DBMS	Database Management System
DBO	Database Owner
DBOO	Database Object Owner
DCA	Defense Communications Agency
DCE	Distributed Computing Environment
DCE	Data Communications Equipment
DD	Double density
DDE	Dynamic Data Exchange
DDL	Data Definition Language
DDM	Distributed Data Management Architecture
DDN	Defense Data Network
DDP	Datagram Delivery Protocol
DES	Data Encryption Standard
DET	Directory Entry Table
DFT	Distributed Function Terminals
DID	Direct Inward Dial
DIMM	Dual, In-line Memory Module
DISA	Defense Information Systems Agency
DIX	Digital, Intel, Xerox
DLC	Data Link Control
DLCI	Data Link Connection Identifier
DLL	Dynamic link library

DMA	Direct Memory Access
DMI	Digital Multiplexed Interface
DML	Data Manipulation Language
DNS	Domain Name System
DOS	Disk Operating System
dpi	Dots per inch
DQDB	Distributed Queue Dual Bus
DRAM	Dynamic Random Access Memory
DS	Data set
DS	Double-Sided
DS1	Digital Signaling Level 1
DS2	Digital Signaling Level 2
DS3	Digital Signaling Level 3
DSA	Directory System Agent
DSDD	Double-Sided, Double-Density
DSE	Data Service Equipment
DSHD	Double-Sided, High-Density
DSP	Digital Signal Processor
DSU	Data Service Unit
DTE	Data Terminal Equipment
DTR	Data Terminal Ready
DUA	Directory User Agent
DXF	Drawing interchange Format
DXI	Data Exchange Interface
-E-	
E-mail	Electronic mail
EARN	European Academic and Research Network
EBCDIC	Extended Binary-Coded Decimal Interchange Code
ECF	Enhanced Connectivity Facilities
EDI	Electronic Data Interchange
EEHLLAPI	Entry Emulator High-Level Language Application Program Interface
EFF	Electronic Frontier Foundation

EGA	Enhanced Graphics Adapter
EGP	Exterior Gateway Protocol
EMS	Expanded Memory
EPS or EPSF	Encapsulated PostScript File
ER Model	Entity/Relationship Model
ES-IS	End System - Intermediate System
ESF	Extended Super Frame
EUnet	European UNIX Network
EUUG	European UNIX Users Group
EWOS	European Workshop for Open Systems
-F-	
FAQ	Frequently Asked Questions
FARNET	Federation of American Research NETworks
FAT	File Allocation Table
FCB	File Control Block
FCC	Federal Communications Commission
FCS	Frame Check Sequence
FDDI	Fiber Distributed Data Interface
FEP	Front End Processor
FFAPI	File Format API
FIPS	Federal Information Processing Standard
FM	Frequency Modulation
FNC	Federal Networking Council
FPU	Floating Point Unit
FRICC	Federal Research Internet Coordinating Committee
FT1	Fractional T1
FT3	Fractional T3
FTAM	File Transfer, Access, and Management
FTP	File Transfer Protocol
FYI	For Your Information
-G-	
GDI	Graphics Device Interface

GIF	Graphics Interchange Format
GOSIP	Government OSI Profile
GUI	Graphical User Interface
-H-	
HAL	Hardware Abstraction Layer
HCSS	High Capacity Storage System
HD	High-Density
HDLC	High-level Data Link Control
HDX	Half-duplex
HFS	Hierarchical File System
HLLAPI	High-Level Language Application Program Interface
HMA	High Memory Area
HPFS	High Performance File System
HTML	Hypertext Markup Language
HTTP	Hypertext Transfer Protocol
Hz	Hertz
-I-	
IAB	Internet Activities Board
ICMP	Internet Control Message Protocol
IDE	Integrated Drive Electronics
IEEE	Institute of Electrical and Electronics Engineers
IESG	Internet Engineering Steering Group
IETF	Internet Engineering Task Force
IFS	Installable File System
IGP	Interior Gateway Protocol
IGRP	Internet Gateway Routing Protocol
IIS	Internet Information Server
IMHO	In My Humble Opinion
INTAP	Interoperability Technology Association for Information Processing
IONL	Internal Organization of the Network Layer
IP	Internet Protocol
IPX	Internetwork Packet Exchange

IPXODI	Internetwork Packet Exchange Open Data-Link Interface
IRC	Internet Relay Chat
IRQ	Interrupt Request Lines
IRTF	Internet Research Task Force
IS-IS	Intermediate System - Intermediate System
ISAPI	Microsoft Internet Server Application Programming Interface
ISDN	Integrated Services Digital Network
ISO	International Standards Organization
ISODE	ISO Development Environment
ISP	Internet Service Provider
IXC	Inter-exchange Carrier
-J-	
JANET	Joint Academic Network
JPEG	Joint Photographic Experts Group
JUNET	Japan UNIX Network
-K-	
KB	Kilobyte
Kb	Kilobit
KBps	Kilobytes per second
Kbps	Kilobits per second
-L-	
L2PDU	Layer Two Protocol Data Unit
L3PDU	Layer Three Protocol Data Unit
LAN	Local Area Network
LAPB	Link Access Protocol Balanced
LAPD	Link Access Protocol Device
LAPS	LAN Adapter and Protocol Support
LATA	Local Access and Transport Area
LCD	Liquid Crystal Diode
LDT	Local Descriptor Table
LEC	Local Exchange Carriers
LEN	Low Entry Networking

LLAP	LocalTalk Link Access Protocol
LMI	Local Management Interface
lpi	Lines per inch
LSL	Link Support Layer
LU	Logical Unit
-M-	
MAC	Media Access Control Sublayer
MAN	Metropolitan Area Network
MAP	Manufacturing Automation Protocol
MAPI	Messaging API
MAU	Multistation Access Unit
MB	Megabyte
Mb	Megabit
MBps	Megabytes per second
Mbps	Megabits per second
MCGA	Multicolor Gate Array
MDI	Multiple Document Interface
MHS	Message Handling System
MHz	Megahertz
MIB	Management Information Base
MIDI	Musical Instrument Digital Interface
MILNET	Military Network
MIME	Multipurpose Internet Mail Extensions
MIPS	Million Instructions Per Second
MLID	Multiple Link Interface Driver
MOO	Mud, Object Oriented
MPEG	Moving Pictures Experts Group
ms	Milliseconds
MTA	Message Transfer Agent
MTU	Maximum Transmission Unit
MUD	Multi-User Dungeon or Dimension
MVS	Multiple Virtual Storage

MVS-CICS	Multiple Virtual Storage-Customer Information Control System
MVS/TSO	Multiple Virtual Storage/Time-Sharing Option
-N-	
NAK	Negative AcKnowledgment
NBP	Name Binding Protocol
NCC	NetWare Control Center
NCP	NetWare Core Protocol
NCP	Network Control Point
NCSA	National Center for Supercomputing Applications
NDS	NetWare Directory Services
NetBEUI	NetBIOS Extended User Interface
NetWare DA	NetWare Desk Accessory
NFS	Network File System
NIC	Network Information Center
NIC	Network Interface Card
NIST	National Institute of Standards and Technology
NLM	NetWare Loadable Module
NLQ	Near Letter Quality
NLSP	NetWare Link Services Protocol
NMS	Network Management Station
NNS	NetWare Name Service
NNTP	Network News Transfer Protocol
NOC	Network Operations Center
NREN	National Research and Education Network
NSAP	Network Service Access Point
NSEPro	Network Support Encyclopedia Professional Volume
NSEPro	Network Support Encyclopedia Professional Edition
NSF	National Science Foundation
NSFnet	National Science Foundation Network
NT	Windows NT
NT1	Network Termination 1
NT2	Network Termination 2

NTAS	Windows NT Advanced Server
NTFS	New Technology File System
NTP	Network Time Protocol
NWADMIN	Network Administrator
-O-	
OBS	Optical Bypass Switch
ODI	Open Datalink Interface
OIW	Workshop for Implementors of OSI
OLE	Object Linking and Embedding
ONC	Open Network Computing
OOP	Object-oriented programming
OPAC	Online Public Access Catalog
OSI	Open Systems Interconnection
OSPF	Open Shortest Path First
-P-	
PAD	Packet Assembler/Disassembler
PAP	Printer Access Protocol
PBX	Private Branch Exchange
PCI	Peripheral Component Interconnect
PCI	Protocol Control Information
PCL	Printer Control Language
PCM	Pulse code modulation
PCMCIA	Personal Computer Memory Card International Association
PDC	Primary Domain Controller
PDF	Printer Definition Files
PDN	Packet Data Network
PDS	Processor-Direct Slot
PDU	Protocol Data Unit
PID	Process Identification Number
PIF	Program Information File
Ping	Packet internet groper
PMMU	Paged Memory Management Unit

POP	Point of Presence
POP	Post Office Protocol
POSI	Promoting Conference for OSI
POST	Power On Self Test
POTS	Plain Old Telephone Service
ppm	Pages per minute
PPP	Point-to-Point Protocol
PPTP	Point-to-Point Tunneling Protocol
PRAM	Parameter RAM
PRI	Primary Rate Interface
PRMD	Private Management Domain
PROFS	Professional Office System
PSN	Packet Switch Node
PU	Physical Unit
PUC	Public Utility Commission
PVC	Permanent Virtual Circuit
-Q-	
QMF	Query Manager Facility
-R-	
RAID	Redundant Array of Independent Disks
RAM	Random Access Memory
RARE	Reseaux Associes pour la Recherche Europeenne
RARP	Reverse Address Resolution Protocol
RAS	Remote Access Service
RAS	Remote Access Server
RBOC	Regional Bell Operating Company
REM	REMARK
RFC	Request For Comments
RFS	Remote File System
RIP	Raster Image Processor
RIP	Router Information Protocol
RIPE	Reseaux IP Europeenne

RISC	Reduced Instruction Set Computer
ROM	Read-Only Memory
ROSE	Remote Operations Service Element
RPC	Remote Procedure Call
RTF	Rich Text Format
RTMP	Routing Table Maintenance Protocol
RTSE	Reliable Transfer Service Element
-S-	
SAA	Systems Application Architecture
SAP	Service Access Point
SAP	Service Advertising Protocol
SAPI	Service Access Point Identifier
SAPS	Service Access Point Stations
SAR	Segmentation and Reassembly protocol
SCSI	Small Computer Systems Interface
SDH	Synchronous Digital Hierarchy
SDI	Storage Device Interface
SDLC	Synchronous Data Link Control
SDN	Software Defined Network
SDU	SMDS Data Unit
SFT	System Fault Tolerance
SGML	Standard Generalized Markup Language
SGMP	Simple Gateway Management Protocol
SID	Security Identifier
SIMM	Single, In-line Memory Module
SIP	SMDS Interface Protocol
SLIP	Serial Line IP
SMDS	Switched Multimegabit Data Service
SMI	Structure of Management Information
SMP	Symmetric Multiprocessing
SMS	Storage Management Services
SMTP	Simple Mail Transfer Protocol

SNA	System Network Architecture
SNMP	Simple Network Management Protocol
SONET	Synchronous Optical Network
SPAG	Standards Promotion and Application Group
SPE	Synchronous Payload Envelope
SPX	Sequenced Packet Exchange
SQL	Structured Query Language
SRAM	Static RAM
SRPI	Server Requester Programming Interface
SS7	Signaling System 7
SSL	Secure Sockets Layer
STDM	Statistical Time Division Multiplexing
STM	Synchronous Transport Module
STS	Synchronous Transport Signal
SVC	Switched Virtual Circuit
Sysop	Systems Operator
-T-	
TA	Terminal Adapter
TAC	Terminal Access Controller
TCP	Transmission Control Protcol
TCP/IP	Transmission Control Protocol/ Internet Protocol
TDM	Time-Division Multiplexor
TE1	Terminal Equipment Type 1
TE2	Terminal Equipment Type 2
Telex	Teleprinter Exchange
TIFF	Tagged Image File Format
TLI	Transport Layer Interface
TNX	Teletypewriter Exchange Service
TP0	OSI Transport Protocol Class 0
TP4	OSI Transport Protocol Class 4
TSA	Target Server Agent
TSR	Terminate and Stay Resident program

TTF	TrueType fonts
TTL	Time to Live
TTS	Transaction Tracking System
TWX	Teletypewriter Exchange Service
-U-	
UA	User Agent
UDP	User Datagram Protocol
UMA	Upper Memory Area
UMBs	Upper Memory Blocks
UNC	Universal Naming Convention
UPS	Uninterruptible power supply
URL	Uniform Resource Locator
UUCP	UNIX-to-UNIX Copy Program
-V-	
VBR	Variable Bit Rate
VCI	Virtual Connection Identifier
VDM	Virtual DOS Machine
Veronica	Very Easy Rodent Oriented Net-wide Index to Computerized Archives
VGA	Video Graphics Array
VLM	Virtual Loadable Module
VLSI	Very Large-Scale Integration
VM/CMS	Virtual Machine/Conversational Monitor System
VMM	Virtual Memory Manager
VNET	Virtual Network
VPI	Virtual Path Identifier
VPN	Virtual Private Network
VRAM	Video RAM
VRC	Vertical Redundancy Check
VRML	Virtual Reality Modeling Language
VSE/CICS	Virtual Storage Extended-Customer Information Control System
VT	Virtual Terminal

-W-

WAIS	Wide Area Information Servers
WAN	Wide Area Network
WATS	Wide Area Telephone Service
WWW	World Wide Web
WYSIWYG	What You See is What You Get

-X-

XDR	External Data Representation
XMS	Extended Memory
XNS	Xerox Network System

-Z-

ZIP	Zone Information Protocol

Index

CONTENTS

S0-BZJ-757

With love to Tom, Emily, Charles, Mom, and Dad

—M.B.

With love to Bruce, Andy, Megan, Mom, and Dad

—J.G.M.

ABOUT THIS BOOK

Dressing up is an integral part of life—especially for a kid. Most parents are surprised at how often the need for costumes comes up (more often than they expect!) and how drastically the requirements vary from occasion to occasion. While some costumes are a snap to make, others make you desperate! When confronted with an insistent, out-of-season, offbeat, or short-notice costume request from your kid or kid's teacher, you may find yourself frantically searching the aisles of novelty stores, shocked by the prices, or worse, stranded at the sewing machine at midnight, spending more money and time than a reasonable person should part with. *The No-Sew Costume Book* is here to help you get through these times with ease and style. Featured in the pages to follow is a cleverly thought-out and designed collection of costumes that highlights classic, fun, kid-chic, and clean design and becomes a new dimension in the art of disguise.

Using simple patterns and easy assembly techniques, basic materials are transformed into memorable costumes that you can make without fuss, aggravation, or a lot of talent. If you can cut, glue, and staple, you can do it.

The appeal and wearability of these costumes is virtually ageless, but the needs of children were considered foremost in the designs. Comfort and safety became prerequisites; faces are unmasked and arms and legs free-moving. The costumes can be slipped on and off with ease and can be worn over indoor and outdoor clothing, as needed. They can also be "hand-me-ups," as well as hand-me-downs. Even with all this factored in, you'll find the designs exciting, charming, and amusing. We've tried to give you a wide variety of possibilities (hopefully, we've covered some of those offbeat requests) and to give you costumes with looks that are not only deceptive disguises but deceptively easy to make. We hope you have as much fun with them as we have.

MATERIALS: The materials in this book are for the most part inexpensive and readily available. Although this is a no-sew book, you'll find fabric stores carry a majority of the materials used, including a myriad of great-looking and useful notions, e.g., sequins, wiggle eyes, round-cord elastic, buttons, etc. Craft and hobby stores, as well as variety, hardware, and stationery stores, are also great sources of supplies. The essential pencil, ruler, and scissors are required for every costume and, therefore, have not been included under the "Materials" listing for each costume. Probably your most important tool is a good pair of scissors; they will save you time and aggravation. A fresh bottle of glue can make a difference, too, when a lot of gluing is required; the glue flows more freely, allowing you more accuracy and speed. When working with glue on felt, make a test swatch first—draw a line of glue on a small square of felt and place another felt square on top to secure. On some polyester felts, the glue will seep through the felt, leaving a mark; if this is the case, be especially careful to apply glue in neat lines along the costume edges, so the seep-through pattern does not detract from the costume. Natural-fiber felt does not have this problem. Fabric netting, often used for veils, comes in fine and large mesh, the fine being softer and less stiff. The type of netting (fine or large mesh) is specified under the "Materials" listing when it affects the outcome.

MAKING PATTERNS:

All of the headgear designs are uni-sized to fit anyone at any age without any pattern alterations. The body patterns have been sized primarily to fit a wide range of children—with or without an overcoat underneath. Most costumes can be worn successfully by adults without any changes; they just don't cover as much of you! To check the fit, try on or hold up the paper pattern before you lay it out. If you think you'll need extra length, hold off on buying the fabric until you've checked, in case you need a little more. If a costume needs to be lengthened or shortened, in most cases the pattern simply can be cut to the desired length or added to with a piece of paper—you can't go too far wrong. If a special adjustment is needed, it is explained under the "For Adult Sizing" section. For mitt patterns, as for the body patterns, hold up to the hand and check for fit, trimming away excess or adding on as necessary.

To make the patterns, you must enlarge the gridded pattern drawings. Most of the costume designs are based on squares, rectangles, and circles, and many of them are symmetrical (both sides the same), making

the enlarging process an easy one. In addition, a half-sheet or whole sheet of newspaper (depending on the format) is just about equal in size to a piece of poster board, which makes enlarging some of the simple poster board patterns, such as the heart, star, robot body, and turtle, very easy. You can enlarge drawings using a photocopy machine with enlarging capacities—enlarging to scale—or by using graph paper. To do this, first mark off as many 1-in. grid squares on the graph paper as shown on the artwork (for patterns that are marked 1 square = 2 in., 2½ in. grid squares for those marked 1 square = 2½ in., etc. Number the horizontal and vertical rows of squares in the margin on the original; then transfer these numbers to the corresponding rows on your graph paper grid. Begin by finding a square on the graph paper that corresponds to a square on the original. Mark the graph grid with a dot wherever a design line intersects a line on the original. (It helps visually to divide the graph lines into fourths to gauge whether the line cuts the grid line halfway or somewhere to the right or left of it.) Working 1 square at a time, mark each grid line where the design intersects it; then connect the dots, following the contours of the original artwork. It's easiest to draw in the straight lines first, then concentrate on the curves and angles.

CONSTRUCTION TECHNIQUES:

Staples: When working with staples, staple with raw edges away from the body. If not possible, tape the staple ends to prevent "catching."

Glue: When making a glue seam, be sure to draw glue in a thin stream, following the edge line. Align and place the piece to be secured directly on top, without shifting, to create a clean seam. When gluing through netting or lace, be sure to use a sufficient amount of glue.

Gathers: Gathers are created by simply bunching the fabric or paper up with the hand to fit.

FINISHING OFF THE LOOK: Since these costumes were designed to be worn over clothes, the clothes you wear should coordinate or blend in with the costume, if possible. Generally, plain clothes are best — turtlenecks or T-shirts and sweatpants or tights. If a storm coat is in order, however, don't fret — the costume will shine through!

ACKNOWLEDGMENTS

The authors' sincerest thanks go to our families and friends for their contributions and generous support throughout this project. Special thanks go to our aunts Joan and Kay for their kind and unfailing support, and to our models, Andy and Megan Macfarlane, Emily and Charles Stanback, Margaret White, Nicole Plumez, Ward Young, Emily Gunther, and Matthew Feldstein.

T H E
NO-SEW
COSTUME BOOK

CHAPTER I

MAJOR AND MINOR ANIMALS

PIG

FIGURE A

Here's a blue-ribbon pig—well rounded, fine looking, and fashionably pink. The easy-to-make three-dimensional headband is whimsical and amazingly piglike (see illustration on front cover).

DESCRIPTION: Pig headband, bodysuit, and cloved hoof bands.

MATERIALS: 1 piece of pink poster board; 2 yds. of 72-in.-wide pink felt; 1 square of black felt; 2 large wiggle eyes; double-stick tape; round-cord elastic; small piece of dry household sponge; hole punch; 4 Velcro circles or gripper snaps or 2 buttons.

PREPARATIONS: Enlarge and trace body pattern piece (figure B); headband pieces 1, 2, 3, and 4 (figure C); a 4-×6-in. tail piece; and a 2-×-5½-in. hoof band piece onto newspaper or brown wrapping paper. Extend headband arrows on pattern pieces 1 and 4 an equal amount on each side to a full length of 18 in. for the eye band and 14½ in. for the ear band. Cut pieces out. Following figure B, lay body pattern piece and hoof band piece on folded pink felt; cut out. Trace the headband pieces 1, 2, 3, and 4 and tail piece onto pink poster board; cut out. Measure and cut 4 cloves, 2¾

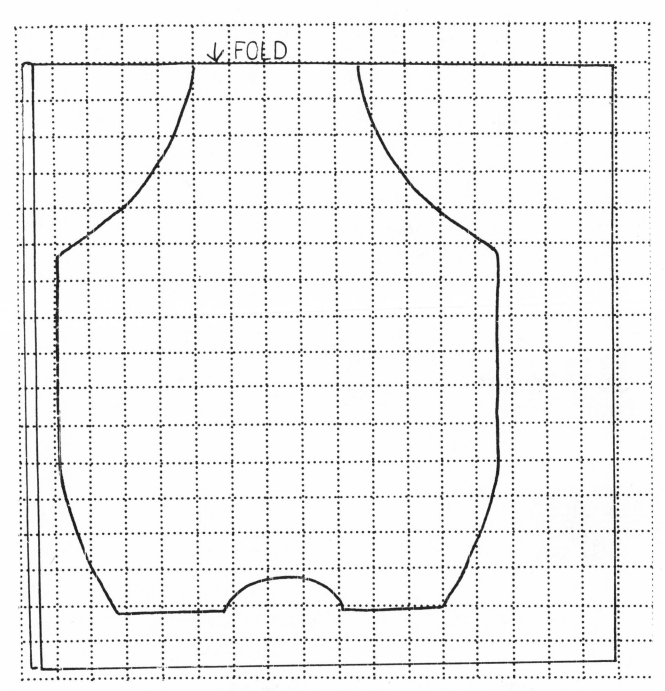

↓ FOLD

FIGURE B (1 sq. = 2 in.)

× 3¾ in., and 2 nostrils, ½ in. circles, from black felt.

TO MAKE HEADBAND: Glue black felt nostrils onto nose piece as shown in figure C. To create the 3-D effect, pieces are stacked and glued on top of each other. To do this, first glue a ½-in. square of dry sponge onto center circle on piece #2, then glue piece #3 (nose) on top of this; let dry. Using double-stick tape, center and attach the constructed nose segment (pieces 2 and 3 assembled) to piece #1. Glue wiggle eyes as shown in figure D. Punch holes at the ends of the band and tie closed to fit around the head with a piece of round-cord elastic. To attach ear band to headband, measure in and mark 3 in. from the headband ends for placement; secure

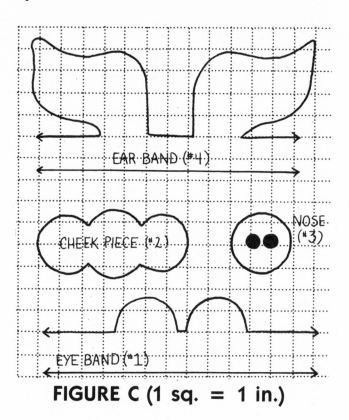

FIGURE C (1 sq. = 1 in.)

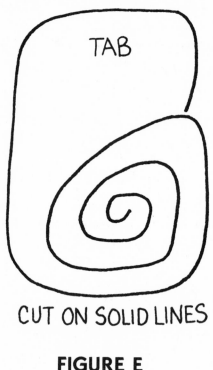

TAB

CUT ON SOLID LINES

FIGURE E

ends of ear bands in place, as shown in figure D, using double-stick tape. Fold ears up for piggy show.

FIGURE D

TO MAKE BODYSUIT: Cut the pink poster board tail piece, following the cut lines, as shown in figure E. Lay bodysuit out flat. Mark tail position by measuring 10 in. up from the center of the crotch; cut a 1-in. slit. Slide the end of the tail coil through the slit until only the tab remains to hold the tail in place (this will be the wrong side of the fabric). Glue the tab in place; let dry. To complete the bodysuit, place front and back together, right sides out. Apply a steady stream of glue ¼ in. from back side edges, align pieces together, and squeeze-press to secure, as shown in figure F; let dry. Pull the tail into a 3-D corkscrew shape. To fasten each shoulder closed for wearing, glue 2 Velcro closures along front and back shoulder edge; let dry. (For gripper snaps, follow same procedure. For buttons, sew button on front and cut a corresponding slit on back shoulder for each side.)

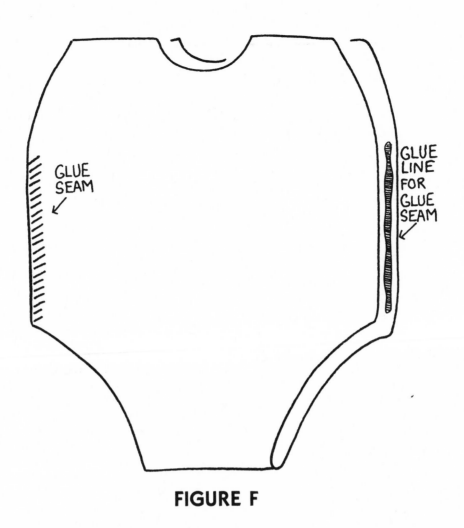

FIGURE F

TO MAKE CLOVED HOOVES: Shape the 4 black felt cloves along the upper lengthwise edges, rounding off the corners (figure G). Glue 2 cloves to each pink felt wristband as shown in figure G; let dry. Punch holes at ends of wristbands and tie closed to fit around the wrist with a piece of round-cord elastic or ribbon.

FOR ADULT SIZING: The bodysuit is the only piece that needs to be adjusted. This can be done easily by adding a minimum of 2 in. to each side and to the length of the bodysuit pattern. Before cutting into felt, hold adjusted pattern up to wearer to assure fit.

SUGGESTIONS: For added fullness, stuff the bodysuit with wadded-up tissue or fabric scraps.

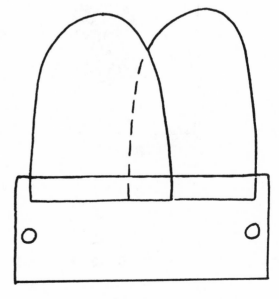

FIGURE G

COW

FIGURE A

Pink-balloon udders add a touch of humor to this classically moo-velous milk machine. The easy-to-make 3-D headband looks like it's right off the farm.

DESCRIPTION: Cow headband and fabric slip-on body with udders.

MATERIALS: 1 piece of white poster board; ½ yd. black, ½ yd. white, and ¼ yd. pink 72-in.-wide felt; black marking pen or black Con-Tact paper in smooth or fuzzy texture; double-stick tape; 4 uninflated, long pink balloons; glue; round-cord elastic; hole punch; dry household sponge.

PREPARATIONS: Enlarge body and tail pattern pieces (figure B) and hat pieces 1, 2, 3, 4, and inner ear (figure C) onto newspaper or brown wrapping paper; extend ear band and nose band arrows an equal amount on both sides for a finished length of 14½ in. for the ear band and 18 in. for the nose band. Cut pieces out. Following figure B, lay body and tail pattern pieces on folded black felt; cut out. Measure and cut a 7-×-10-in. oval from pink felt for the udders. Trace the headband pieces 1, 2, 3, and 4 onto white poster board (figure C); cut out. Cut inner ears from pink felt.

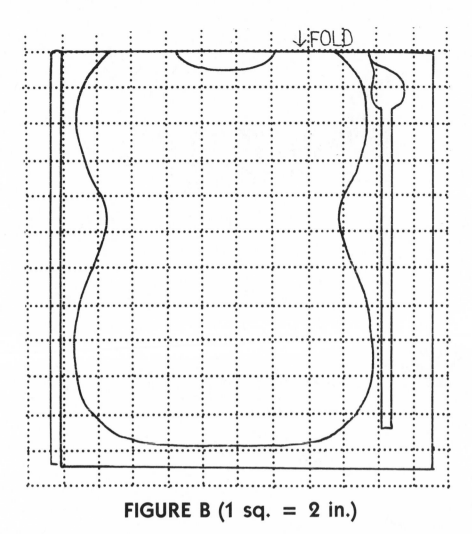

FIGURE B (1 sq. = 2 in.)

TO MAKE HEADBAND: First apply black coat markings to the nose band and ear band, using the placement in figure C as a guide and black Con-Tact paper (preferably) or an intense black marker. If using Con-Tact paper, trace part of the band edge and then draw an irregular shape using the straight edge as the base. Affix the Con-Tact paper in place on the bands and trim if necessary. Make the eyes by tracing the eye design shown in figure D onto eye pieces 3 and 4. Go over the tracing with a black marker and color in the eye; add black felt eyelids if desired. Using pink felt, cut nostrils (2 narrow 1¾-in. ovals) and 2 inner ears (as shown on earband). Glue or double-stick tape nostrils and inner ears in place (figure A). If desired, outline the nostrils with black marker. To create the 3-D effect, pieces are stacked and glued on top of each other. To do this, first glue a ½-in. piece of dry sponge to the back of the nose at both eye positions as shown in figure E. Glue right side of each eye piece to sponge along the lower edge, making sure that the right eye is on the right and the left eye is on the left and that the eye projection sticks up above the nose section (figures E and F). Let dry. Punch holes at the ends of the band and tie closed to fit around the head with a piece of round-cord elastic. To attach ear band to headband, measure in and mark 4 in. from the headband ends for placement; using double-stick tape, secure ends of ear band in place as shown in figure F. Ears and horn should be along the back edge of the band; fold them up and your cow head is complete.

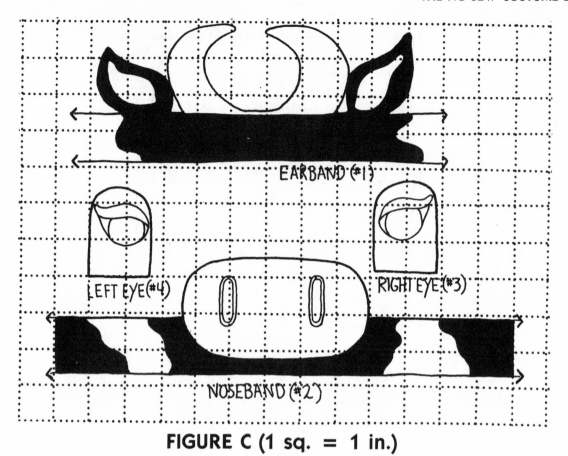

FIGURE C (1 sq. = 1 in.)

EARBAND (#1)

LEFT EYE (#4)

RIGHT EYE (#3)

NOSEBAND (#2)

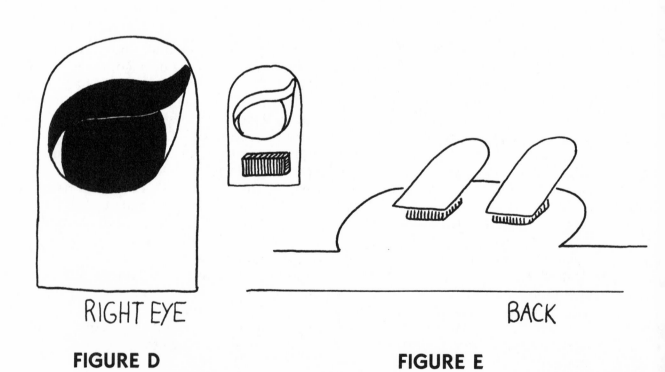

RIGHT EYE

BACK

FIGURE D

FIGURE E

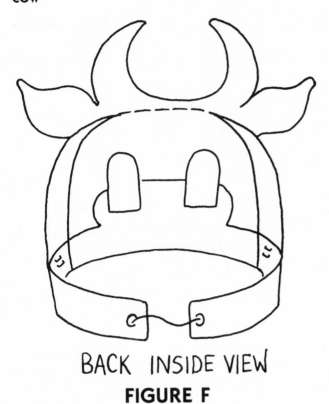

BACK INSIDE VIEW
FIGURE F

TO MAKE BODY: Lay body base piece out flat. Cut a 4-in. slit as shown in figure G at center of circle edge (when you wear the slip-on body, the slit will be in the back); try the body on the wearer and extend the slit if necessary to pull it over the head. Cut white felt coat markings (as for headband markings above) and glue to body base as shown in figure G. On the pink felt udder base, make four ¼-in. slashes across the middle. Slide the balloons through the slashes, leaving balloon neck on the back side. Glue the oval onto the body front, positioning and hiding the balloon necks as shown in figure G. On the back, glue the tail in place.

FOR ADULT SIZING: The slip-on body is the only piece that needs to be adjusted. Simply lengthen the body pattern piece.

SUGGESTIONS: A cow bell laced on a ribbon makes a nice addition to this costume.

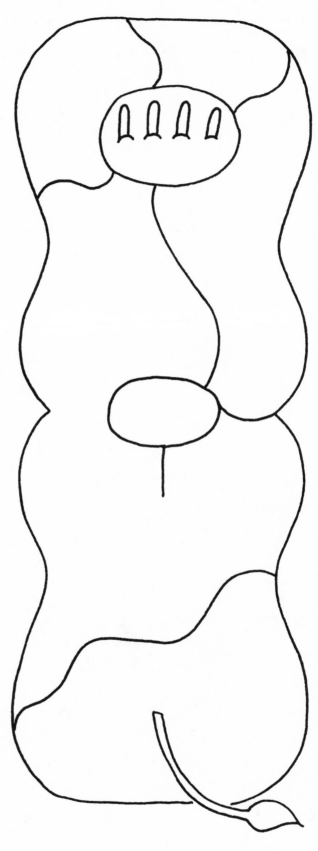

FIGURE G

PALOMINO

FIGURE A

This unique, one-person-horse costume is worn upright for total comfort. The wearer's face is concealed, but vision is unimpaired.

DESCRIPTION: Horse headpiece, slip-on felt body, and hooves.

MATERIALS: 1 piece of white poster board; 1 yd. gray and ½ yd. white 72-in.-wide felt; 1 square each of black and purple felt; glue; hole punch; round-cord elastic; double-stick tape.

PREPARATIONS: Enlarge body, hoof, horseshoe, and tail pieces shown in figure B and head, neck, mane and bangs, eye, pupil and eyelash pieces, nostril, bit, and rein pieces in figure C onto newspaper or brown wrapping paper; cut out. Hold up hoof pattern to the wearer's hand to check fit; if the pattern is more than 1 in. larger than the hand all around, trim to fit. Following figure B, lay body, 2 hooves, 2 tails, and head pattern pieces onto folded gray felt; cut out. Following figure B, lay out neck, mane and bang pieces, horseshoe, tail, eye, and nostril pattern pieces onto folded white felt, placing pieces close together to allow enough remaining fabric to make coat markings for the body; cut out. Trace two base head pattern pieces (figure C) and a 2-×-18-in. band piece onto white poster board; cut out. Lay out and cut bit and rein pattern pieces (figure C) twice from purple felt and pupil, eyelashes, mouth, and nostril pattern pieces twice from black felt.

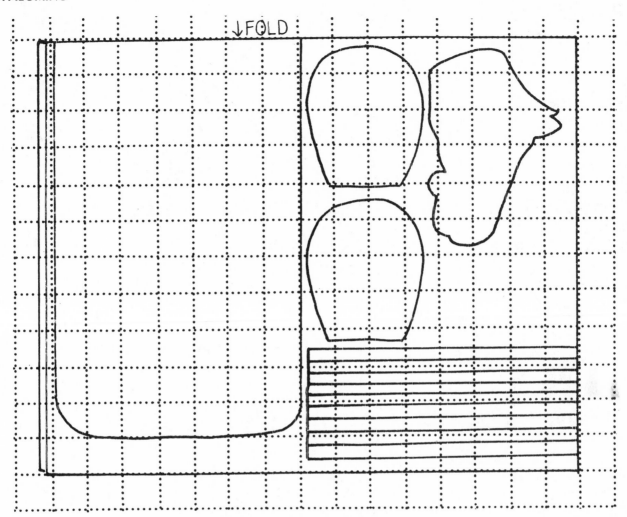

FIGURE B (1 sq. = 2 in.)

TO MAKE HEADPIECE: Cover the base head poster board pieces with gray felt head-pieces, making a right and left face (mirror image) as shown in figure D and aligning the edges; glue in place and let dry. To make each eye, layer and glue the eyelash, eye, and pupil together, aligning lower edges. For each nostril, cut white nostril piece slightly smaller all around and glue onto black nostril piece. Position and glue eye, nostril, mouth, bit and rein pieces, and mane and bang pieces onto each headpiece as shown in figure D. For left and right headpieces, glue neck piece onto wrong side of headpiece, positioning it along the lower edge as shown by the dotted line in figure D. The lower edge of the mane will overlap the neck piece slight-ly. To complete, lay one headpiece, wrong side up, and apply small pieces of double-stick tape from the nose/mouth edge to just past the bit. Place the two headpieces together, right sides out and edges aligned; finger-press to secure together. Fold poster board band in half and place between attached headpieces, positioning as shown in figure E. Using double-stick tape, secure band in place. Punch holes at the ends of the band and tie closed to fit around the head with a piece of round-cord elastic.

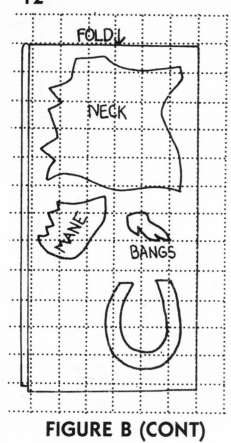

FOLD ↓

NECK

MANE

BANGS

FIGURE B (CONT)

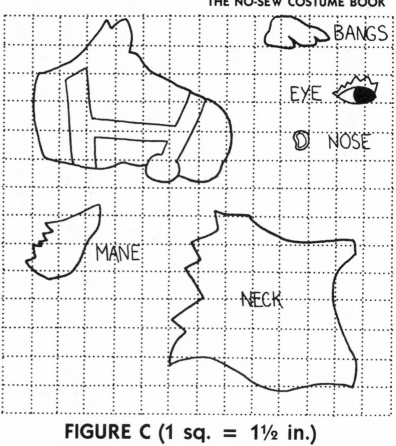

BANGS

EYE

NOSE

MANE

NECK

FIGURE C (1 sq. = 1½ in.)

FIGURE D

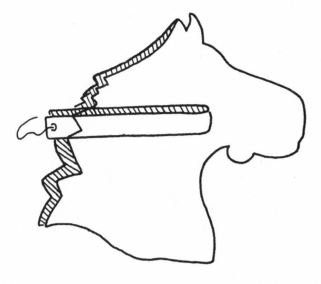

FIGURE E

TO MAKE BODY: Lay body piece out flat. Cut a 4-in. slit as shown in figure F at center of circle edge (when you wear the slip-on body, the slit will be in the back); try the body on the wearer and lengthen the slit if necessary to pull it over the head. Cut white felt coat markings — irregularly cut pieces of felt — as shown in figure F and glue to body base; trim along edges as necessary. On the back, position and glue tail pieces together; cut a small piece of white felt to cover upper tail edges and glue in place as shown in figure F.

TO MAKE HOOVES: For each hoof, place two hoof pieces together. Apply a steady stream of glue ¼ in. from the edge, along the inside (do not glue the wrist edge); align and squeeze-press to secure. Position and glue horseshoe in place as shown in figure A; let dry.

FOR ADULT SIZING: The slip-on body is the only piece that needs to be adjusted. This can easily be done by adding a few inches to the width and lengthening the body pattern piece as desired.

SUGGESTIONS: This great-looking horse can be made in brown, black, tan, or any color you choose, with markings or without.

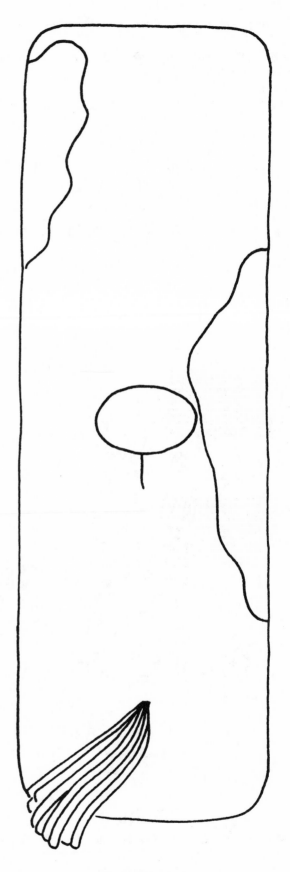

FIGURE F

LEOPARD

This fast-footed and spotted beast of the jungle is purr-fectly adorable, unbelievably easy to make, and easier yet to wear.

DESCRIPTION: Leopard headband, slip-on felt body, and claw paws.

MATERIALS: 1 piece of tan-colored (or yellow) poster board; ¾ yd. of tan (or yellow) and ½ yd. of black 72-in.-wide felt; ⅛ yd. black Con-Tact paper, optional; small piece of white Con-Tact paper or plain white paper; glue; hole punch; round-cord elastic.

PREPARATIONS: Enlarge body, tail, paws, and headband pieces as shown in figures B and C onto newspaper or brown wrapping paper; extend headband arrows an equal amount on both sides to a finished length of 18 in. Cut pieces out. Hold paw pattern up to wearer's hand; if paw is more than 1 in. bigger than hand all around, simply trim away the excess. Following figure B, lay out body, tail, and paws onto folded tan felt; cut out. From black felt, cut 75+ irregularly shaped ¾- to 1-in. spots, ten ¾-in. circular paw pads, two 1-×-2-in. oval paw pads, and 10 skinny 1-in. triangular claws. Trace headband pattern (figure C) onto tan poster board; cut out. From black Con-Tact paper or felt, cut 25 irregularly shaped ½- to ¾-in. spots, a ¾-×-1⅛-in. oval nose, 2 almond-shaped ¾-×-1¼-in. eyes, and 2 triangular 2-×-1½-×-1½-in. ear pieces. From white Con-Tact paper (or plain paper), cut 2 almond-shaped ½-×-⅝-in. pupils for the eyes.

FIGURE A

14

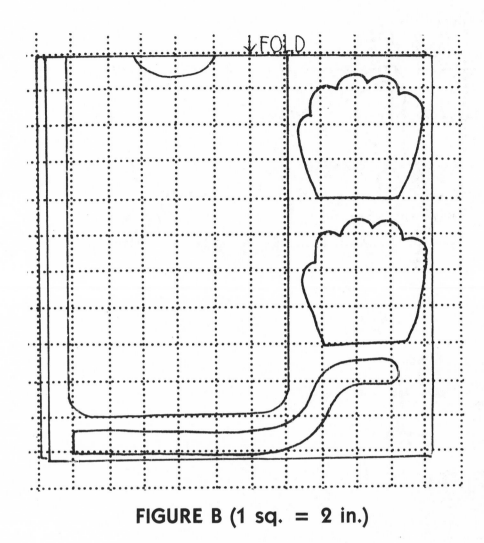

FIGURE B (1 sq. = 2 in.)

TO MAKE HEADBAND: Affix ear pieces, eyes, and pupils (glue on if plain paper) onto the headband as shown in figure C; for nose only, remove half the Con-Tact paper backing, affixing only this much to the headband and leaving the remaining half nose extending below the headband edge. Affix Con-Tact paper spots in a pleasing pattern on the headband (figure C). Punch holes at the ends of the band and tie closed to fit around the head with a piece of round-cord elastic.

TO MAKE PAWS: For each paw, glue 5 felt claws along the scalloped edge, 1 on each scallop (this will be the wrong side). Place a plain paw on top of this, aligning the edges; apply a steady stream of glue ¼ in. from the edges, along the inside (do not glue the wrist edge), and squeeze-press to secure (figure D). To complete each paw, position and glue spots on the paw front and circular and oval paw pads on the paw back as shown in figure D.

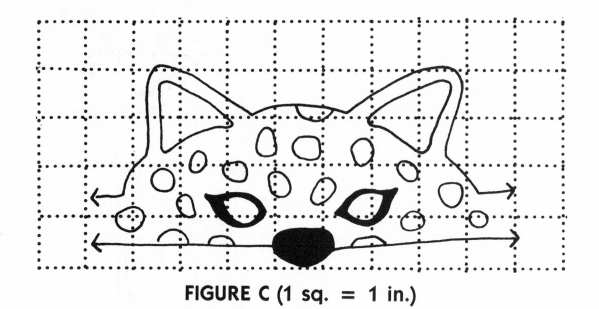

FIGURE C (1 sq. = 1 in.)

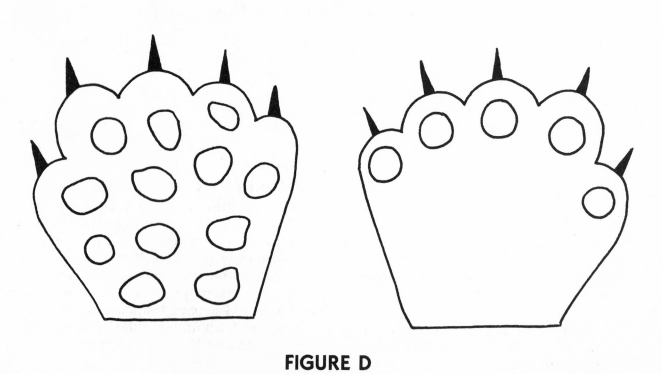

FIGURE D

TO MAKE BODY: Lay body piece out flat. Cut a 4-in. slit as shown in figure E at center of circle edge (when you wear the slip-on body, the slit will be in the back); try the body on the wearer and lengthen the slit if necessary to pull it over the head. With body piece laid flat, add the details—spots all over and the tail in the back—and glue in place (figure E).

FOR ADULT SIZING: Simply lengthen and widen the body and paw pattern pieces.

SUGGESTIONS: For a humorous, cartoon look, this costume could be made in hot pink and purple, yellow and red, or whatever you fancy.

FIGURE E

LION

FIGURE A

Making a dramatic, lionesque statement comes easily with this colorful, paper-sculpted mask and slip-on body. Because of the unique hat construction, vision remains unobstructed and unimpaired.

DESCRIPTION: Lion headdress, slip-on felt body, and claw paws.

MATERIALS: 1 piece of yellow or orange poster board; ½ yd. of matching-colored 72-in.-wide felt; ⅛ yd. of black Con-Tact paper and/or a square of black felt; 1 sheet of white crepe paper; 2 large wiggle eyes; double-stick tape; staples; hole punch; round-cord elastic; glue.

PREPARATIONS: Enlarge body, tail, paws, and eye/nose piece as shown in figures B and C onto newspaper or brown wrapping paper; cut out. Hold paw pattern up to wearer's hand; if paw is more than 1 in. bigger than hand all around, simply trim away the excess. Following figure B, lay body, tail, and paw pattern pieces on folded yellow (or orange) felt; cut out. Trace eye/nose piece and a 1¾-×-24-in. mane band onto poster board; cut out. From black felt or Con-Tact paper, cut two 1½-in. circles for eyes and a 2½-×-7-in. rectangle for whiskers. Cut 10 skinny triangular claws from black felt.

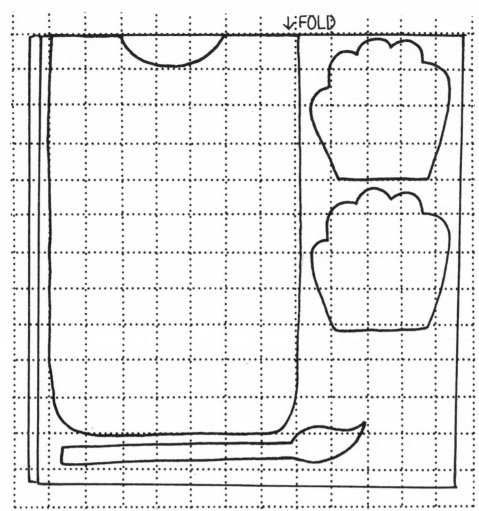

FIGURE B (1 sq. = 2 in.)

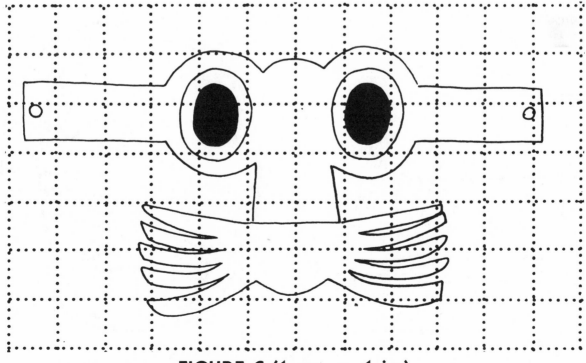

FIGURE C (1 sq. = 1 in.)

TO MAKE HEADDRESS: Make the mane by folding the sheet of crepe paper in half lengthwise; then fold in half again. Along one lengthwise edge, clip all 4 paper layers with 2-in.-deep grass cuts, 1½ to 2 in. apart (figure D). Align unclipped edge of mane close to mane band edge; staple together, leaving ½ in. at the ends of the band free (figure D). Overlap ends of band together, mane facing out, to form a circle; staple closed (figure E). Staple crepe paper over band closure, then "fluff" out mane, gently pulling the crepe paper layers apart and toward the front and back band edges to create fullness. Affix eye circles to eye/nose band (glue, if using felt) and glue wiggle eyes onto circles (figure C). Center whisker piece onto band whiskers and cut nose shape; affix (glue, if felt) to nose/whiskers; let dry and trim along whisker edges (figure C). To assemble the headdress, adhere eye/nose band to mane band, using double-stick tape, as shown in figure F (hold headdress up to wearer's face to be sure the wearer's eyes are not covered; adjust, if necessary). Punch holes at the ends of the band and tie closed to fit around the head with a piece of round-cord elastic.

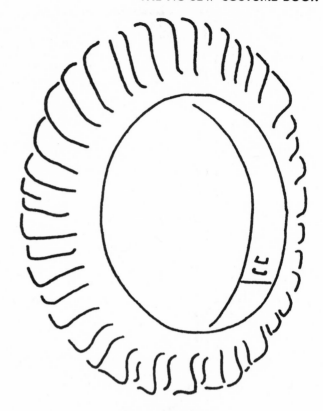

FIGURE E

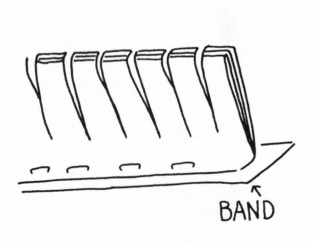

FIGURE D

FIGURE F

TO MAKE BODY: Lay body piece out flat. Cut a 4-in. slit as shown in figure G at center of circle edge (when you wear the slip-on body, the slit will be in the back); try the body on the wearer and lengthen the slit if necessary to pull it over the head. Glue tail to back as shown; let dry.

TO MAKE PAWS: For each paw, glue 5 claws along scalloped paw edge (figure H). Place a plain paw on top, aligning the edges. Apply a steady stream of glue ¼ in. from the edges on the inside (but not along the wrist edge); squeeze-press to secure together. Let dry.

FOR ADULT SIZING: Lengthen the mane band piece 2 in. and lengthen (and widen, if desired) the body pattern piece.

SUGGESTIONS: This lion is quite adorable as is, but for an added touch, you could add a medallion of courage.

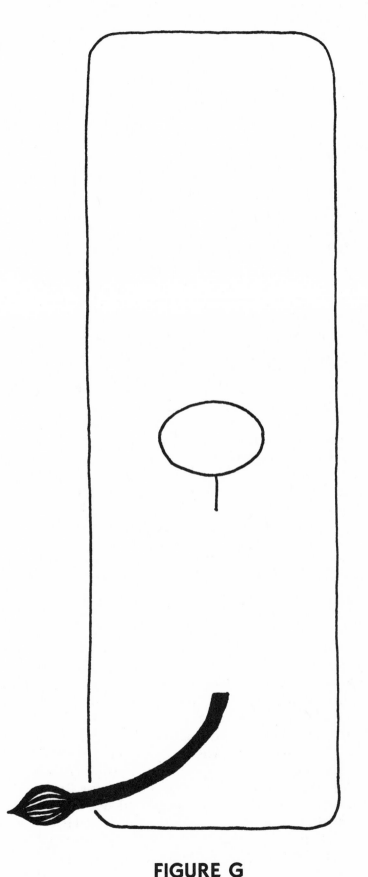

FIGURE G

FIGURE H

ELEPHANT

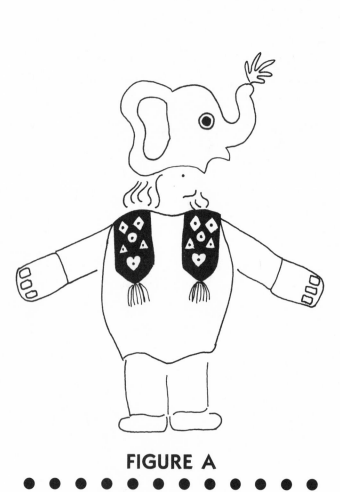

FIGURE A

This jolly elephant is colorfully dressed in circus attire with tasseled sashes hanging from the shoulders and a feather in his trunk. If you like the big look, this one's a winner.

DESCRIPTION: Elephant-head hat, body-suit with colorful circus sashes, and felt feet.

MATERIALS: 2 yds. of gray and ¼ yd. of black 72-in.-wide felt (for adult sizing, see below); 1 square of pink felt; an assortment of colorful felt scraps, yarns, and/or trims; glue; 2 large wiggle eyes or large sequins; double-stick tape; round-cord elastic; hole punch; two 4+-in. tassels, bought or hand-made; feather; 4 Velcro circles..

PREPARATIONS: Enlarge body and head pattern pieces shown in figures B and C onto newspaper or brown wrapping paper; cut out. Measure and cut a 4-×-14-in. sash pattern. Following figure B, lay body, head, and two 5-×-8-in. foot pieces onto folded gray felt; cut out, trimming away felt along inner ear and eye lines and rounding the edges of the foot pieces. Check fit of foot on wearer's hand; if more than 1 in. bigger than the hand all around, trim to fit. Lay out and cut sash pattern twice from black felt, and cut out eight 1-in. square toenails from pink felt. Trace the head pattern and a 2-×-18-in. hatband onto pink poster board; cut out.

TO MAKE HAT: On pink poster board headpieces, outline the eyes and mouth, creating a left and right face (mirror image) as shown in figure C. Position gray felt headpieces on poster board headpieces, aligning the outer edges and maintaining a left and a right face; pink will show through at the eye, inner ear, and mouth. Glue the layers together; let dry. Cut ear along trim line (beginning at bottom edge) to make it free-moving. From black felt, cut mouth and eye circle details shown in figure C and glue in place on headpieces, then glue wiggle eyes

22

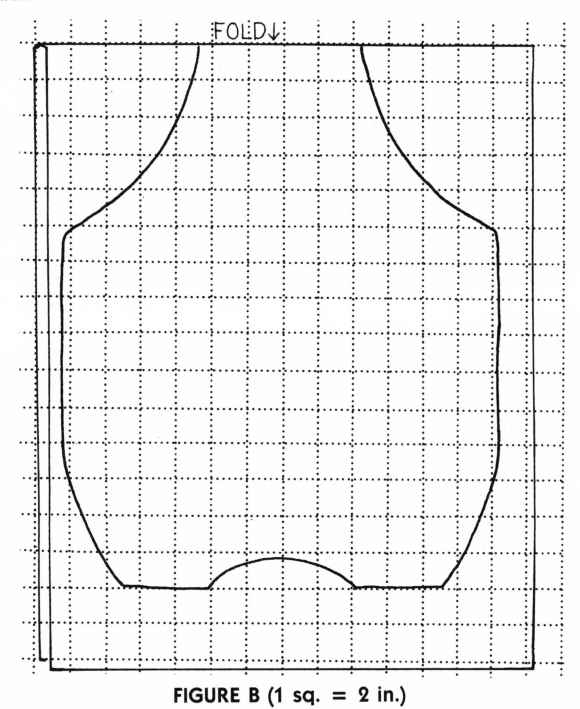

FIGURE B (1 sq. = 2 in.)

or sequins within eye circles. To construct hat, lay one headpiece, wrong side up (pink), and apply small pieces of double-stick tape from the front of the eye, top to bottom, through the trunk, leaving 1 in. untaped at the trunk end. Place the 2 headpieces together, right sides out (gray) and edges aligned; finger-press to secure together. Fold hatband in half and place between attached headpieces, along the lower edge and halfway in, as shown in figure D. Using double-stick tape, secure band in place, making sure not to attach it to the ears. Punch holes at the ends of the band and tie closed to fit around the head with a piece of round-cord elastic.

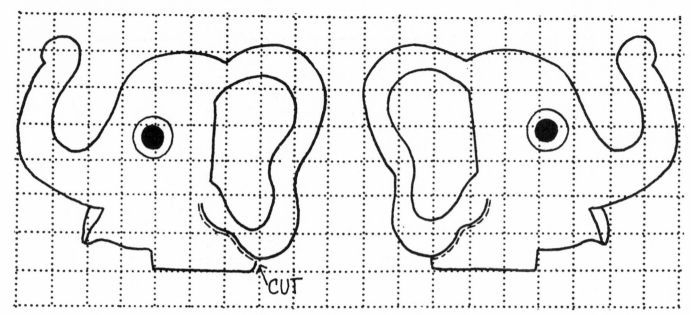

FIGURE C (1 sq. = 1½ in.)

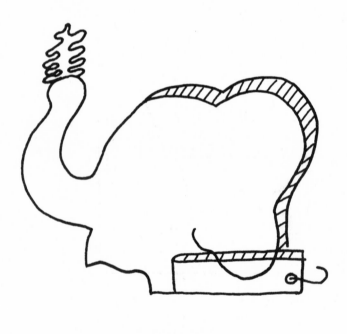

FIGURE D

TO MAKE BODYSUIT: First make the decorative sashes. Using scissors, angle the corners at one end of each sash, forming a V. Cut out an assortment of shapes—hearts, diamonds, squares, triangles, circles—from different colors of felt; the pieces should be approximately 1 to 1½ in. in size. Lay these out on the sash in a pleasing arrangement and add sequins or other decorative trims if desired; glue in place. Punch a hole near the end of each sash and carefully tie tassel in place. Lay bodysuit out flat. Align shoulder edge and top edge of sash, right sides together. Glue sash in place, applying a steady stream of glue ¼ in. from shoulder edges; repeat for other sash (this will be the back of the bodysuit) as shown in figure E. To complete the bodysuit, place front and back together, right sides out. Apply a steady stream of glue ¼ in. from back side edges, beginning at top of leg hole and extending up for 12 in. (Be sure to leave leg and armholes open.) Align pieces together and squeeze-press to secure as shown in figure F; let dry. To fasten shoulder closed for wearing, glue 2 Velcro closures along front and back shoulder edge (on wrong side of back edge); let dry.

TO MAKE FEET: For each foot, place 2 foot pieces together. Apply a steady stream of glue ¼ in. from the edge, along the inside (do not glue wrist edge); align and squeeze-press to secure. Glue 3 or 4 toenails along upper edge (figure A).

FOR ADULT SIZING: The bodysuit is the only thing that needs to be adjusted. This can be done easily by adding a minimum of 2 in. to each side and to the length of the bodysuit pattern. Before cutting into felt, hold adjusted pattern up to wearer to assure fit.

SUGGESTIONS: For a whimsical touch, this elephant can be made in pink all over, or it can take on the look of a storybook character with the addition of appropriate clothes, e.g., vest, tie, king's cape and medallion, etc. For a chubby look, stuff with wadded-up tissue paper or netting.

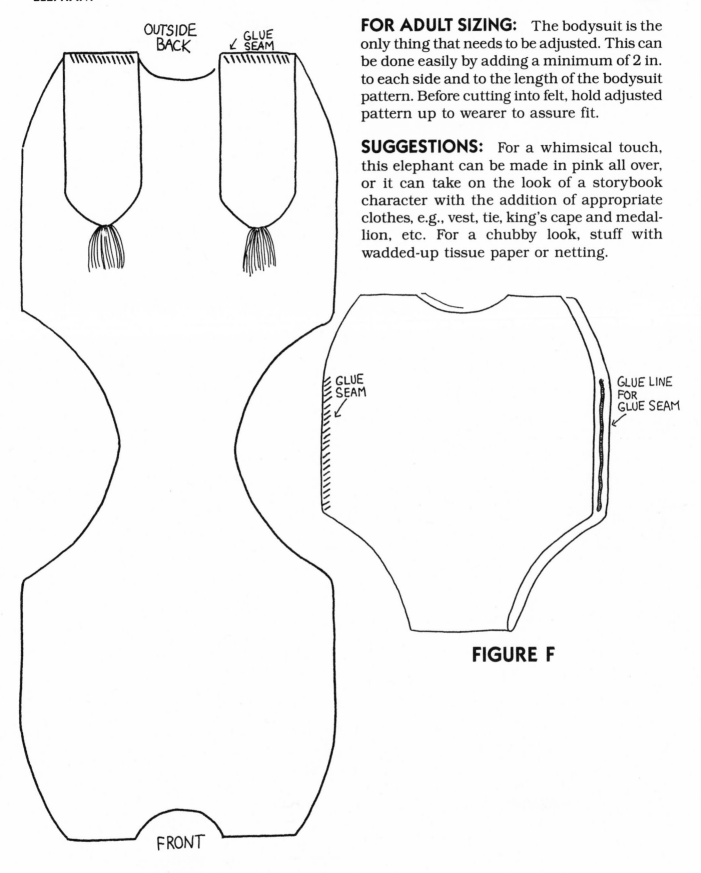

OUTSIDE BACK

GLUE SEAM

FRONT

FIGURE E

GLUE SEAM

GLUE LINE FOR GLUE SEAM

FIGURE F

HIPPO

FIGURE A

This hippy hippo takes on a real personality with accessories of your choice, whether it be a tutu or a necktie. The simple "shoebox" hat evokes the true image of this favored animal.

DESCRIPTION: Sponge-printed hippo-head hat and slip-on body with tutu or tie.

MATERIALS: 6 pieces of pink poster board; black and white poster paints (or gray poster paint); household sponge; 1 square each of black and white felt; round-cord elastic; staples; double-stick tape; adhesive or other thick tape; ½ yd. hot pink netting (for tutu), plus 2 yds. of coordinating-color 1-in.-wide ribbon, or a necktie, plus 2 yds. of coordinating-color 1-in.-wide ribbon.

PREPARATIONS: Lightly sponge-print 4 pieces of pink poster board on one side. To do this, pour and mix some black and white (or gray) poster paint into a shallow, wide bowl or plastic container. Dip one side of the sponge into the paint, then lightly press the paint-coated side onto the poster board to cover with a bit of the pink showing through. Let dry. Enlarge head pattern as shown in figure B onto newspaper or brown wrapping paper (note, this hat is a combination of simple shapes, making pattern enlargement an easy task); cut out. Trace head pattern (marking in the fold lines), 2-×-18-in. headband, and two 2-×-12-in. shoulder bands onto unpainted side of poster board; cut out. From remaining painted poster board, cut twenty-six 2-×-20-in. strips. For the body base, cut 2 rectangles from unpainted poster board, 18 × 22 in., and round off the corners. From black felt, cut two 1-in. circles for the eyes, two ¾-in. circles for the nostrils, two 1¼-×-1¼-×1¾-in. triangular-shaped inner ears (see figure B), and a ⅛-×-12-in. strip for the mouth. Cut 2 teeth, 1 × 1¼ in., from white felt.

26

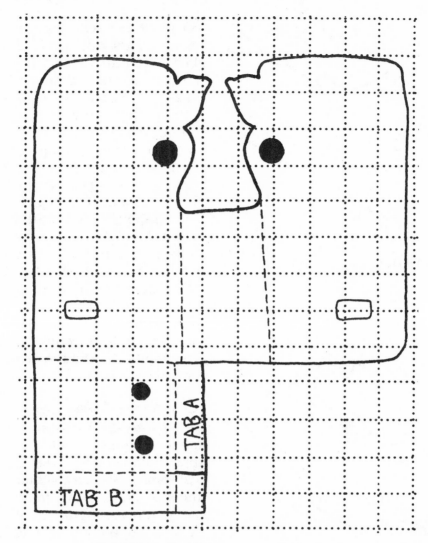

FIGURE B (1 sq. = 1½ in.)

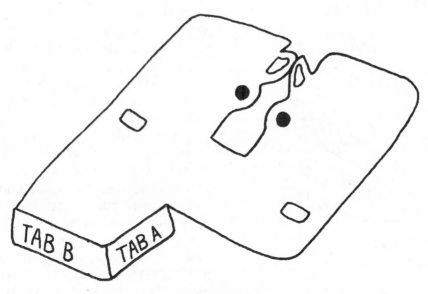

FIGURE C

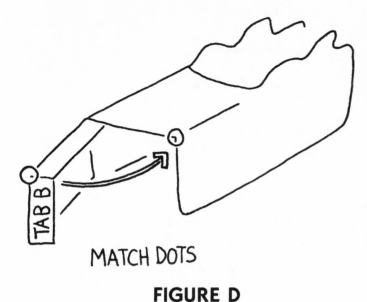

MATCH DOTS

FIGURE D

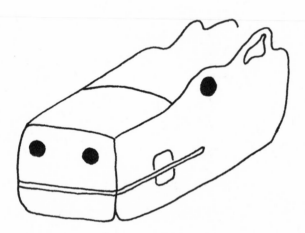

FIGURE E

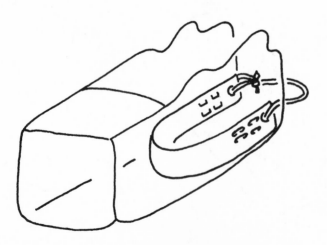

FIGURE F

TO MAKE HAT: Position and glue eyes, nostrils, ears, and teeth onto headpiece as shown in figure B; let dry. Crease the hat along the fold lines (note, there are 5); cut slits along lines A and B, as marked (figure B). Fold Tab A under Tab B (figure C) and Tab B under front face edge (figure D). Staple together at lower front face edge; tape tab down along the inside. Looking in from underneath, the hat resembles an open shoebox. Position and glue felt mouth strip in place, starting on one face, wrapping around the snout, and finishing on the opposite face, as shown in figure E. To complete the hat, fold poster board band in half and position along the inside face sections as shown in figure F. Staple the band to the face on each side, 3 in. and 4 in. from the band end, stapling from the inside. Punch holes at the ends of the band, and tie closed to fit around the head with a piece of round-cord elastic.

TO MAKE BODY: Cover base body pieces with 2-×-20-in. strips, starting from the top and overlapping each preceding strip by approximately ½ in. To secure strips and conceal staples, place unpainted side of strip end under body base, 1 in. in from the side edge; staple in place (figure G). Wrap strip across right side of body base, fold end under, and staple from underneath. Continue in this manner as shown in figure G until the front and back are completed. Hold one body piece up to the wearer and mark the position of the shoulder edges onto the top edge; transfer these marks onto the top edge of the back body piece. Staple the ends of the shoulder bands to the wrong side of the front and back body pieces at the shoulder marks to fit, stapling under the strips, as shown in figure H. Cover staples on the inside, if desired, with long, neatly laid strips of adhesive tape. Punch a hole approximately halfway up both sides of the front and back body pieces; lace one piece of ribbon on each side, through front and back, and tie closed when worn. Tying the pieces together makes the body bow out, creating a fat appearance. To make a tutu, fold netting in half lengthwise and lace a 45-in. piece of round-cord elastic ½ in.

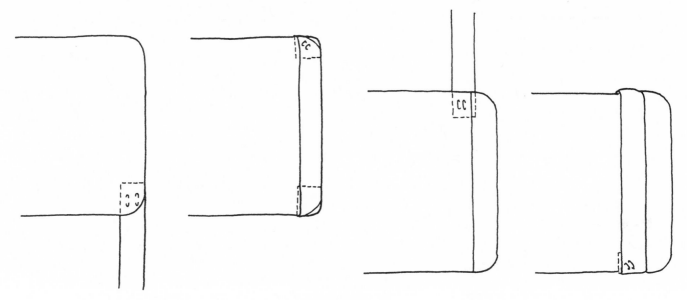

FIGURE G

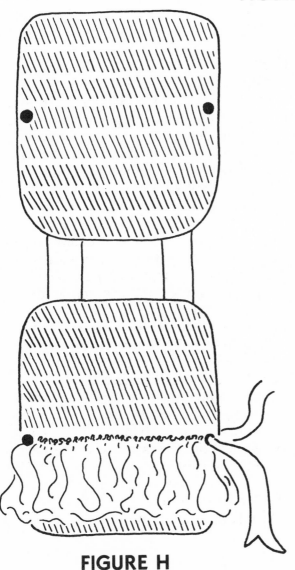

FIGURE H

FIGURE I

from the cut edges through both layers, weaving in and out of the holes, every inch or so, as shown in figure I. Repeat this procedure ¼ in. away from first gathering line. Gather the netting up to fit across the width of the body front and tie the remaining elastic ends together on the wrong side. For a masculine effect, simply tie on a necktie.

FOR ADULT SIZING: The slip-on body is the only piece that needs to be adjusted. Simply lengthen body pattern pieces.

SUGGESTIONS: Although the painted body strips add a lot of texture and an appearance of fullness, the front and back body pieces can simply be sponge-painted and the hippo will still be a winner.

BEAR

FIGURE A

Cuddly, comfortable, and cute beyond compare, who could find fault with this adorable bear? The three-dimensional headband, round-bellied body, and claw mitts are all easy to make and are a hit at any age.

DESCRIPTION: Bear headband, slip-on felt body, and claw mitts.

MATERIALS: 1 piece of brown poster board; ⅓ yd. light brown and ½ yd. dark brown 72-in.-wide felt; 1 square black felt; glue; dry household sponge; round-cord elastic; double-stick tape; hole punch.

PREPARATIONS: Enlarge body pattern piece and inner circle in figure B; headband pieces 1, 2, 3, and 4 (figure C); and mitt (figure G) onto newspaper or brown wrapping paper. Extend ear band and eye band arrows an equal amount on both sides for a finished length of 14½ in. for the ear band and 18 in. for the eye band. Cut out all pieces. Hold mitt pattern up to wearer's hand to check for fit. If the mitt is more than 1 in. bigger than hand all around, simply trim away the excess. Lay out body pattern piece (figure B) and 2 mitt pieces (figure G) onto dark brown folded felt; cut out. From the remainder, cut a 4-×-4-in. tail on the fold (figure F). From light brown felt, cut 1 body inner circle piece, 1 muzzle (piece #4), two 1¼-in. circles for the eyes, and two 1½-in. circles for the ear pads, trimming ear-pad circles to create a straight edge as shown (figure C). From black felt, cut two ¾-in. eyeballs, the nose—1-×-1-in. rounded square, trimmed along one long edge at both sides to form the lower nose area—as shown in figure C, and 10 small skinny triangles for the mitt claws (figure G). Trace headband pieces 1, 2, 3, and 4 onto brown poster board; cut out.

30

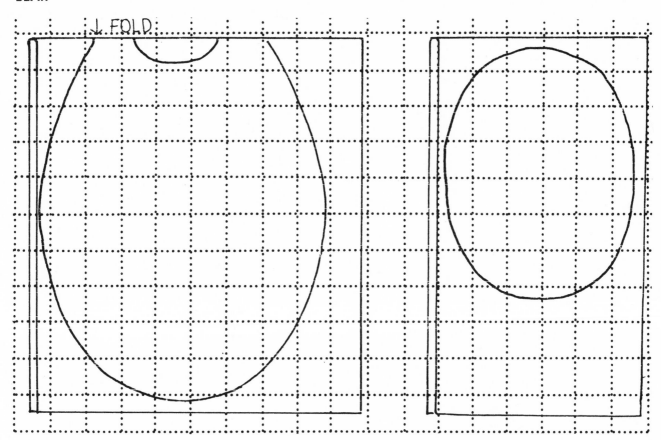

FIGURE B (1 sq. = 2 in.)

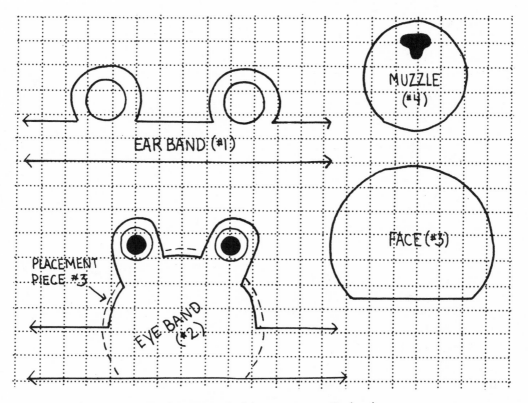

FIGURE C (1 sq. = 2 in.)

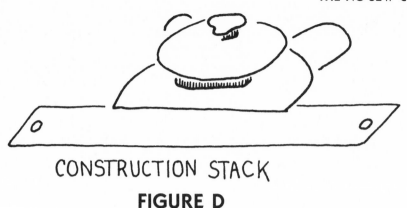

CONSTRUCTION STACK
FIGURE D

TO MAKE HEADBAND: Glue ear pads onto the ears. Glue black felt eyeballs onto brown felt eye circles and position and glue onto eye band as shown in figure C. Glue felt muzzle (piece #4) onto poster board muzzle and black nose onto a piece of brown poster board, trimming to the edge of the felt; let all pieces dry. To create the 3-D effect, the pieces will be stacked and glued on top of each other (figure D). To assemble, first glue face (piece #3) onto eye band; center and align straight bottom edges, as shown by the broken line in figure C. Cut a 2-in. circle of sponge and glue to center of face. Center and glue muzzle (#4) on top of sponge. Cut a ¼-×-¾-in. rectangle of sponge; glue sideways to muzzle at nose placement. Glue nose to sponge; let dry. To finish assembly, punch holes at the ends of the band and tie closed to fit around the head with a piece of round-cord elastic. To attach ear band to eye band, measure in and mark 3 in. from the eye band ends for placement; secure ear band ends in place, using double-stick tape. Fold ears up, perpendicular to ear band, as shown in figure E. Optional finishing touch: To conceal sponge from view, cut narrow strips of felt and glue to sponge edge.

FIGURE E

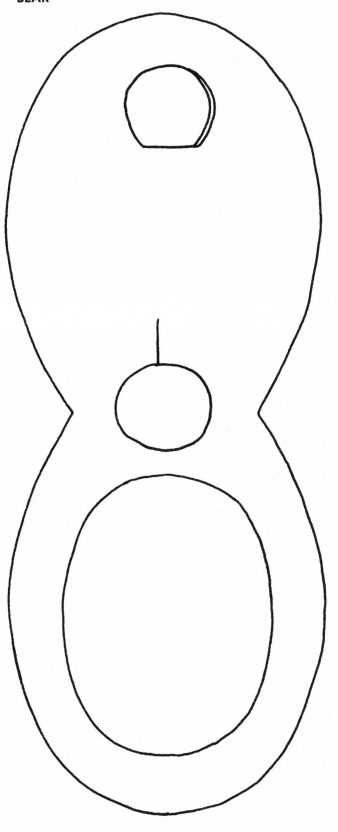

TO MAKE BODY: Lay body piece out flat. Cut a 4-in. slit as shown in figure F at center of circle edge (when you wear the slip-on body, the slit will be in the back); try the body on the wearer and lengthen the slit if necessary to pull it over the head. Glue felt inner belly piece in center of body front and tail piece on body back (figure F).

TO MAKE CLAW MITTS: For each mitt, place two mitt pieces together. Apply a steady stream of glue ¼ in. from the side edges on the inside (but not along the wrist edge); align pieces together and squeeze-press to secure. Glue black felt claws in place (figure G). Let dry.

FOR ADULT SIZING: The slip-on body is all you need to adjust. Simply lengthen the body pattern piece.

SUGGESTIONS: For a nontraditional teddy bear look, this costume can be made in whatever colors you choose.

FIGURE F

FIGURE G

HOUND DOG

FIGURE A

For a domestic-animal lover, this all-American hound dog is a comfortable, easy-to-wear costume, particularly appealing to young children.

DESCRIPTION: Tricolored dog-head hat, slip-on felt body with tail, and paws.

MATERIALS: 1 piece of brown poster board; ½ yd. brown, ¼ yd. black, and ¼ yd. white 72-in.-wide felt; white (and black, optional) Con-Tact paper; large wiggle eyes; 1½

ft. ribbon for collar (optional); double-stick tape; glue; round-cord elastic; hole punch.

PREPARATIONS: Enlarge body, tail, and paw (figure B) and dog head, nose mask, ear, and chin pattern pieces (figure C) onto newspaper or brown wrapping paper; cut out. Hold paw pattern up to wearer's hand to check for fit. If the paw is more than 1 in. bigger than the hand all around, simply trim away the excess. Following figure B, lay body, paw, and tail pattern pieces on folded brown felt; cut out. Cut 2 ears, eight 1-in. paw spots, and eight small triangular claws (figure G) from black felt and 2 noses (figure D) from black felt or Con-Tact paper. Cut tail tip (figure F) from white felt, 2 nose masks from white Con-Tact paper or felt, and 2 neck pieces from white Con-Tact paper. Save remaining white felt for body and paw spots (figures F and G). Trace head pattern piece and a 2-×-18-in. headband onto brown poster board; cut out.

TO MAKE HAT: Affix Con-Tact paper nose mask and neck piece, glue ears, and double-stick tape nose and ribbon collar (optional) to right and left dog head face pieces as shown in figure D. Optional: Using a hole punch, punch 8 to 10 brown dots from scrap poster board or felt; double-stick tape in place around the nose for freckles. Glue eyes in place; let dry. To construct hat, lay one face piece, wrong side up, and apply small pieces of double-stick tape to cover the snout area. Place the 2 face pieces together, right sides out and edges aligned; finger-press to secure together. Fold poster board headband in half and place between attached face pieces,

34

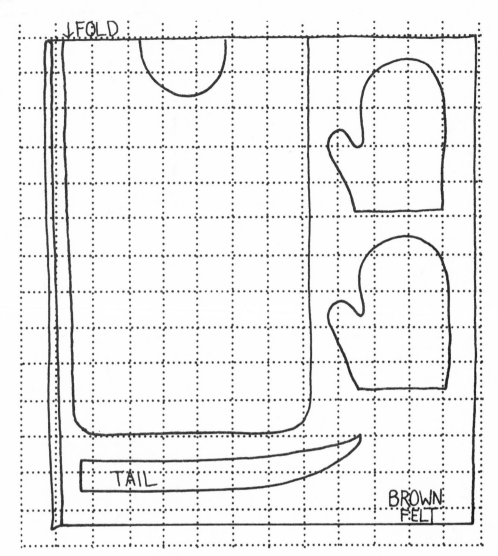

↓FOLD

TAIL

BROWN FELT

FIGURE B (1 sq. = 2 in.)

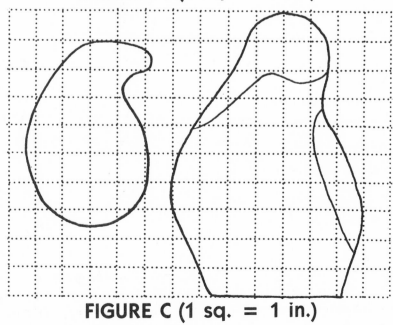

FIGURE C (1 sq. = 1 in.)

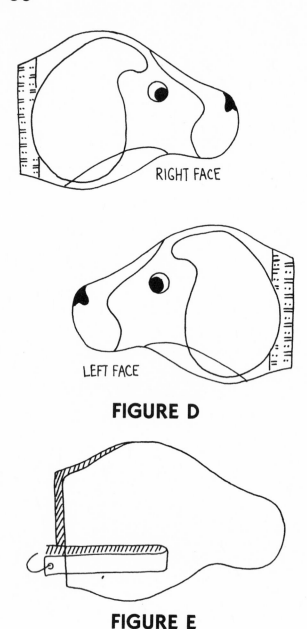

RIGHT FACE

LEFT FACE

FIGURE D

FIGURE E

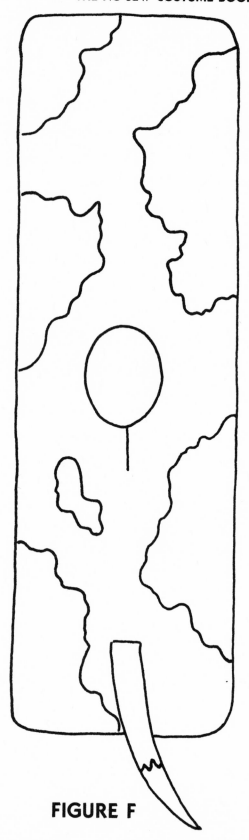

FIGURE F

along the lower edge and about halfway in, as shown in figure E. Using double-stick tape, secure band in place. Punch holes at ends of band and tie closed to fit around the head with a piece of round-cord elastic.

TO MAKE BODY: Lay body piece out flat. Cut a 4-in. slit as shown in figure F at center of circle edge (when you wear the slip-on body, the slit will be in the back); try the body on the wearer and lengthen slit if necessary to pull it over the head. Cut white felt spots and glue to body front and back as shown (figure F); trim along edges as necessary. Glue white felt tail tip onto brown tail piece; glue tail to body back as shown (figure F); let dry.

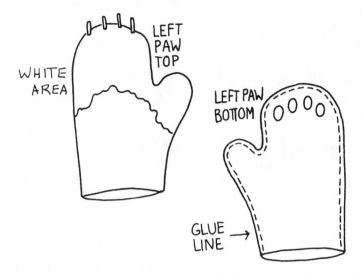

FIGURE G

TO MAKE PAWS: Cut 2 white felt spots equal to the paw width and about ⅓ the length, as shown in figure G; glue in place on a right and left paw piece, trim along edges if necessary, and let dry. For each paw, place a spotted (top) paw piece and plain paw piece together, right sides out. Apply a steady stream of glue ¼ in. from the side edges on the inside (but not along the wrist edge); align the pieces together and squeeze-press to secure; let dry. Glue 4 black paw spots to plain side and 4 claws along white-spotted paw edge as shown (figure G); let dry.

FOR ADULT SIZING: All you need to do is lengthen the body pattern as desired and widen the paws, using your own hand as a guide.

SUGGESTIONS: You can use fun fur for the body, ears, and paws instead of felt, or you can substitute fun fur for the ears only.

CHAPTER II

CREEPERS, CRAWLERS, SWIMMERS, AND FLIERS

OCTOPUS

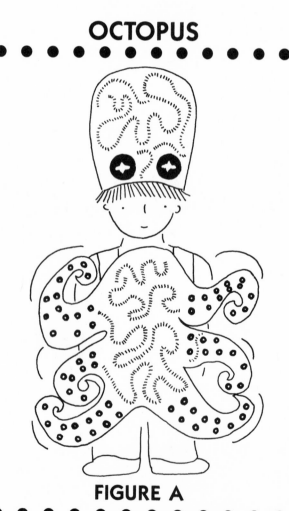

FIGURE A

For all you salty dogs, this whimsical bottom dweller is a real kick! Neon or metallic details give this octopus an electric presence (see illustration on front cover).

DESCRIPTION: Octopus headband and slip-on octopus body.

MATERIALS: 3 pieces of black poster board; small pieces of fluorescent poster board or metallic paper in assorted colors; small piece of black Con-Tact paper or poster board; small piece of dry household sponge (for eye foundation); round-cord elastic; glue; staples; hole punch.

PREPARATIONS: Enlarge body and head pattern pieces in figures B and C onto newspaper or brown wrapping paper and cut out. Trace 2 body patterns, 1 head pattern, and two 2-×-12-in. shoulder bands onto black poster board. Trace two 3-in.-round eye circles onto 1 color of fluorescent poster board. Cut all pieces out (figures B and C). Trace and cut approximately 75 circles, ranging in size from ½ in. to 1¼ in., from fluorescent poster board or metallic paper for the suckers.

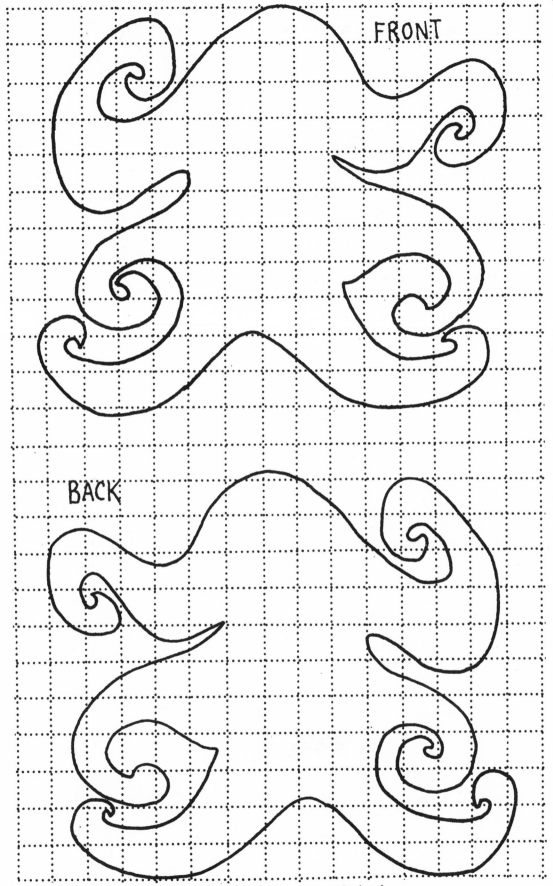

FRONT

BACK

FIGURE B (1 sq. = 2 in.)

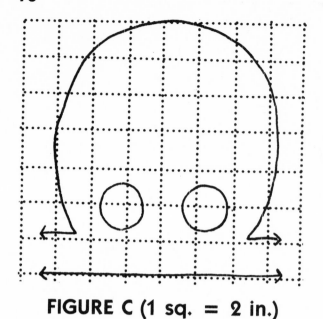

FIGURE C (1 sq. = 2 in.)

TO MAKE HEADBAND: First make the eyes. Trace the 2 poster board eye circles onto the black Con-Tact paper and cut out. One at a time, fold the Con-Tact paper circles in half and cut a narrow 2-in.-long slit along the fold line; then cut a small notch at the center of the slit as shown in figure D. Align and affix the black circles onto the poster board eye pieces. To attach the eyes to the headband, glue two 1-in.-square pieces of dry sponge onto band at eye locations; center and glue eye pieces onto sponge and let dry. Punch holes at the ends of the band and tie closed to fit around the head with a piece of round-cord elastic.

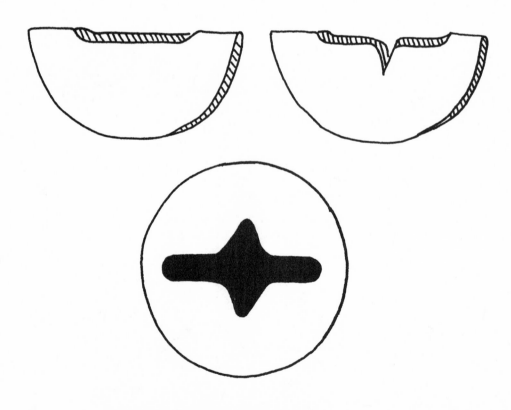

FIGURE D

TO MAKE BODY: On the front body piece, glue circular poster board suckers onto the arms in random fashion as shown in figure E; let dry. Hold this piece up to the wearer and mark the position of the shoulder edges onto the top edge; transfer these marks onto the top edge of the back body piece. Staple the ends of each shoulder strap to the wrong side of the front and back body pieces at the shoulder marks to fit, as shown in figure E.

FOR ADULT SIZING: No changes are necessary.

SUGGESTIONS: This octopus looks terrific made in any fluorescent color.

FIGURE E

LOBSTER

FIGURE A

Slipping into this red-hot lobster with menacing pincer claws, a nicely flanged shell, pop-out eyes, and tentacles is a lot more comforting than a plunge into boiling water! This costume ranks very high on ease of wearability and comfort (see illustration on front cover).

DESCRIPTION: Lobster headband, slip-on fabric shell body, with fins and pincer claws.

MATERIALS: 1 yd. of 72-in.-wide red felt; 1 piece of red poster board; clear Con-Tact paper (optional); 2 large wiggle eyes; round-cord elastic; hole punch; straight pins; ruler or measuring tape; glue.

PREPARATIONS: To maximize the use of the red felt, enlarge body, fin, and claw pattern pieces in figure B onto newspaper or brown wrapping paper; cut out. Following the layout (figure B), pin the patterns onto the folded felt and cut out. Note fin pattern is laid out 3 times for a total of 6 pieces. Enlarge and trace the headband onto red poster board as shown in figure C, extending the band arrows an equal amount on each side to a full band length of 18 in. Affix a piece of clear Con-Tact paper over the tracing to cover the headband (optional) and cut out. The addition of Con-Tact paper makes the headband more durable, but it will survive many wearings without this backing.

TO MAKE HEADBAND: Glue wiggle eyes onto eye projections as shown in figure C; let dry. Punch holes at the ends of the band and tie closed to fit around the head with a piece of round-cord elastic.

TO MAKE BODY: Lay body piece out flat. Cut a 4-in. slit as shown in figure F at center of circle edge (when you wear the slip-on body, the slit will be in the back); try the body on the wearer and extend the slit if necessary to pull it over the head. To make the flanges, following figure D, place pins along both side edges of the front and back shell body. For each side edge, work from the bottom edge up and measure and pin in this sequence: ½

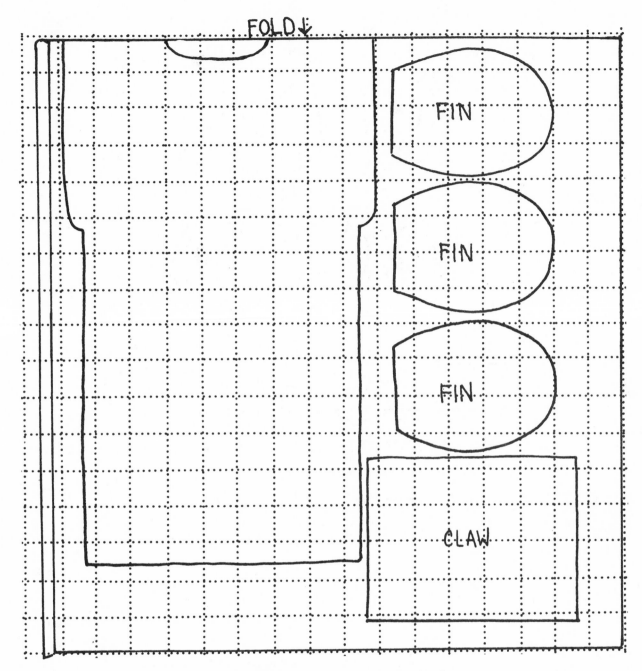

FIGURE B (1 sq. = 2 in.)

in., 3½ in., 4 in., 2¼ in., 4 in., 1¾ in., and 2½ in. You will have 7 pins on each side edge for a total of 28. Working with the shell front first, on each side edge, match up pins as shown in figure E, matching pin 2 to 1, 4 to 3, and 6 to 5; secure with pins. When both front side edges are matched and pinned a fold is created across the shell body. Glue the underside of the fold in place as shown in figure E. Pin #7 marks the hemline; turn up and glue the hem edge in place (figure E). Repeat this same procedure for the shell back. Flip the shell body right side out (the previous folding and gluing created the wrong side), and, using scissors, scallop the edges of the flanges as shown in figure F. Add 3 fins each to the wrong side of the front and back hem edge, angling them as indicated in figure F (center straight and side fins angling outward); glue in place and let dry.

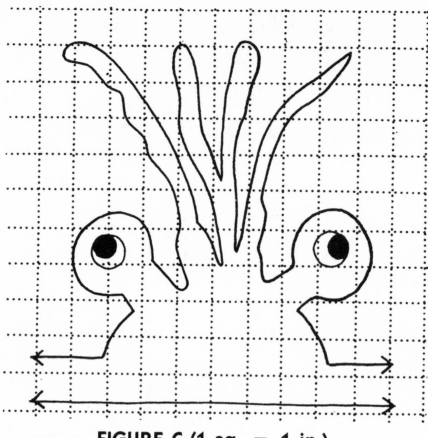

FIGURE C (1 sq. = 1 in.)

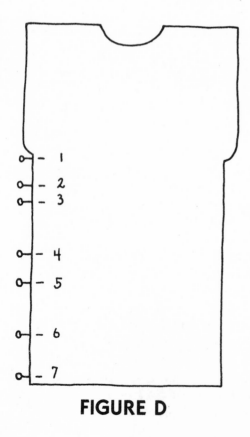

FIGURE D

PLEAT & HEM
CONSTRUCTION

1/2

3/4

5/6

7

FIGURE E

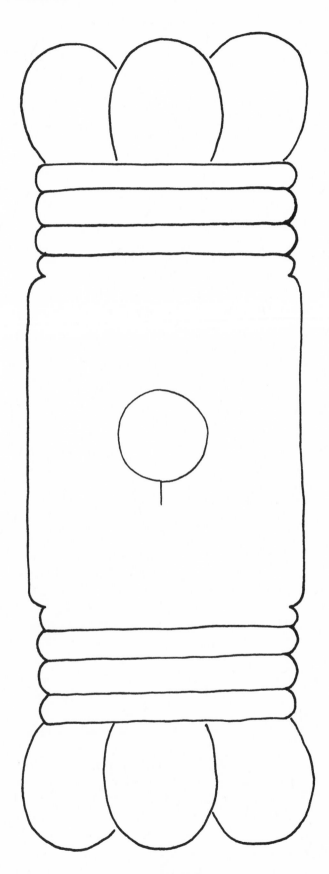

FIGURE F

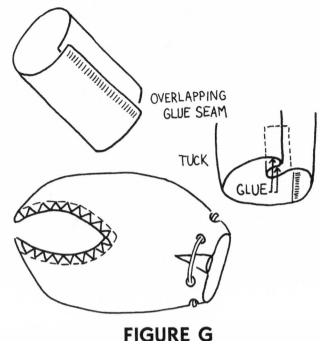

FIGURE G

TO MAKE CLAWS: For each claw, overlap long edge of felt approximately ½ in., forming a tube, and glue in place (figure G). Flatten tube with seamed edge at one side; at opposite side along one top edge, form a ½-in. tuck as shown in figure G and glue tuck in place. Keeping tube in same flattened position, cut claw shape through both layers at untucked edge as shown in finished claw view. Glue these two cut layers together about ½ in. from claw edge; let dry. To form zigzagged edge, pink the claw edge with pinking shears or cut out notches, being careful not to cut into the glue "seam." To finish each claw, using a hole punch, make 4 holes, ½ in. in from wrist end as shown. Lace an 8-in. piece of round-cord elastic through holes, place claw on hand, and tie elastic closed to secure (figure G).

FOR ADULT SIZING: Lengthen the body piece by adding to the top (neck) edge of the pattern—a few inches should be more than sufficient. The claw pattern can easily be lengthened and widened a few inches to accommodate a larger hand.

SUGGESTIONS: Dress this lobster up, if you wish, with a shell necklace or lobster bib or simply carry a shell in your claw.

SEA HORSE

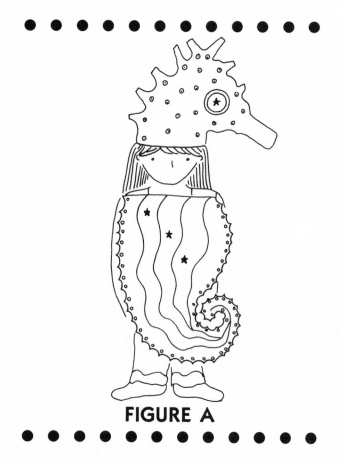

FIGURE A

The ancient-looking, almost mythical sea horse is reinterpreted here for a shimmery look. Simple cutout detailing and decorations make this costume stand out in the crowd.

DESCRIPTION: Sea horse slip-on body and headband.

MATERIALS: 3 pieces of green poster board; 6 yds. of strung sequins (2 yds. per color, preferably hot pink, turquoise, and yellow or green); 4 large pink star sequins or sequin-style plastic stars or gummed stick-on stars (optional); glue; round-cord elastic; staples; double-stick tape; hole punch.

PREPARATIONS: Enlarge head and body pattern pieces shown in figures B and C onto newspaper or brown wrapping paper; cut out. Measure and cut out a 2-×-18-in. headband pattern and a 2-×-12-in. shoulder band pattern. Trace head pattern and the shoulder band twice and body pattern and the headband once onto poster board; cut out. Cut notches around edge of 1 body piece as shown in figure E; transfer these cut lines onto second body piece and cut out these notches.

TO MAKE HEADBAND: Add face details as shown in figure B as follows. Affix star eye in position with glue or tape; then glue strung sequins in circles around the eye. Glue individual sequins—removed from the strings—randomly on the face, mixing the colors; let dry. Center the face on the poster board headband and attach with double-stick tape (indicated by shading) as shown in figure D. Note that the right (nose side) extreme corner of the face bottom will not be secured to the band. Punch holes at the ends of the headband and tie closed to fit around the head with a piece of round-cord elastic.

TO MAKE BODY: Before adding details to the front of the body, correctly position the piece so that the belly/tail edge is on the same side as the nose of the finished headband, creating a profile view of a sea horse as in figure A. To add front body details, draw a thin, wavy line of glue, following figure E,

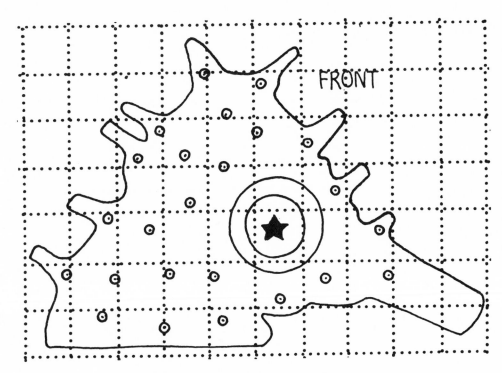

FIGURE B (1 sq. = 1½ in.)

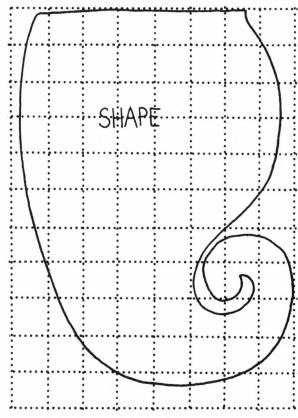

FIGURE C (1 sq. = 2 in.)

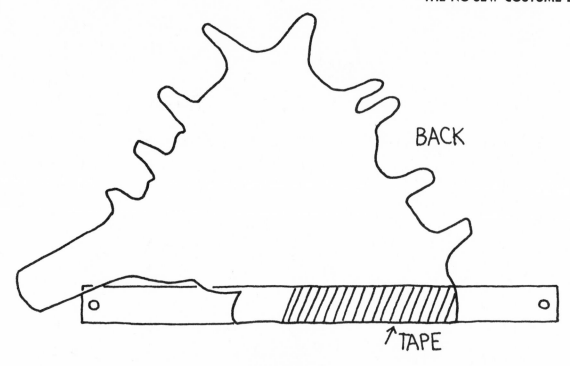

FIGURE D

down the body for the first strand of sequins. Lay the strung sequins, thread side down, carefully in place on the glue line. Repeat this procedure for the remaining 3 lines of alternating sequin colors. Add 3 stars as shown in figure A (optional). Let dry. Hold the front up to the wearer and mark the position of the shoulder edges onto the top edge; transfer these marks onto the top edges of the back body piece. Staple the ends of each shoulder band to the wrong side of the front and back body pieces at the shoulder marks to fit, making sure that the back belly/tail is positioned on the same side as the front as shown in figure E.

FOR ADULT SIZING: To add length to the pattern, draw a line across the body at the level of the star on the right. Cut the pattern in 2 pieces along this line. Create the new pattern by laying the 2 pieces 2 to 4 in. apart, depending on the desired finished length. Complete body edge, repeating the notch pattern freehand.

SUGGESTIONS: Although green seems to be a very seaworthy color for a sea horse, you may choose any color. If strung sequins are not available in your color choices, you can get the same effect using individual sequins or you can use glitter glue.

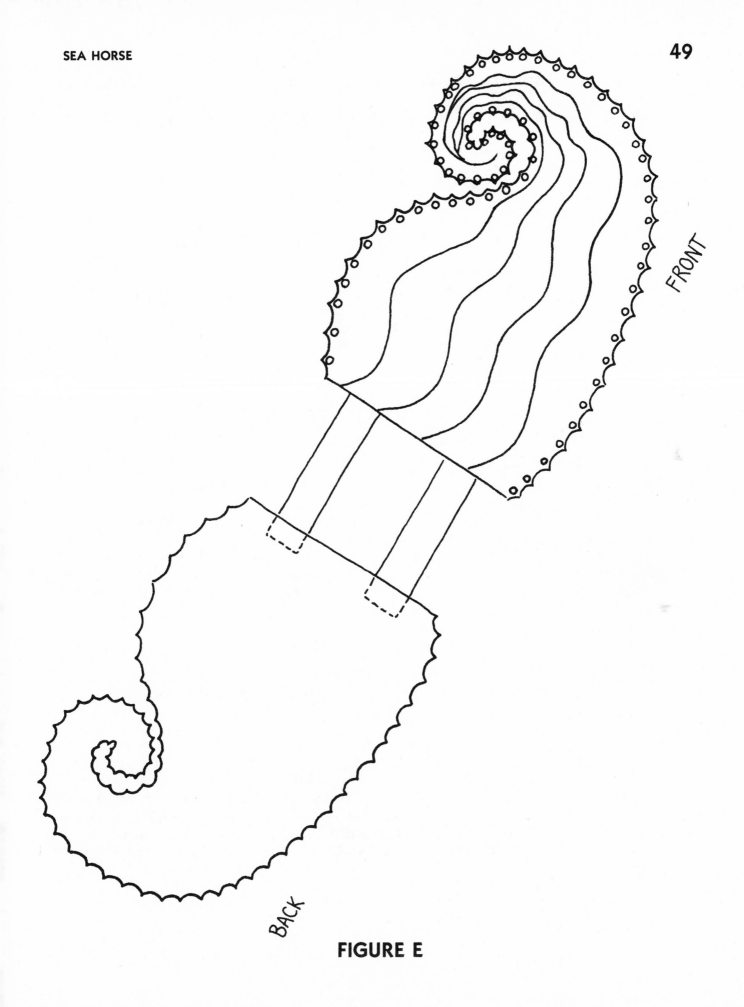

FRONT

BACK

FIGURE E

FROG

FIGURE A

This not-so-slimy frog is really sweet. It's got real frog looks—warts and all—and it can be worn comfortably at any age, from toddler to adult!

DESCRIPTION: Frog headband, slip-on fabric body, and webbed feet.

MATERIALS: Green poster board; 2 small squares light green felt; 1 yd. of 72-in.-wide dark green felt; ⅛ yd. 72-in.-wide black felt; silver-metallic or black-chenille pipe cleaners; 2 large wiggle eyes; round-cord elastic; hole punch; glue; 2 black checkers (optional).

PREPARATIONS: Enlarge body and foot pattern pieces in figure B and headband pattern piece in figure C, extending the band arrows equally on each side to a full band length of 18 in., onto newspaper or brown wrapping paper; cut out. Following the layout in figure B, pin the patterns onto the folded, dark green felt and cut out. Cut ½-×-18-in. strips and ½-×-5-in. strips from black felt for rib detail to be used on body; cut mouth and nose details. Save the remaining fabric for the details that will be cut as you are making the costume. Trace headband pattern onto green poster board; cut out.

TO MAKE HEADBAND: Glue wiggle eyes to checker centers; glue checkers onto headband at eye positions. Affix nose and mouth as shown (figure C). Cut approximately fifty ½-in. light green felt circular dots and 30 slightly larger black felt dots. Ten green and 4 black dots are used on the head; set aside remaining dots for use on the body and feet. Lay out an assortment of single green dots and double dots (green dots glued onto black dots) on frog face to create a warty effect and glue all dots in place. Punch holes at the ends of the band and tie closed to fit around the head with a piece of round-cord elastic.

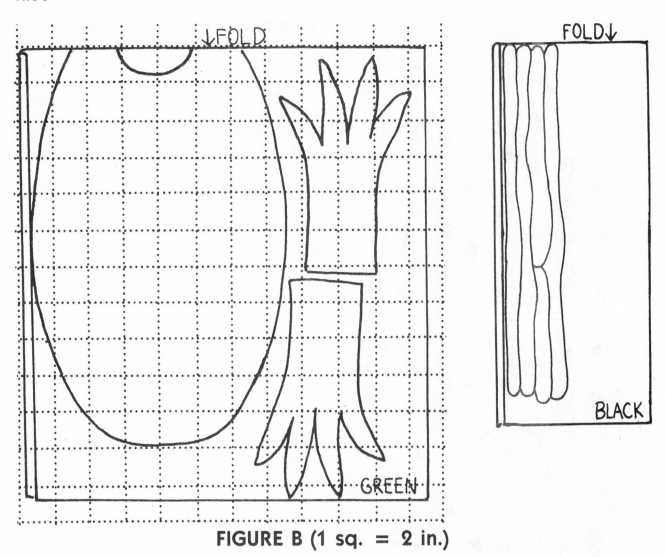

FIGURE B (1 sq. = 2 in.)

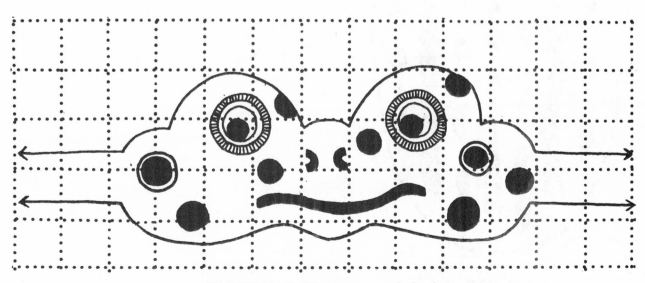

FIGURE C (1 sq. = 1 in.)

TO MAKE BODY: Lay body piece out flat. Cut a 4-in. slit as shown in figure D at center of circle edge (when you wear the slip-on body, the slit will be in the back); try the body on the wearer and lengthen the slit if necessary to pull it over the head. With body piece laid out flat, add the details—warts (dots, single and double) and ribs—and glue in place (figure D).

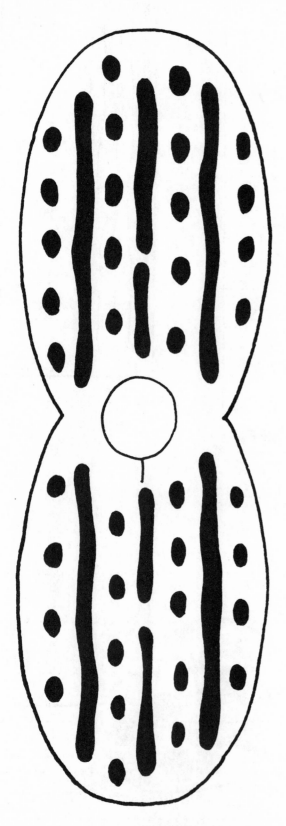

FIGURE D

TO MAKE WEBBED FEET: Lay the 2 foot pieces out flat and position and glue warts in place as desired (figure E). Push (poke) pipe cleaner ends through felt in positions indicated and pinch into a hook to secure in place on wrong side of feet (figure E). Trim ends of pipe cleaners to ¼ in. Punch holes along both side edges and tie with an 8-in. piece of round-cord elastic to form a wristband-type closure (figure E).

FOR ADULT SIZING: The slip-on body is the only piece that needs to be adjusted. This can be done easily by adding a few inches to the width and lengthening the pattern as desired.

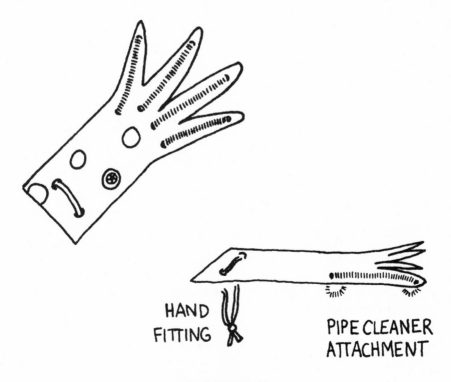

HAND
FITTING

PIPE CLEANER
ATTACHMENT

FIGURE E

CROCODILE

FIGURE A

You can smile at this crocodile and chances are, he won't bite. The body of this costume requires a little more time to put together, but it's easy to do and very effective.

DESCRIPTION: Crocodile-head hat, sponge-painted (optional) and rippled slip-on body, and slithery hands.

MATERIALS: 5 pieces of green poster board; 3 yds. of green and a small piece of white Con-Tact paper; green acrylic or poster paint and a household sponge (optional); 2 large wiggle eyes; double-stick tape; staples; hole punch; round-cord elastic.

PREPARATIONS: Enlarge head pattern piece shown in figure B onto newspaper or brown wrapping paper; cut out. Measure and cut 2 rectangles from green poster board for the front and back body pieces, one 14 × 22 in. (front) and one 14 × 30 in. (back). Trace these rectangles onto green Con-Tact paper; cut out. Lightly sponge-print all of the remaining pieces of poster board (optional) on one side. To do this, pour some of the green paint into a shallow, wide bowl or plastic container. Dip one side of the sponge into the paint, then lightly press the paint-coated side onto the poster board in random fashion, leaving green poster board showing through; let dry. Trace a left and right head (mirror image) from the head pattern piece, a 2-×-18-in. headband, and two 2-×-12-in. shoulder bands onto the unpainted side of the poster board; cut out along outer edges (do not cut teeth). Trace a left and right mouth outline onto white Con-Tact paper; cut out. Using the remaining poster board, cut six 2-×-8-in. pieces for the hands and the rest into strips, 2 in. wide and 22 in. long or more—these strips will be used to form the ripples on the body.

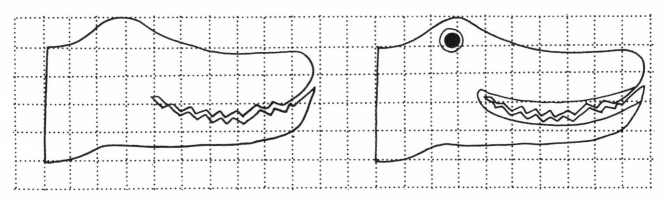

FIGURE B (1 sq. = 1½ in.)

TO MAKE HAT: On painted side of each face piece, affix mouth piece in position; cut upper and lower jagged teeth within the mouth as shown in figure B. The teeth don't need to look perfect, simple triangular cuts will do. Glue eyes in place (figure B). To construct hat, lay one face piece, wrong side up, and apply small pieces of double-stick tape along the entire upper snout. Place the 2 face pieces together, right sides out and edges aligned; finger-press to secure together. Fold poster board headband in half and place between attached face pieces, along lower edge and about halfway in, as shown in figure C. Using double-stick tape, secure band in place. Punch holes at the ends of the band and tie closed to fit around the head with a piece of round-cord elastic.

TO MAKE BODY: First, shape front and back body pieces. For front, simply round off the corners at one 14-in. end of the rectangular front piece; for the back, measure down the sides, lengthwise, and mark off 17 in. At this point, trim each side down to the bottom, forming a tail as shown in figure D, narrowing the width to approximately 4 in. at the bottom. Next, add the textured ripples as follows. Starting with the top back body edge, align and staple one narrow end of a 2-in. precut and sponge-painted strip along side edge. Curve the strip into 4 to 5 waves across the width of the back, stapling in place as you go; staple strip at opposite side edge and trim (figure E). Repeat the procedure of applying the strips in waves to cover the back, aligning strip ends with side edges and butting strips up against each other across the width; staple in as far as possible and then use double-stick tape where necessary to secure waves to body piece. Trim strips along side edges where necessary. Repeat this entire process to cover the body front. To attach front to back, hold the back body piece up to the wearer and mark the position of the shoulder edges onto the top edge of the back piece; transfer these marks onto the top edge of the front. Staple the ends of each shoulder strap, painted side up, to the wrong side of the front and back body pieces at the shoulder marks to fit, as shown in figure D. To finish body and cover staples, align and affix green Con-Tact paper rectangular pieces to wrong side of body front and back; trim along side edges as necessary.

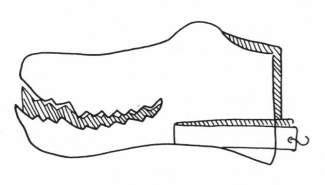

FIGURE C

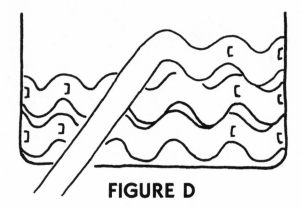

FIGURE D

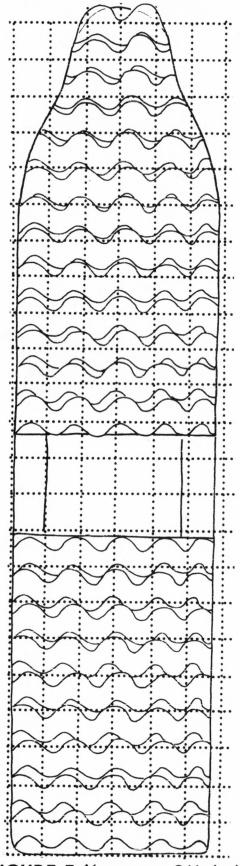

FIGURE E (1 sq. = 2½ in.)

TO MAKE HANDS: Using scissors, taper each 2-×-8-in. hand piece along one end into 2 pointed claws as shown in figure F. For each hand, align and overlap the uncut (wrist) end of 3 pieces; staple together. Punch 2 holes about 1 in. in from side edges and wrist edge, thread an 8-in. piece of round-cord elastic through, and tie to form a wristband closure (figure F).

FOR ADULT SIZING: Widen and lengthen body pieces if desired.

SUGGESTIONS: Although this crocodile is sensational with sponge-printing and ripple strips, it can be made without either or both of these additions and still look terrific (for children under 4, this is probably preferable). Another option is to leave the back plain but jazz up the front.

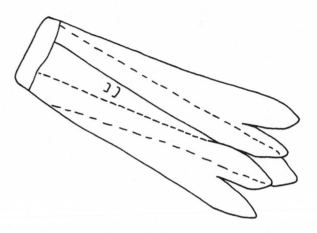

FIGURE F

TURTLE

FIGURE A

This turtle flaunts a showcase house. The stomach evokes the image of a painted turtle, and the 3-D back springs to life. Both effects are created using cutting methods even children can do.

DESCRIPTION: Turtle-head hat and slip-on "box" turtle body (front and back detailed).

MATERIALS: 2 pieces each of black and yellow poster board; 2 yds. yellow and ¼ yd. each of red and black Con-Tact paper; 2 large wiggle eyes; round-cord elastic; double-stick tape; staples; hole punch.

PREPARATIONS: Enlarge head pattern piece shown in figure B onto newspaper or brown wrapping paper; cut out. Measure and cut out a 2-×-18-in. hatband pattern, a 5-in.-square pattern and a 3-×-6-in. rectangular pattern for the back shell details, and a 4-in.-square pattern for the front shell details. Trace head pattern twice, the hatband once onto black posterboard; cut out. Trace the 5-in. square 7 times, and the 3-×-6-in. rectangle twice onto yellow poster board; cut out all pieces. Trace the 4-in. square 6 times and the 5-in. square 4 times onto yellow Con-Tact paper; cut out all pieces. To form the shell body base, fold 1 piece of black poster board in half crosswise; round off the corners to make an oval, approximately 22 × 14 in. (figure C), and cut along the fold to separate the 2 shells. Cut 2 shoulder straps, 2 × 12 in. long, from the remaining poster board.

TO MAKE HAT: Cut a mouth and eye socket for both faces from red Con-Tact paper and affix to right and left face as shown in figure B. Cut neckline scale details, irregularly shaped spots (from yellow Con-Tact paper), and affix to necks following an impression of figure B. Center and tape wiggle eyes in place with double-stick tape. To construct hat, lay one face piece, wrong side up, and apply small pieces of double-stick tape from the back side of the eye socket to the nose, including the

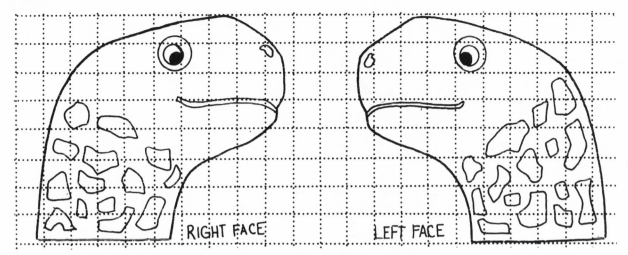

FIGURE B (1 sq. = 1 in.)

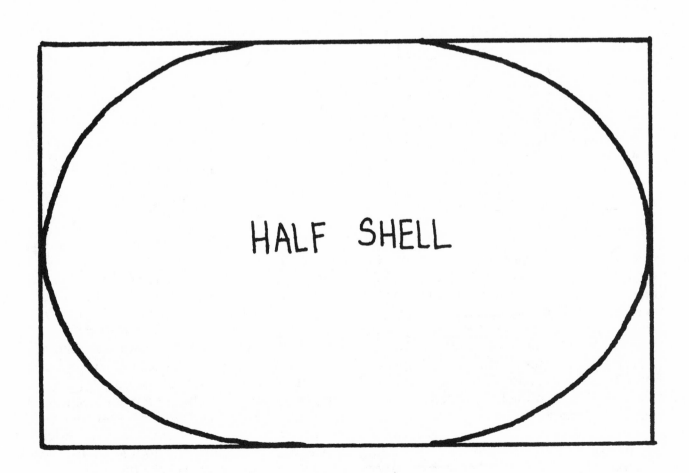

FIGURE C

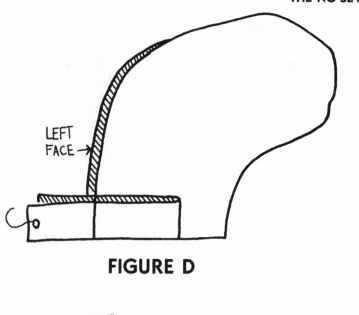

FIGURE D

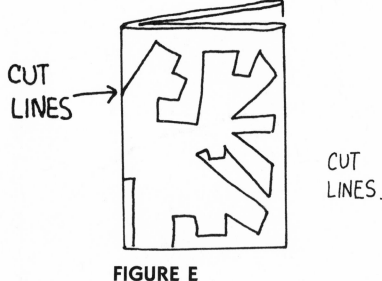

FIGURE E

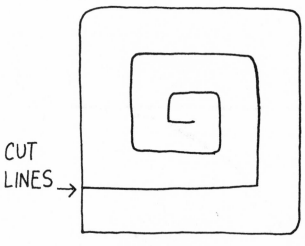

FIGURE F

front neck edge. Place the 2 face pieces together, right sides out and edges aligned; finger-press to secure together. Fold poster board hatband in half and place between attached face pieces, along lower edge and about halfway in, as shown in figure D. Using double-stick tape, secure band in place. Punch holes at the ends of the band and tie closed to fit around the head with a piece of round-cord elastic.

TO MAKE BODY: Round off all corners on detail poster board and Con-Tact paper squares. Beginning with the front shell half, fold each Con-Tact paper square in quarters

and cut into a snowflake pattern (figure E). Following figure G, snowflakes a, b, c, and d are 5-in. rounded squares and e–j are 4-in. rounded squares; affix on shell as shown in figure. Cut and affix small bow-shaped pieces from red Con-Tact paper to decorate the blank edge spaces. For the back shell half, using the rounded poster board squares, cut along the cut lines as shown in figure F to form spirals (springs) in each. Position pieces on shell as shown in figure G, working from the center to the edges; attach with double-stick tape placed along the upper edge of the spiral only, leaving inner cuts free. When pulled from the center, the spirals create three-dimensional springs. Cut small triangles from red Con-Tact paper to decorate outer blank edges of the shell. To attach front shell to back, first hold the front shell up to the wearer and mark the position of the shoulder edges onto the top shell edge; transfer these marks onto the top edge of the back shell. Staple the ends of each shoulder strap to the wrong side of the front and back shells at the shoulder marks to fit, as shown in figure G.

FOR ADULT SIZING: Lengthen and widen the shells by cutting each oval on a separate piece of poster board. Make additional snowflake squares and springs to fit.

SUGGESTIONS: The colors chosen here create a dramatic, yet realistic, effect, but turtles come in many colors and sizes, so you may choose whatever color suits your fancy. An option for the decorative detailing shown here (snowflakes and springs) is sponge-painting, which would add a colorful, textured effect in very quick time.

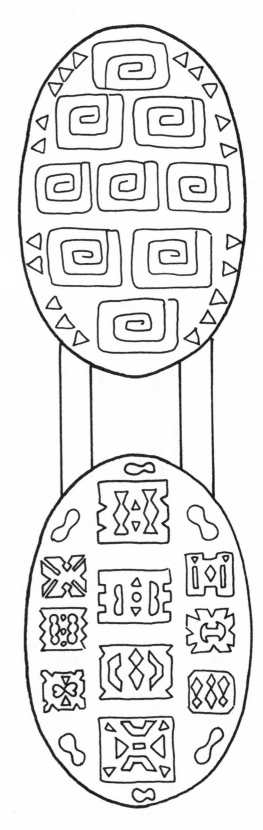

FIGURE G

BEETLE

FIGURE A

A common garden-variety beetle comes alive with uncommonly good looks, parading a shell full of glittering spots. This costume takes almost no time to make, and it rates high on ease of wearability.

DESCRIPTION: Beetle headband and spotted slip-on body.

MATERIALS: 2 pieces of green and 1 piece of blue poster board (or colors of your choice);

50+ large sequins; 2 large wiggle eyes; small piece of metallic Con-Tact paper or aluminum foil; double-stick tape; glue; staples; hole punch; round-cord elastic.

PREPARATIONS: Enlarge eye/horn and headband pattern pieces as shown in figure B onto newspaper or brown wrapping paper; extend arrows an equal amount on each side to a finished length of 17¾ in. for the eye/horn band and 18 in. for the headband. Cut out. Trace head pieces and two 2-×-12-in. shoulder bands onto green poster board; cut out. Fold second piece of green poster board in half crosswise; round off the corners to make an oval, approximately 22 × 14 in., and cut along the fold, creating 2 ovals. One oval will be used for the front body piece; cut the other oval in half, lengthwise, to form the wings. Trace the body front onto blue poster board for the body back; cut out. Cut four ¼-×-18-in. front body stripes from remaining blue poster board. Cut two 1½-in. circles for the eyes from Con-Tact paper or foil.

TO MAKE HEADBAND: Position and affix Con-Tact paper eyes (or glue foil eyes) to eye/horn piece as shown in figure B. Arrange sequins on eye/horn and headband pieces in a pleasing arrangement as shown. To attach eye/horn band to headband, measure in and mark 4 in. from both headband ends for placement; using double-stick tape, secure ends of eye/horn band in place as shown in figure C. Horns should be along the back edge of the band; fold the horns up and the eyes down. Punch holes at the ends of the headband and tie closed to fit around the head with a piece of round-cord elastic.

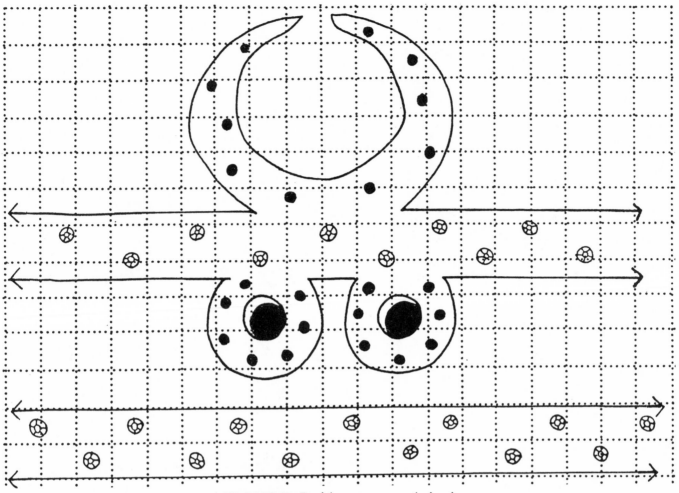

FIGURE B (1 sq. = 1 in.)

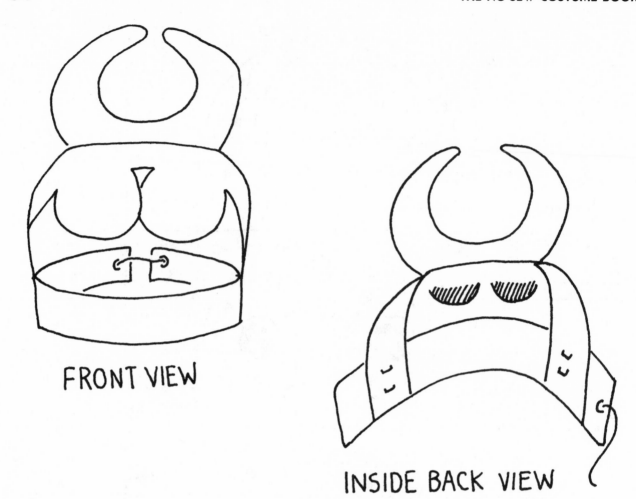

FRONT VIEW

INSIDE BACK VIEW

FIGURE C

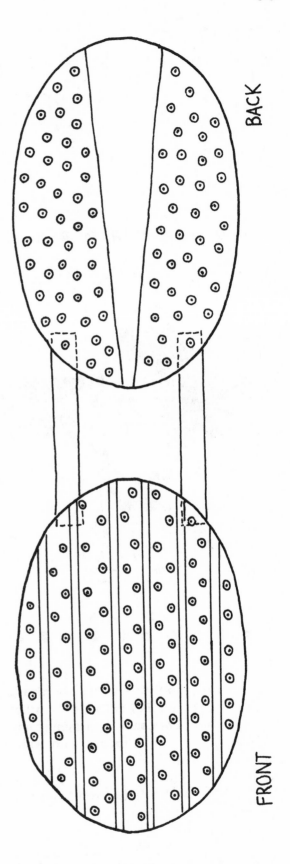

TO MAKE BODY:
Position and align green poster board wings on top of blue body base; separate the straight, inner wing edges slightly (pushing the wings out a bit) to reveal the blue underbody and secure wings in place at the top, using double-stick tape or staples (figure D). Position and secure sequins on wings in a pleasing fashion, using glue or double-stick tape (figure D). Position and glue blue poster board body stripes on body front as shown in figure D. Add sequins between the stripes as shown in figure D. Hold front body up to wearer and mark the position of the shoulder edges onto the top edge; transfer these marks onto the top edge of the body back. Staple the ends of the shoulder bands to the wrong side of the front and back body pieces at the shoulder marks to fit, as shown in figure D.

FOR ADULT SIZING:
Lengthen, if desired, by cutting each oval on a separate piece of poster board, utilizing the full length of the board.

SUGGESTIONS:
For a ladybug, use red and black colors. For your own, special, imaginary beetle, use your favorite coordinating colors.

FIGURE D

PREDATORY BIRD

FIGURE A

This generic, high-flying predatory bird takes on a different look and mood, depending on the colors you choose—from menacing (red and black) to patriotic (brown and white) to ethereal (pastels).

DESCRIPTION: Bird headpiece and 2-piece slip-on felt body.

MATERIALS: 1½ yds. black and ⅓ yd. red 72-in.-wide felt; 1 piece of red poster board

(or contrasting felt and poster board colors of your choice, substituting lighter color for red and darker for black); small piece of aluminum foil; glue; double-stick tape; hole punch; round-cord elastic.

PREPARATIONS: Enlarge body, wing, shield, wristband, and overbody shown in figure B, and the neck, neck feathers, face, eye pupil, and eyebrow shown in figures C and D onto newspaper or brown wrapping paper; cut out. Following figure B, lay body pattern onto folded black felt; refold remaining black felt as shown and lay out wing (twice), shield, neck, wristband, pupil, and eyebrow patterns; cut out. Lay overbody and neck feathers onto folded red felt as shown; cut out these and fourteen 1½-in. teardrop-shaped feathers. Trace headpiece twice and 2-×-18-in. band once onto red poster board; cut out.

TO MAKE HEADPIECE: Cut 2 eye-base circles from aluminum foil, making them ¼ in. larger than the pupil circles. Glue eye base, pupil, and then eyebrow in position on the poster board face pieces as shown in figure D, creating a left and right face (mirror image). For each face piece, position and glue felt neck-feather piece to face, placing "unfeathered" edge along broken line mark as shown in figure D. Position black felt neck piece on top of feather piece so that cut-feather portion shows; glue in place. Along lower neck edge, glue teardrop-shaped feathers onto scalloped areas; let dry. To construct headpiece, lay one face piece, wrong side up, and apply small pieces of double-stick tape on the beak. Place the two face pieces together, right sides out and edges aligned; finger-press to secure together. Fold poster board band in half and place between attached face pieces, positioning as shown in figure E (broken line marks edge of poster board face piece). Using double-stick tape, secure band in place. Punch holes at the ends of the band and tie closed to fit around the head with a piece of round-cord elastic.

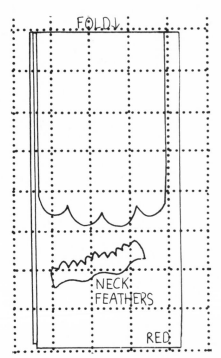

FIGURE B (1 sq. = 3 in.)

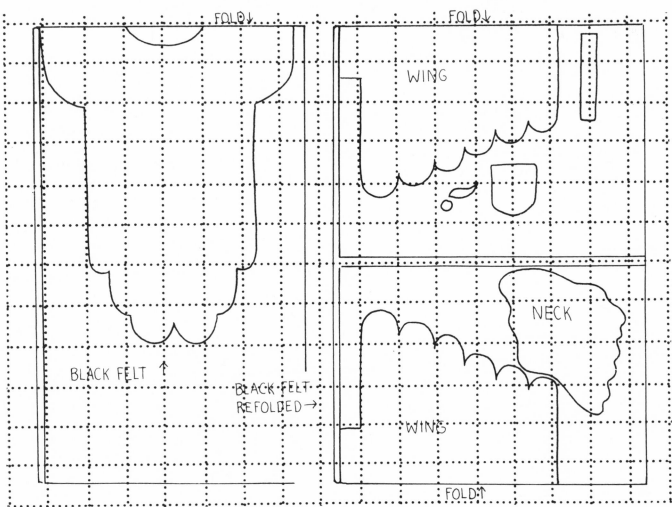

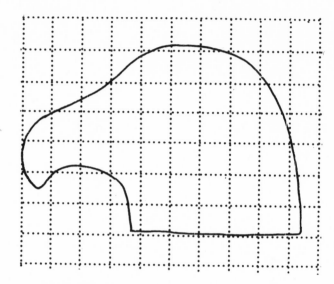

FIGURE C (1 sq. = 1½ in.)

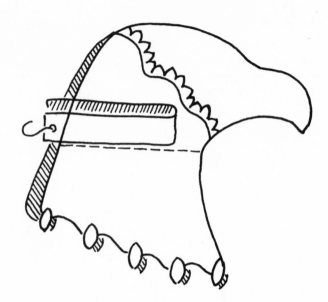

FIGURE E

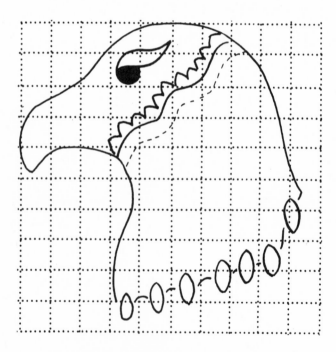

FIGURE D (1 sq. = 1½ in.)

TO MAKE BODY: Lay body piece out flat. Cut a 4-in. slit as shown in figure F at center of circle edge (when you wear the slip-on body, the slit will be in the back). Repeat this same procedure for the overbody, making the slit at the center circle edge. Position overbody onto body base, aligning neck edges

and slits; glue together by applying a steady stream of glue ¼ in. from the neck and slit edge on the inside; squeeze-press to secure (figure F). Try the 2-piece body on the wearer and lengthen slit if necessary to pull it over the head. Create a design on the shield piece, folding it in half and cutting flame shapes out from the center or free-hand-cut your own design as desired. Position and carefully glue shield to overbody front as shown in figure F. Position wristbands on wing pieces and glue at ends as shown in figure G. To complete body, position right side of each wing along upper tab edge onto wrong side of body piece at sleeve cap, overlapping as shown (figure G); glue in place. Let dry.

FOR ADULT SIZING: Lengthen and widen the body and overbody pattern pieces and lengthen the wing piece at the upper edge (below the tab), widening as you go to continue the shape design of the wing.

SUGGESTIONS: As suggested above, you can vary the colors for a different effect. For the shield, you can purchase a decorative badge, instead of making a cutout.

FIGURE F

FIGURE G

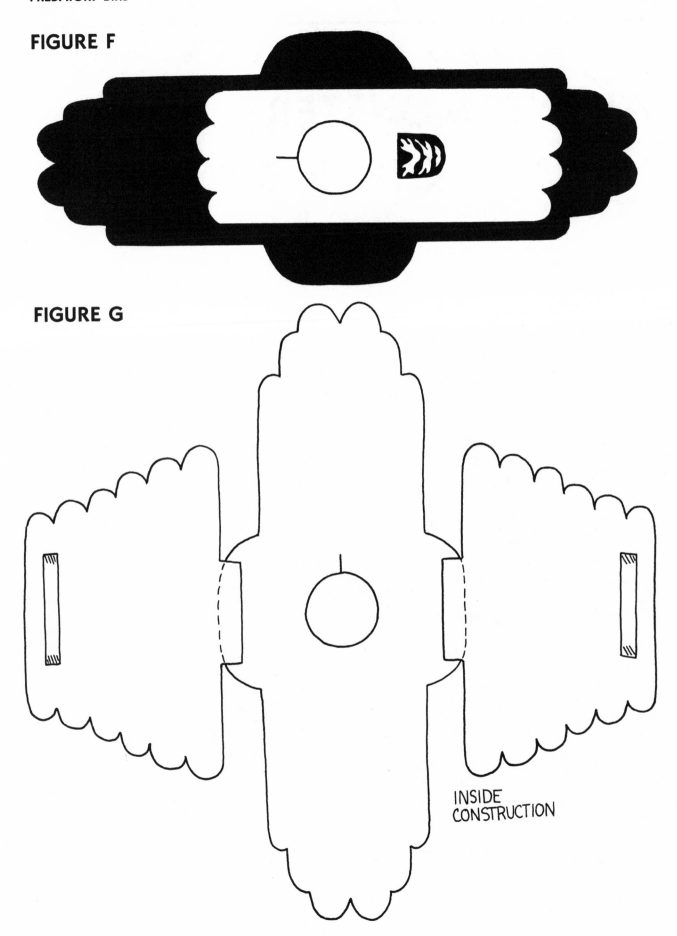

INSIDE
CONSTRUCTION

CHAPTER III

ALIENS, MONSTERS, FAERIES, AND OTHER BEINGS

AQUA ALIEN

• • • • • • • • • • • • •

FIGURE A

• • • • • • • • • • • • •

From out of the depths, this water-loving creature emerges for all to admire and enjoy. It's easy to see, "Aqua's" a comfortable sort of being.

DESCRIPTION: Coral hat and 2-piece felt slip-on body.

MATERIALS: 1 piece of lime green or peach poster board; ⅔ yd. gray or turquoise and ½ yd. lime green 72-in.-wide felt; ¼ yd. each of any 4 colors large-mesh fabric netting; 8–10 large wiggle eyes; glue; round-cord elastic; hole punch; small pieces of string, yarn, or 4 rubber bands.

PREPARATIONS: Enlarge body, sleeve, wristband, and alien emblem in figure B and headband in figure C onto newspaper or brown wrapping paper; extend headband arrows an equal amount on each side to a finished length of 18 in. Cut all pieces out. Following the layout in figure B, pin the body, sleeve, and wristband patterns onto folded gray felt; cut out. Pin emblem pattern onto folded green felt; cut out. Trace headband pattern onto green poster board; cut out.

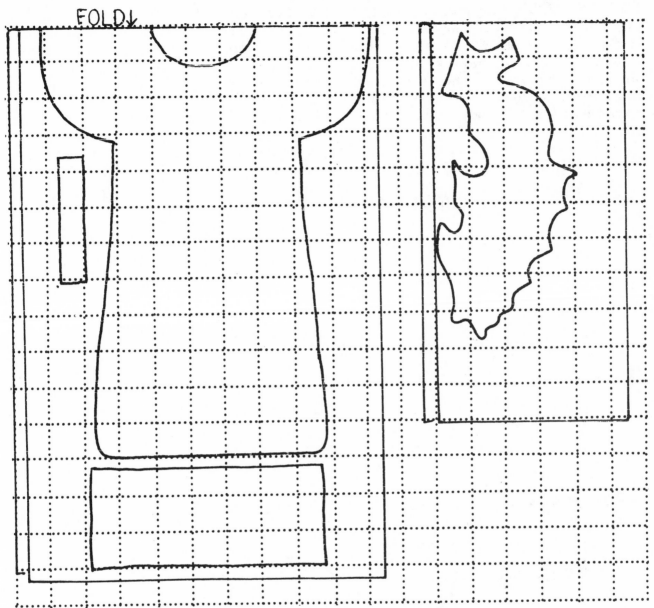

FIGURE B (1 sq. = 2 in.)

TO MAKE HEADBAND: Glue eyes in place on headband as shown in figure C.

Punch holes at ends of band and tie closed to fit around the head with a piece of round-cord elastic (figure C).

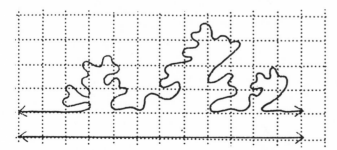

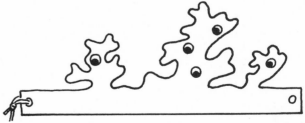

FIGURE C (1 sq. = 2 in.)

TO MAKE BODY: Lay body piece out flat. Cut a 4-in. slit as shown in figure D at center of circle edge (when you wear the slip-on body, the slit will be in the back); try the body on and lengthen the slit if necessary to pull it over the head. To construct body, position each sleeve piece on body sleeve cap edge, overlapping as shown in figure D; glue in place. Position wristbands on sleeves, gluing ends in place as shown in figure D. Let dry. On the right side of the front and back, add the felt emblem as shown in figure E, gluing only the top ¼ of the emblem to the body. Position and glue eyes in place on emblem. Cut 4 pairs of 1-in. slits—2 on each sleeve— for weaving the netting through (figure E). For each pair, space the slits ½ in. apart. Gather each piece of netting into a 14-in. (approximately) tube and weave it through a pair of slits. Bunch the netting together and tie tightly on the right side, close to the sleeve, with string, yarn, or a rubber band (figure F); trim ends.

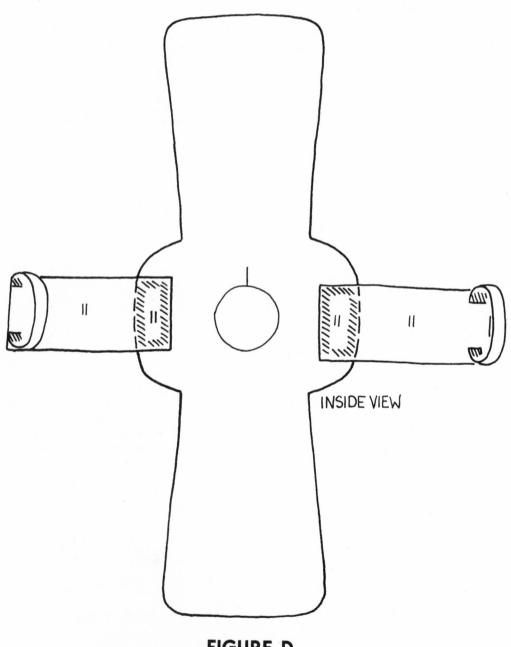

INSIDE VIEW

FIGURE D

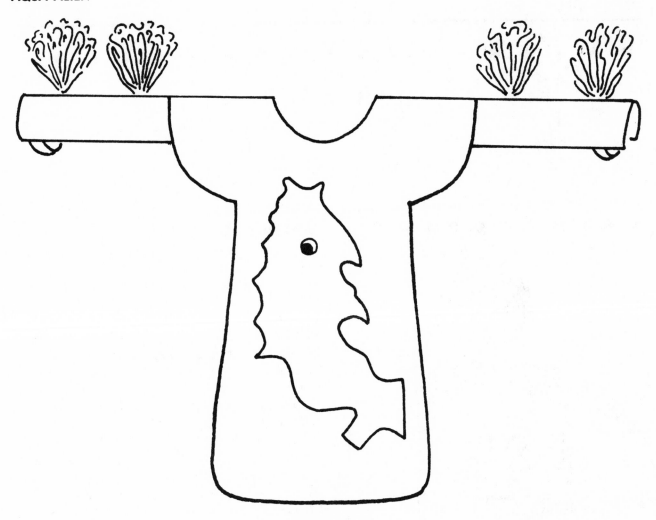

FIGURE E

BUNCH NET

TIE TIGHTLY

FIGURE F

ADULT SIZING: No alterations are necessary, although you may choose to lengthen the body.

SUGGESTIONS: Water colors have been chosen for this alien, although you may choose other colors to your taste. The emblem can be dressed up with the addition of shiny green and blue sequins.

ROBOT

FIGURE A

A product of today's technical world, this industrial-looking robot is programmed and ready to go. You don't need to be an electronics genius to make a copy.

DESCRIPTION: Sensor headgear and metallic slip-on body.

MATERIALS: 3 pieces of red, blue, or yellow poster board; 4 yds. silver Con-Tact paper; 1 yd. black and ¼ yd. each red, blue, and yellow Con-Tact paper; 2 flexible straws; staples; hole punch; black shoelaces (optional).

PREPARATIONS: Enlarge the body and headgear pattern pieces in figures B and C onto newspaper or brown wrapping paper; cut out. Cover 1 side of 2 pieces of poster board with silver Con-Tact paper. Trace body pattern onto paper side of each covered poster board; cut out. Trace headgear pieces onto remaining poster board; cut out. Trace 6 backwards 1's and six 0's, using the pattern in figure F, onto yellow Con-Tact paper. Cut an 11-×-10-in., a 2-×-22-in., and a ⅝-×-18-in. rectangle and two 4¼-in.-diameter circular discs from black Con-Tact paper. Cut ½-×-12-in. and ⅜-×-12-in. strips of yellow, blue, and red Con-Tact paper and two 24-×-27-in. and one 2½-×-18-in. rectangles from silver Con-Tact paper.

TO MAKE HEADGEAR: Using scissors, make a small slit on the short, top end of each straw. Slip the cut straw end onto the barbell-shaped headpiece, positioning as shown in figure D; tape ends flat on front and back. Peel backing from one 7-×-24-in. rectangle of silver Con-Tact paper and lay flat, adhesive side up. Center and secure barbell-shaped headpiece onto Con-Tact paper; trim along poster board edges, being careful not to cut the straws. Repeat this procedure to cover the other side of the headpiece. To create audio sensor, punch 2 circles on each black Con-Tact paper disc as shown in figure D.

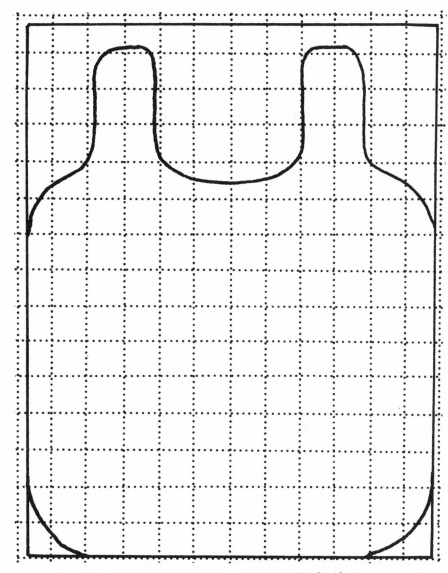

FIGURE B (1 sq. = 2 in.)

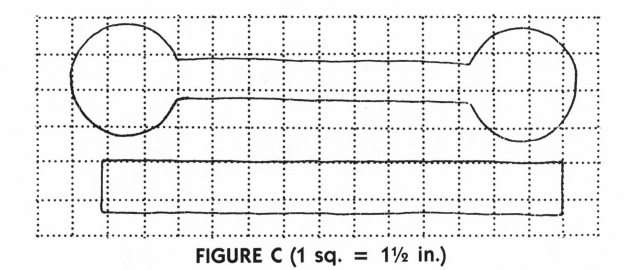

FIGURE C (1 sq. = 1½ in.)

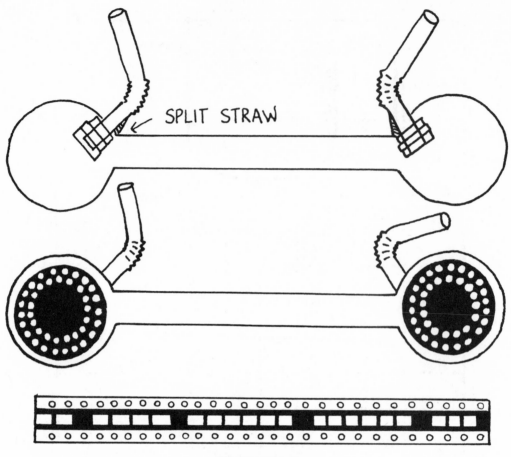

SPLIT STRAW

FIGURE D

Center and secure the discs onto the head-piece as shown. Cover the headband with the 2½-×-18-in. piece of silver Con-Tact paper; trim along poster board edges. Then, center and adhere the ⅝-×-18-in. black Con-Tact paper rectangle on top of the covered head-band. Using colored ⅜-×-12-in. strips, cut and adhere ½ in. pieces in a random pattern on top of the black strip as shown in figure D. Punch holes along the band edges, ½ in. apart (figure D). Staple the disc piece to the headband as shown in figure E. Punch holes at the ends of the band and tie closed to fit around the head with a piece of round-cord elastic.

FIGURE E

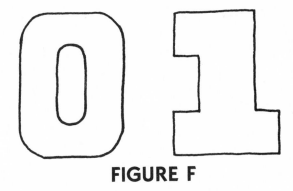

FIGURE F

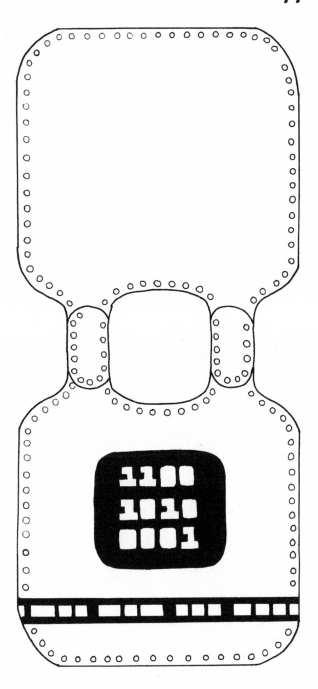

FIGURE G

TO MAKE BODY: Position and adhere the 10-×-11-in. black Con-Tact paper rectangle onto the metallic body front as shown in figure G. Center and adhere the numbers (figure F), in groupings of 4, on the black rectangle. Position and adhere the 2-×-22-in. black Con-Tact paper rectangle 2 in. up from the bottom edge; trim at sides. Using the colored Con-Tact paper strips, cut and create patterns of rectangles and squares as for the headband and secure on lower black strip (figure G). Punch holes around the front and back edges, ½ in. in from edge and approximately 1 in. apart. Staple front and back together to fit as shown (figure G). If desired, secure sides together by lacing through the front and back holes with shoelacing; tie.

ADULT SIZING: No alterations are necessary, although you can lengthen the body if desired. To do this, you will need to tape 2 pieces of poster board together for the front and back. The tape will be concealed by silver Con-Tact paper.

SUGGESTIONS: Dark or shiny, irridescent clothes lend the perfect foil to this high-tech costume. For added fun, fluorescent tape strips can be added in bands to your clothes.

DRAGON

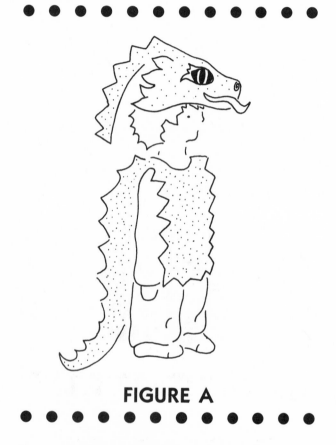

FIGURE A

This fire-tongued dragon is a truly good-looking "fellow," even from the back. Catch him on the run, and you'll see a spiny trail!

DESCRIPTION: Dragon headdress and spiny-backed felt slip-on body.

MATERIALS: 1 piece of green poster board; 1 yd. 72-in.-wide matching green felt; 2 squares of dark pink and 1 square each of blue and purple felt; small piece of white Con-

Tact paper, jumbo rickrack, or felt (for teeth); glue; round-cord elastic; double-stick tape.

PREPARATIONS: Enlarge body front, back, head, mouth, and teeth patterns as shown in figures B and C onto newspaper or brown wrapping paper; cut out. Trace the 4 eye pieces (figure D); cut out. Following the layout plan in figures B and C, first cut a 30-×-43-in. rectangle from the corner of the green felt, fold it, and pin the back pattern on it as shown; cut out. Next, lay the body pattern on the remaining piece of felt; cut out. Trace the head pattern twice and one ½-×-2-in. and two 1-in.-square stiffeners from green poster board; cut out, being careful when making the interior head cut near the spines. Using the mouth (figure C) and eye (figure D) patterns, pin and cut 2 tongues from dark pink felt, teeth from white felt (or rickrack or paper), 2 eye bases from green felt, 2 eyes from blue felt, 2 eye ovals from dark pink felt, and 2 pupils from purple felt. Also cut two 1½-in. ovals from dark pink felt for the nostrils.

TO MAKE HEADDRESS: Lay one face out flat. Tape ½-×-2-in. stiffener at first spine base as shown in figure E. Then, apply double-stick tape along the front half of the face and spine area, starting above the ears, as shown (figure E). Align and adhere second face/spine piece to the taped face/spine. Using a small piece of double-stick tape, secure 1-in. stiffener piece inside lower back edge of both faces as shown in figure E. Make each eye, layering and gluing the eye base, eye, oval, and pupil. Position and glue the eye, tongue, and teeth on both faces. Spiral-cut the nos-

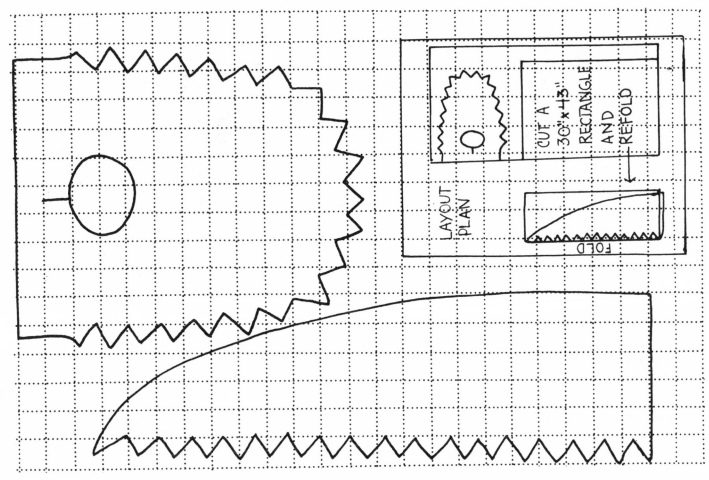

FIGURE B (1 sq. = 2 in.)

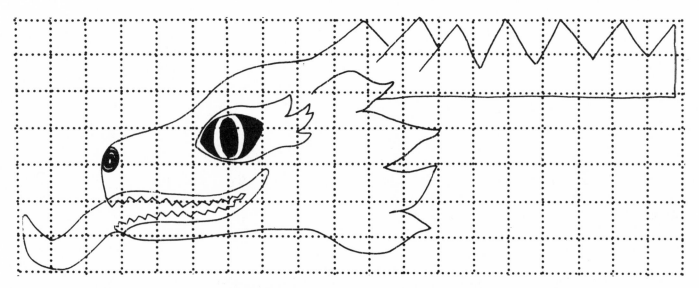

FIGURE C (1 sq. = 1½ in.)

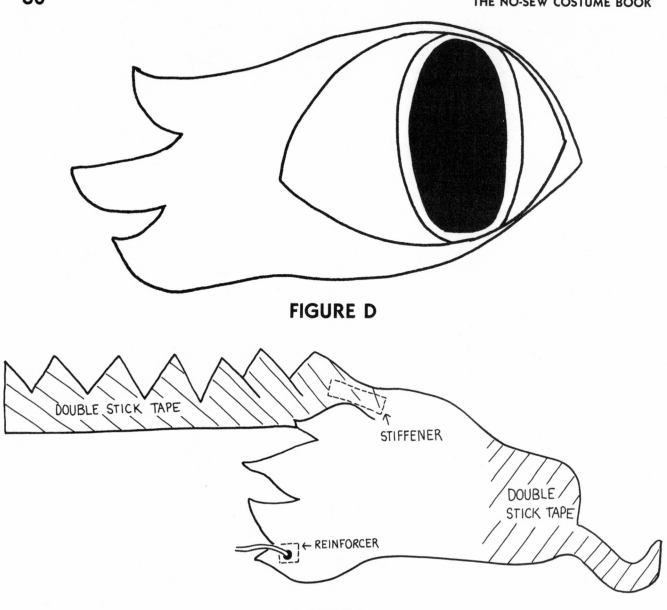

FIGURE D

FIGURE E

trils as shown in figure C and glue along outer edge in place. Punch holes through each face at position of lower edge stiffener; tie closed to fit around head with a piece of round-cord elastic.

TO MAKE BODY: Lay one back piece out flat. Squeeze glue onto piece as shown in fig-

ure F, leaving 3 top spines glue free. Carefully align second back piece and squeeze-press spines together; let dry. Try on front piece; lengthen neck slit if necessary to fit over the head. Lay front piece out flat and overlap the back onto the front, aligning the front neck cut with the unglued spines; glue together as shown in figure G and let dry.

ADULT SIZING: The slip-on body is the only piece that needs to be adjusted. Simply add to the length of the front and back pattern pieces to fit.

SUGGESTIONS: This traditional-looking dragon comes in green, but can be made in any color that is available in both poster board and felt. The dragon's spines can be jazzed up with glued-on sequins or other sparkly notions of your choice.

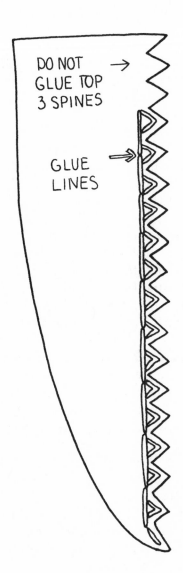

DO NOT GLUE TOP 3 SPINES →

GLUE LINES →

FIGURE F

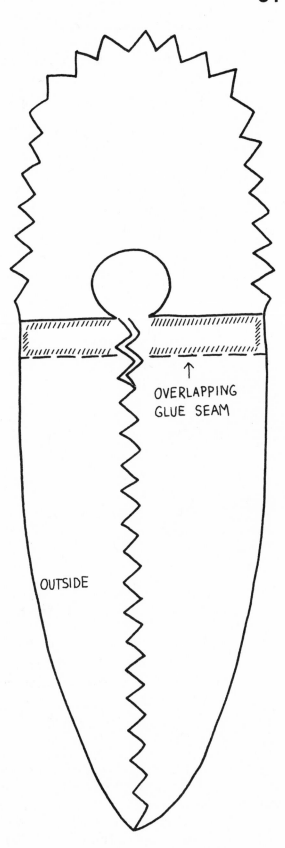

OVERLAPPING GLUE SEAM

OUTSIDE

FIGURE G

MERMAID

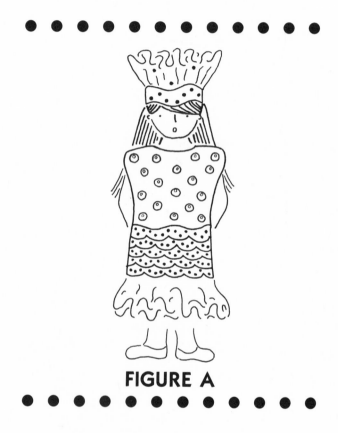

FIGURE A

A shimmering vision from out of the sea, this mermaid has no trouble getting around on land.

DESCRIPTION: Sea foam headband and shimmery felt slip-on body.

MATERIALS: ¾ yd. green and ¼ yd. blue 72-in.-wide felt; 6 yds. green fine-mesh netting; blue poster board; 50+ (1 bag) green and blue ½-in. sequins; twenty 20MM flat silver sequins; glue; staples; round-cord elastic; ribbon (optional).

PREPARATIONS: Enlarge body, wave, and headband patterns in figures B and C onto newspaper or brown wrapping paper; cut out. Following the layout in figure B, pin body pattern once and the wave pattern twice onto green felt; cut out. Pin and cut 3 waves from blue felt, using wave pattern (figure B). Trace headband pattern onto blue poster board; cut out. Cut net into 2 equal pieces (3 yds. each).

TO MAKE HEADBAND: Gather 1 piece of netting into accordion folds to reduce its size to 16 in. (most of the length of the band). Staple folded edge of netting to the headband, 1 in. in from the ends and at 2-in. intervals (figure D). Lay band out flat. On right side, glue green sequins on band in random fashion, covering staple ends when possible. Add 12 to 15 blue sequins to the outermost layers of netting, using double-stick tape (optional). Punch holes near the ends and tie around head to fit with a piece of round-cord elastic.

TO MAKE BODY: Lay body piece out flat, as shown in figure G. Cut a 4-in. slit at center back neck edge (when you wear the slip-on body, the slit will be in the back). Try the body on the wearer and lengthen the slit if necessary to fit over the head. Lay body piece out flat again. Working from the bottom up, position the upper edge of 1 blue wave 2 in. from the bottom edge of the body; trim wave at side edge. Using a thin line of glue along upper edge only, secure wave to body (figure E). Repeat procedure, positioning and gluing upper edge of green wave 2 in. from upper edge of blue wave; repeat procedure, alter-

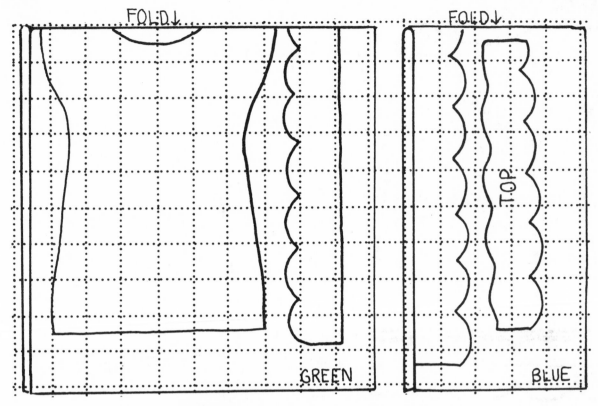

FIGURE B (1 sq. = 2½ in.)

FIGURE C (1 sq. = 2½ in.)

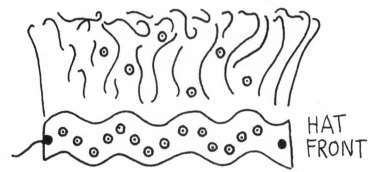

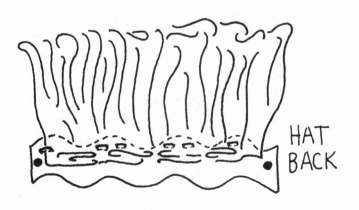

FIGURE D

nating colors, until all 5 waves are attached. Cut remaining netting into 3 pieces of equal length. Fold each piece in half crosswise and hand-gather each piece along the crosswise fold. Lift and pin lower blue wave back onto the body; apply a thin line of glue along body edge close to upper edge of wave. Place folded edge of gathered netting onto glue line, positioning center section first and then the 2 side sections. Apply a thin line of glue near folded edge of wave, remove pin, and press wave down onto netting (figure F). Weight down until dry. Glue sequins onto body as shown, green on blue waves, blue on green, and silver on the upper body (figure G).

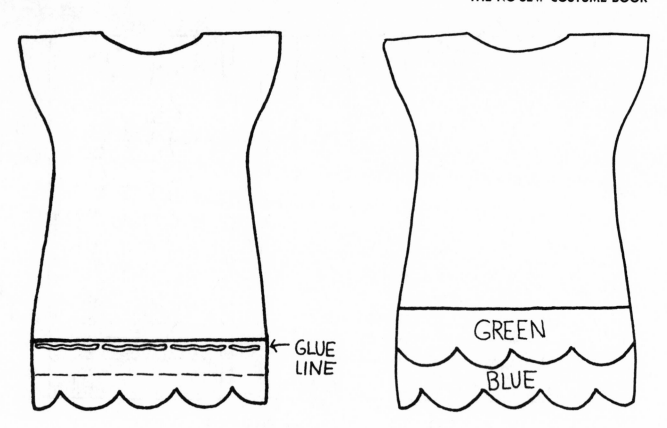

FIGURE E

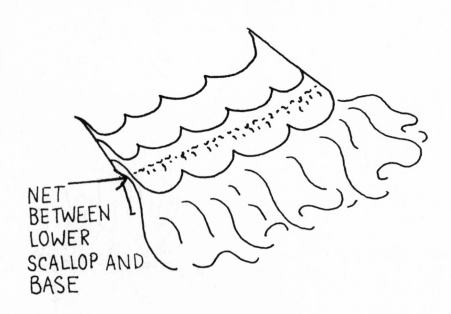

FIGURE F

ADULT SIZING: Alterations are not necessary, unless you want a full-length (below knee) body. For this, simply lengthen the body pattern and allow for extra felt if necessary.

SUGGESTIONS: For a more fitted look, you can attach the front and back together at the sides. To do this, punch a hole 1 in. in from the side edge to match on front and back of both sides; lace a ribbon through and tie closed.

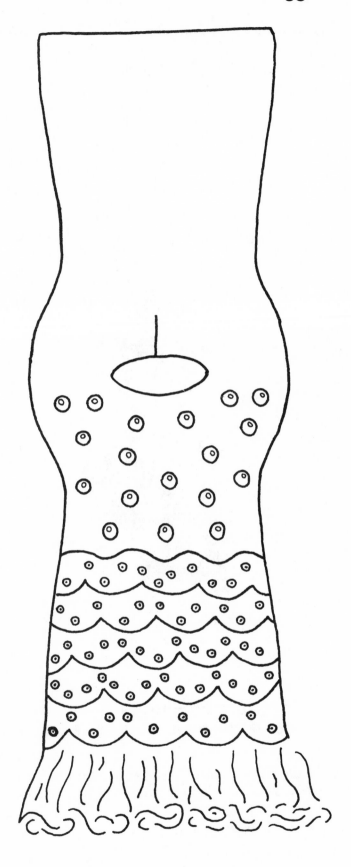

FIGURE G

MONSTER

FIGURE A

A bit more humorous than scary, this monster, nonetheless, has a look that's far from ordinary.

DESCRIPTION: Multi-eyed monster headband and slip-on body pelt.

MATERIALS: 1½ yds. brown or black fun fur; 1 small plastic Slinky; 8 or more green, screw-back cat's-eyes or large wiggle eyes; brown or black poster board; red or other contrasting-color poster board; small piece of silver Con-Tact paper (preferably) or aluminum foil; double-stick tape; glue; staples; round-cord elastic.

PREPARATIONS: Enlarge body, base headband and ear band, and ear patterns in figures B and C onto newspaper or brown wrapping paper; extend headband arrows an equal amount on each side to a finished length of 18 in. Cut out all pieces. Following the layout in figure B, pin the body pattern onto a single layer of fur; cut out. Trace the base headband pattern, 2 ears (including interior spiral cuts), and a 2-in. circle for the tongue onto red poster board and the ear band pattern onto brown or black poster board; cut out. Cover a large (6-in.) scrap of poster board with silver Con-Tact paper and cut it into 2-in. (approximately) irregularly shaped triangles. Cut the Slinky into 6 to 8 pieces.

TO MAKE HEADBAND: Beginning with the ear band, curl the center projection into a tube and staple it in place (figure D). Attach each spiral-cut ear piece to the ear position, using double-stick tape along the outermost edge to secure. Gently pull unattached ear spirals out from the ear band, forming a 3-D coil. Center and align ear band onto headband; secure, using double-stick tape, leaving the ear flaps free. Curl center and left-side

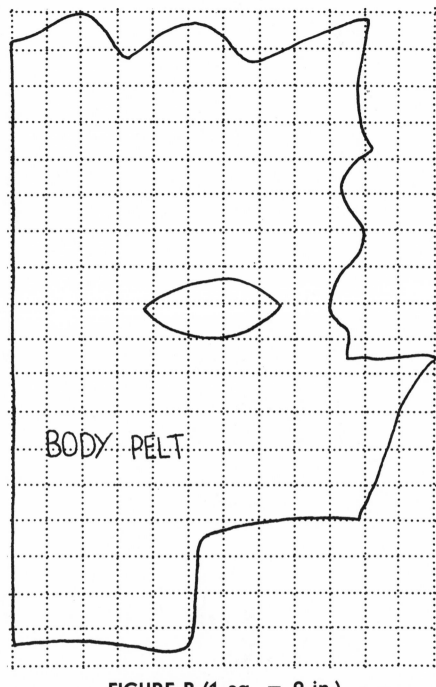

FIGURE B (1 sq. = 2 in.)

headband projections into a tube; staple in place as shown in figure D. Spiral-cut the 2-in. red poster board circle (same as for ear) and attach along outermost edge to mouth position, using double-stick tape. Coil, same as for ears (figure E). To create eyes, use scissors to carefully punch a small hole in the center of 4 metallic triangles. Push a cat's-eye screw-back through each hole. Then, punch a hole on the headband projections and push screw-back through as shown in figure E. Secure in place with metal clasp that's provided with eye (which threads on the screw-back) or by putting small pieces of double-stick tape under the triangles. Lace one cut Slinky "earring" onto each coiled ear.

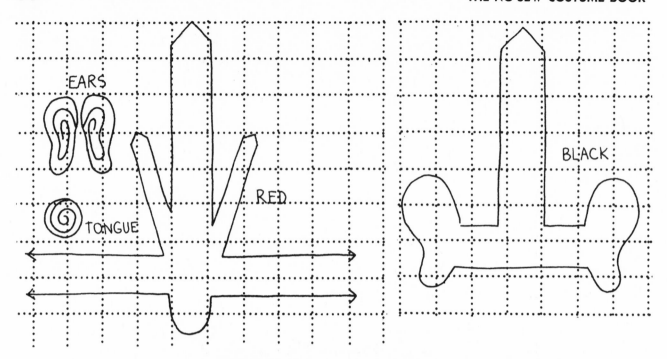

FIGURE C (1 sq. = 2 in.)

FIGURE D

FIGURE E

TO MAKE BODY: Create several eye pieces, same as for headband. Attach the eye pieces to the body front, positioning as shown (figure F), by poking small holes in the fur backing with scissors or by just pushing the screw-back through. Secure eye pieces on back with clasps provided. Position and secure Slinkys on fur, making a hole same as for eyes and sliding a coil of the Slinky through to the back. Work with the Slinky on front, stretching and twisting it to form the desired, wacky appearance.

ADULT SIZING: No alterations necessary.

SUGGESTIONS: Using the fur remnant, you can make a hand flap—furry covering for top of hand—by cutting an irregular shape to fit the upper hand. Punch 2 holes at the wrist edge, lace a piece of round-cord elastic through the holes, and tie closed to fit.

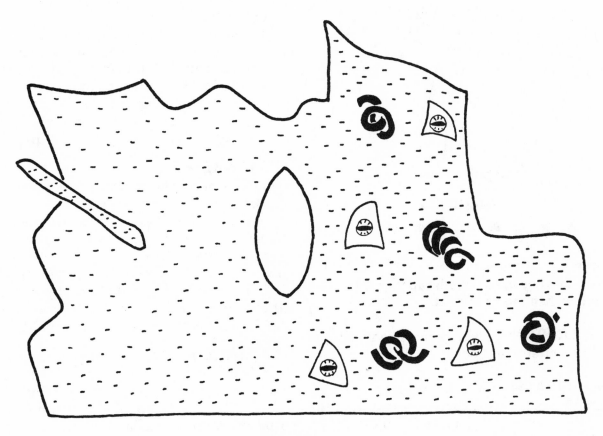

FIGURE F

FAERIE

FIGURE A

From out of a dream comes this diaphanous wisp of a costume, unbelievably easy to make and enchanting to look at.

DESCRIPTION: Beribboned headband and icicle net slip-on body.

MATERIALS: 6 yds. white (cut into 1½-yd. lengths) or 1½ yds. each of 4 coordinating colors of netting (preferably fine mesh); ½ yd. white or coordinating-color 72-in.-wide felt;

5 yds. of ¼- to ½-in.-wide ribbon; decorations for ribbon ends—flowers, stick-on stars, etc.; rubber band or tie.

PREPARATIONS: Enlarge body and collar patterns in figure B onto newspaper (attached together) or brown wrapping paper; cut out. Align and place 4 single layers of netting together; randomly pin through all layers—this will help prevent slippage. Fold the pinned netting in half, and following the layout in figure B, pin the body pattern to the netting, pinning along all pattern edges; cut out along outer, solid lines only. Remove pattern, but keep body netting layers randomly pinned together. Save netting remnants for the headband. Pin petal collar to folded felt (figure B); cut out along outer edges and inner circle. On one collar, using a hole punch, punch holes ½ in. from petal points as indicated by X's in figure B. Cut ribbon into 7 pieces.

TO MAKE HEADBAND: Tie 1 piece of ribbon around the wearer's head as shown in figure A, tying it loosely enough so it can be slipped off the head but still feels comfortable on the wearer; make a knot and remove the headband. Gather up some of the remaining netting in a small bunch and secure it to the headband at the knot by knotting the ribbon around it. Tie a bow and glue or stick on decorations at ribbon ends (figure A).

TO MAKE BODY: The body is made by sandwiching and gluing netting between 2 collars and trimming away the netting at the neck hole area for the head opening. To do this, working on a large surface, lay the unpunched collar out flat. Center and posi-

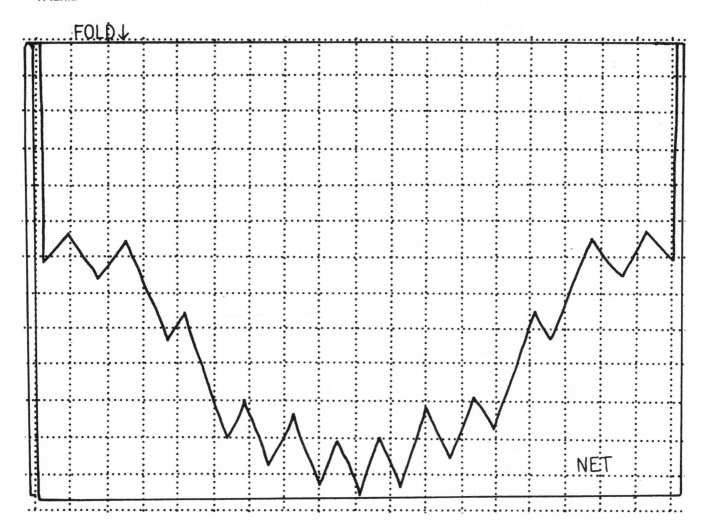

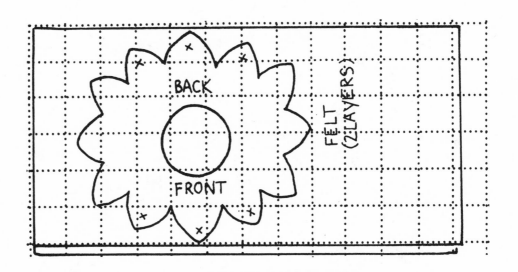

FIGURE B (1 sq. = 2½ in.)

tion the pinned, layered body piece on top of the collar, orienting the front and back of the collar to the body as shown in figure C. Remove the pins in the collar area, then generously apply glue through the netting onto the collar, leaving the petal points glue free (figure D). Align the outer edges of the remaining collar piece on the glued collar, sandwiching the netting in between. Squeeze-press together (figure E). Before glue dries, stick 1 end of each ribbon length through the petal-point hole, approximately 1 to 2 in., lifting the petal point to do this (figure F). Apply a bit more glue on petal underside to hold ribbon in place; finger-press petal point flat and let dry. Attach decorations to ribbon ends (same as for headband), gluing in place to the top layer of netting or to the ribbon end only for a dangling effect; let dry (figure G). Trim away netting from neck hole area. Then, cut a slit in neckline at center back as shown, cutting through all layers, but not extending the slit beyond the collar edge (figure G). Try

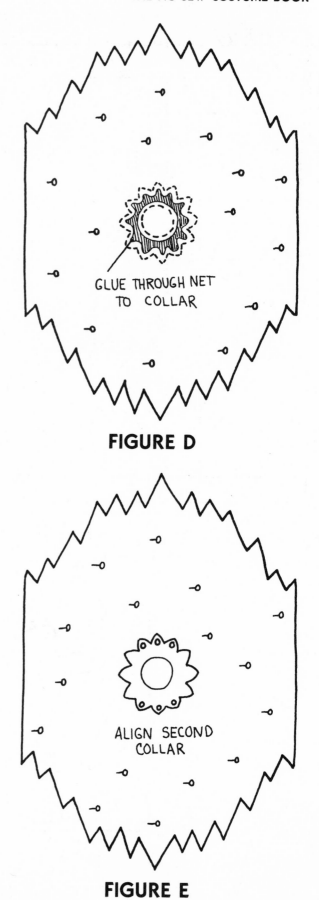

GLUE THROUGH NET TO COLLAR

FIGURE D

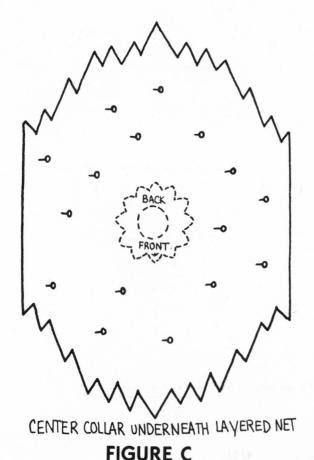

CENTER COLLAR UNDERNEATH LAYERED NET

FIGURE C

ALIGN SECOND COLLAR

FIGURE E

body on wearer and extend slit if necessary to fit over the head. While still on, carefully cut angled slashes—approximately 9 in. long—along the bottom edge through all layers, lifting the ribbons out of the way and holding the netting taut (figure G). These slashes allow for easier movement and the optional use of a belt. Remove all pins.

ADULT SIZING: The slip-on body can be worn very effectively as is over a flowing gown or dress, or it can be lengthened. To do this, make the body pattern, hold it up to the wearer, and determine how long you want the body to be. Measure the difference in length and double it (to account for front and back). Cut the pattern in half along the straight edge and add a piece of paper between the 2 cut edges equal to the width and the determined extra length; tape in place. Allow for extra length when purchasing netting and continue same as above.

SUGGESTIONS: Additional decorations (stars, hearts, flowers) can be added to the netting layers as desired. Ribbons and netting can be tied together for wristlets.

FIGURE F

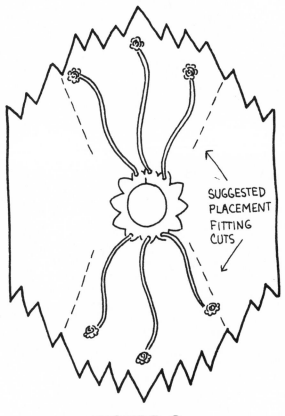

SUGGESTED PLACEMENT FITTING CUTS

FIGURE G

UNICORN

FIGURE A

In a world of their own, unicorns will ride on, forever capturing the imaginations of young and old alike. Simple, but beautiful, this unicorn can be ultrafeminine or dramatically masculine, depending on the colors used.

DESCRIPTION: Unicorn head and felt slip-on body.

94

MATERIALS: ½ yd. white and ¼ yd. pink 72-in.-wide felt; 2 sheets pink poster board (close in color to felt); 3½ yds. turquoise or purple silk cording; 5 yds. gold strung sequins; gold glitter (optional); 2 large wiggle eyes; glue; double-stick tape; hole punch.

PREPARATIONS: Enlarge body, saddle, and wing pattern pieces shown in figures B and C and the head and mane patterns in figure D onto newspaper or brown wrapping paper; cut out. Following the layout in figure B, pin body and mane pattern to folded white felt and saddle pattern to folded pink felt; cut out. Carefully cut neck hole in the body and save the circular remnant for use on wing piece. Trace and cut wings, 2 headpieces, and a 2-×-18-in. rectangular band from pink poster board.

TO MAKE HEAD: Glue eyes and mane in place to create a right and left face as shown in figure D. Draw a fine line of glue along outline of each mane and lay silk cording or strung sequins (string side down) on glue line; trim ends and let dry. To create gold horn, cover horn with a thin layer of glue and apply glitter and/or loose sequins (unstrung) generously to horn; let dry, shake to remove excess. To construct hat, lay 1 face, wrong side up, and apply pieces of double-stick tape to cover the facial area in front of the neck and all of the horn. Place the 2 faces together, right sides out and edges aligned; finger-press to secure together. Fold poster board band in half and place between attached face pieces, along lower edge and starting approximately 6¼ in. in from the back edge, as

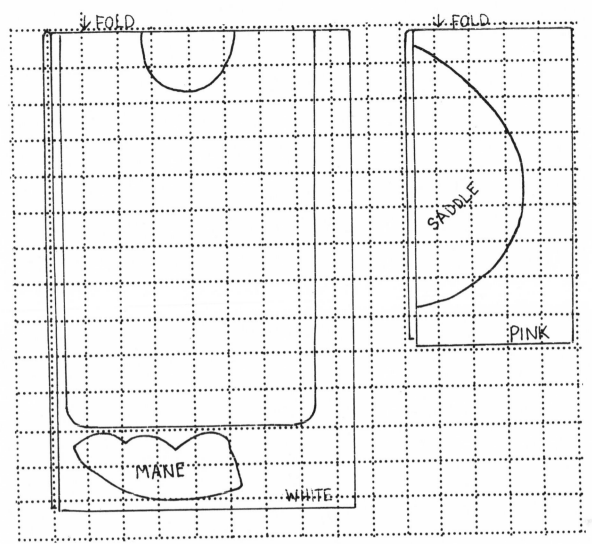

FIGURE B (1 sq. = 2 in.)

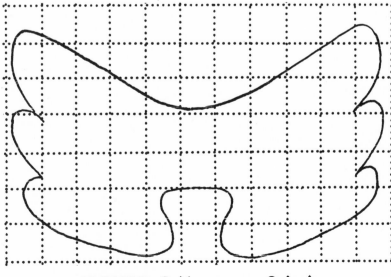

FIGURE C (1 sq. = 2 in.)

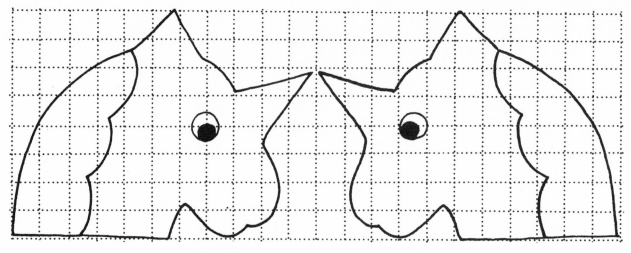

FIGURE D (1 sq. = 1¼ in.)

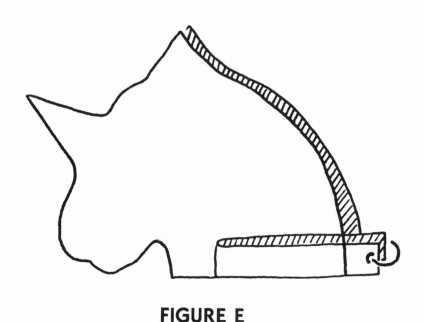

FIGURE E

shown in figure E. Using double-stick tape, secure band in place. Punch holes at the ends of the band and tie closed to fit around the head with a piece of round-cord elastic.

TO MAKE BODY: Lay body out flat. Cut a 3-in. slit as shown in figure F at center of circle edge (when you wear the body, the slit will be in the back). Try body on wearer and extend slit if necessary to fit over the head. To make saddle, lay and glue pink saddle pieces in place as shown. For each saddle piece, draw a thin line of glue 1 in. in from the rounded edge on saddle, following the curve (figure F). Affix strung sequins, string side down, onto glue line; trim. Draw a thin line of glue onto white body along rounded saddle edge; affix silk cording onto glue line, trim, and let dry. To make wings, work on one side at a time, and starting at the center, draw a glue line 1 in. from the outer wing edge; affix strung sequins onto glue and trim (figure F). Trim felt neck hole remnant to a 4-×-6-in. oval. Lay wings onto body back, sequin side up, and secure to body, gluing as shown. Cover felt oval with glue and lay over center of wings, hiding sequin ends and overlapping onto body piece (figure F). Cover with plastic wrap and weight down with books until dry.

ADULT SIZING: No alterations are necessary, although you may lengthen the body if you wish.

SUGGESTIONS: For a more dramatic, masculine look, make a black felt body and head with red or purple details.

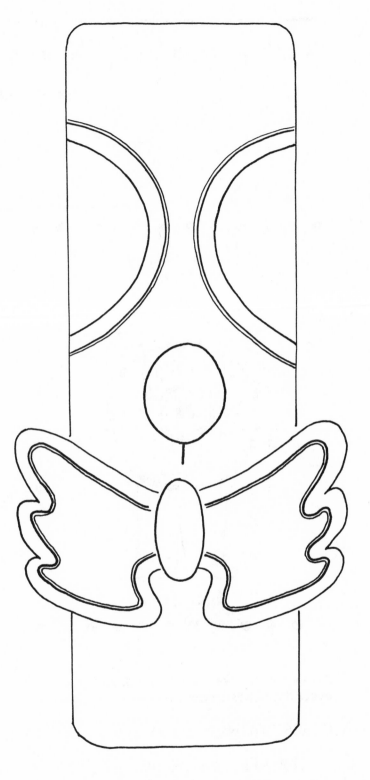

FIGURE F

EYEBALL

FIGURE A

Always on the watch, this bulging, bloodshot eyeball catches people by surprise.

DESCRIPTION: Slip-on bloodshot eyeball.

MATERIALS: 3 pieces white poster board; 1 yd. red and ¼ yd. black Con-Tact paper; 1 sheet metallic blue wrapping paper or ¼ yd. blue Con-Tact paper; double-stick tape; red marking pen; ¼-in. or round-cord elastic; staples; hole punch.

PREPARATIONS: Measure and draw 2 rounded ovals on white poster board, one 22 × 24 in., the other 18 × 20 in., and 2 strips, each 9 × 26 in. On the 18-×-20-in. oval only, extend the side edges out 3 × 3 in., forming 2 tabs as shown in figure B; cut out all pieces. Measure and cut a 3-in. and an 8-in. circle from black Con-Tact paper and a 7¾-in. circle from metallic blue paper. Cut 8 slightly curved slivers of Con-Tact paper, approximately 2 in. long, for detailing the iris of the eye. Trace outer edge of the 22-×-24-in. oval onto red Con-Tact paper, piecing as necessary. Measure in 2 in. from the outline and cut out, forming an eye ring.

TO MAKE EYEBALL: Position and affix large Con-Tact paper circle in the middle of the large oval eyeball. Center the blue paper iris on top of the black circle and secure with small pieces of double-stick tape. Center and affix small black circle (pupil) onto the blue iris. Position and affix Con-Tact paper slivers on the iris, radiating from the pupil (figure C). Using red marker, draw broken blood vessels (jagged lines that resemble tree branches) on the white eye area as shown. Turn the eye over to the wrong side. Fold each poster board 9-×-26-in. strip into thirds, forming a 3-×-26-in. strip; fold up 1½ to 2 in. on each end of 1 strip. Center strip with folded ends on back of eye, so it goes across the eye (shorter, 22-in. width) and the fold lines are aligned with the side edges; staple the ends to the eye 1 in. in from the edge (figure D). The eye will bulge outward. Lay the remaining strip lengthwise over the first, on center and with ends aligned with upper and lower edge of eye; staple ends to eye (figure D). Draw broken blood vessels on remaining oval with tabs (the back of the eyeball). Position oval on top of the crossed strips, slipping tabs between the eye and the folded strip ends on the sides; staple all 3 layers together close to the edge (figure E).

Punch 2 holes along the upper edge of back eyeball, 1 in. from the edge and 5 in. from center on either side. Tie a 20-in. piece of elastic (or doubled round-cord elastic) through 1 hole, weave it under the strip at the top of the front eye, and then pull it through the other hole and tie loosely. Slide the eyeball onto the wearer, over the head; the crossed strips will rest on the front upper body. Adjust elastic to fit and tie securely (figure F).

ADULT SIZING: No changes are necessary.

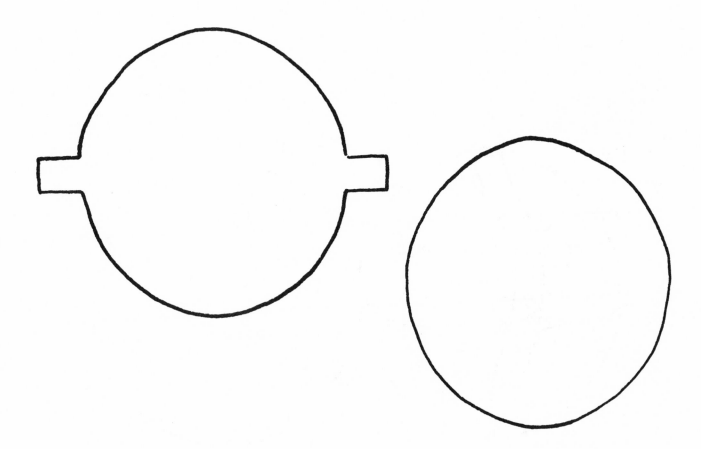

FIGURE B

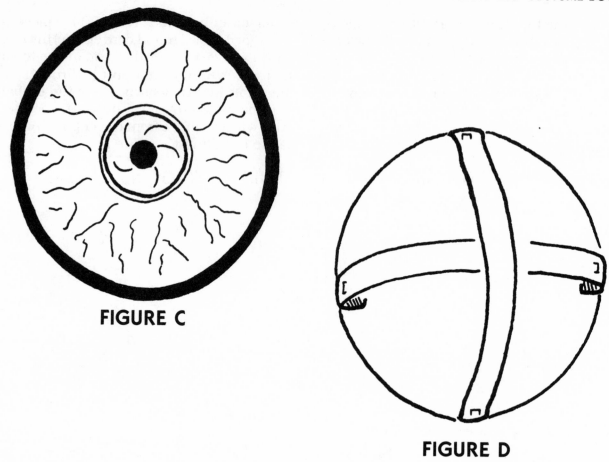

FIGURE C

FIGURE D

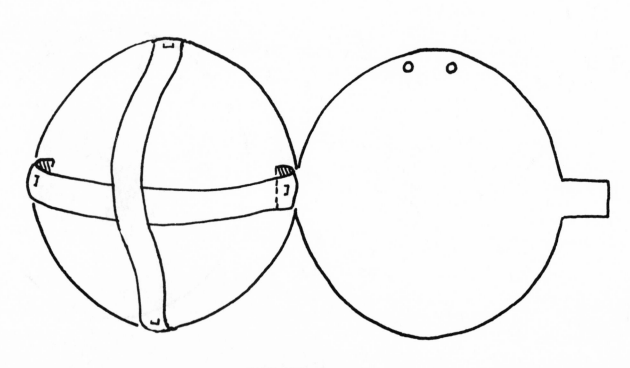

FIGURE E

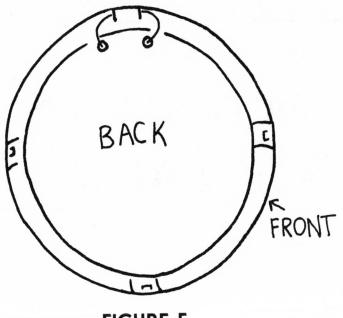

FIGURE F

CHAPTER IV

FICTIONAL AND NONFICTIONAL CHARACTERS

CLEOPATRA

FIGURE A

A figure from the past, the beauty and allure of Cleopatra are captured with simplicity in this colorful and comfortable costume (see illustration on front cover).

DESCRIPTION: "Hair" band/felt wig and felt, "jewelled" slip-on tunic.

MATERIALS: ½ yd. navy, ¼ yd. gold (or 3 squares), ½ yd. white, and ¼ yd. black 72-in.-wide felt (if navy felt is not available by the yard and gold is, reverse these yardages); 1 or 2 squares turquoise felt; metallic notions, such as 1½ yds. strung gold sequins, metallic gold slick fabric pen, or glitter; jewel notions, such as glue-on rubies, rhinestones, large sequins, or glitter; small piece of gold Con-Tact paper (optional); aluminum foil; 2-×-20-in. band of poster board or similar weight cardboard; round-cord elastic; staples; hole punch.

PREPARATIONS: Enlarge tunic and collar patterns (include dotted lines and numbers) shown in figures B and C onto newspaper or brown wrapping paper; cut out. Following the layout in figure B, pin tunic pattern onto folded white felt; cut out. Then pin collar, folded in half, onto folded navy felt as shown in figure B and cut out along outside lines

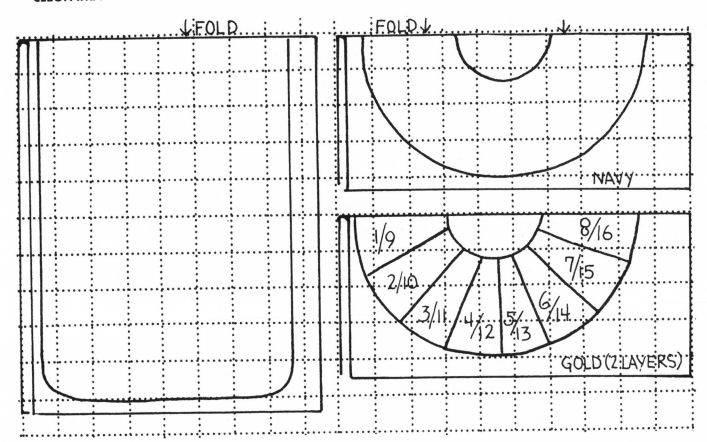

FIGURE B (1 sq. = 2 in.)

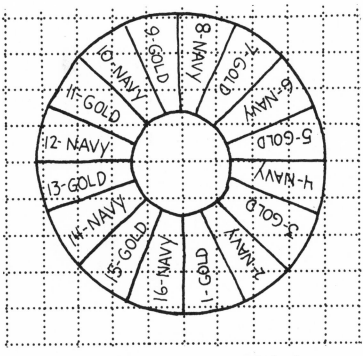

FIGURE C (1 sq. = 2 in.)

only. Using the collar pattern again and folded gold felt, lay out pattern as shown and cut along outlines and inner lines; leave pattern attached to pieces until time of assembly. Cut turquoise felt into ¼-in. strips. Hold the poster board strip up to the head of the wearer, across the forehead, and trim to 1 in. less than the circumference of the head. Cut a piece of black felt the length of the strip and 10 in. wide. Cut a 1¼-×-14-in. strip of gold Con-Tact paper (optional).

TO MAKE HAIR BAND: Align and staple black felt to poster board band. To create the face opening, measure the distance from eyebrow end to eyebrow end on the wearer; this is the width of the face opening. Measured from the bottom, the height is 5 in. on both sides. Center and cut the face opening as shown in figure D. Then, make ½-in. grass cuts on the black felt sides and edge above opening, creating hair and bangs (figure D). Try on hair band to determine desired hair length, remove, and trim accordingly. Center

and adhere Con-Tact paper strip ¼ in. from the top of the hair band. Then, cut a 26-in. piece of foil and roll it lengthwise into a 2-in. tube; fold the tube along the center and crimp together for 2 in. from the fold, forming a snake head. Crimp the remaining foil into 2 separate bodies coming out from the head; center the snake head on the hair band strip and staple in place (figure D). Punch holes near end of band and tie closed to fit around the head with a piece of round-cord elastic (figure D).

TO MAKE TUNIC: Lay navy collar piece out flat. Arrange the gold felt pieces (with patterns attached) numerically around the navy collar, as shown in figure C. The even-numbered pieces are used for positioning only; when all pieces are placed, remove the even-numbered pieces and glue the odd-numbered pieces in place on the collar. The collar will now have an alternating gold and navy pattern. Working from the neck opening edge, lay turquoise strips along the gold edges;

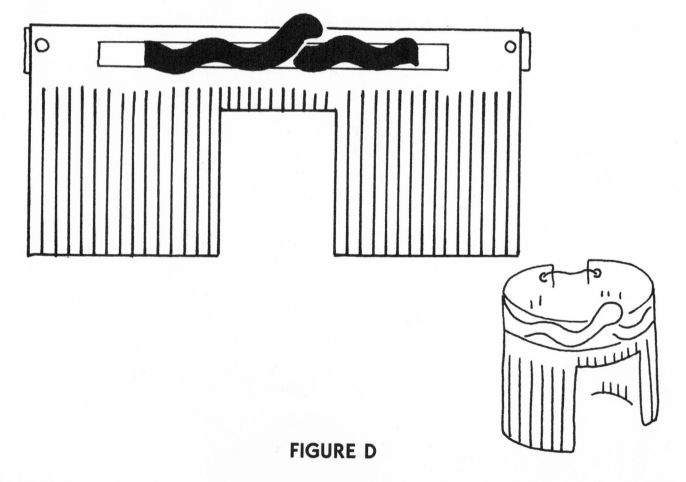

FIGURE D

trim along outer collar edges and glue in place (figure E). On each gold felt segment, draw a thin line of glue from the neck opening to the collar edge; lay strung sequins on glue, thread side down, trim, and gently finger-press to secure. Position and glue jewels, large sequins, or glitter (or, draw on jewels with slick fabric paint) in place on navy segments as shown in Figure E. To complete, lay the white felt tunic out flat. Position decorated collar on tunic, right side up and centered, and glue in place; let dry. Trim away tunic neck hole area along collar neck edge and cut a 4-in. slit along the center back neck edge—through both layers—as shown (figure F). Try tunic on wearer and extend slit if necessary to fit over the head.

ADULT SIZING: Use the full 72-in. felt width to make a longer version of the tunic.

SUGGESTIONS: Make foil snake arm bands and/or add a gold belt to the tunic.

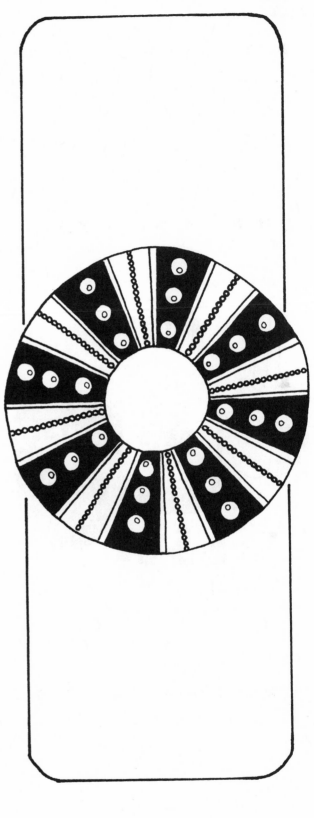

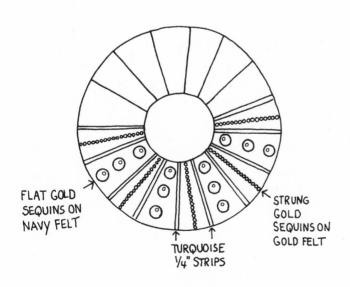

FLAT GOLD SEQUINS ON NAVY FELT

STRUNG GOLD SEQUINS ON GOLD FELT

TURQUOISE 1/4" STRIPS

FIGURE E

FIGURE F

KNIGHT

FIGURE A

Fearless and brave is the knight who wears the emblem of the double-headed dragon. Very little effort is required, however, to pull this garb together!

DESCRIPTION: Double-headed dragon tabard and shield.

MATERIALS: ⅔ yd. black and ⅓ yd. red 72-in.-wide felt; 2 pieces black poster board; glue; tape; staples.

PREPARATIONS: Enlarge tabard, overbib, and dragon emblem as shown in figures B and C on newspaper or brown wrapping paper; cut out. Following the layouts in figure B, pin the tabard onto folded black felt and the overbib onto folded red felt; cut out. Pin and cut 1 dragon from remaining black felt and 1 or 2 dragons from red felt. Measure and cut two $2\frac{1}{4}$-×-14-in. arm bands from 1 piece of black poster board.

TO MAKE TABARD: Lay black felt tabard out flat. Draw a thin line of glue around the neck, ¼ in. in from the edge. Center and align red felt overbib on top of tabard; finger-press together at neck area; let dry. Turn tabard over and trim away overbib neck area along tabard neckline. Make a 4-in. slit through both layers at center back neck edge (figure E); try on wearer and lengthen slit if necessary to fit over head. Position and glue the black felt dragon emblem on the overbib as shown in figure E.

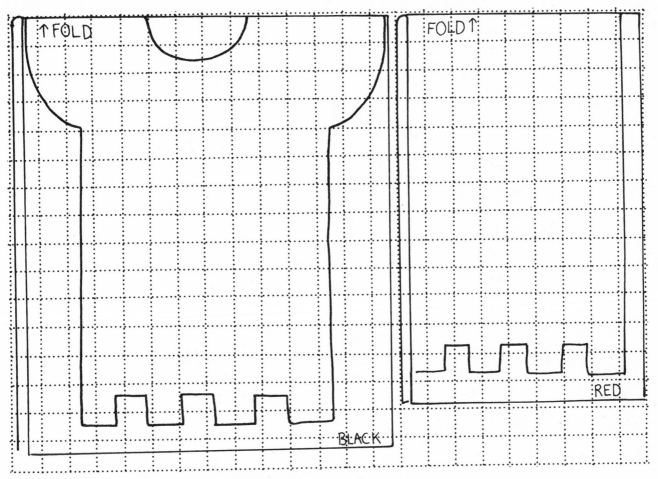

FIGURE B (1 sq. = 1½ in.)

TO MAKE SHIELD: Fold the uncut black poster board in half. Cut a shield shape, using the full width and height of the folded board, as shown in figure D. Position and staple ends of arm bands to the shield, stapling through 1 layer only; tape ends of bands to shield (figure D). Glue or staple the 2 shield layers together along the cut edges; let dry if glued. Position and glue 1 or 2 red dragon emblems on the shield front (figure D).

ADULT SIZING: No alterations are necessary, although you may lengthen the tabard if desired.

SUGGESTIONS: The remaining poster board can be used to make a sword or lance. For a shiny blade, cover with silver Con-Tact paper or foil. Other royal colors that are good choices for this costume are royal blue and black, purple and black, green and black, or purple and red.

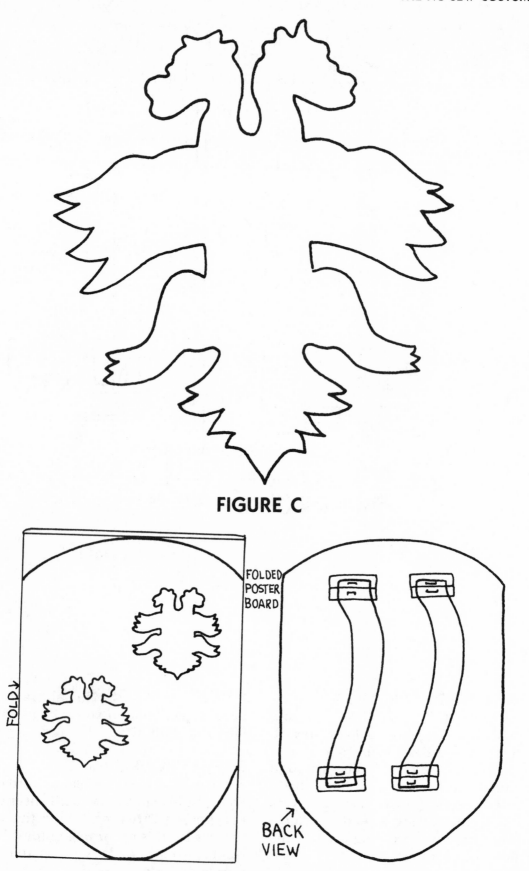

FIGURE C

FIGURE D

FIGURE E

BALLERINA

FIGURE A

A new turn on a classic, this all-season ballerina costume comes with legs included, toe shoes and all. Its slip-on design allows for easy movement.

DESCRIPTION: Bow band and felt slip-on ballerina body.

MATERIALS: ⅔ yd. bright pink and ¼ yd. each of light pink, black, and white 72-in.-

wide felt; black or navy yarn; glue; strung sequins (optional); round-cord elastic.

PREPARATIONS: Enlarge body, collar, leg, and shoe patterns in figure B onto newspaper or brown wrapping paper; cut out. Following the layout in figure B, pin the body piece on a single layer of bright pink felt as shown; cut out. Fold the remaining bright pink felt, and following the layout, pin the collar onto it as shown; cut out. Pin legs to the folded white felt; cut out. Pin the shoe pattern to folded black felt; cut out shoes and three ⅝-×-16-in. strips for the shoe ties. For the headband, measure and cut a 1½-×-16-in. black felt rectangle and a 1-×-14-in. bright pink felt rectangle. For bows, cut twelve 1-×-4½-in. rectangles and one 1-×-6-in. rectangle plus a 2-×-14-in. belt from light pink felt. Cut one 1½-×-9-in. black felt rectangle for the belt bow.

TO MAKE HEADBAND: Center and glue the 1-×-14-in. pink rectangle on top of the 1½-×-16-in. black rectangle. Add a single strand of strung sequins—if desired—on center, using a thin line of glue to secure; let dry (figure C). On wrong side, reinforce each band end with a small square of poster board or cardboard; glue in place and let dry. Make a bow, using the 1-×-6-in. light pink felt rectangle; overlap the ends, glue, and press together to make a tube (figure D). Tie a 6-in. piece of black yarn around the middle of the tube tightly, knotting to make a bow (figure D). Glue the bow on front of band in position shown (figure C); let dry. Punch holes at band ends through the poster board; tie closed to fit around the head with a piece of round-cord elastic.

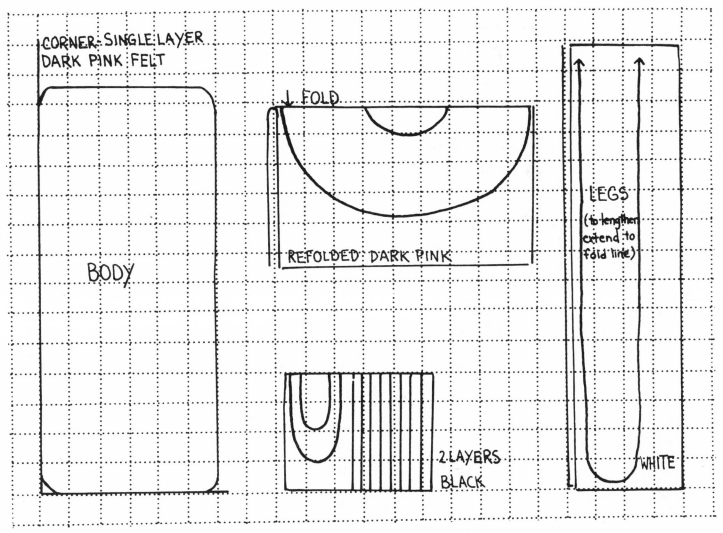

FIGURE B (1 sq. = 2½ in.)

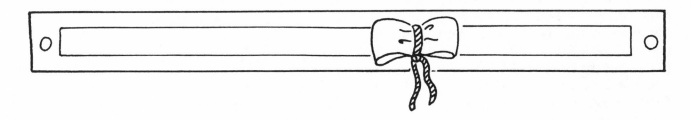

FIGURE C

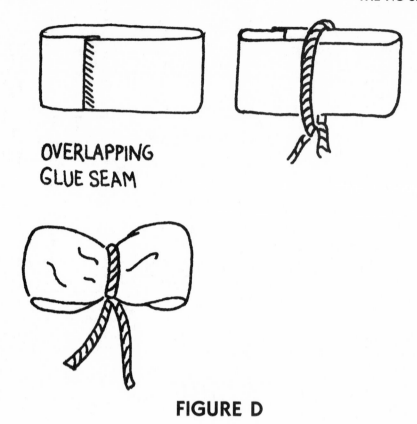

OVERLAPPING
GLUE SEAM

FIGURE D

TO MAKE BODY: Lay body piece out flat. Position open collar on body, centering and aligning the back edges; glue in place around neck hole, shoulder edges, and back edge of body; let dry. Cut away neck hole from body piece and cut a 4-in. slit at center back neck edge as shown in figure E. Try on, lengthening the slit if necessary to fit over head, and check the body length. If the length is longer than midthigh, shorten it, cutting off the excess. Using the 1-×-4½-in. rectangles, make 12 bows, same as for headband. Position around the edge of the collar and glue in place (figure E). Position and glue belt to body. Make a bow from the 1½-×-9-in. black felt rectangle, same as for headband; glue to side of belt and let dry. Decorate legs. Position and glue on shoes first, then laces (⅝-×-16-in. strips), crisscrossing them up the lower leg as shown (figure E). Cut remaining black strip into 4 equal pieces for leg ties. Position and glue these to wrong side of legs as shown in figure E. To determine the leg length, try the body on the wearer and hold the legs up so that the ballet slippers extend from the bottom of the body to the top of the wearer's feet. Pin legs in place with excess on wrong side of body. Remove costume and lay out flat, wrong side up. Trim leg if necessary and glue in place (figure E).

ADULT SIZING: Lengthen the body front and legs.

SUGGESTIONS: Although the legs add a special touch to this costume, they can be eliminated. The colors chosen are very feminine but can be changed to your liking.

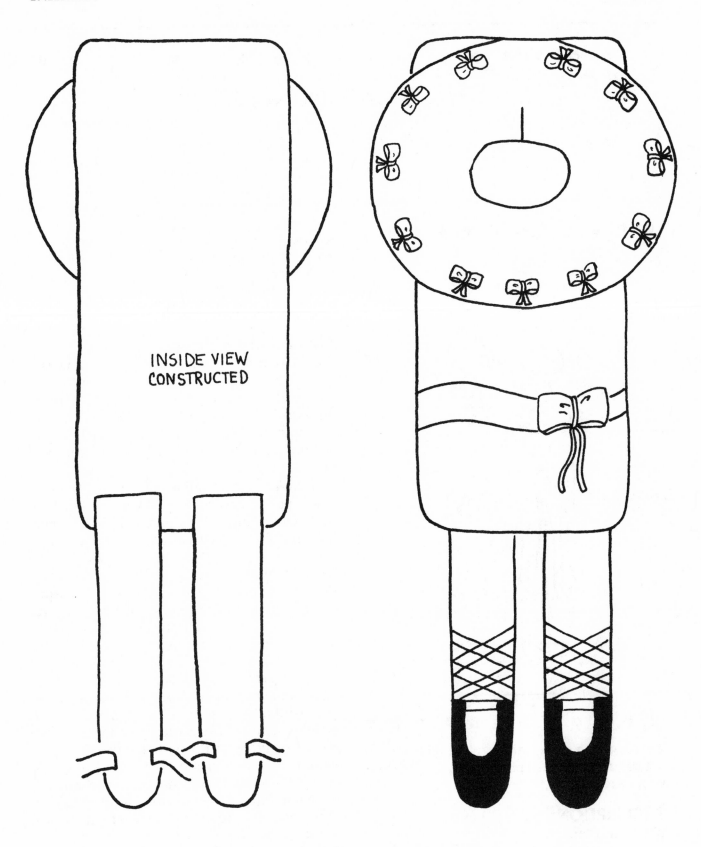

INSIDE VIEW
CONSTRUCTED

FIGURE E

HAWAIIAN PRINCESS

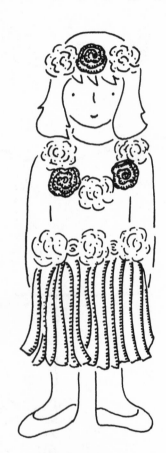

FIGURE A

Bursting with color, this floral delight is fit for a most royal Hawaiian princess. It's easy to make and easy to wear.

DESCRIPTION: Floral headband, grass skirt, and lei.

MATERIALS: 1 piece pink poster board; 3 sheets each of light green and dark pink tissue paper (or colors of your choice); 1 roll each of purple, dark pink, light pink, and green crepe paper streamers; craft knife; staples; double-stick tape; hole punch; round-cord elastic.

PREPARATIONS: Measure and cut a 1½-×-16-in. headband, a 1¾-×-24-in. waistband, and a 10-in.-diameter circle (for the lei) from pink poster board; forty-five 5-in. squares from dark pink tissue paper; and approximately four 40- to 42-in. lengths each of both pinks, purple, and green streamers.

TO MAKE HEADBAND: Make 9 pink tissue paper flowers, using 4 squares for each and positioning them 1 on top of the other as shown in figure B. Grasp and squeeze the center of the tissue layers to resemble a flower; set aside. Make 4 purple streamer flowers. To do this, wrap the streamer into a cone shape; then, wrap the streamer around the cone 10 or more times, securing the bottom edge with your fingers and tapering the upper edge out into a petal shape (figure C). Staple bottom edges together to secure; set aside. Gather up 1 sheet of green tissue paper crosswise to fit the headband; staple in place 1 in. from each edge. Starting at the center, position and staple a pink flower to the gathered tissue. Then, working out to each end, position and staple a purple flower and then another pink flower as shown in figure D. Carefully secure the gathered tissue (between the staples) to the headband, using a few small pieces of double-stick tape. Punch holes near the ends of the headband and tie closed to fit around the head of the wearer with a piece of round-cord elastic.

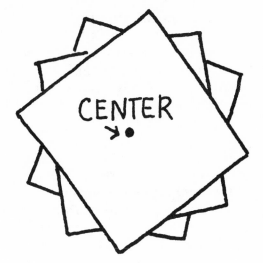

CENTER

SQUEEZE CENTER

FIGURE B

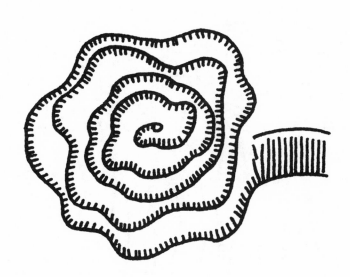

FIGURE C

FIGURE D

TO MAKE GRASS SKIRT: First make slashes in the waistband for weaving the "grass" through. To do this, work from the center out to each side. Using a craft knife, carefully cut a 2-in. slash ½ in. below the top waistband edge, then cut the next 2-in. slash ½ in. below the first and starting ⅝ in. in from the upper slash edge. By doing this, the upper grass pieces will partially overlap the ones below, creating a fuller look. End slashes 1½ in. in from band ends. There will be approximately 17 slashes. Using the 4 colors of streamer lengths, form the grass skirt by pulling 1 streamer approximately halfway

through each slit, varying the colors as you go (figure E). Gather up 1 sheet of green tissue paper lengthwise to fit the waistband; staple in place 1 in. from each end. Starting at the center, position and staple 1 pink flower to the gathered tissue and then another halfway between the center and end on each side as shown in figure E. Carefully secure the gathered tissue to the waistband at the flower positions only, using a small piece of double-stick tape. Punch holes near the ends of the waistband and tie closed to fit around the wearer's waist or hips with a piece of round-cord elastic.

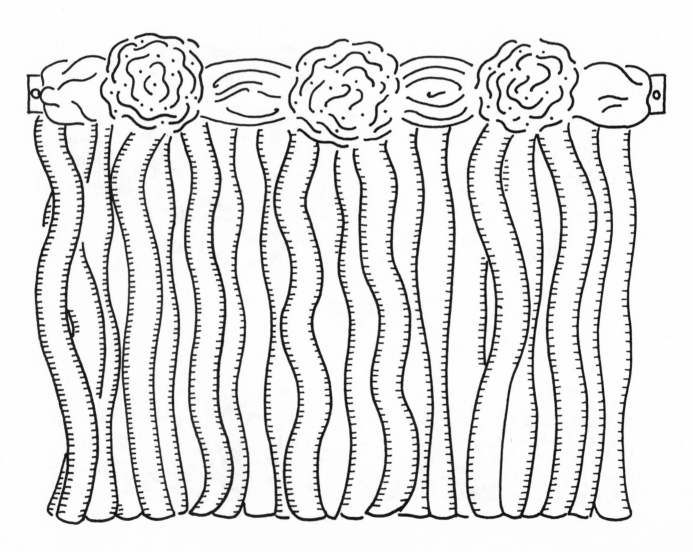

FIGURE E

TO MAKE THE LEI: Measure in 2 in. from the edge of the pink poster board circle all around and draw another circle, squaring off the sides slightly as shown in figure F; cut out inner circle to form a ring and cut across the ring at the top edge to form an opening. Gather, position, and staple 1 sheet of green tissue paper onto the ring, same as for the headband (figure G). Starting at the center and working out same as for the headband, staple pink and purple flowers to the gathered tissue. Cut approximately fifteen 2- to 2½-in. triangular leaf shapes from green crepe paper streamers. If desired, cut each leaf individually on a small piece of folded streamer, posi-

tioning the leaf tip on the fold (this gives a double-leaf effect). Tuck 2 or 3 leaves under each flower as shown in figure G and secure to the tissue with small pieces of double-stick tape. Tape the tissue to the poster board ring under the flowers, same as for the grass skirt. Punch holes near the ends of the lei and tie closed with a piece of round-cord elastic.

ADULT SIZING: Widen the waistband to fit and lengthen the grass streamers.

SUGGESTIONS: Wear a coordinating bathing suit, leotard, or simple shirt with or without tights for the best effect.

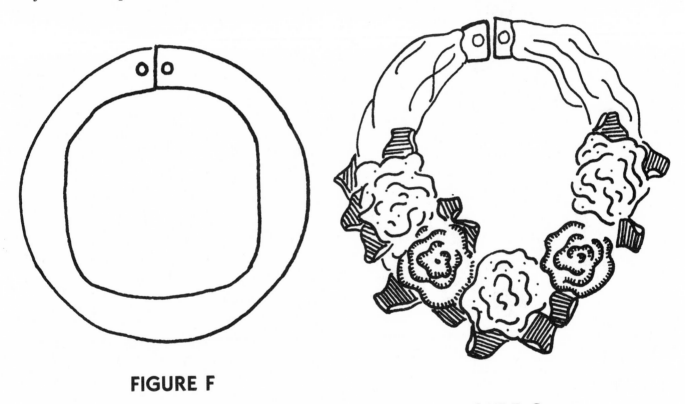

FIGURE F

FIGURE G

SNOWMAN

FIGURE A

This snowperson couldn't be much "cooler," parading around in his tropical shades! The face is attached to the hat for a very comfortable fit.

DESCRIPTION: Snow face/hatband and snowball slip-on body.

MATERIALS: 3 sheets of white and 1 sheet of black poster board; small pieces of yellow and orange poster board (preferably) or construction paper; 2 yds. of 45-in.-wide batting or fluffy interfacing; five 1-in. black or blue buttons (optional); black fabric tape; ½ yd. red dotted or plaid (or color and design of your choice) 1-in.-wide ribbon; 1 package red or green jumbo rickrack; 3 or more stick-on decorations for glasses (optional); small piece of green cellophane or plastic wrap; feather (optional); scarf or fabric remnant; double-stick tape; staples; hole punch; round-cord elastic; glue.

PREPARATIONS: Enlarge hat, sunglasses, body, face, and nose pattern pieces as shown in figures B, C, D, E, and F onto newspaper or brown wrapping paper; cut out. Trace the face pattern once (including face opening); body pattern twice, and two 2-×-12-in. shoulder bands onto white poster board; cut out. Apply glue or double-stick tape generously to the face, body, and shoulder band pieces; lay the pieces glue (or tape) side down on the batting and trim away excess along edges. Trace the hat and hat brim patterns onto black poster board, the sunglasses onto yellow poster board (or white poster board if using construction paper), and the nose patterns onto orange poster board (or white); cut out all pieces. (If using yellow and orange construction paper, trace and cut glasses pattern from yellow and nose patterns from orange; align and glue these pieces to the matching white poster board pieces.)

118

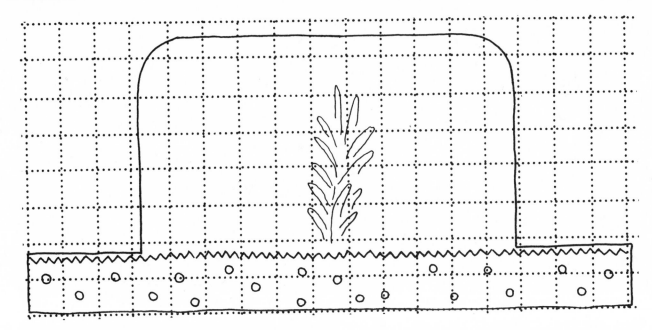

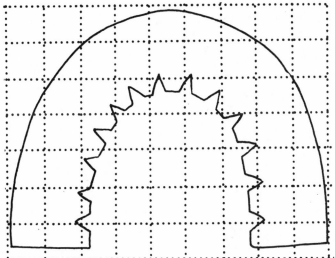

FIGURE B (1 sq. = 1 in.)

TO MAKE HATBAND/FACE: Assemble the hat first, beginning by fitting the brim to the hat base. Bend the notched (inner) edge up on a 90-degree angle to the brim and place this edge along the inside lower edge of the hat, curving the hat to fit. Tape notches to hat as shown in figure G. To decorate hat, run a line of double-stick tape around the hat, 1 in. from each end and just above the brim; affix ribbon to tape, trimming ends as necessary. Punch holes near the ends of hatband and tie closed to fit around the head with a piece of round-cord elastic.

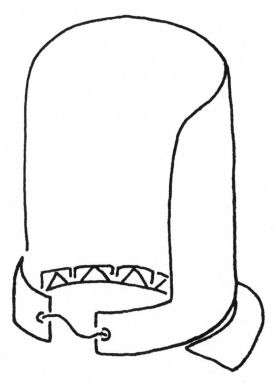

FIGURE E (1 sq. = 1½ in.)

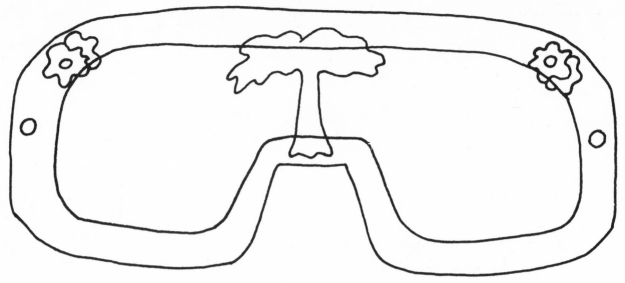

FIGURE C

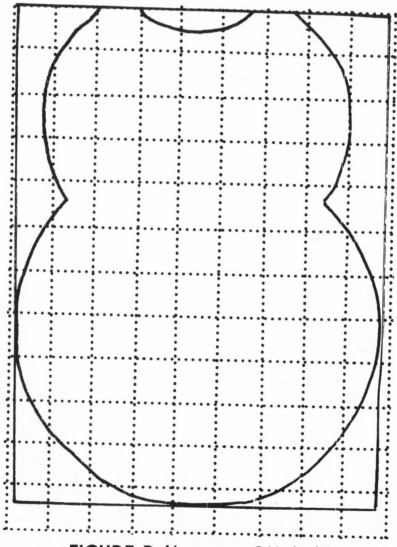

FIGURE D (1 sq. = 2½ in.)

Assemble the face pieces next, beginning with the nose. Fold nose base at tip as shown in figure H. Squeeze small beads of glue along one edge of nose base and affix upper nose piece in place; let dry (figure H). To assemble sunglasses, place small pieces of double-stick tape on the back side of the frame, and lay the frame, tape side down, onto a piece of cellophane or plastic wrap cut slightly larger than the frame. Trim the cellophane or wrap along the outside edge of the frame. Punch holes at the sides of the frame as indicated and tie a 14-in. piece of round-cord elastic through the holes to form a band (figure C). Decorate frame with stickers.

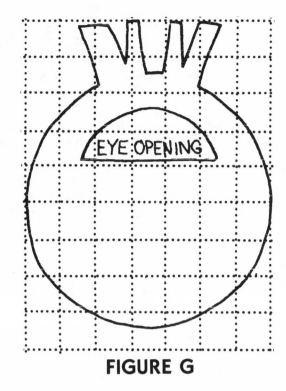

FIGURE G

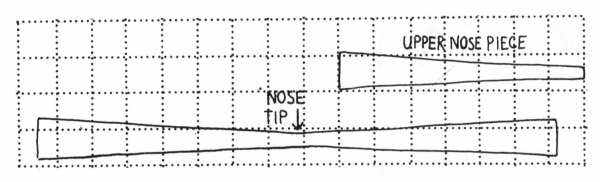

FIGURE F (1 sq. = 1 in.)

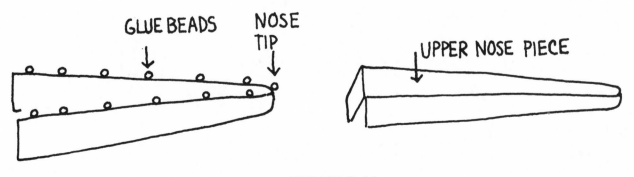

FIGURE H

To assemble the face, position and glue 2 button eyes (or 1-in. poster board circles) slightly below the face opening as shown in figure I. Fold in the ends at the base of the nose ¼ in. and position and glue to face; let dry. Position and glue rickrack mouth in place; let dry (figure I). Slide the sunglasses on over the head, tightening the elastic if needed. To attach face to hatband, place the notched face extension along the inside lower edge of the hat, centering the face; tape in place (figure J). Finish off the inside with black fabric tape for a smooth, clean look.

FIGURE I

FIGURE J

TO MAKE BODY: Position and glue 3 buttons (or 1-in. poster board circles) onto body front. Hold the front up to the wearer and mark the position of the shoulder edges onto the top edge; transfer these marks onto top edge of back body piece. Staple or tape ends of shoulder bands to wrong side of front and back body pieces at shoulder marks to fit as shown in figure K. Finish off costume with a scarf tied loosely around the neck.

ADULT SIZING: If necessary, enlarge facial opening to allow maximum visibility.

SUGGESTIONS: You can dress this ''person'' up to fit your fashion sense—change the color of the hat or decorate it with sequins . . .use your own sunglasses. . .put on a bow tie. . .add a polka-dot bikini!

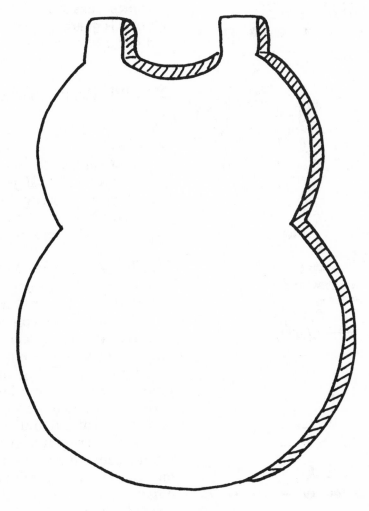

FIGURE K

• • • CHAPTER V • • •

BOTANICALS AND EDIBLES

COCONUT TREE

FIGURE A

A tropical sensation, this walking, talking coconut tree is guaranteed to raise a few eyebrows and get a few laughs.

DESCRIPTION: Leaf headband and slip-on tree trunk.

MATERIALS: 5 pieces of fluorescent green or leaf green poster board; 7 sheets green tissue paper (only 2 if using leaf green poster board); brown corrugated box cardboard; 1 brown, orange, or yellow balloon plus 1 dark stocking; tape; staples; glue; hole punch.

PREPARATIONS: Enlarge 2 leaf and headband patterns shown in figures B and C onto newspaper or brown wrapping paper; cut out along outer edges only (do not make leaf cuts). (For fluorescent green poster board only, cover white side of poster board with green tissue, affixing them together with glue; let dry.) Trace 5 large leaves, 3 small leaves, and 1 headband pattern onto green poster board; cut out. Measure and cut 2 pieces of corrugated cardboard for the tree trunk, each approximately 14 × 26 in.—cutting slightly wavy along the lengthwise edges for a more realistic look—and 2 shoulder bands, 2 × 12 in.

124

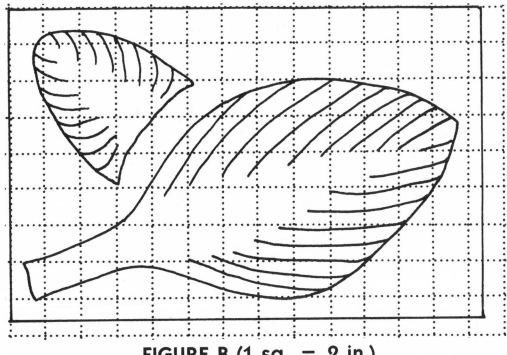

FIGURE B (1 sq. = 2 in.)

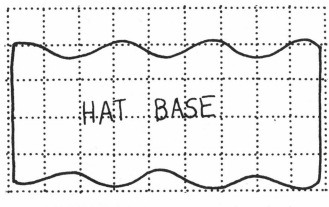

FIGURE C (1 sq. = 1¾ in.)

TO MAKE HEADBAND: For each large leaf, gently fold in half lengthwise just enough to make a slight crease in the poster board. Then, beginning at the leaf tip, make leaf cuts on each side of the crease as shown in figure B. Fold the headband in half, so scalloped edges meet; finger-crease, then open up again. Fold 1 sheet of tissue paper crosswise 2 times and gather it up along one edge to fit on the wrong side of the headband as shown in figure D; tape in place. Position 5 large leaves, wrong side up (if tissue-covered) onto wrong side of headband as shown; staple in place (figure D). Refold the headband and staple together at both ends. Punch holes near the ends and tie closed to fit around the head with a piece of round-cord elastic (figure E). When worn, the leaves will gently fold over the band as shown in figure A.

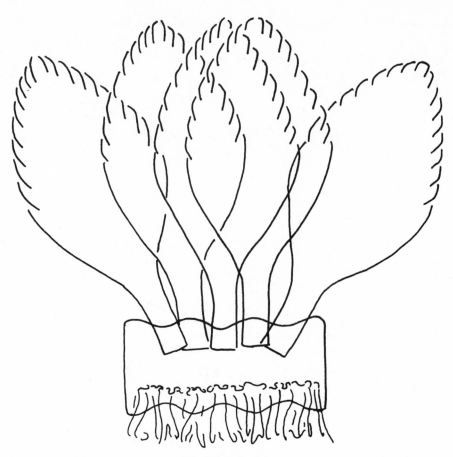

FIGURE D

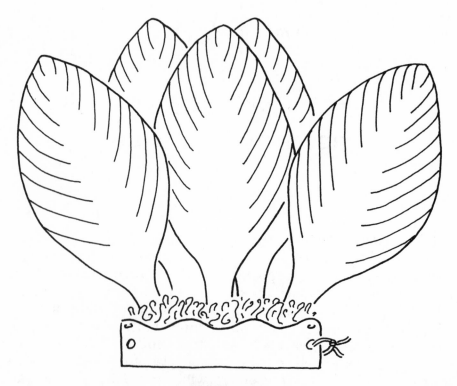

FIGURE E

TO MAKE TREE TRUNK: First create the bark texture. To do this, peel strips of the top paper layer from the corrugated cardboard trunk, starting from the side edge as shown in figure F. Then, join the front and back together. Hold the front up to the wearer and mark the position of the shoulder edges on inner top edge; transfer these marks to wrong side of back top edges. Staple the ends of each shoulder band to wrong side of the front and back at shoulder marks to fit. Crease and cut the small leaves, same as for headband leaves. Cut 1 leaf along crease to form 2 halves. Staple these leaves to front neck edge as shown in figure F. To make the coconut, blow the brown balloon up until slightly full and staple end under the small coconut leaves. If using orange or yellow balloon carefully pull a stocking over it; twist the excess of the stocking at both ends, join them together at the knotted end of the balloon, and staple together. Trim away all but 1 in. of the stocking ends and inconspicuously staple to tree trunk so coconut hangs out from under the leaves (figure A). To complete the trunk, gather up a sheet of green tissue or cut a piece of poster board to fit the lower edge of trunk, glue at bottom, and let dry; grass-cut gathered tissue or poster board as shown in figure F.

ADULT SIZING: If desired, you can lengthen the tree trunk.

SUGGESTIONS: For ease in sitting, the back trunk can be made shorter, so that it ends at the waist. For a small child, 3 headband leaves would be sufficient.

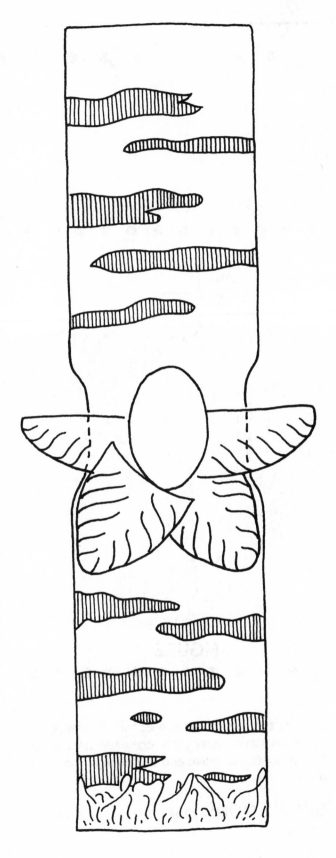

FIGURE F

CACTUS

FIGURE A

From out of the desert comes this southwestern motif—a stately plant that commands respect. It's lots of fun to make and deceivingly comfortable to wear.

DESCRIPTION: One-piece felt-covered cactus.

MATERIALS: ⅔ yd. light green 72-in.-wide felt; 2 pieces green poster board; 8 yds. strung green sequins; 18-×-24-in. piece of corrugated box cardboard; 1 square of red, yellow, or pink felt, or small pieces of red and yellow cellophane wrap, or netting for the flower (optional); glue; staples; craft knife (optional); hole punch; round-cord elastic or ¼-in. elastic.

PREPARATIONS: Enlarge cactus pattern in figure B onto newspaper or brown wrapping paper; cut out. Open up the felt and lay out flat; pin cactus pattern to felt as shown and cut out. Cut a 2½-in. band from the top edge of 1 piece of poster board as shown in figure C. Join 2 pieces of poster board together, overlapping slightly as shown in figure C, and tape securely together.

TO MAKE CACTUS: Using a thin layer of glue along the felt edges, secure the upper portion of cactus to poster board as shown in figure C; let dry. Cut the face hole 4¾ in. from the top of the cactus and attach the headband to the wrong side, stapling near the center of the face opening as shown. Working with cactus right side up (felt up), draw straight glue lines, 6 to 12 in. at a time, following the line patterns in figure D, and lay on strung sequins, string side down; let dry. Trace the midsection of the cactus (arms included) onto the corrugated board. Cut out carefully with a craft knife or scissors. Punch 4 holes in the board 1 in. from the top and bottom edges as shown. Tie 2 pieces of elastic diagonally across the board to fit across the back of the wearer as shown. Then, draw a glue line along the inside edges and affix the board to the wrong side of the cactus as shown in figure E; let dry. Punch holes near the ends of the headband and tie closed to fit around the wearer's head with a piece of round-cord elastic. The head closure serves merely to hold the cactus top in place; the support for the costume comes from the elastic cross straps.

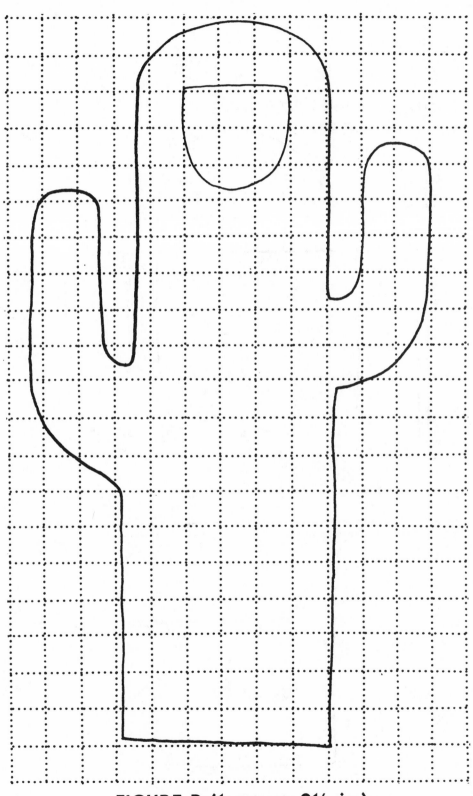

FIGURE B (1 sq. = 2½ in.)

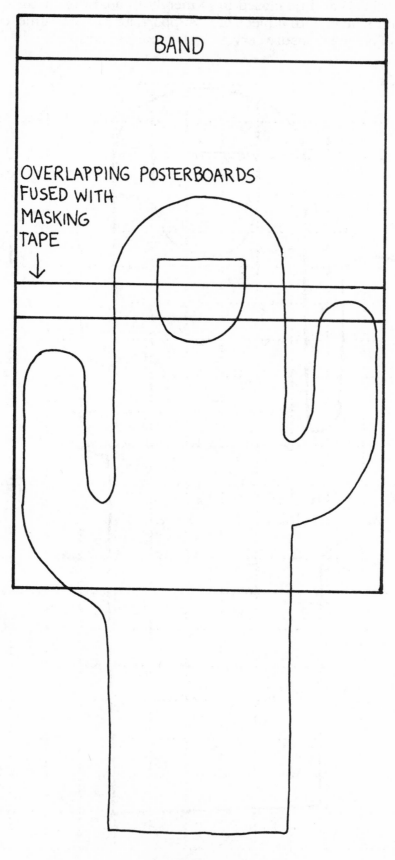

FIGURE C

TO ADD CACTUS FLOWERS (optional):

Make a few layers of small felt, cellophane, or netting squares, and gather the squares up from the center, securing them together with a staple, string, or rubber band. Position on cactus as desired and staple or glue in place.

ADULT SIZING: No alterations necessary, although you can lengthen the cactus if you wish.

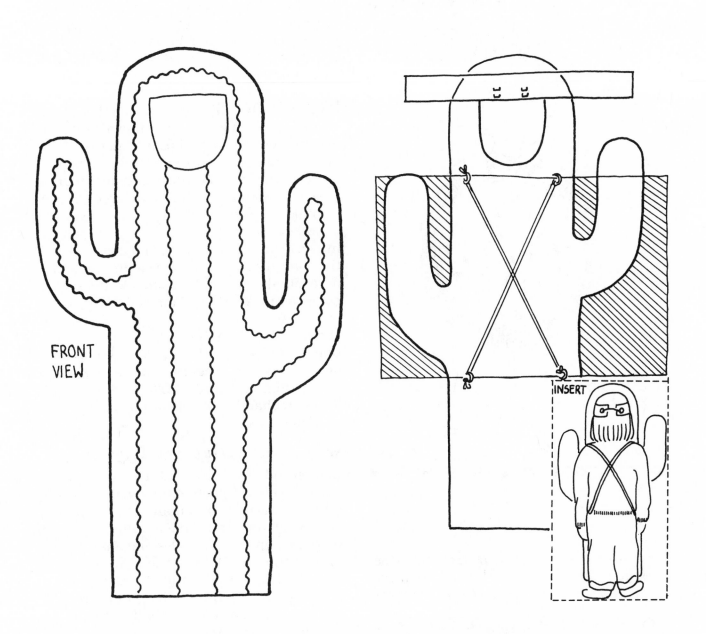

FIGURE D

FIGURE E

WATERMELON

FIGURE A

Fresh from the patch, this melon really does look good enough to eat. If you can trace a circle, you'll find this costume a snap to make.

DESCRIPTION: Leaf-top headband and slip-on watermelon slice.

MATERIALS: 2 pieces each of white and red and 4 pieces of green poster board; 1 piece of black poster board or 1 yd. black Con-Tact paper; staples; glue or double-stick tape; 1 or 2 green pipe cleaners; hole punch.

PREPARATIONS: Draw and cut two 20-in. circles from red poster board, two 22-in. circles from white poster board, and two 26-in. circles from green poster board (2 pieces of poster board must be taped together securely to accommodate each of these large circles). To make circle drawing easier, use a pail, lid, or other large round object that is comparable in size to one of the circles, and use it to draw that one. Then, draw the remaining circles accordingly. Or, make a pencil and string compass, making the string half the diameter (width) of each circle. Trace two 2-×-14-in. shoulder bands, a 2-×-16-in. headband (optional), and leaf (optional) shown in figure B onto green poster board; cut out. Trace the seed pattern in figure C 20 to 40 times or cut it out freehand from black poster board or Con-Tact paper.

TO MAKE THE WATERMELON SLICE: Center and attach each of the white circles to the green and each of the red circles onto the white, using glue or double-stick tape and creating a front and back. Arrange the seeds randomly on the red circles and glue or stick in place (figure D). Hold the front up to the wearer and mark the position of the shoulder edges on the top inner edge; transfer these marks to the back top inner edges. Staple the shoulder band ends at the front and back shoulder marks to fit as shown in figure D.

132

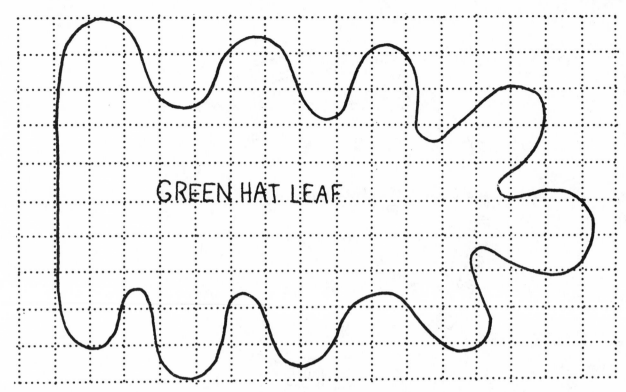

FIGURE B (1 sq. = 1 in.)

FIGURE C

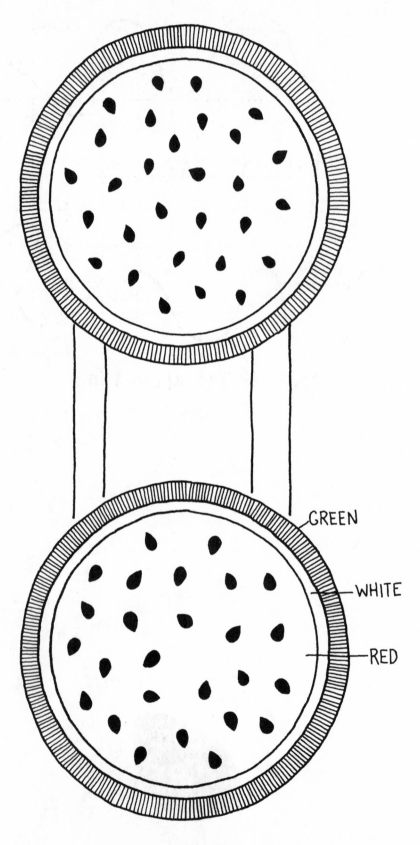

FIGURE D

TO MAKE THE HEADBAND (optional):
Punch holes near the ends of the headband and tie closed to fit around the head with a piece of round-cord elastic. Mark the position just above one ear on the headband, remove, and staple the leaf end in place on this mark as shown (figure E). Punch a hole close to stapled leaf edge, push a bit of pipe cleaner through to the wrong side to secure, and coil the rest as shown.

ADULT SIZING: No alterations necessary.

SUGGESTIONS: Simple green or black clothing is most effective with this costume—tights and a leotard or turtleneck are ideal.

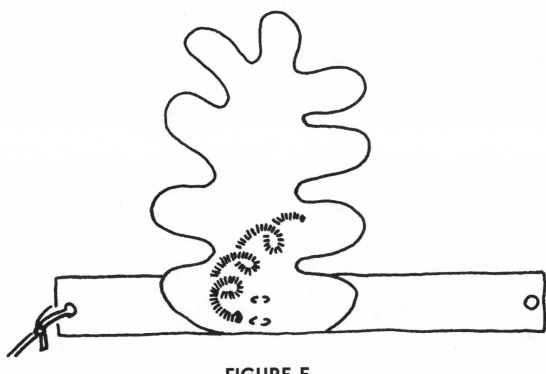

FIGURE E

SALAD

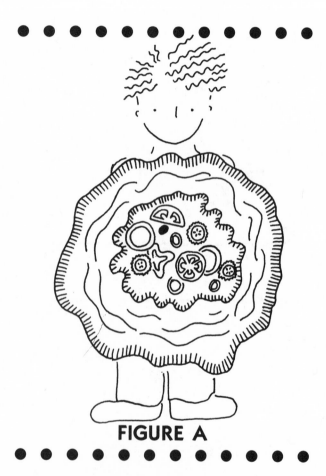

FIGURE A

A gardener's delight, this freshly tossed green salad is all the dressing you'll need (see illustration on front cover).

DESCRIPTION: Slip-on tossed salad.

MATERIALS: 2 pieces medium green and 1 piece each of fluorescent or bright green and fluorescent or bright red poster board; roll of green cellophane wrapping paper; ¼ yd. each green and red Con-Tact paper; small piece of yellow and black Con-Tact paper or

construction paper; plain white paper; tape; staples; double-stick tape or glue.

PREPARATIONS: Enlarge 2 lettuce leaves and the additional leaf ring shown in figures B and C and trace the tomato, pepper, cucumber, olive, radish, and onion in figure D onto newspaper or brown wrapping paper; cut out. Trace the larger, "base" leaf 2 times and two 2-×-12-in. shoulder bands onto medium green poster board; cut out. Trace the smaller lettuce and additional leaf ring onto fluorescent green poster board; cut out. Trace tomato pattern along outside edge only onto fluorescent red poster board 3 or 4 times; cut out. Trace the outer and inner lines of the tomato onto red Con-Tact paper 3 or 4 times and the outer and inner lines of the pepper onto green and yellow Con-Tact paper 2 times each; cut all pieces out. Trace 5 or 6 radishes from red Con-Tact paper, 5 or 6 cucumbers from green, 5 olives from black, and 6 or 7 onion rings from white paper; cut out.

Make the vegetables. For each tomato, align and adhere the Con-Tact paper tomato piece to the poster board tomato, trimming if necessary; cut tiny seeds from red Con-Tact paper and secure on poster board section of tomato. For each cucumber, cut an inner circle from the green Con-Tact paper, approximately ¼ in. from the edge, forming a ring; stick ring onto a piece of white paper that is slightly larger than the ring, and trim away excess along outer green edge. Cut 4 to 6 small seeds from green Con-Tact paper and stick on cucumber as shown. Treat radishes same as cucumbers, forming a ring that sticks on white paper and is trimmed.

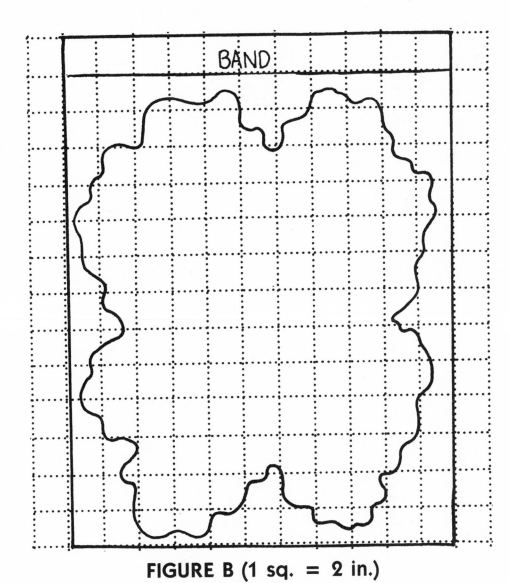

BAND

FIGURE B (1 sq. = 2 in.)

FLUORESCENT GREEN LEAF

← ADDITIONAL LEAF PIECE (RING)

FIGURE C (1 sq. = 2 in.)

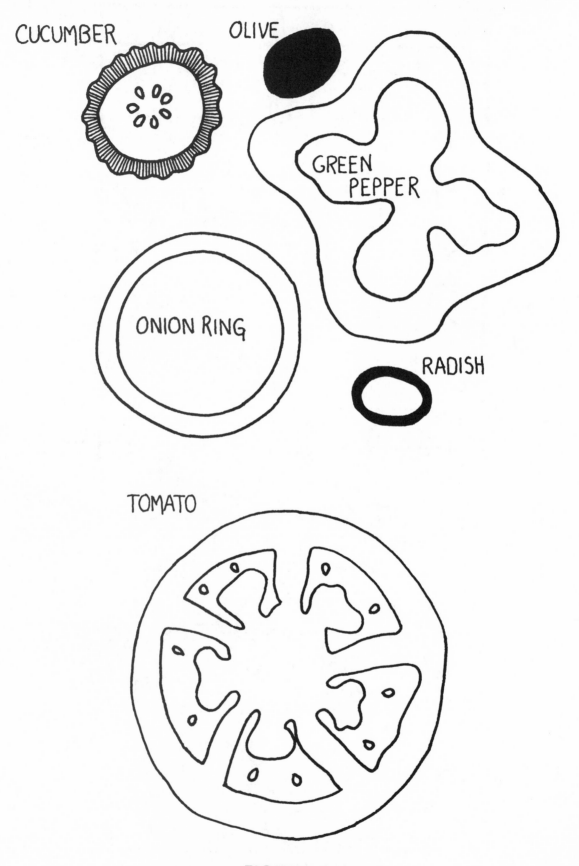

FIGURE D

TO MAKE THE SALAD:
Lay 1 of the large lettuce leaves on a flat surface. Unroll the green cellophane and fold it lengthwise, not quite in half, finger-creasing the folded edge. Beginning a few inches from the center of the lettuce leaf and working around in a circle, gather and tape the creased cellophane edge to form a double layer of lettuce on top of the poster board lettuce (figure E). Arrange the tomatoes, green and yellow peppers, cucumbers, radishes, olives, and onion rings onto the fluorescent green leaf as shown in figure E. Secure with small pieces of double-stick tape or glue (stick on the peppers). Center the vegetable-topped leaf on top of the cellophane lettuce and secure well with double-stick tape. Tuck the extra lettuce ring between the 2 layers of cellophane lettuce to give the illusion of an additional layer of lettuce; tape inconspicuously. Hold the completed salad front up to the wearer and mark the position of the shoulders on the inner top edges; transfer these marks to the inner top edges of the back leaf. Staple the ends of the shoulder bands at the marks on the front and back to fit as shown in figure E.

ADULT SIZING: No alterations necessary.

SUGGESTIONS: Dressing in green complements this delicious salad.

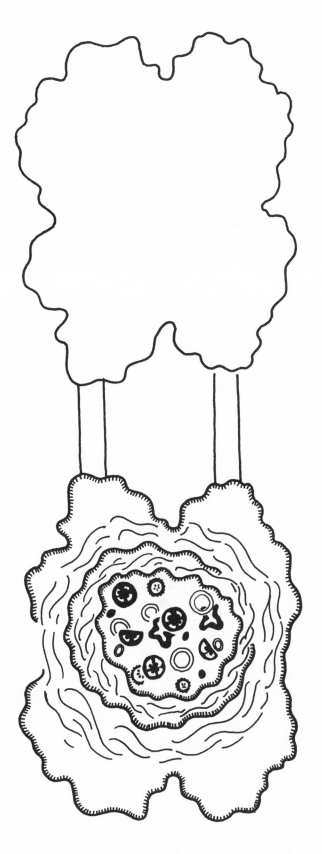

FIGURE E

BURGER

FIGURE A

This burger comes with the works—lettuce, tomato, and a sesame-seed bun! The burger meat sandwiched in between is the wearer of the disguise.

DESCRIPTION: Slip-on burger fixings.

MATERIALS: ½ yd. tan, ¼ yd. green, and ⅛ yd. red 72-in.-wide felt; 2 pieces tan or brown poster board; small bag of polyester filling; gold sequins; glue; straight pins; staples; tape.

PREPARATIONS: Measure and cut 3 oval pattern pieces—1 (the bun top) 20 × 24 in., the second 1 in. smaller all around than the first, and the third 1 in. smaller all around than the second—from newspaper or brown paper; cut out. Following the layout in figure B, pin the largest oval pattern onto folded tan felt and cut out. Trace the second oval 3 times and the third (smallest) oval 2 times and two 2-×-12-in. shoulder bands from tan or brown poster board; cut out. Cut the green felt in half lengthwise, forming 2 strips, each 4½ × 72 in.

TO MAKE BURGER: For top bun half, lay tan or brown bun felt out flat and cover with polyester filling, leaving outer felt edge uncovered approximately 1 in. all around. Make the filling deeper in the middle, tapering out to the edges to form a typical bun shape. Place 1 of the second ovals over the filling, centering it over the felt. Working on a small section at a time, squeeze a thin line of glue ½ in. from the poster board edge, fold 1 in. felt edge over onto the poster board, gathering as needed, and finger-press to adhere. Pin felt edge to poster board if necessary to hold in place; continue all the way around, let dry, then remove pins (figure C). To add the tomato, fold the red felt in half lengthwise and position it with raw edges in and folded edge extending beyond the outer bun edge by 1 in. or more. Glue, position, and pin a small section at a time, same as for bun edge (figure D); overlap slightly where the ends meet and trim. Let dry and remove pins. Add the green felt lettuce leaf (not folded), same as for tomato, gathering the inner leaf edge as you

140

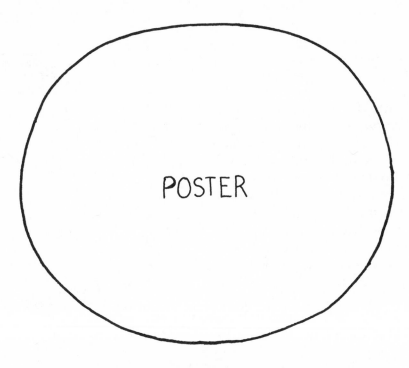

FIGURE B

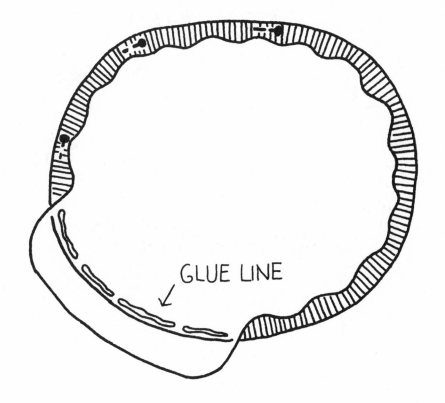

FIGURE C

secure it to the tomato with glue and pins and extending beyond the tomato 2 in. or more (figure E).

Make bottom bun half same as for top, eliminating the tomato and lettuce and applying the filling evenly across the bun. To attach the buns together, position and secure the shoulder bands. To do this, mark the center along the top edge of one of the third (smallest) ovals, then measure and mark 5 in. from the center on both sides. Center 1 end of each shoulder band on each mark overlapping the oval by 1 in. or more; staple in place (figure F). Apply a generous layer of glue to the underside of the top bun along poster board at the leaf edges. Align and lay the banded oval (with stapled bands end in) on top of the glue; finger-press and let dry. Hold the top and bottom bun halves up to the wearer, and tape the remaining band ends to the inner edge of the bottom (back) bun to fit; remove.

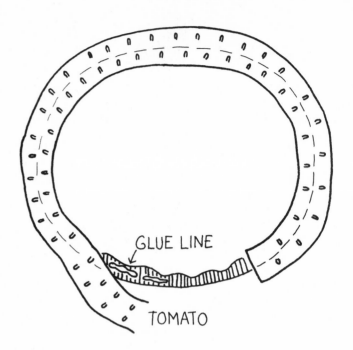

GLUE LINE

TOMATO

FIGURE D

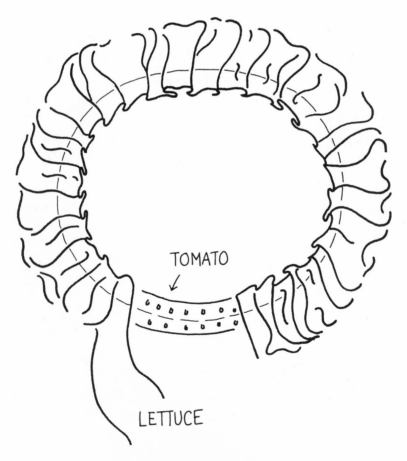

TOMATO

LETTUCE

FIGURE E

BURGER

Apply a generous layer of glue to the poster board on the bottom bun, and align and lay the remaining oval on top of the glue, same as for top. Let dry.

To finish off bun, add the sequin sesame seeds, arranging small drops of glue and applying sequins as shown in figure F.

ADULT SIZING: No alterations are necessary.

SUGGESTIONS: Since the wearer is the burger in this costume, brown clothing is preferable but not essential.

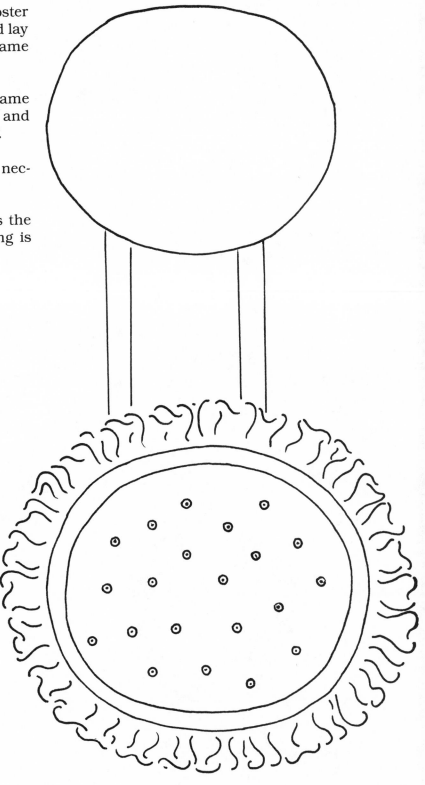

FIGURE F

CHAPTER VI

INANIMATES

ALARM CLOCK

FIGURE A

This elegant timepiece is right on the number for good looks and easy wearability (see illustration on front cover).

DESCRIPTION: Slip-on alarm clock.

MATERIALS: ¾ yd. black and ⅔ yd. white 72-in.-wide felt; 4 yds. strung gold sequins; 20 MM flat black sequins (optional); 1 piece of black poster board; glue; gold glitter and loose sequins.

PREPARATIONS: Enlarge clock pattern shown in figure B onto newspaper or brown wrapping paper; cut out. Make a 19-in. circle and trace the letters and clock-hand patterns in figure C onto newspaper or brown wrapping paper; cut out and fold circle in half. Following the layout in figure B, pin the clock pattern on the folded black felt and the half-circle pattern on the folded white felt; cut out. Using the number and clock-hand patterns, cut 17 I's, 5 V's, 4 X's, and 2 hands from black felt. Trim 1 in. from end of 1 clock hand to make the shorter hand as shown.

TO MAKE CLOCK: Lay white circle flat. This will be the face of the clock. Arrange the numerals around the edge of the face, evenly

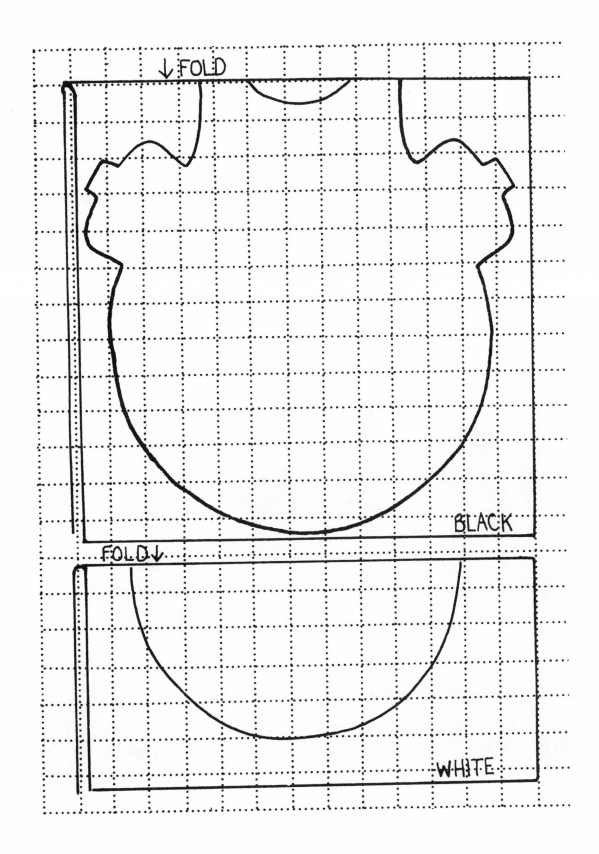

FIGURE B (1 sq. = 2 in.)

spaced and in proper sequence; glue in place (figure E). Lay the 12-hour dots—the flat black sequins—next to the numerals (optional); glue in place. Lay the hands on to read 11:55 as shown; glue in place. Cover the center where the clock hand ends intersect with a flat black sequin; glue and let dry. Lay the black felt clock base out flat. Trim off 1 set of bells to create the back side, and cut a 4-in. slit at the center back neck edge as shown in figure D. Cut a 12-in.-wide scoop to a depth of 2 in. from the center of a piece of 10- × -24-in. black poster board. Slide the poster board under the clock base, below the neck, making sure the bell caps are completely on the poster board. (The center of the scoop will be 4 in. below the center of the neckline.) Glue the felt to the poster board and trim to the edge of the felt (figure D). Lay the clock face on the front of the clock base (side with bells),

1½ in. from the bottom edge; center and glue in place. Draw a thin line of glue onto clock base, along the edge of the face; lay the strung sequins, string side down, onto the glue, encircling the face 2 times. Press down carefully and allow to dry. Cover 1 bell portion at a time with a layer of glue and cover with a mixture of gold glitter and loose gold sequins; let dry (figure E). Try not to use too generous an amount of glue for this process, as it may cause the poster board to warp. Try the clock on the wearer, and lengthen back slit if necessary to fit over the head.

ADULT SIZING: No alterations necessary.

SUGGESTIONS: The use of black and white with gold accents gives a sharp, clean look to this clock. It can, however, be made in the colors of your choice.

FIGURE C

ALARM CLOCK

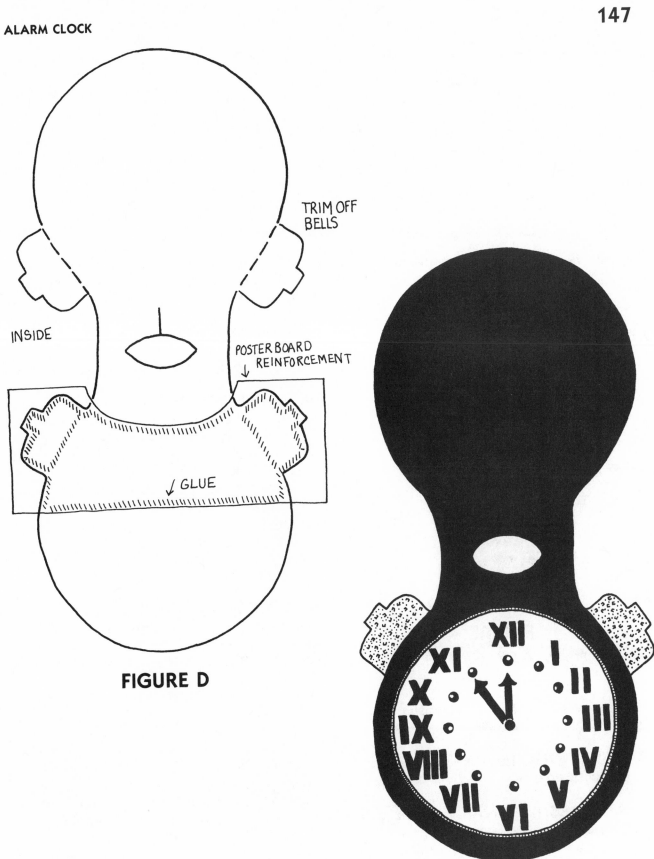

TRIM OFF
BELLS

INSIDE

POSTER BOARD
REINFORCEMENT

↓ GLUE

FIGURE D

FIGURE E

GRAVESTONE

FIGURE A

Beware the deadly hands that grasp the gravestone. What's to follow?!!

DESCRIPTION: Humorous slip-on gravestone with flowers.

MATERIALS: 2 pieces of black poster board; stainless steel, silver, or gray and black acrylic paints; 2 sheets each of white, pink, and red tissue or crepe paper; small piece of green poster board (or white, plus a green marker) for flower stems; heavy white paper; small piece of red paper; clean kitchen sponge; small paintbrush or cotton swab; double-stick tape; staples.

PREPARATIONS: Using a sponge and gray acrylic paint, completely sponge-print one side of 2 black pieces of poster board; let dry. Measure and mark a 2-in.-wide shoulder strap as shown in figure B on 1 piece of the poster board. On the remainder, draw the gravestone shape by simply rounding the corners as shown (figure B); cut out gravestone and strap. Cut strap in half. Trace the gravestone onto the second piece of poster board; cut out. Make 1 or more left and right hands, tracing your own hands on heavy white paper, including 2 in. of arm above the wrist (figure C); cut out. Cut out 4 to 6 strips of green poster board, each ¼ ×16 in.

TO MAKE GRAVESTONE: With a small paintbrush or cotton swab, letter the gravestone in black paint, using the inscription shown in figure E — "Here lies Justin Time, beloved father of Noah Moore, RIP" — or another of your choice. While the lettering is drying, make a limp bunch of flowers. For each flower, roll and bunch a piece of tissue or crepe paper together and sandwich it between the ends of one of the ¼-in. green strips; staple together (figure D). Tie 4 to 6 flowers together with string and staple to the bottom of the gravestone front (figure E). Position and adhere hands, using double-stick tape, onto upper gravestone front, trimming excess hand and arm parts at the edge. From red paper, cut ten 3-in. fingernails to fit hands; adhere. Note that the appearance of

148

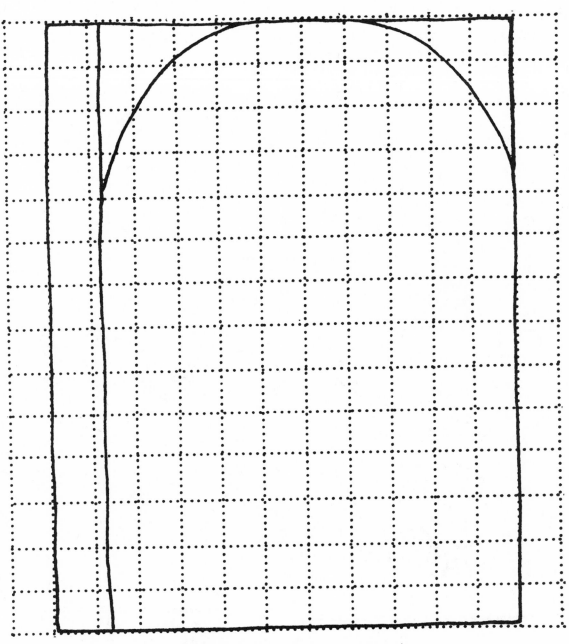

FIGURE B (1 sq. = 2 in.)

the thumbnails may vary depending on the position of the thumbs.

Hold the front up to the wearer and mark the position of the shoulder edges on the inner top edge; transfer these marks to the inner top edge of the back. Staple the shoulder band ends to the front and back at the marks to fit.

ADULT SIZING: No alterations are necessary.

SUGGESTIONS: The wearer can be made up to look like the person rising out of the grave with a bit of white face makeup and white, messy hair. The number of hands can vary—5 look great. Scars and dripping blood can be added for a gorier effect.

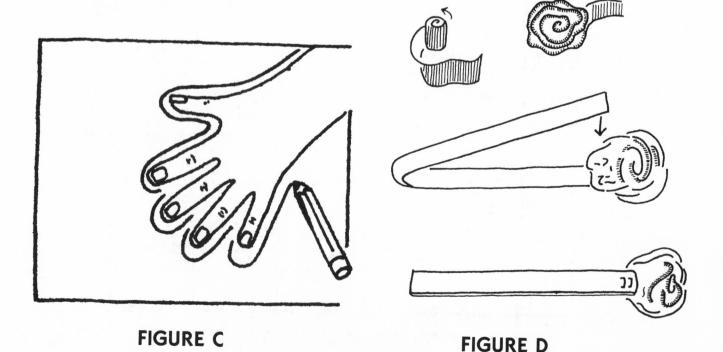

FIGURE C

FIGURE D

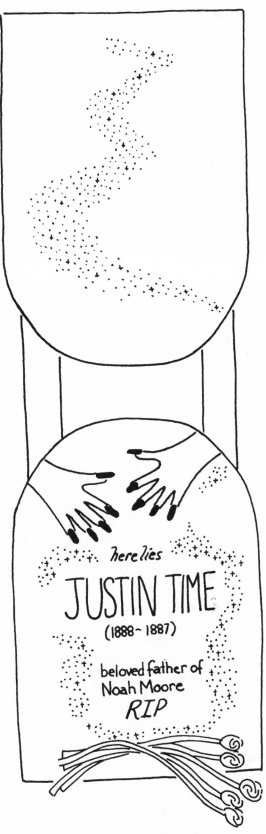

FIGURE E

OLD WOMAN'S SHOE

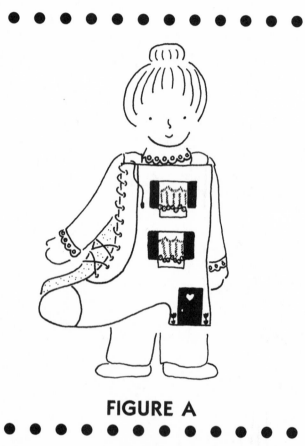

FIGURE A

Move into the old woman's renovated shoe—it's comfortable living!

DESCRIPTION: Decorative slip-on fairy-tale shoe.

MATERIALS: 1 yd. brown 72-in.-wide felt; 1 square each of dark brown, light brown, pink, yellow, white, and green felt; 1¼ yds. brown or black strung sequins; 5 yds. black lacing cord; ½ yd. of 2¼-in. lace edging or two 4-in.-square lace remnants; 3 pieces of brown poster board; masking or other strong tape; staples; glue; hole punch.

PREPARATIONS: Enlarge the boot and toe patterns in figure B onto newspaper or brown wrapping paper; cut out. Following the layout in figure B, trace 2 each of the boot and toe patterns and two 3-×-15-in. shoulder bands; cut out. Align and attach toes to boots, overlapping the poster board edges and securing with masking tape (figure B), to create 2 shoes. Open brown felt out flat. Draw a line of glue along each shoe edge, creating a left and right shoe. Place shoes, glue side down, on the felt, finger-press to secure, and let dry. Trim felt along shoe edges. Using felt squares for the windows, cut two 4¾-in. pink squares for the base, two 4¾-in. white squares for window frame, and six 1½-×-4¾-in. light brown rectangles for shutters and window boxes. Cut one 4-×-6¼-in. light brown rectangle for the door frame, one 3½-×-6-in. rectangle for the door, and two 4-in. lengths of lace edging.

TO MAKE SHOE: You will be adding details to the front shoe only. Set aside second shoe. Draw a thin line of glue 2½ in. in from the inner (lacing) edge of the shoe and lay strung sequins, string side down, onto the glue (forming a seam) as shown in figure C; trim at edges as necessary. Repeat this procedure for the decorative toe seam. Next, create 2 windows as shown in figure D. Lay lace edging over pink felt base. Cut a 3-in. square from the center of the white felt square and lay the resulting frame on top of lace. Glue along inner edges to secure (figure D) and trim edges if necessary. Position windows and

152

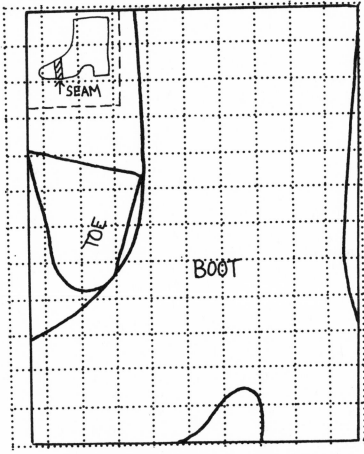

FIGURE B (1 sq. = 2½ in.)

FIGURE C

brown felt window boxes onto shoe as shown in figure E, and glue in place; position and glue shutters along side edges of windows. Position and glue door frame and then door in place on shoe (figure E). Make multicolored tulips and circular flowers (¼-in. felt circle glued on ⅝-in. felt circle) as shown in figure F. Glue tulips along sides of door and circular flowers on top edge of window boxes as shown in figure E. If desired, add a small, circular felt doorknob and heart on the door.

Make lacing holes on front shoe, using a hole punch, 1 in. from the edge and 2 in. apart (figures E and G). Align back shoe with front and mark placement of holes; punch holes where marked. Hold shoe up to the wearer and mark shoulder position on inside upper edge. Staple 1 end of each shoulder strap at mark. Hold shoe up to wearer again, align back shoe with front, and staple remaining strap ends to back shoe. Beginning at the bottom, lace shoes together loosely, up to slightly above wearer's waist. Continue threading 1 lace only up the front and the other only up the back as shown (figure G) to leave room for the wearer's arms. (For tiny children, lace individual shoes all the way up, rather than together, for easy movement.)

TO MAKE CHILDREN (optional): Trace children, clothes, and hair patterns as shown in figure H; cut out. Pin and cut 2 each of children 1 and 2, and 1 each of children 3 and 4 (or more or less according to your preferences) from white felt. Pin and cut clothes patterns from colored felt and hair patterns from black, brown, or yellow felt. Assemble children by lightly gluing their clothes and hair on; let dry. Arrange the completed children in logical places on the shoe; glue to shoe.

ADULT SIZING: No alterations are necessary.

SUGGESTION: To add a bit of humor, the wearer can dress like an old woman. Or, for a totally different look, eliminate all details (windows, door, lacing) and decorate the shoe with sequins to look like a western boot.

FIGURE D

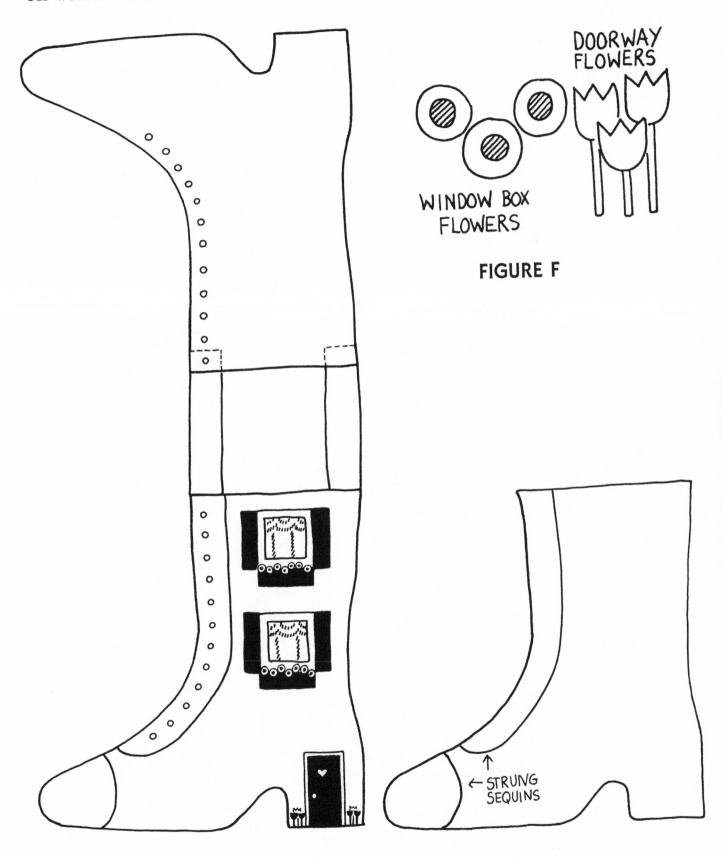

DOORWAY FLOWERS

WINDOW BOX FLOWERS

FIGURE F

← STRUNG SEQUINS

FIGURE E

FIGURE G

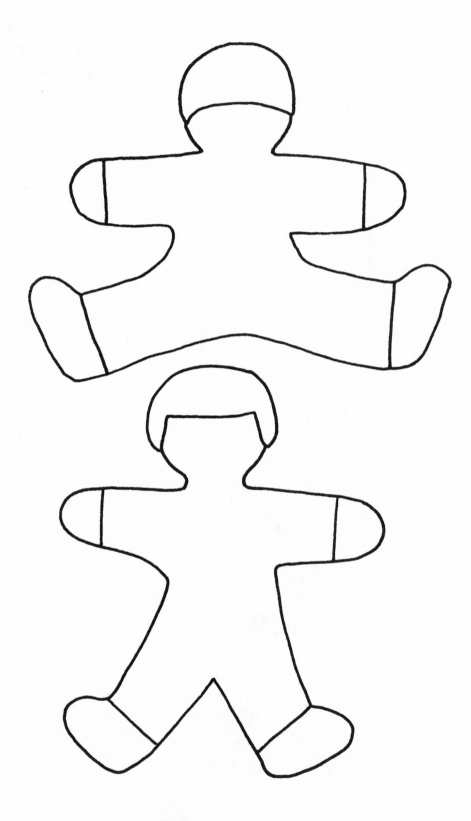

FIGURE H

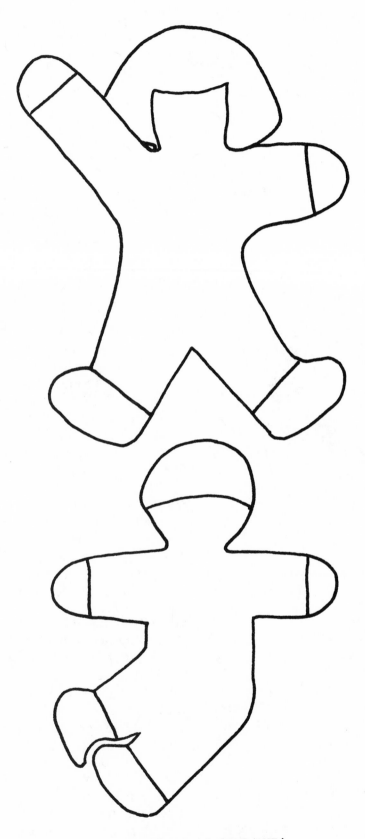

FIGURE H (CONT.)

SATURN

FIGURE A

A cosmic wonder, planet Saturn comes to earth in all its splendor. Encircled by 7 rings, this costume is amazingly comfortable to wear and easy to get around in.

DESCRIPTION: Slip-on Saturn with rings.

MATERIALS: 4 pieces of black poster board; stainless steel, silver, or gray acrylic paint; 4⅔ yds. each of 3 different iridescent or metallic-colored strung sequins; blue and/or deep pink glitter (optional); ¼ yd. each of yellow and violet (or 2 colors of choice) felt, or comparable amount of paper; two 20-in.-square or larger pieces of corrugated card-board; tape; double-stick tape; glue; staples.

PREPARATIONS: Cut two 20-in.-diameter circles from black poster board and two identical circles from corrugated cardboard. Completely sponge-paint black poster-board circles on 1 side with acrylic paint. Lightly dust with glitter while paint is wet (optional). Enlarge ring-structure pattern shown in figure B onto newspaper or brown wrapping paper; cut out along outside edges only. Trace ring-structure pattern 2 times and two 2-×-12-in. shoulder bands onto black poster board; cut out along outside lines only. Cut ring-structure pattern along ring #1 and #3 lines. Pin or trace pattern for ring #1 onto yellow felt or paper; cut 4 rings. Pin or trace pattern for ring #3 onto purple felt or paper; cut 4 rings.

TO MAKE SATURN: Trim away the outer straight edges of each black ring structure, ¾ ×4⅜ in. on each side, as shown in figure C. Then, slash the midsection, cutting on the solid lines; the slashes must be cut the same depth (approximately ¾ in.). On each side of each ring structure, secure rings #1 and #3, using dots of glue or double-stick tape for paper, and positioning same as for pattern (figure B). There will be a ring of black poster board between the felt rings. Draw a thin line of glue along the center of the black ring (dividing it into 2 rings), and lay strung sequins, string side down, on the glue (figure D); trim.

158

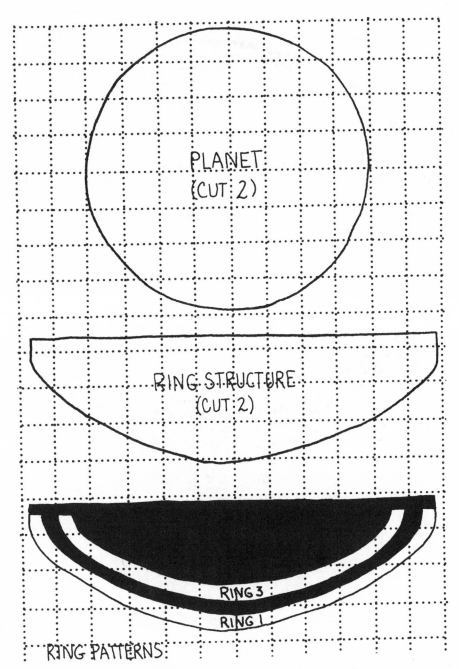

FIGURE B (1 sq. = 2½ in.)

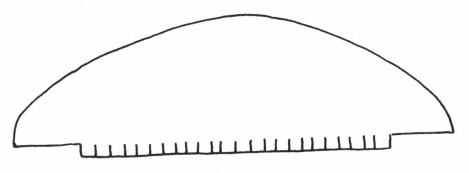

FIGURE C

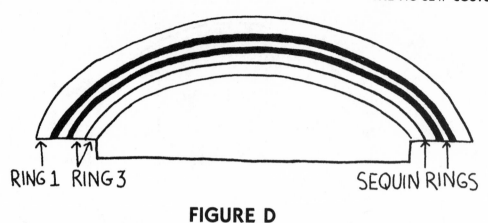

RING 1 RING 3   SEQUIN RINGS

FIGURE D

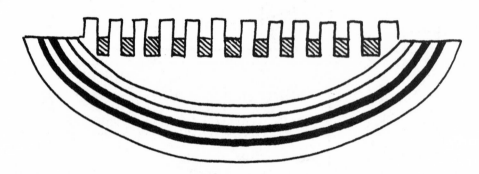

FIGURE E

Repeat the glue and strung-sequin procedure, drawing the line of glue along the center of ring #3 (figure D). You will now have 7 rings on the ring structure. Allow 1 side of the ring structure to dry before turning over and repeating the procedure.

When both sides of each ring structure are completed and dry, prepare the straight, slashed edges for assembly. To do this, simply fold up every other tab (created by the slashes), as shown in figure E. Position each ring structure on the 20-in. corrugated-cardboard circles, so that standing perpendicularly it visually and actually bisects (halves) the planet. Making sure that the tabs are alternating and laying flat on each side, tape all of the tabs securely in place, securing the ring structures to the corrugated cardboard (figure F). Both completed planet faces should be identical. To conceal the tabs and tape, cut the 20-in. sponge-painted poster-board circles in half so that each half covers the area above and below the ring structure. Adhere poster board to corrugated cardboard with staples or double-stick tape.

SATURN

Hold the planet up to the wearer, aligning the rings at the proper angle (figure A), and mark the position of the shoulders along the inside upper edge. Staple end of each shoulder band to planet at mark. Hold planet up again and staple the remaining band ends to the other planet, aligning the front and back ring structures to create a complete ring (figure G).

ADULT SIZING: No alterations necessary.

SUGGESTIONS: A headband with styrofoam balls attached to represent the moons of Saturn is an amusing touch, as are stick-on stars on the face.

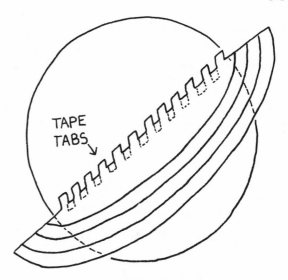

FIGURE F

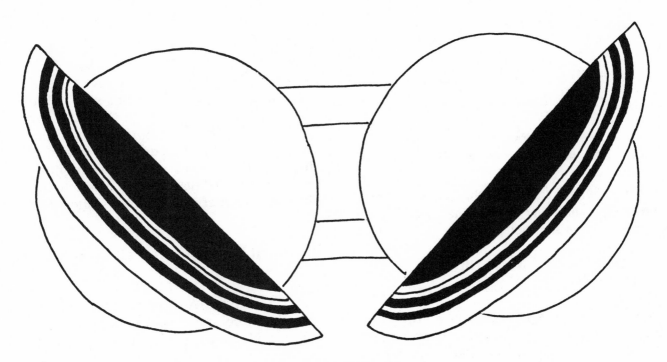

FIGURE G

STAR

FIGURE A

Twinkle, twinkle little star, this disguise shows how bright and shiny you are. The beauty of this costume is its simplicity.

DESCRIPTION: Shiny slip-on star and headband.

MATERIALS: 3 pieces of shiny silver (preferably) or white poster board; 3½ yds. silver Con-Tact paper, if not using metallic poster board; staples; round-cord elastic; hole punch; metallic sequins or glitter and glue, plus stick-on stars (optional).

PREPARATIONS: Enlarge the star and headband patterns in figures B and C onto newspaper or brown wrapping paper; cut out. If not using shiny silver poster board, cover 1 side of 3 pieces of poster board with silver Con-Tact paper. Trace headband, 2 star patterns, and two 2-×-12-in. shoulder bands onto poster board; cut out.

TO MAKE HEADBAND: Punch holes near the ends of the headband and tie closed to fit around the head with a piece of round-cord elastic (figure C).

TO MAKE THE STAR: Hold 1 body piece up to the wearer (front) and mark the position of the shoulder edges onto the inner top edge; transfer these marks onto the top edge of the other body piece (back). Staple the ends of the shoulder bands to the wrong side of the front and back body pieces at the shoulder marks to fit, as shown in figure D. For a special, optional touch, star dust can be added by lightly gluing a spray of sequins or glitter across the star and headband. Complete the look with 1 or 2 stick-on stars as shown in figure A.

FOR ADULT SIZING: No alterations are necessary.

SUGGESTIONS: Although a shiny star is featured, any color can be used, and it could get its sparkle from the added sequins or glitter. A simple, shiny star with stick-on stars on the wearer's face is also quite appealing.

162

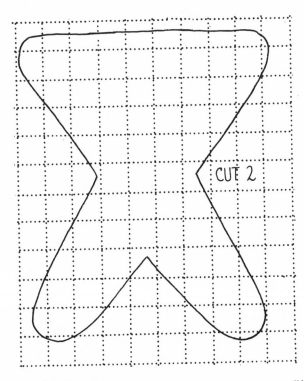

CUT 2

FIGURE B (1 sq. = 2 in.)

FIGURE C (1 sq. = 1½ in.)

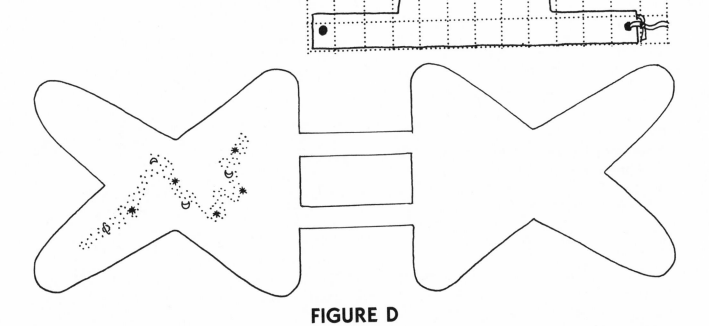

FIGURE D

HEART

FIGURE A

Surrounded by ruffles and glistening with shiny streamers and jewels, this heart comes from a long line of beloved Valentines. Its great looks disguise its easy assembly.

DESCRIPTION: Ruffled slip-on heart.

MATERIALS: 2 pieces of pink or red poster board; 4 or five 14½-in. paper doilies (any shape) with a 3-in. decorative border (or comparable amount in any size with a 2- to 3-in. border); 1 roll or 4 yds. of shiny silver curling ribbon; 2 fake silver 1-in. jewels (optional); double-stick tape; staples.

PREPARATIONS: Enlarge heart pattern piece as shown in figure B onto newspaper or brown wrapping paper; cut out. Trace 2 heart patterns and two 2-×-12-in. shoulder bands (positioned along the top edge) onto pink poster board; cut out. Trim the doily borders from the doilies, cutting ½ in. in from the inner border edge.

TO MAKE HEART: Attach doily border ruffle to outer edge of front heart piece. Starting at the center V and working with 1 doily border piece at a time, slightly gather (inner) undecorated edge of the border and position it ½ to ¾ in. in from the outer heart edge; using small pieces of double-stick tape, secure the gathered edge to the heart. Continue adding gathered border all the way around the heart, beginning each new border piece where the previous one ended for a continuous appearance (figures C and D). To finish off the gathered edge, add the silver ribbon, beginning at the center V. Place the ribbon on top of the gathered edge to form a wave pattern all the way around; secure the bottom of each wave to the gathered edge with small pieces of double-stick tape, as shown in figures C and D. Using the remaining ribbon, tie a small bow with long streamers. Carefully curl the streamers, using the edge of a scissors or blunt knife. Secure the bow at the center V and the ends of the streamers along

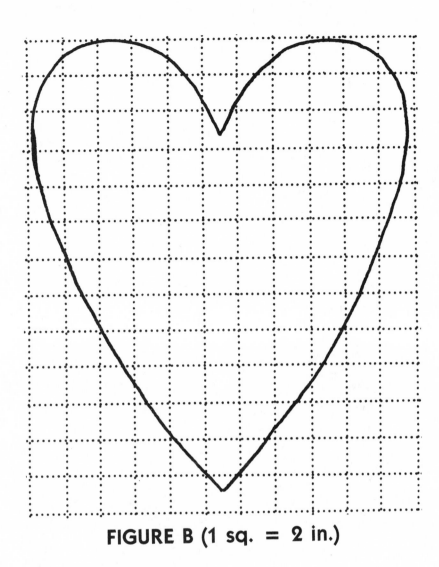

FIGURE B (1 sq. = 2 in.)

the side edges as shown in figure D, using double-stick tape. Add the jewels (optional), using double-stick tape.

To complete the heart, hold the front up to the wearer and mark the position of the shoulder edges onto the inner top edge; transfer these marks onto the top edge of the back heart. Staple the ends of the shoulder bands to the wrong side of the front and back at the shoulder marks to fit, as shown in figure

D, concealing the front staples under the ruffle edge.

FOR ADULT SIZING: No alterations are necessary.

SUGGESTIONS: Instead of fake jewels, sequins or glitter can be used for extra sparkle. Decorating the face with small, painted or stick-on hearts adds a bit of whimsical charm to the total look.

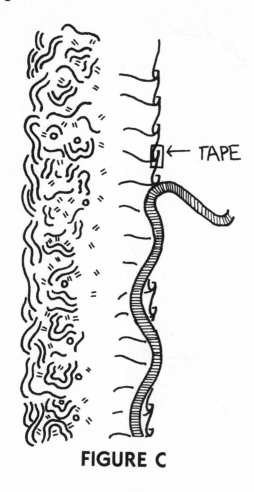

FIGURE C

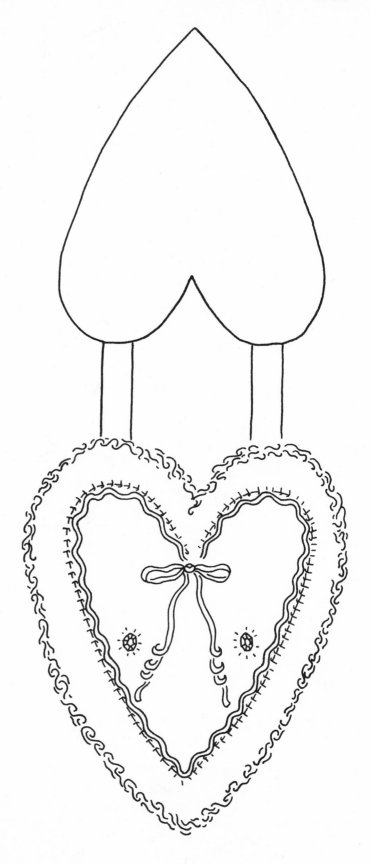

FIGURE D